# AGENT-BASED METHODS IN ECONOMICS AND FINANCE: Simulations *in* Swarm

# Advances in Computational Economics

VOLUME 17



*The titles published in this series are listed at the end of this volume.*

# Agent-Based Methods in Economics and Finance:
## Simulations *in* Swarm

*edited by*


**Francesco Luna**
*International Monetary Fund*
*EU2 Eastern Division*

*and*

**Alessandro Perrone**
*Università di Venzia Ca'Foscari*
*Venice, Italy*



Springer Science+Business Media, LLC

**Library of Congress Cataloging-in-Publication Data**
Agent-based methods in economics and finance: simulations *in* Swarm / edited by Francesco Luna and Alessandro Perrone.
p.cm--(Advances in computational economics; v. 17)
Includes bibliographical references and index.
ISBN 978-1-4613-5238-9 ISBN 978-1-4615-0785-7 (eBook)
DOI 10.1007/978-1-4615-0785-7
1. Economics--Computer simulation. 2. Economics--Mathematical models. I. Luna, Francesco, 1963- II. Perrone, Alessandro. III. Series

HB143.5.A44 2001
330'.01'13--dc21 2001038822

---


**Originally published by Kluwer Academic Publishers in 2002**
**Softcover reprint of the hardcover 1st edition 2002**



*Printed on acid-free paper.*

# Contents

# List of Figures

# Preface

This second book on financial and economic simulations in Swarm marks the continued progress by a group of researchers to incorporate agent-based computer models as an important tool within their discipline. It is encouraging to see such a clear example of Swarm helping to foster a community of users who rely on the Swarm framework for their own analyses.

Swarm aims at legitimizing agent-based computer models as a tool for the study of complex systems. A further goal is that a common base framework will lead to the growth of user communities in specific areas of application. By providing an organizing framework to guide the development of more problem-specific structures, and by dealing with a whole range of issues that affect their fundamental correctness and their ability to be developed and reused, Swarm has sought to make the use of agent-based models a legitimate tool of scientific investigation that also meets the practical needs of investigators within a community.

To accomplish these goals, Swarm is very careful about the extent of system structure that it imposes or requires while leaving open the flexible assembly and combination of elements that carry the problem-specific features of an application. The ability of Swarm to serve across many disciplines is a strength in helping to assure completeness of a common starting point. However, for wider adoption of Swarm it has always been assumed that specific disciplines would build and share their own structures on top of Swarm just as Swarm builds on its own foundations.

Swarm's principal foundation is an object-oriented representation for the state of a world composed of active agents in some environment. To this base layer it adds its own structures to represent and drive the events that occur across this world, and to observe both the state and activity of this world in some experimental context. The specific contents of any world, however, are up to the experimenter to provide, either by themselves or by tapping previous contributions.

This book and its predecessor are notable in assembling a rich array of such contributions, which are significant in their own right, but which can also be mined to determine a progression of successive layers that package the reusable elements in their respective areas of finance and economics. It also begins to examine the responsibilities that a program to build these successive layers might entail. Whether they come from Swarm itself or from foundations that Swarm itself is built on, techniques such as object-oriented analysis and framework design and new forms of user support such as visual and web interfaces and more explicit declaration of model structure can all be expected to take prominent roles as Swarm continues to move upward into the needs of specific communities.

The quest for a "common language" for agent-based computational economics, which drove the selection of Swarm by many of the contributors to these books, must start with a base grammar and set of initial terms, which Swarm supplies, but a living language must grow into the ever richer and increasingly more specific structures that occupy the concerns of a research community in its own discipline. The Swarm community at large can benefit greatly from the lead that the growing field of computational economics is taking to address its own needs, as represented by this book.

Roger Burkhart
Swarm Development Group

to

Katia, Lionello, Nicoletta
Manuele, Mariangela, Vela
Michele, Paolo, Lorenzo

# Contributing Authors

**Riccardo Boero**. Phd student in Economics at the University of Pavia, Italy, Boero is interested in theoretical issues and empirical applications of agent based models and experiments for the study of social sciences. He has also focused on the evolution of cooperation and coordination between agents and on the emergence and propagation of innovations.

**Charlotte Bruun**. Associate Professor of Economics at the Department of Economics, Politics and Public Administration of the University of Aalborg, Denmark. Her main scientific contributions are in Monetary Economics with simulation studies on pure-credit economies and Macroeconomics in a Keynesian approach. An early and enthusiastic supporter of Agent-Based Economics, before discovering Swarm she wrote her programs in Object-Oriented Pascal.

**Roger Burkhart**. Technical architect and consultant at John Deere and VantagePoint Network. He was part of the original team that developed Swarm and wrote some of its core libraries. In his current work he is continuing to research the use of shared computer models in a wide variety of potential applications.

**Alessandra Cassar** is a graduate student in International Economics at the University of California, Santa Cruz. Cassar's primary interest is in the effect that the network architecture, the pattern of links between individuals, has on coordination and cooperation. She is currently working on testing in the economic laboratory some recent network hypotheses focusing on local communities of interactions—in comparison to random and small-world networks—as a way to model sustainable cooperation in Prisoner's Dilemma games and relatively fast coordination on the risk-dominant equilibrium in Coordination games. She is also interested on how the pattern of relations linking financial institutions affects the diffusion of financial crises.

**Marco Corazza**. Associate Professor of Financial Mathematics in the Department of Applied Mathematics at the University "Ca' Foscari" of Venice, Italy. In 1994 he obtained a Ph.D. in Mathematics for the Analysis of Financial Markets. Corazza's main research interests are in numerical and computational methods for finance, insurance and economics, non-standard approaches for quantitative finance (fractals and deterministic chaos), and, more recently, in web-economics.

**Domenico Delli Gatti**. Associate Professor, Università Cattolica, Milan, Italy. Associate editor of JEBO, Delli Gatti has published extensively on financial fragility, monetary economics, and non-linear dynamics. He has published a book on "Capital Accumulation and Crises" (NIS, 1992) and edited a book on "heterogeneity and interaction" (Springer, 2000)

**Nigel Duffy**. Graduate student in the Department of Computer Science at the University of California, Santa Cruz. Duffy's primary interest is in theoretical machine learning with applications to computational economics, computational biology and data mining.

**Davide Fiaschi**. Assistant Professor in the Department of Economics at the University of Pisa. Fiaschi is interested in theoretical issues of coalition formation, agent-based modeling, growth theory and fiscal policy.

**Magda Fontana**. Assistant professor at the Department of Economics "S. Cognetti De Martiis", University of Turin. Fontana holds an MA in Political Economy, University of East Anglia (UEA) and a PhD in European Economic Studies, University of Turin. Fontana is member of the Swarm Users Group GTUS at the University of Turin. Her principal areas of interest are Institutional Economics, Evolutionary Game Theory, and in particular applications seeking to explain the emergence of conventions. She is currently working on agent based models for the analysis of job search processes.

**Mauro Gallegati**. Professor of economic dynamics, University of Teramo, Italy. He has extensively published on financial fragility, business cycle fluctuations, and non-linear dynamics. Gallegati has published a book on "Fluctuations in Italy" (Giappichelli, 1998) and has edited two books on "heterogeneity and interaction" (Elgar, 1999; Springer, 2000)

**Nicolas Garrido.** System Analyst, Information System Engineer with specialization in Artificial Intelligence, Master in Business Administration, Master in Economics and Ph.D. Candidate in Economics at the University of Alcala de Henares, Spain. Garrido has worked on Object Oriented Analysis and Design developing software under different environments. Currently he is working on agent-based simulation modeling of coalition formation, information technology market, and financial markets.

**Laszlo Gulyas.** Research fellow at the Computer and Automation Research Institute of the Hungarian Academy of Sciences. Gulyas headed the Telemodeling project at the Complex Adaptive Systems Laboratory, Central European University. A Ph.D. candidate in Computer Science at the Lorand Eotvos University of Sciences, Budapest, Hungary, Gulyas's main interests include multi-agent systems with social emphasis on agent-based simulation and coordination, mobile computation, and programming languages.

**Michael Harrington.** Visiting lecturer in the Department of Political Science at the University of California Los Angeles. Harrington is interested in the dynamics of wealth distributions and the political economy of public policies dealing with income security. His empirical work in these areas has focused on comparative policies in advanced democracies. His dissertation, titled "Trade and Social Insurance: the Development of National Unemployment Insurance in Advanced Industrial Democracies", received the Harold D. Lasswell Prize from the American Political Science Association for Best Dissertation completed in 1998/1999 in the field of Policy Studies.

**Darold Higa.** PhD candidate at the University of Southern California School of International Relations. Higa's primary areas of interest include environmental security and the use of agent-based models in international relations. Higa is currently finishing his dissertation which uses agent-based models to integrate spatial, social, economic and political factors to refine theories about the relationship between violence and environmental scarcity

**Roberto Leombruni.** Ph.D student at the Department of Economics of the University of Ancona, Research Associate at the Laboratorio Revelli - Centre for Employment Studies (Turin) and member of the Group of Swarm Users at the University of Turin. Leombruni is interested in agent-based simulations, firm demography and labour market mobility.

**Francesco Luna.** Economist at the International Monetary Fund. Luna has taught International Economics, Transition Economics and Computational Economics at the University of Venice "Ca' Foscari" and at Oberlin College, Ohio. His interests and publications revolve around computability theory for economics, learning as induction, the emergence of institutions and mechanism design in transition economies.

**Pier Mario Pacini.** Associate Professor of Economics at the University of Pisa (Italy). His current research focuses on theoretical issues and agent-based modeling of coalition formation in a non-cooperative setting, evolutionary game theory and the emergence of stable conventions. Pacini is also interested in general equilibrium and chaos theory.

**Alessandro Perrone.** An ITC consultant for various private enterprises, Perrone has been a programmer since 1990. He has contributed numerous computer programs for the Department of Economics and Business Administration of the University of Venice "Ca' Foscari" where he is currently working on a dissertation based on Swarm. One of Swarm's earliest "beta testers" outside Santa Fe, Perrone has acquired a large experience on Unix-like operating systems (such as Linux, MacOSX Server, BSD and its variants) and various simulation tools. Perrone is beta tester of Metrowerks products, and, as a hobby, maintains a FAQ section for the mailing list of Italian Macintosh developer.

**Massimo Daniele Sapienza.** Ph.D. candidate in Economics of Institutions, Monetary and Financial Markets at the University of Rome "Tor Vergata". He is currently completing his dissertation on "Real Options, Rational Bubbles and the New Economy". In 1999 Sapienza joined McKinsey & Co as a business analyst. His research focuses, on real options theory and asset pricing, Computational Economics and Political Economy.

**Marco Tenuti.** Independent software developer since 1995. Tenuti owns a degree in Computer Engineering from the University of Padova,

Italy, and concentrates on application development for MacOS. Devoted to user interfaces and object oriented programming techniques, he specialized in C++, PowerPlant, and Metrowerks Codewarrior development platform for MacOS, and Visual Studio for the Windows environment. Tenuti is currently project manager and design coordinator of some commercial projects of Concrete, a civil engineering and CAD software house located in Padova, Italy.

**Pietro Terna.** Associate Professor of Mathematical Economics and of Economic Dynamics at the University of Torino, Italy. He was previously external Professor of Mathematics for economics and Associate Professor of Mathematics for economics. His recent works are in the fields of (i) artificial neural networks for economic and financial modeling and (ii) social simulation with agent-based models. Terna is one of the pioneers in the use of Swarm for economic modeling.

**Tibor Vincze.** B.Sc. in Computer Science, Lorand Eotvos University of Sciences, Budapest, Hungary. Vincze was a member of the Artificial Intelligence Research Group at Lorand Eotvos University where he is currently pursuing a M.Sc. degree. Vincze's fields of interests are artificial intelligence, multi-agent systems and neural networks.

# Introduction

The Editors

## 1. Evolution and continuity in a competitive environment

This volume serves a double purpose. On the one hand, it is a natural sequel to the companion book *Economic Simulations in Swarm*–published by Kluwer in this series as number 14–presenting various simulation models in Swarm for financial economics. On the other hand, it offers an original contribution to the debate on the emergence of a simulation *language* for agent-based computational economics. Swarm, as every language that is alive, has evolved and the current compiler will not understand correctly the codes for the models presented in the first volume. The latest Swarm version allows the programmer to use Java code in addition to the less popular Objective-c. Obviously, the potential number of Swarm users is greatly increased by this innovation. Fortunately, Paul Johnson, one of the most active members of the Swarm community, has recently "translated" those programs (http://lark.cc.ukans.edu/~pauljohn/Swarm/).

The wealth of examples and software capital available for Swarm agent-based economists is steadily accumulating. The models presented in this volume will be found both on the Swarm organization web page (http://www.swarm.org) and on the page devoted to new tools for economics (http://www.econ-pol.unisi.it/newtools).

Tesfatsion's introduction to the JEDC special issue[1] expertly summarizes four key strength points of the agent-based approach to economics. Heterogeneity, adaptive dynamics, (co-)evolution and emergence, and observability of the history of the artificial world while it unfolds, step by step. The possibility of genuine surprises (events that the researcher had not ingeniously designed the model to generate) offers a promising way out of what Axel Leijonhufvud called the "clock-work" mechanics of most economic models. Furthermore, the constructive nature of the models—forced by the computer finite automaton environment—will eventually force the economic theorist to investigate computability constraints in human economic behaviour.

Far from imposing a straightjacket to theoretical insight, a computable approach encompasses the wealth of possibilities described above. The equivalence of dynamic systems and Turing machines, the parallel between surprises/emergence and the halting problem and the link between heterogeneity and NP-complex problems is explored in the literature.

However, despite the highly favourable prospects for an agent-based *discourse* in economics, the lack of a mother tongue of agent-based economics has hindered the emergence of a school of thought. Clearly, the special issues mentioned above would have been much more effective had they been based on simulations written in a common language! Unfortunately, the probability that those models will be re-used by other researchers is very low and this reduces the chances of a cumulative process of experience and knowledge acquisition.

The need of a common language for agent-based economic simulations is, by now, widely recognized and several attempts are under way to identify the fundamental characteristics that such language should have. Between the two extremes of "just add water" and "do it yourself" several options have emerged in the last few years. Swarm, Ascape, Repast, Starlogo, Agent Sheet and few other simulation platforms are, as of today, the most credible contenders.
From the on-going discussion, a new trade-off has emerged. It is no longer a matter of deciding whether the researcher should be constrained by the rules of an all encompassing software environment (the "just-add-water" option) or, rather s/he should painstakingly construct every soft-brick of the artificial world modeled (the "do-it-yourself" alternative). Rather, the trade-off is between the ease of programming on the one hand, and the sophistication of the obtainable end-product on the other hand.

Swarm in particular has attracted substantial interest from the economic profession for its inherent modeling potential, but is now challenged by simulation platforms like Ascape and Starlogo which are proposed as more "user-friendly" insofar as they can reduce the initial investment for the professional economist (but amateur programmer).

Part I is devoted to Charlotte Bruun's provocative and inspiring piece. She suggests a somewhat different approach. The impasse facing the emergence of a common language could be overcome by borrowing another concept from software design: the *framework*. An extensive economics library could then be used to flesh out in different ways a well-known and generally accepted structure. Her paper discusses the feasibility of this library and studies the recent production of models to identify those elements that may have the necessary characteristics to belong to such a collection.

In the economic history of the introduction of innovations, the adoption of a particular new technology over a contender has seldom been dictated by its ascertained superiority. More often than not, other factors like network effects and hysteresis played a more fundamental role. In a decentralized fashion—typical of the GNU philosophy that has inspired the design and diffusion of Swarm—several researchers have worked to make Swarm meet the challenges launched by other user-friendly competitors.

Part II of this volume proposes three different avenues followed by the Swarm community. MAML designed by Laszlo Gulyas is a meta-language offering a set of commands whose wording and syntax are much closer to those of a "natural language." At the same time, its adoption will free the user from the need to keep up with the subsequent Swarm versions. Riccardo Boero pursues a different goal. His SWIEE (Swarm Web Interface for Experimental Economics) enlarges Swarm's audience and potential users proposing Swarm as the standard for experimental economists. SWIEE builds an environment amenable to the design and management of economic experiments. The interactions of human subjects will be observed in a laboratory-like situation (over the internet). By using Swarm as the background (and playing field) of the experiment, individual actions and simulations merge in a new tool for the study of economic behavior. Perrone's and Tenuti's Visual Swarm Builder offers the next step in the quest for simplicity. VSB is an integrated environment for the design and realization of Swarm code based on a menu-driven selection of objects like schedule of events, graphics, lists and arrays. A visual building tool is clearly a useful extension to any programming environment, the more so for a large, complex and powerful simulation platform like Swarm. The absolute beginner will find VSB easy to use, while the expert programmer will appreciate the speed with which VSB allows him/her to obtaina prototype.

Part III of the volume presents a series of original contributions dealing with financial economics and international finance. Cassar and Duffy question the role of networks in the spreading of financial crises. Their conclusion seems to indicate that the tendency towards globalization in capital markets will ease and improve the allocation of financial resources. However, there is a trade-off. The domino effect of bankruptcies may become more pervasive. Corazza and Perrone exploit Swarm's flexibility to study the implications of a time-varying dependence in financial returns. Agent-based techniques prove in this case very precious also in analyzing the behaviour of a fractional stochastic process. Financial fragility in a contestable market is the source of complex dynamics in the entry-exit model proposed by Leombruni, Delli Gatti, and Gallegati. Equity rationing and the need to base entry and exit decisions on the lagged profitability of the market lead to unexpected distributions of the equity base of firms. The simulation results, somewhat in contrast with the simplified analytical model presented as benchmark, appear strictly related to the heterogeneity of firms. Clearly, the agent-based approach is the most natural way to study the implication of such heterogeneity. Terna's contribution further elaborates his previous work on the functioning of a real stock market and on the behaviour of cognitive agents. The computerized book of a real stock market is coded (another precious volume in Bruun's suggested library). Artificial agents are then endowed with increasing degrees of complexity from a simple random buy-sell choice to a cross-target learning mechanism. The aim is to investigate some empirical puzzles like the apparent time series predictability and volatility persistence observed in stock prices.

Part III collects three more papers that range from labor economics to microeconomics and industrial organization/game theory. Fiaschi, Garrido, and Pacini tackle the problem of coalition formation in a non-cooperative environment, where increasing returns to scale on the one hand and free-riding on the other render coalitions unstable. The paper tries to identify the relation between the distributive rule and the coalition structure. Who is more loyal to the coalition, a partner contributing physical capital or one inputing labor? Will the answer change if the output distribution is egalitarian rather than "productivity" driven? Heterogeneity in risk preferences is the topic analyzed by Harrington and Higa. Boundedly rational agents adapt their gaming strategies to maximize survival. The result is that "rational" behaviour (as emerging from experimental economics as well as evolutionary psychology) and luck can determine persistent wealth inequality. Heterogeneity in skill and endowment is exploited also in Fontana's and Sapienza's model of a labor market. Their *Labor Sim* implements sequential search processes for boundedly rational agents and is compared with a more "orthodox" structure with maximising actors. The authors proudly state that this model may significantly contribute a new foundation to labor economics.

We believe that this volume will significantly enrich the endowment of agent-based studies *in* Swarm further enlarging the audience of practitioners or, better, of "Swarmophones".

## 2. Acknowledgments

We would like to thank the contributors for the effort invested in this endeavour and for their patience. The Swarm community at large offered support for this project. Roger Burkhart wrote the preface despite his many commitments. Nicoletta Pireddu read and commented on parts of the draft. Alessandro would like to thank his family for enduring his many sleepless nights while working on this volume.

It should be expressly noted that we alone are responsible for the contents of this book.

Naturally, we hope the reader will find that its value greatly outweighs its errors, and we apologize for any error it contains.

The usual disclaimer applies.

The Editors

## Notes

1. Tesfatsion, L. 2001, "Introduction to the special issue on agent-based computational economics," *Journal of Economic Dynamics and Control*, 25, pp.281-293.

I

# A MODEST PROPOSAL ...

# Chapter 1

# PROSPECT FOR AN ECONOMICS FRAMEWORK FOR SWARM

Charlotte Bruun
*Department of Economics, Politics and Public Administration*
*Aalborg University*
*9220 Aalborg*
*Denmark*
cbruun@socsci.auc.dk

**Abstract** Will the economic agent-based simulation community ever conquer the Tower of Babel effect - and what does it take to succeed in this quest? These are the topics for this paper where it is argued that settling on a common programming language - or even a common platform as Swarm, is not sufficient for reaching a satisfactory level of communication between modelers. With this lack of communication, agent-based simulation models runs the risk of being perceived as *one damned thing after the other*, without ever accumulating a set of broadly accepted conclusions. A solution to this problem is suggested in the adoption of the framework concept from computer science. A sketch of an application framework for doing economic simulations in Swarm is presented and tested (in a virtual sense) on existing economic Swarm models

## 1. Introduction

With the recent book edited by Luna and Stefansson (2000), Swarm is making its entry to economics on a broader scale. Finance still appear to be the dominant field for economic Swarm applications, but also traditional areas within macroeconomics as well as microeconomics are now being subjected to Swarm modeling. With a variety as that displayed by the articles in "Economic Simulations in Swarm", one may ask, whether a programming platform is sufficient common ground for a book. Should not the collecting force be the economic content rather than the tool? The point is that builders and users of economic simulation models still hope to concentrate around a single programming platform. As mentioned in Leijonhufvud's preface to Luna and Stefansson (2000), CCE and CEEL[1] have recommended Swarm as a common platform for economic simulations. Seen in this light it makes sense to try to collect models written with Swarm in a book.

The questions to be posed here is whether the simulation models in "Economic Simulation in Swarm" have gained from being written in Swarm, and whether an application framework for economics can be developed within the Swarm platform so that the gains from using Swarm for economic simulations will increase. In section 2 we shall discuss aspects of the Tower of Babel effect and Swarms potential for overcoming such negative effects. Next we turn to application frameworks (section 3) and search for building blocks (section 4) to be used in prospecting a Swarm framework for economics (section 5). Finally we discuss how existing Swarm models might have benefited from a Swarm framework for economics (section 6).

## 2. Swarm and the Tower of Babel

As has been discussed in several articles on the methodological aspects of simulation (e.g. Axelrod (1997), Bruderer and Maiers (1997) and Terna(1998)), there are advantages to be collected by joining around a single programming environment for economic simulation. There is a Tower of Babel effect if we all concentrate on our own models and our own modeling language. In this case it will be difficult for others to completely understand and replicate our models - and this will weaken the conclusions obtained from applying simulation models.

There are, at least, three different aspects of the Tower of Babel effect, of which we shall only deal with two here. *First* there is an effect from the fact that we use different models. If we could all agree that e.g. a Walrasian setting is the optimal way of describing an economic system, we could all join forces in exploring this setting. This Babel effect is, we believe, inevitable since we need the pluralism; without it we run the risk of losing important information about economic systems. The *second* effect is a language effect as the original Babel effect. Builders of simulation models use separate languages and their own way of implementing the language. This makes it difficult to read and understand code written by other programmers. The *third* Babel effect lies between the first two. It refers to what we have chosen to call institutional settings, i.e. small and apparently unimportant details of simulation models. Some researches may agree on using a Walrasian setting, but still it may not be possible to compare their results because different institutional settings are chosen, e.g. different ways of implementing the Walrasian auctioneer, or different updating mechanisms. We are not suggesting that model builders should choose the same institutional settings, but our work would be easier if we had a typology of different settings to choose from, and to refer to in communicating with other model builders.

## 2.1. Programming Economic Simulation Models

Most builders of economic simulation models do not have any formal education in programming, and are not very aware of the principles they apply in developing simulation models. This enlarges the Babel effect due to difficulties in reading program code. In his discussion of programming simulation models, Axelrod (1997) claims that the programming of a simulation model should achieve three goals;

**Validity** The program must correctly implement the model. This is a self-evident goal, but as noted by Axelrod, not at all an easy goal to reach.

**Usability** It must be easy to run the program, interpret the output and understand how the program works.

**Extensibility** It must be possible for future users to adapt the program for new uses.

Axelrod's goals are not controversial, but in spite of this, very few economic simulation models achieve the goals to a satisfactory degree. We hope that the models we study have a high validity, but due to a low degree of usability it is hard for us to check the validity ourselves. Further more, if we would like to make some changes in a model pursuing our own research, models are generally hard to extend.

As a consequence of this, the important thing to discuss is not so much the goals of programming as it is discussing how the goals may be reached. We shall concentrate on how to achieve the goal of having extensible models - not because validity and usability are trivial or unimportant goals, but because validity and usability are bound to increase if we start reusing building blocks from each other models. Hence, it is likely that, we shall get the highest pay-off if we concentrate on increasing extensibility.

Unfortunately Axelrod is not very specific on how to reach his goals, but we suggest the following intermediate aims for improving extensibility;

**Modularity** By encapsulating details behind stable interfaces, it becomes easier to understand the code, and to reuse elements. Object-oriented programming, and hence Swarm, is in its essence modular, and programmers need to work with this feature, not against it.

**Increase communication** Only make new models when there is a need to. Make models as similar to already existing models as possible.

**Reuse of code and design** This is the essential intermediary aim in reaching Axelrod's goals. Reuse of code and design will increase validity since it will reduce the number of bugs[2], and increase usability and extensibility because of the modularity required for reuse. As a side effect, efficiency of model building will increase.

Fulfilling these aims requires that programmers of simulation models are patient and that they do not start programming before the ground of already existing models is explored. With a multitude of programming languages and modeling platforms, a complete exploration, however, becomes intractable. Consequently, there is no doubt that positive feed back effects à la Brian Arthur applies to the choice of programming language in economic simulation models. The more people use a specific programming language or platform, the easier it becomes to fulfill the goals above, and the larger the payoff from choosing that particular language will be.

## 2.2. Determining Institutional Settings of Agent-based Simulation Models

Axelrod's discussion is on the programming of a simulation model, but in agent-based simulations, the programming of a simulation model and the simulation model itself become inseparable. Agent-based models need so many details that it is impossible (or at least impractical) to specify the model without considering the programming of the model. Furthermore the agent-based methodology and object-oriented programming has so much in common that specifying a model is also the first step in actually programming the model. As a consequence you cannot understand all the details of the model without being able to read the code. This also implies that the goals of programming a simulation models should also apply to the specification of the model. There is no use being a good programmer making valid, usable and extensible programs, if the specification of the implemented model does not make the final product usable and extensible.

With respect to the specification of simulation models, Axelrod's advice is the KISS principle[3]. But when an agent-based model needs to be run, there is a limit to how simple models can be. In the article "Artificial worlds and economics" David A. Lane illustrates this aspect:

> Artificial economies have to be "playable" - and so a lot of institutional details have to be explicitly specified. For example, events have to be scheduled to occur in a logically meaningful and physically realizable order - a firm cannot produce until it has hired the workers it will use to do so. Also, market rules have to spell out how prices are formed and who ends up trading with whom, as a function of the allowable actions of the agents who trade in the market. And if firm can borrow, some form of bankruptcy law has to be implemented, since a firm might find itself unable to make good on the terms of its loans. (Lane(1993)p. 189).

Lane suggests two complementary research strategies for dealing with the arbitrariness of all the microlevel details that are a necessary part of economic simulation models in order to make them *playable.*

1 [develop] functional taxonomies of the various institutional arrangements that have to be introduced into an artificial economy. For example, is there a minimal characterization of the functionally different types of market rules or bankruptcy laws? Similarly, one might try to construct a typology of "nonoptimizing" decision making strategies (or perhaps orientations) that are economically relevant.(p.194)

2 Second one could change the notion of what an artificial economy is away from the idea of a single parameterized model that specifies a priori its institutional forms and agent behaviors. Instead, imagine an artificial economy as an experimental environment in which users can easily tailor models designed to suit their own particular research agendas. Object-oriented programming techniques can be used to construct such an environment, which would consist of a library of different kinds of modeled institutions and agent types, together with an interface that makes it easy for users to combine different items from this library to make particular experimental economies. (p.194)

Notice the potential complementarity of the two strategies. Lane is advocating an artificial economy which is NOT *a single parameterized model*[4], but an environment where different institutional arrangements can easily be implemented. The taxonomies and typologies are for taking more qualified decisions on institutional settings, and communicating the choices made. The artificial economy is where you implement the choices. An "economics" framework for Swarm should encapsulate both of Lane's visions. The framework must include a collection of taxonomies and typologies, within which each individual element is provided with similar interfaces so that they are easily exchangeable.

Unfortunately, seven years later we still do not have such a system. Lane's perception of an artificial economy is, furthermore, not what we intend to suggest with the economics framework for Swarm, since Lane hopes for a model based on real world data. Our suggested framework does not contain any real world data[5].

The Tower of Babel effect thus, not only makes it difficult for us to read and understand the programs of one another - it also makes us choose different institutional settings. This is appropriate in cases where the institutional settings in question have a specific role to play in the model, but in cases where they do not, e.g. in cases where there just needs to be a bankruptcy mechanism, we are, as a community, better off choosing similar mechanisms[6]. Thus the goals of usability and extensibility should apply, not only to our choice of programming language and programming technique, but also to our choice of institutional settings. This implies that we must communicate institutional settings to other programmers, and that we must program our models in such a way that institutional settings are easily exchanged.

## 2.3. Economic Swarm models

How fit, then, is Swarm for fulfilling the task of conquering the Tower of Babel? Looking through the libraries of Swarm, there is no doubt that focus is on more technical aspects of agent-based simulation. People outside the Swarm community easily overestimate the contents of Swarm. Swarm is an objective-C library for agent-based simulations in the broadest sense of the term. An agent may be a biological cell as well as an economic agent. It is therefore on a very general level that Swarm has its advantages; all agent-based simulation models need to have a user interface, a graphical presentation of results, a random number generator, ways of handling large numbers of agents etc.[7]. There is a clear advantage in using libraries for such things - a recognition that has dominated the software industry in general for the past decades.

With respect to the aim of increasing communication, Swarm certainly is a step in the right direction. There is an active Swarm community, and mailing lists make it easy to check whether certain program elements have already been made, or whether other *swarmites*[8] are working with similar models. The fact that practically all users have learned swarm using the same models (e.g. `heatbugs`) also means that they develop similar ways of doing things. This makes it easier to read programs developed by other modelers, which must be the first condition for reaching the remaining goals.

As a subgroup under the Swarm community we need, however, not content ourselves with these more general and technical gains from using Swarm. As a subgroup defined by our interest in economics we have much more to share. The gains we would like to discuss here are gains that *economic* Swarm models have achieved from being written in Swarm due to the increase in communication between modelers and possible reuse of code, and not just the more technical advantages of using Swarm.

If we evaluate the benefits of using Swarm presently, gains are limited. The following economic Swarm models are identified[9]:

1 ASM (Arthur et al. (1997))

2 BankNet (Askenazi (1996))

3 ABCDE (Terna (1998))

4 BP-CT (Terna (2000))

5 Economic Growth (Bruun and Luna (2000))

6 Tax Evasion (Mittone and Patelli (2000))

7 Sapienza's version of BankNet (Sapienza (2000))

8 Jares' finance model (Jares (2000))

9 Monopolistic Markets (Corazza and Perrone(2000))

10 Supply Chain (Lin, Strader and Shaw (2000))

11 ORECOS (Schlueter-Langdon, Bruhn, and Shaw (2000))

12 Human Capital and Firm Structure (Luna and Perrone (2000))

What is the extent of reuse, modularity and communication in these models? There is some overlap between the models. Sapienza (2000) uses the BankNet model, but here one cannot talk about two separate models. The model in Jares (2000) has many similarities with the ASM model, but in this case no code has been reused. Neural nets are used by Terna's BP-CT model and the Bruun/Luna growth model, but there is no reuse of code. Bruun/Luna and Luna/Perrone use the same neural network analogy for modeling learning. There is some reuse of design between the two supply chain models (10 and 11 above).

Has communication improved? As a Swarm programmer, it is easier to understand more technical aspects of the Swarm programs, but among the eleven[10] models we find very little reuse of code or design. Even when it appears obvious to reuse code, as in the case of financial market modeling, reuse is absent. Similar market mechanisms are written several times in the models.

One may choose to conclude that Swarm has failed to serve one of its purposes - that even models written within the same platform have not succeeded in conquering the Babel effect. It is, however, far too early to draw any conclusions with respect to Swarm's ability to increase communication and reuse of code. Secondly, since one cannot expect any other programming platform to perform any better, a more constructive approach is to ask what could increase gains from using Swarm.

## 2.4. Extending Swarm for Economic Simulation Models

In their introduction Luna and Stefansson (2000) present two different ways of providing economics with a common language; just-pour-water models, where a pre-defined set of parameters are manipulated, and a more general platform as Swarm. Not surprisingly they vote in favor of the latter. And, rightly, there is a risk that in "just-pour-water models" the implemented model will dominate the theoretical model. Just as Keynes criticized Tinbergen for letting the tools of the statistician rule rather than economic reasoning (Keynes(1939)), there is a risk that "just-pour-water models" will assign an inferior role to economic reasoning by reducing it to the dimensions that can be handled by the specific model.

There is, however, also the possibility of extending Swarm for economic simulations to get some of the advantages of "just-pour-water models". This could be done by making a library for economics. If we take a look at the latest developments in the software industry, there has, however, not been full contentment with the library solution. Apparently, reuse of code is not promoted enough by making components available in a library. The structure in which the elements from the library is to be integrated must also be taken into consideration. From the software industry the suggested solution has been frameworks[11] and patterns[12].

By making an economics framework for Swarm one may enable the model-builder to add much more than just water to a predefined structure. Components already existing may be combined to make a new model, but for special features the user may apply his own components to the predefined structure. The predefined structure must be so flexible that it can handle fix-price as well as flex-price systems, systems emphasizing exchange as well as systems emphasizing production. In this way the tyranny of "just-pour-water models" can be avoided while the advantages can still be collected.

The ultimate goal of the suggested framework is to conquer the Tower of Babel; to make economic simulation models a acumulative activity. Beyond this ultimate goal, there is a number of possible gains from using a common framework:

**usability** Make it easier for newcomers to construct their first model, and make it easier to replicate models written outside the framework. In the software literature, the advantages of black box design, which does not require full information about what is in the code, only knowledge of how to use it (i.e. the interface), is often emphasized. In research the advantage of encapsulating details behind interfaces in this way, is not that we do not need to know the details - since we do need to know everything. The advantage is, that we do not need to know everything at once. As beginners we can implement a `consumer` agent and have our first model running without knowing how exactly the consumption decision is taken.

**typology** Develop certain standard ways of handling different auction types, different ways of performing bankruptcies etc. This will ease model construction but also increase communication and reduce the risk of bugs. It will also make causes for differences between model results more transparent, i.e. reveal whether differences are due to small deviations in the auction mechanism or the updating mechanism.

**testing** Make it possible to test a model against different model components. It will be easier to test the sensitivity of a model to specific model elements, e.g. bankruptcy rules or behavioral assumptions. It will also be easier to compare models and perform what Axtell et al. (1996) call *alignment and equivalence testing of computational models.*

**transversal studies** Make it easier to study effects of certain institutional setting across different simulation models. E.g. can we say anything general on synchronous versus asynchronous updating, the number of agents or the auction mechanisms across models.

**macro-foundation** Make it easier to provide microeconomic models with a macro-foundation. As a way of testing partial models, they may be completed (closed) by adding standard components from a framework, and in this way check feedback effects from the macrolevel[13].

By having a framework within the agent-based computational economics community, some standard models for addressing families of problems could emerge and a positive feedback mechanism set off. Models can no longer be accused of being *one damned thing after the other*[14] since modelers extends and modifies each others models in order to reject or strengthen their conclusions. In this way the community can accumulate knowledge in a set of conclusions that are developed, not by one model-builder in one model, but by a number of model-builders making a number of variations of a given model.

## 3. What's in a Framework?

It is not only builders of economic simulation models who seek to promote reuse and extensibility of programs - economics has picked up the discussion from software engineering. The widespread use of object-oriented programming today, partly stems from the possibility of reusing object classes, and the belief that this will improve productivity in the software industry. The industry is, however, realizing that object-oriented programming does not do the job on its own and focus has shifted from reuse of code to reuse of design[15]. Application frameworks is a method for reusing design as well as code[16].

It would be wrong to present frameworks as a completely new way of writing software applications. Instead of being a new method, frameworks should be perceived as a plea for focusing on the architecture of the complete object-oriented systems rather than focusing on the objects in isolation. The idea is that object classes will only be reused if it is possible to reuse the way they are meant to interact as well. By focusing on architectural aspects, reuse becomes a question of making reusable designs as well as reusable code. Figure 1.1 illustrates the idea of using frameworks rather than class libraries. In using a class library the programmer writes a structure e.g. the main program, and uses components from the class library whenever they fit into his structure. The same component may be used in different structures. In using a framework the programmer would have a predefined structure, e.g. a main program that is already written - the job of the programmer is to modify existing components or develop new components so that the structure fits his specific needs. The programmers code get called by the framework code rather than letting the programmers code call the code from class libraries[17]. The same structure is thus used with different

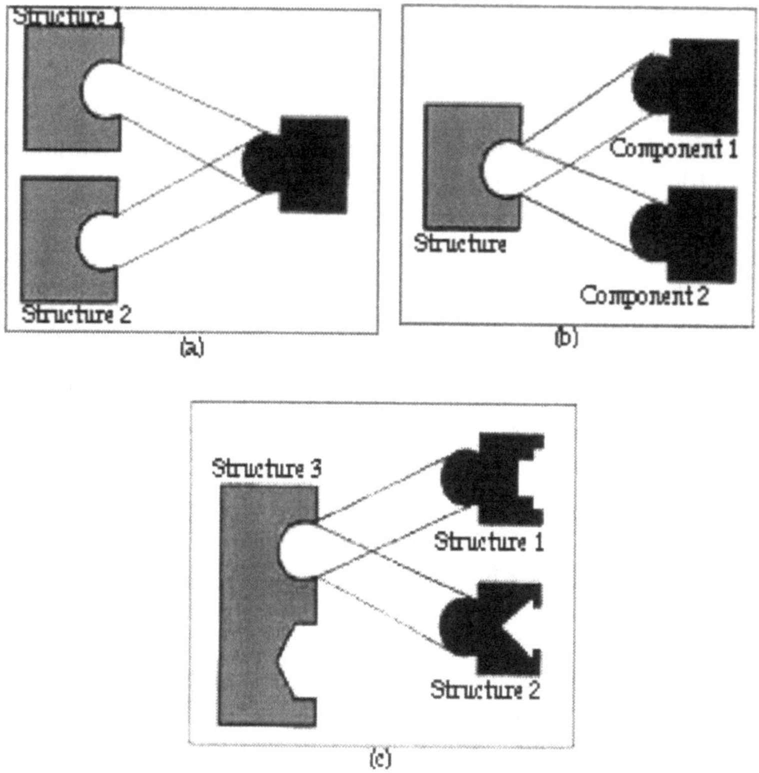


*Figure 1.1.* Component reuse and structural reuse: (a) component reuse, (b) intentional structural reuse, and (c) extensional structural reuse. This figure is from Erdogmus and Tanir(1999).

components. Frameworks normally come with a class library, but what is important in a framework is the structure of object interaction, rather than the contents of the library.

The use of inheritance is essential for the working of a framework. In a framework inheritance is not only applied for reusing code, it is also used for setting up protocols or creating templates. Protocols are placed in the interface of abstract classes. Abstract classes are classes that are not implementable, i.e. cannot be used for creating objects. Instead abstract classes are used as super-classes for implementable classes. The advantage of inheriting from the abstract class, is not a reduction in the number of lines of code to be written. The implementable subclass is provided with a list of methods that it must implement. In the implementation part of the abstract superclass, the implementation of some methods may be completely absent. In this case we talk about a virtual or a template method. It is placed in the interface part of the abstract class, simply to remind the programmer that all subclasses of the abstract class must provide an implementation part for the given method. In this way an interface is created that all subclasses must respect.

Abstract classes may thus be characterized as skeletons or templates for making objects - and it is these templates that allow the user to add his own components to a framework. Since that part of a class, which is essential to an object's interaction with other objects in the system, is defined by the abstract classes, it is easy for the user of a framework to define his own subclasses. The collection of abstract classes becomes more than a conventional class library because patterns of object interaction are contained in the abstract classes.

An example of the contents of an economics framework would be an object class called **agent**, an object class called **market**, and interfaces specifying the way instances of these two object classes interact. One can imagine many different ways for an agent to determine quantities to buy or sell at a given price[18]. By fixing an interface, for instance by forcing all imaginable agent types to have a method called **giveQuantity** with an input called **price**, all details of the decision making process is hidden behind this interface. We cannot be sure whether the agent actually uses the price information in setting its quantity. What we do know, is that if we need to interact with an **agent** subclass, we can provide it with a price and it will give us a quantity. This will be the case no matter where we get the **agent** from, e.g. whether it has been supplied by another user of the framework. The **agent** can interact with different market mechanisms, i.e. it does not care whether it is asked for a quantity by another **agent**, a Walrasian auctioneer, or a fix-price market-maker.

To some extent Swarm itself may be perceived as a framework; Swarm is not just a collection of independent class libraries, but a set of class libraries that are designed to be used together (Minar et al.(1996)). The division between **ModelSwarm** and **ObserverSwarm** and Swarms support of hierarchical modeling are examples of design reuse. But apart from these optional structures, Swarm is not characterized by a predefined organizational structure and the focus is on component reuse.

Since frameworks will move the focus from the actual source code to the software design or architecture, it becomes just as important to have good tools for software design as it is to have good programming languages. In the present work, the Unified Modeling Language (UML) is used. This language was developed, not merely in order to improve software design, but also in order to ease communication between modelers. Figures representing program design in this article are UML class diagrams, where each bow represents a class, the upper part denoting

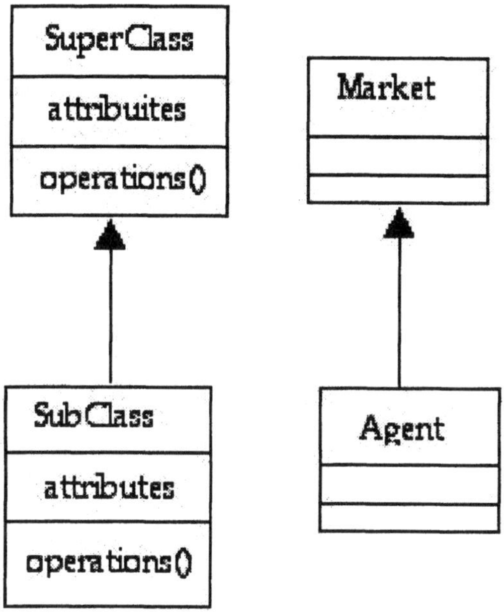


*Figure 1.2.* Elements of Unified Modeling Language (UML).

the name of the class, the middle part its state variables (attributes) and the third part its methods (operations). A hollow arrow illustrates inheritance, where the superclass is the class the arrow points at. Other lines between classes represent association, where aggregation is a special form of association.

## 4. Collecting Building Blocks for a Framework for Economics

In object oriented software design it is often recommended to perceive the activity of writing programs as an activity of building models. If you cannot think of a good name for your object - reconsider whether you really want to create it, trained object oriented programmers claim. Following this advice in considering the architecture of a Swarm framework for economics, the main source of inspiration must be the real world economy and consumers, production units, market etc. obvious candidates for object classes.

Another important source of inspiration must be models already written in Swarm. For an economics framework to offset the necessary positive feedback effects, it must start off as a unifying framework and not just hope to become one. There has been several attempts at making unifying modeling platforms for agent-based simulation modeling[19], and their apparent lack of success in spreading suggests that the ambition should not lie in providing a good framework for doing agent-based simulation within the social sciences, but in unifying aspects of simulation models already existing[20]. Thus the aim is not to provide agent-based computational economics with a new tool, but in gathering the building blocks and tools that are already there. Compared to other platform enterprises, our suggested application framework, is also more focussed on the economics contents.

We have chosen to search for building blocks in four different economic Swarm models that all claim to have a generality that make them useful to other modelbuilders; ASM, BP-CT, BankNet and ORECOS. We shall also discuss the Evo artificial life framework to see how a framework may be implemented within the Swarm platform.

Our two sources of inspiration comply with two existing strategies for framework development; a refactoring approach, where a framework is extracted from a number of related implementations, and an a priori approach where the framework is developed by studying the domain of the framework (in our case the economy) (Miller et al.(1999)). This is not the place for making statements about framework development, but in this section we shall, in accordance with the refactoring approach, attempt to extract building blocks for the suggested framework. Extracting components or program elements from already existing models, is also a way of encouraging the bottom up generation of a swarm framework for economics. In their *Agenda to bring simulation into the mainstream*, Bruderer and Maiers (1997) opt for the bottom up generation (or emergence) of a java platform for simulation models rather than a top-down platform design, to which they claim Swarm belongs. By encouraging users to contribute components to a Swarm framework, a bottom up development of the framework is made possible.

## 4.1. Building Blocks Supplied by the ASM

One model that it is hard to disregard when it comes to economic Swarm models, is the Artificial Stock Market (ASM) developed by Arthur, Holland, LeBaron and Palmer (1997). Their aim in building the model was not merely to build a model applicable to some specific financial market simulations, but to build a simulation model to which other users could contribute new types of agents, new types of market mechanisms etc.

The ASM model thus in itself holds many of the features described as characterizing an application framework. The model provides a predefined structure and a predefined interface for agents - the user can then add different components, in this case different agents, to the model. The spreading of the ASM model made possible by this structure, does, however, not appear to have happened yet and the fact that financial swarm models are being written without any reference to ASM, illustrates how difficult it is to increase communication and reuse of code among model-builders.

What can be used from the ASM model, is the way that a market is modeled. The ASM is built upon the following elements:

**agent** The agents of the ASM have standard demand functions based on their prediction of asset price and dividend next period. Agents submit their demand to a specialist.

**specialist** The specialist is an auctioneer whose purpose it is to clear the market by varying prices. The exact mechanism may take various form, but follows the same procedure:

1 Set a trial price.

2 Ask each agent for demand at that price.

3 set a new trial price or return to the last trial price.

**world** Controls the state of the world. It is not an active agent, but primarily used for storing data.

**dividend** the dividend is a random process of some sort.

The relation between these four basic classes of the ASM is illustrated in figure 1.3[21]. Some of the state variables and methods of the various classes have been displayed to give the reader an idea of their content, but it is far from a full listing. The `agent` demands assets from the `specialist` and gets the input for the demand decision from the `world` class. The `world` does not generate this information itself, but obtains information on dividends from the `dividend` class and information on asset prices from the `specialist` class.

Four different `agent` subclasses and five different `specialist` subclasses are displayed. Note that all methods that handle the relation to other classes, are placed with the superclasses `specialist` and `agent`. One may denote these methods *the interface elements* as these methods are always present and thus can be relied upon for interaction purposes. Also note that all the subclasses of the `agent` have a method

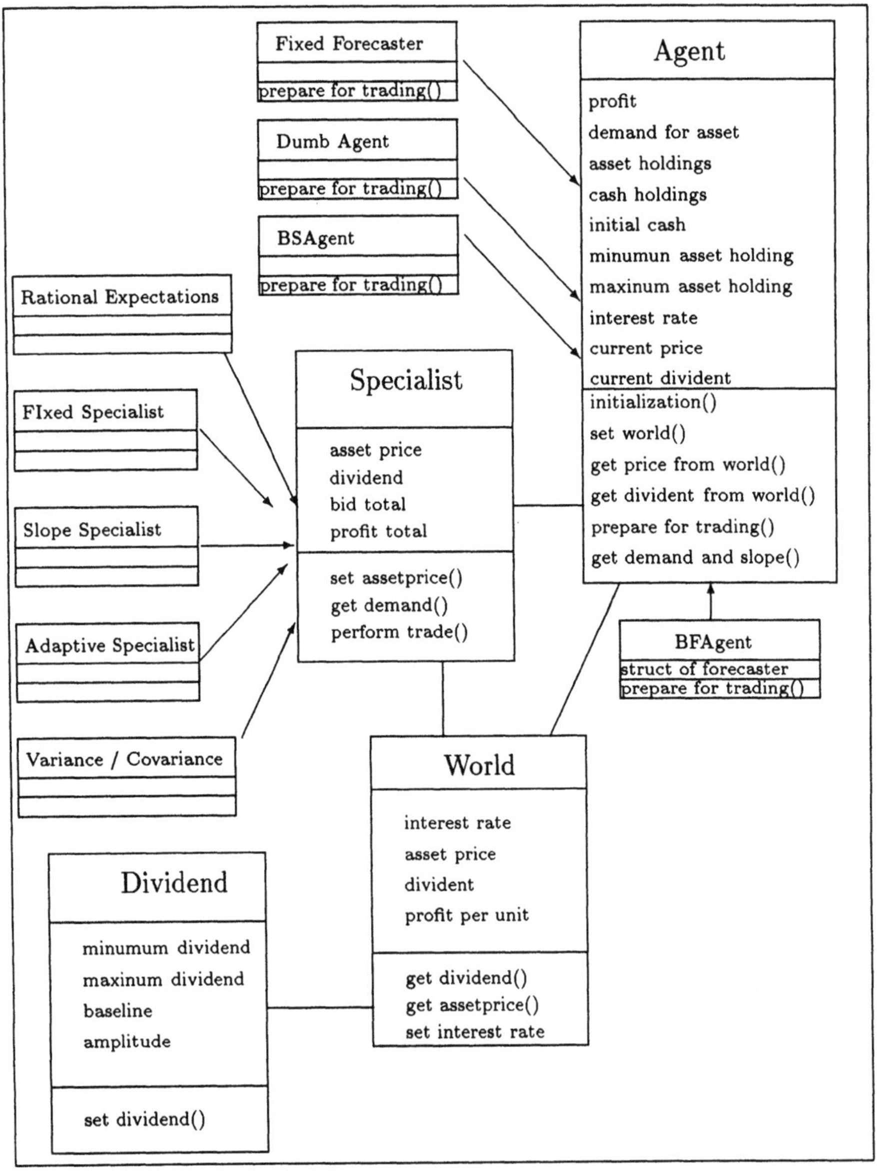


*Figure 1.3.* The structure of ASM

called **`prepare for trading`** a method that in all cases overrides a similar method in the superclass. As a matter of fact the **`prepare for trading`** method in the **`agent`** class is empty - it is placed there to remind developers of new agents that all agents must have a method called **`prepare for trading`** - a very simple way of communicating interface requirements as described above in section 3.

## 4.2. Building Blocks Supplied by Askenazi's BankNet

BankNet is a graph-based simulation systems that obtains its graph structure by letting agents have links to each other. The model is supposed to illustrate the emergence of banking, but as a matter of fact all agents start out as being banks. Agents are given an income each period, and this income is lent to members of the `investLink` of the agent. Some agents are then presented with an investment opportunity, but in order to carry out the investment, the agent in question needs to borrow money. The following agent sends a borrow request to members of its `borrowLink`. Agents presented with a borrowing request, divide their money holdings equally among all agents requesting to borrow. The investment may generate a profit, and this profit is divided among the sources of the financing (members of the `borrowLink`). Finally agents must get back the money they "invested" in members of their `investLink`.

The model is developed by a pleaded non-economist, and for an economist the model is not very intuitive. There are a number of questions to be posed; why do agent engage in this double-lending process - why not keep the income until borrowing requests are made? Where does the income come from, and where does it go?

An element from BankNet that could be transformed to a more general framework is the idea of having links between borrowers and investors, and the possibility of moving these links from one agent to another. In a cellular structure the same principles could be applied - only in this case it would only be possible to link with neighboring cells. The tools that come with the BankNet `DiGraph`, may also be useful. To use this tool, the agent designed by the user (`myAgent`), however, needs to inherit from the class `DiGraph`. Since an economics framework would also require `myAgent` to inherit from an **`agent`** class, this creates problems in objective-C which does not support multiple inheritance.

## 4.3. Building Blocks Supplied by Terna's ERA Scheme and his BP-CT (Hayek)Model

Terna's BP-CT model is a model of agent behavior based on neural networks. Terna applies an Environment-Rules-Agent (ERA) Scheme; a scheme that may be considered a framework. The environment of the ERA scheme is what is normally contained in `ModelSwarm`. Rules are an abstract representation of the cognition of agents. `RuleMasters` determine agent behavior whereas `RuleMakers` changes the rules of the `RuleMasters` (e.g. by updating neural nets). This division into `RuleMaker` and `RuleMaster` appear to be very potent whenever learning is applied to agent behavior. The modularity obtained by dividing into `agent`, `RuleMaster` and `RuleMaker` is exactly the kind of structure which characterizes frameworks. The interface between `Agent` and `RuleMaker` remains the same no matter which `RuleMaster` is used.

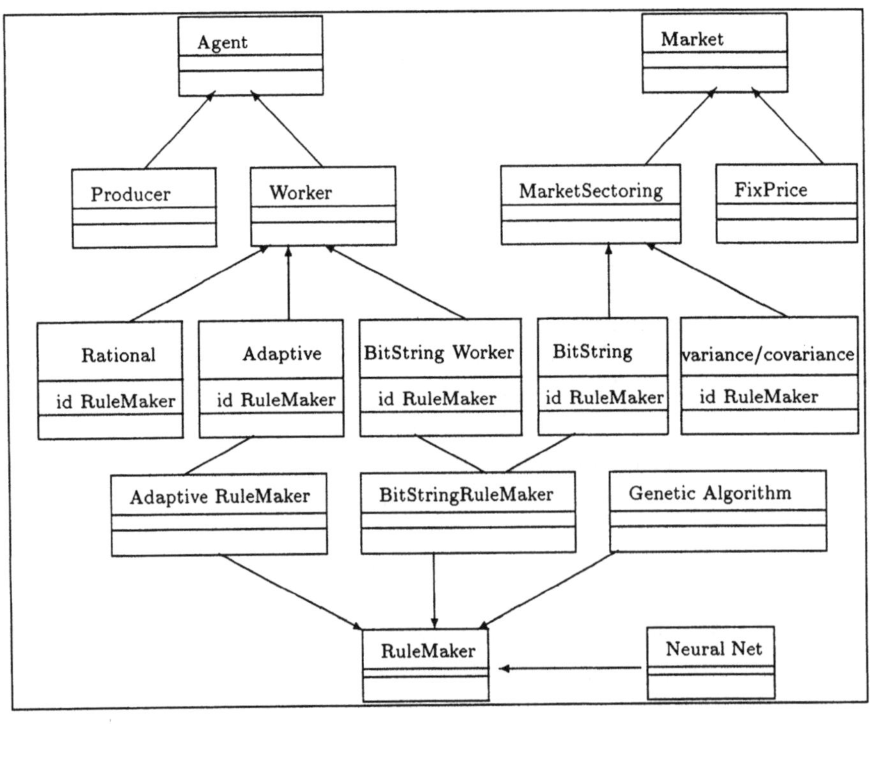


*Figure 1.4.* A possible implementation of the ERA scheme

In Figure 1.4 we see an example of how Terna's scheme may be applied. We have defined a `RuleMaker` superclass and different `RuleMaker` subclasses like neural net and genetic algorithm. These `RuleMaker` classes may be used by different `Agents` and `Markets` (called specialist in the ASM model). In our example, `RuleMasters` are subclasses of `agents` or `markets`. We associate a `RuleMaker` to the `RuleMasters` if rules are evolving in any way. In this way, the updating mechanism of the `bitString ruleMaker` can be used by both the `bitString worker ruleMaster` and the `bitstring market ruleMaster`.

Besides his ERA scheme, Terna has another architectural suggestion; that agents should have two associated classes; `dataWarehouse` for storing all data and `interface` for handling an agents interaction with the environment and thus with other agents. The idea is that the contents of the `dataWarehouse` and the `interface` need not change in case one wants to substitute a neural network agent for a genetic algorithm agent.

Terna applies his ERA scheme in the BP-CT package which is used for making artificial neural networks in Swarm. BP-CT is referring to the techniques applied in training the neural nets (Back Propagation - Cross Targets). BP-CT is applied to the modeling of markets (Hayek model) where consumer agents make buying proposals and producer agents make selling proposals. Terna applies a very simple trading rule; exchange is possible if the price proposed by the producer is less than, or equal to, the price proposed by the consumer. The final price is that suggested by the producer and the quantity exchanged is the minimum of the two.

It is clear that Terna's focus is on learning by economic agents, and unfortunately this focus hides away the actual economic interaction of his Hayek model in the `consumerInterface` rather than making an intermediary agent as the specialist trader in the ASM. This is NOT a critique of the fact that Terna uses complete decentralized coordination (no auctioneer), but a critique of the fact that it is made rather difficult to implement other ways for agents to meet than his list shuffling device. It could also be easier to introduce different trading rules to the model. This is particularly unfortunate since Terna in other respects successfully obtains the modularity which is a prerequisite for reuse of code.

## 4.4. Building Blocks Supplied by ORECOS

The developers of ORECOS (ORganizational ECOsystems Simulator) describe it as a toolkit designed to facilitate organizational analysis (Schlueter-Langdon, Bruhn and Shaw (2000)). The organizational structure analyzed is supply chains, and the elements that this toolkit can supply to an economics framework, are methods for handling industry level and input-output systems.

ORECOS contains three different types of agents; `enterprises`, `processes` and `markets`. The market agents clear the individual `markets` using a two-sided competitive sealed-bid auction mechanism. `Enterprises` are both buyers and sellers since they buy their input and sell their output. The functional relation between input and output of an `enterprise` is determined by one or more of the `process` agents. The `enterprise` plan and manage production, `process` agents executes the production.

The implementation of production as a relation between an `enterprise` agent and a number of production processes (`process` agents), and the interdependence of `enterprises` is something that could be applied to an economics framework. Since relations between `enterprises` is modeled as markets, a more general market structure may be applied. The difference here is not the market-clearing mechanism, but the fact that it may be applied at different hierarchical levels.

## 4.5. The Evo Artificial Life Framework

The Evo framework that has been developed by Michael A. Krumpus is a framework developed in order to ease implementation of decentralized evolutionary computation (Krumpus(2000)). Since the framework has no economics content, it is the implementation of a framework that may help us design an economics framework for Swarm. The primary method for reusing code implemented in the Evo framework is inheritance. The framework defines a number of superclasses; `Agent`, `Population`, `Environment`, and the user of the framework lets his own classes inherit from these super-classes.

In the Evo framework one may find a structure similar to Terna's division into `RuleMaster` and `RuleMaker`, although in this case it is a little more complex than in Terna's example. An `Agent` in the Evo framework has the following general characteristics:

**instructions;** actions that the agent can perform.

**senses;** the methods the agent can use to learn about its environment.

**observables;** characteristics of the agent that can be observed by other agents.

**traits;** characteristics of the agents that do not change and are transmitted to offsprings. May be observables.

**targeters;** the methods the agent can use to learn about other agents.

From these characteristics Evo generates a genome for the agent divided into a trait chromosome and a behavior chromosome. It is on these chromosomes that evolution operates.

Krumpus has implemented a version of `SimpleBug`; a population of bugs that eat, move and mate in an environment containing food. There is no doubt that the complexity and the size of the code to be written to perform this simulation is reduced by using the Evo framework rather than using Swarm directly.

The idea of Evo is to let the classes of your model inherit from Evo classes rather than from `Swarm` and `SwarmObject` as is standard in Swarm modeling. In the case of `SimpleBug`, `ModelSwarm` is a subclass of the Evo class `EnvironmentDiscrete2d`, but since `EnvironmentDiscrete2d` is a subclass of `Swarm`, `ModelSwarm` still has all the Swarm features. In the same way `Bug` inherits from the Evo class `Agent`, but `Agent` is itself a subclass of `SwarmObject`.

In this way the Swarm community may develop frameworks for different types of simulations. The lack of multiple inheritance, however, makes the combination of different frameworks rather cumbersome. There are ways of overcoming the problem, but the different frameworks must be adopted for it. Once a solution to this problem is found, one could picture a situation, where economic models using neural nets or genetic algorithms would combine two frameworks; one for economics and one for neural nets or genetic algorithms.

## 5. An Economics Framework

Judging from our experience with the Evo framework, and with ASM and other economic Swarm models, we feel confident that it is possible to build an economics framework that would be useful to most economic simulation models. Learning from ASM and other economic Swarm models, we suggest a basic structure with an `Agent` class and a `Market` class. As illustrated in figure 1.5 the relation between the two classes is one of aggregation; a `Market` class consist of a number of `Agents`.

In figure 1.5 we have made some suggestions of the type of state variables and methods that our two base classes may contain. An `Agent` has a money balance, a number of financial assets, which may be contained in a linked list so that they may be heterogeneous, e.g. linked to specific issuers. An `Agent` must be able to make offers of sale or purchase to a `Market`. For this activity we have reserved two state variables; `offerPrice` and `offerVolume`. We have also provided the `Agent` with a list of associates; this list may contain neighbors or preferred trading partners. We have provided the `Agent` with two methods as examples;

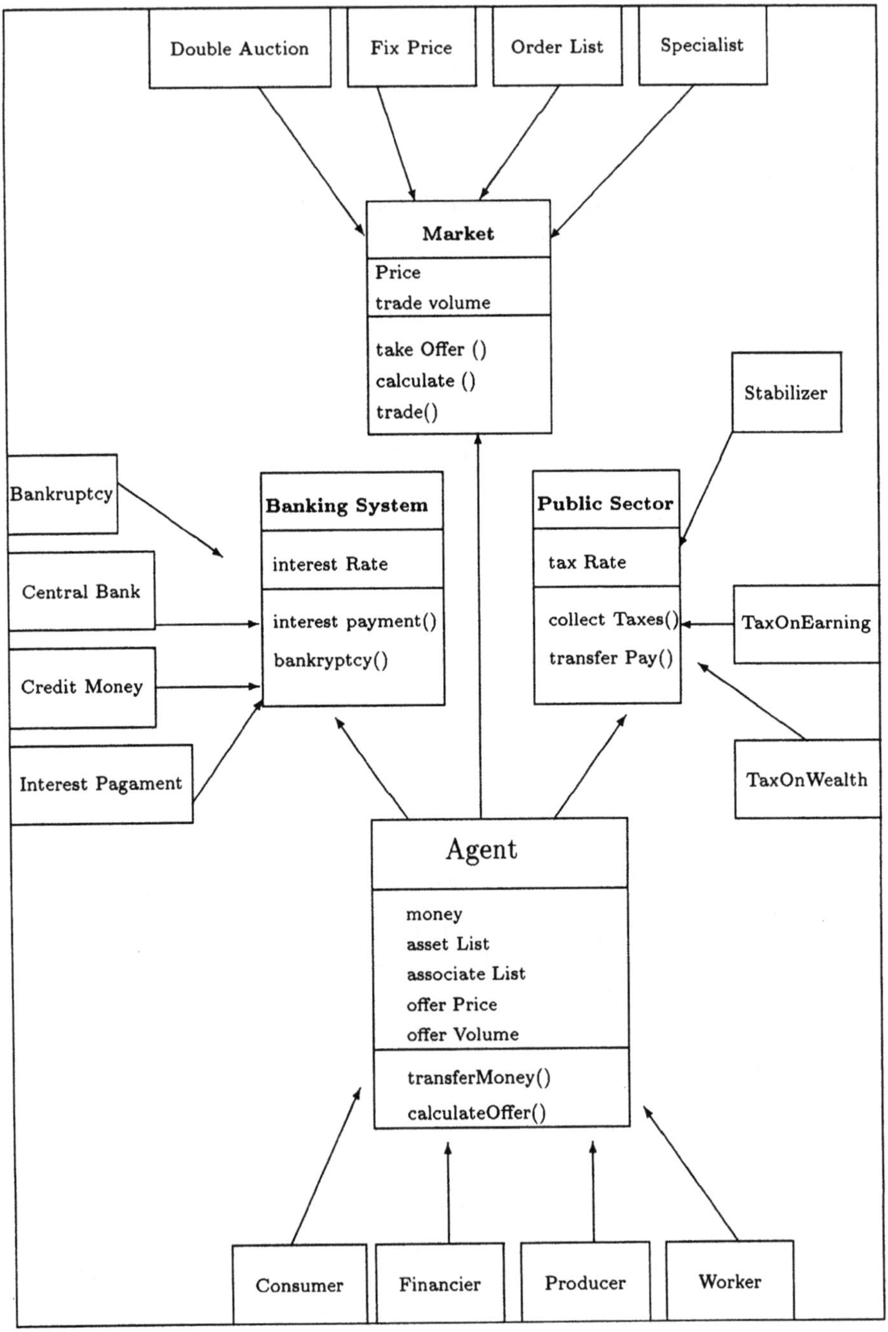


*Figure 1.5.* Suggestion for an economics framework

`transferMoney`, which will assure that accounting identities are always respected (no money disappears). The `calculateOffer` method, used for signaling offers to buy or sell, is a template method that must be overridden by its subclasses.

The framework should have a number of different agent types that all inherit from the `Agent` class. Obvious candidates for agent types are `Producer`, `Consumer`, `Financier`, and `Worker`. They will all use the `offerPrice` and `offerVolume`, but it is different things the subclasses offer for sale or purchase, and in some cases `offerPrice` or `offerVolume` may be fixed. A `worker` may offer a fixed volume of 8 hours a day, and a `Producer` may offer goods at a fixed price. A user of the framework will need to make his own subclasses of the four subclasses of `Agent` suggested here.

We have also made a few suggestions with respect to the contents of the `Market` class. We have a `price` which may be a centrally determined market clearing price, or it may be calculated as an average of decentralized trading prices. The `Market` will also register the trade volume. The `Market` must take orders from its `Agent` members, calculate prices and volumes, and perform the actual trade. These methods may apply to the case of a centralized market clearing mechanism, but the same methods may apply to decentralized trade. As suggested by Terna (2000) we do not allow agents to interact directly, but let our `Market` communicate with them.

The framework should also contain a number of subclasses of the `Market` class. Here we have suggested a double auction market, a fix-price market, a market which is a linked list of offers to buy and sell and a specialist trader market. Note that it is a mixture of completely decentralized trading mechanisms, and mechanisms that use a centralized market maker of some sort. All three methods of the `Market` are template methods that must be overridden by the subclasses. A model may of course have several markets with different characteristics.

Economies are not pure market economies and therefore we have made room for other institutions at a market level. Other classes could be; `Central Banking System`, `Public Sector` (with tax collection and public spending/transfer payments). Again figure 1.5 contains suggestions for subclasses; one may have different public sectors e.g. different tax systems. A subclass of `BankingSystem` could hold methods for performing bankruptcy.

Besides these two layers of classes; `Agent` and `Market`, an economics framework should embrace a number of classes of a more auxiliary nature. Such classes could take care of the learning aspects of agent behavior, i.e. classes for neural networks, genetic algorithms, etc. Here a structure similar to Terna's ERA scheme could be useful. One could also have a set of classes holding different formalizations of agent preferences. Another set of classes could hold the characteristics of different financial assets or the characteristics of different consumer goods. There must, of course, be a correspondence between different ways of perceiving human preferences and different ways of describing a good[22].

The framework should be designed in such a way that the modeling of feedback effects from macrolevel to microlevel is encouraged. Important information may be lost if these effects are not enforced. In this context we are mainly thinking about respecting the accounting rules of real world economies. Much too often agent-based models are partial, for instance they let consumers receive incomes that arise out of the blue (i.e. they are not an expense to another agent in the system) - even in models where the production side is modeled. One may find models where agents pay taxes that just disappear, or entrepreneurs that pay wages that are not received by other agents. As far as possible such holes in the accounting system should be avoided. By letting all agents have accounts in one big accounting system, and by only changing these accounts if money is transferred from one agent to another, many fallacies can be avoided. The big advantage of agent-based computational economics is precisely the possibly to model the interaction of micro- and macro-level, and the potential of this fact reaches far beyond respecting accounting identities. Where general equilibrium systems must accept technology and preferences as being exogenously determined, agent-based models can allow these magnitudes to be generated through interaction between micro- and macrolevels.

A widely discussed topic in the simulating community is the importance of scheduling, e.g. differences in results between synchronous updating, and event-driven updating. The framework should not limit Swarm's support of different types of scheduling, but hopefully contribute to making users more aware of their choices.

## 6. Testing our virtual framework

In this section we shall search through existing economic swarm models for program elements that could be replaced by our virtual economics framework.

### 6.1. Terna's ABCDE Model

Terna's ABCDE model (Terna(1998)) is a very simple market model which could easily be fitted into our virtual framework. Terna has two main agent classes; `Consumers` and `Vendors`. Instances of these classes meet randomly and trade takes place if the price demanded by the `vendor` is lower than the maximum price accepted by the `consumer`. Both types of agents will lower or raise their price according to their past experience - e.g. no success in selling will make a `vendor` lower its price and vice versa.

In an economics framework it should be possible to implement such a simple model with only few lines of code. The simplicity of the model however also reveals an important aspect of simulation modeling, namely the method by which agents meet. Terna uses a list shuffling device similar to what is found in several other Swarm models. As shown by Huberman and Glance (1993), how updating takes place (synchronous or asynchronous) may be very important to the results obtained, and how agents meet is likely to be important as well. A fundamentally different method for agents to meet is by event-driven simulation, where agents will have to find an agent to trade with when THEY have the need to trade, and not when their number happens to turn up in the lists of some market-maker. Different scheduling methods have to be integrated in the framework. Simple models as Terna's ABCDE are ideal for getting to understand such different scheduling principles.

## 6.2. Bruun and Luna's Endogenous Growth Model

The central object in the growth model (Bruun and Luna (2000)) is the producer, which could be made a subclass of the suggested `Producer` class. The model uses neural nets for modeling learning by producers, and this might be imported from another framework. As is suggested in the economics framework, the model operates with an `agent` class which takes care of money transfers etc.. All instances of the `agent` class have a consumer side and a production side. The production side is either an `independent` producer, a `worker` or an `entrepreneur` who has hired other agents to work for him. The different producer types are all subclasses of the `agent`. The status of the production side of an `agent` changes during runtime. Such a structure would also be possible under the economics framework.

Consumers in the model are very simple, and in a framework setting it would be an easy task to substitute the existing `consumer` with other types to investigate the importance of consumption to growth. As is the case with the different `producer` subclasses, the consumer is also a subclass of the `agent` class.

The model also uses other features planned to be part of the framework; a bankruptcy mechanism, a public sector with transfer payments. The payment system of the model is a pure credit system.

A weak aspect of the model is its market mechanisms. A very simple mechanism is used for the labor market whereas the market for consumption goods is fix-price demand-determined. In a framework more complex market mechanisms would probably be chosen.

## 6.3. Mittone and Patelli's tax evasion model

In Mittone and Patelli's tax evasion model (Mittone and Patelli), a fiscal system collects taxes from different types of agents in order to finance the production of a public good. The population is composed of three different types of agents; honest taxpayers, imitative taxpayers and free rider taxpayers, and the relative weight of the three types is determined by their fitness through a genetic algorithm. The question to be answered is what effect can be expected from an increase in the tax rate.

Agents derive utility from an externally determined income and from the consumption of a public good and dis-utility from the payment of taxes. Some agents (honest), furthermore, derive utility from being honest, other agents (imitative) derive utility from being close to the average, whereas the last group (free riders) derives utility from not paying taxes. It would be nice if this model could make use of a standardized way of handling utility. The utility functions used are probably close to the literature, but it seems strange to have this mixture of goods and income in a utility function[23].

Modeling utility is a vital part of an economics framework since utility constitutes probably the weakest element in economic simulation approaches. For applying evolutionary optimization tools, as in this case genetic algorithms, one must be able to define a fitness function - and as the most natural thing in the world many economists turn towards the well-known utility function. But can the goals of human behavior really be reduced to such a one-dimensional structure? The suggested framework has no easy way of solving this problem, but it must contain a number of different ways of representing utility, e.g. as a binary string[24].

Since we are dealing with a partial model, where taxes are somehow transformed into capital - a capital which is the only input in the production of public goods: using the suggested framework could provide the model with a macro-foundation. Another way of phrasing the partial non-monetary picture is that agents assign part of their labor to the production of a public good. If money and tax-payment are to be introduced, the fiscal system would collect taxes and spend the taxes in order to pay labor to produce the public good. At least in a less than full employment setup, this would make the story of tax evasion a little different since, now, agents income can no longer be exogenously given. Income and tax-payment become mutually dependent - at least at the aggregate level. The model thus constitutes a good example of a traditional microeconomic problem which can be given a macroeconomic foundation in a simulation model.

## 6.4. Corazza and Perrone on counterfeiting in monopolistic markets

This model (Corazza and Perrone (2000)) stands out from the remaining models a non agent-based, but a simulation model used for numerical analysis of a system of non-linear differential equations. The model has three agents; a monopolist, a counterfeiter and a consumer. The consumer is also perceived as a *market*. The monopolist and the counterfeiter could be modeled as a subclass of the `producer` class, but due to the aggregate nature of the market mechanism, there is not much to be won by letting the consumer/market agent inherit from the market class.

It would be interesting to carry out similar simulations in an agent-based setting. A number of stochastic variables is used to generate the dynamics of the system. Such use of the random generator may be replaced by endogenously arising dynamics in an agent-based model. In an agent-based setting it would also be possible to operate with more realistic behavior. In the present setting it is not easy to justify that the monopolist perform reputation investment when a counterfeiter enters the market, since the consumer is assumed not to be able to tell the difference between products supplied by the monopolist and products supplied by the counterfeiter. In an agent-based setting these assumption could be modified.

## 6.5. BankNet by Sapienza

An economist has adopted the BankNet model and placed it in a context of theory of financial intermediation (Sapienza(2000)). The actual model has not been changed, and the mechanisms of the model are still as described in section 4.2. The model could gain by being placed in the context of an economics framework, since it might provide a rationale for the behavior of agents. What is special about the BankNet model is the relations or links between agents, and these links need not be studied in the context of lending and investment as suggested by Askenazy.

Instead Askenazy's model could be applied to a Minsky world where all agents are perceived as financial intermediaries with assets and liabilities, and the structure for making such agents should be present in the `agent` class.

## 6.6. Financial Market simulation by T.E. Jares

Jares (2000) investigates the effects of having noise traders in a financial markets. The model has three main classes; a `trader` class, a `marketMaker` and a `marketStatistician`. In his code, Jares operates with a number of different trader types, but they are reduced to a fundamental trader and a noise trader in the final simulations. Besides these main classes, Jares operates with a number of classes of an auxiliary nature; a `shareRequest` is used for communicating asset demand from `trader` to `marketMaker`, and a `ClearingInfo` class is used by the `marketMaker` for storing information about asset demand.

It is evident that Jares' simulation model is similar to the ASM model. Where ASM has an `Agent`, Jares has a `Trader`, where ASM has a `Specialist` Jares has a `MarketMaker`, and where ASM has a `World`, Jares has a `MarketStatistician`. Jares has, however, not split out his stochastic dividend process in an independent and replaceable class.

It seems more than likely that the time and effort spent in developing Jares' model could have been reduced by reusing the design and some of the code of the ASM model. It is therefore a good example of the importance of increasing communication between builders of simulation models.

## 6.7. Supply Chain Management by Lin, Strader and Shaw

We already presented the ORECOS model as a supply chain model. Another supply chain Swarm model (Lin et al.(2000)) has a more complex subdivision of an enterprise since focus is on demand management policies / supply chain modeling. A business entity (enterprise) here consists of a number of different agents being responsible for different decisions (e.g.. capacity planning agent, production planning agent etc.). Since focus is on demand management, the interrelatedness of enterprises is not as well specified here as in the ORECOS model. Whereas the ORECOS model has both "upstream" (input) and "downstream" (output) relations, Lin et al. only model the upstream relations.

The suggested frameworks for economics is not ideal for modeling a structure as the supply chain, but still the model may benefit from different aspects of the framework. Again the basic agent can be used, but

Lin et al. also express a desire to extend their model with market mechanisms, and these could be provided by the framework. Links similar to those of the BankNet model may also be used for modeling the relations between different business entities in a supply chain.

## 6.8. Luna and Perrone on Coevolution of Human Capital and Firm Structure

This model (Luna and Perrone (2000)) operates at a higher level of abstraction than any of the remaining models discussed. A worker is perceived as a particular skill whereas entrepreneurs represent a particular firm-structure. The worker can change its skill by imitating other workers. Entrepreneurs hire an ex ante determined number of agents. The entrepreneur is a neural net connecting to the workers, and changing the weights assigned to the individual workers. At the end of the period, only effective firms survive.

Due to the level of abstraction, there is not much an economics framework could provide for this model. There is no actual production or consumption decision, no monetary accounting and no market mechanisms.

# 7. Conclusion

After replicating 8 different models within social sciences in Swarm, Axelrod (1997) concluded; *"We hoped to find some building blocks that were shared by several of these models that could provide the basis for a set of useful simulation techniques. Instead we found little overlap."* Our conclusion from looking at 11 different economic simulation models written in Swarm is not similar. There are a lot of common elements in economic simulation models, and there are advantages to be collected if we use a common programming platform.

Programming economic simulation models in Swarm in itself, however, does not lead us to a collection of these advantages. Swarm does not have any economics content, and the benefits from using Swarm are derived at a more technical level. Neither, it has been argued here, can it be expected to be sufficient to develop an economics library where components with a content from economics can be made available. In order for the benefits to be collected, one must have a framework that can give economic simulation models a common structure.

An economics framework is not meant to affect the theoretical content of economic simulation model. It must not function as a strait jacket and make us develop similar models. An economics framework is meant to reflect the structure of real world economies, and builders of economic simulation models must be able to put on different spectacles to focus on different aspects of the economic reality. But because economics is about a real world phenomena, we do have some structures that we can use as a common starting point.

## Notes

1. Center for Computable Economics originally at UCLA and Computable and Experimental Economics Laboratory, University of Trento, Italy

2. Program elements will be tested by more than one programmer.

3. Keep It Simple, Stupid!

4. Later we shall call such models "just-pour-water" models, meaning that you just add your values for a limited number of parameters.

5. Implementations of the framework may, of course, contain real world data.

6. This, of course, leaves an important work to be done in studying the institutional settings that the community chooses as standards. As noted by Lane, institutional settings matter, and therefore we must be very aware which settings we choose.

7. On top of this, Swarm takes care of memory allocation.

8. Users of the Swarm mailing lists often refer to themselves as *swarmites*.

9. Stefansson (1997) also presents two Swarm models; oligopolistic competition and a principal-agent model. These models are, however, presented as tutorials.

10. The two versions of BankNet are regarded as one model.

11. For frameworks the most popular reference is Fayad, Schmidt and Johnson(1999) building Application Frameworks - Object-Oriented Foundations of Frameworks Design.

12. For patterns the most popular reference is Gamma, Helm, Johnson and Vlissides (1995).

13. Schelling(1978) and Lane(1993) both emphasize the importance of allowing for feedback effects from macro to micro. One way of implementing such feedback effects is by modeling money flows.

14. This phrase originates from H.Putnam according to Bonabeau and Theraulaz(1995).

15. Fayad et al.(1999a) talk about a "distributed software crisis" since hardware gets smaller, faster and cheaper whereas distributed software gets larger, slower and more expensive.

16. The present focus on frameworks is primarily due to Fayad, Schmidt and Johnson (see Fayad et al. (1999a+b)).

17. This is often referred to as the *Hollywood principle*; don't call us - we'll call You!

18. We may of course also talk about a number of different goods and a price vector.

19. Mass (Multi-Agent Survivability Simulator) and its successor (Horling and Lesser (1998)), MIMOSE (MIcro- and multilevel MOdelling SoftwarE)(Möhring(1992)) and its successor (`http://www.uni-koblenz.de/~moeh/projekte/framework.html`), GEAMAS (`http://www.univ-reunion.fr/~mas2/geames`), Boxed Economy at the following URL (`http://www.boxed-economy.org`), DESIRE (Brazier, van Eck and Treur (1997)), DMarksII (Kutschinski, Polani and Uthman), Lsd (Laboratory for Simulation Development) (`http://www.business.auc.dk/lsd/`).

20. Some of these platforms are quite recent, so they may be successful in spreading in the future.

21. The content of the scheme is mine, and may be different from what the developers of ASM would put there. For information on ASM I therefore refer the reader to the documentation of ASM, which is extensive.

22. If human preferences are a binary string, one must also describe goods by a binary string.

23. The literature quoted does not have public goods in the utility function at all - what seems to be even more strange.

24. Such an approach to utility is taken in Zambelli and Hjortlund (1998)

# References

Arthur, W.B. , Holland, J.H., LeBaron, B., Palmer, R. and Taylor, P. (1997). Asset Pricing under Endogenous Expectations in an Artificial Stock Market. in *The Economy as an Evolving Complex System II.* ed. by Arthur, W.B., Durlauf, S. and Lane, D.. Addison-Wesley.

Askenazi, M, *Some Notes on the BankNet Model*, available at `http://www.santafe.edu/~manor/banknet.html`.

Axelrod, R. (1997). Advancing the Art of Simulation in the Social Sciences, in *Simulating Social Phenomena* ed. by Conte, R., Hegselmann, R. and Terna, P.. Lecture Notes in Economics and Mathematical Systems 456, Springer 1997.

Axtell, R, Axelrod, R., Epstein, J.M. and Cohen, M.D. (1996). Aligning Simulation Models: A Case Study and Results. In *Computational and Mathematical Organization Theory.* Vol 1.

Bonabeau, E.W., and Theraulaz, G.(1995). Why do we need Artficial Life? In *Artificial Life - An overview* ed. by Langton, C.G..

Brazier,F.M.T., van Eck, P.A.T. and Treur, J. (1997). Modelling a Society of Simple Agents: From Conceptual Specification to Experimentation. In *Simulating Social Phenomena* ed. by Conte, R., Hegselmann, R. and Terna, P. Lecture Notes in Economics and Mathematical Systems 456, Springer.

E. Bruderer and Maiers, M. (1997). From the Margin to the Mainstream: An Agenda for Computer Simulations in the Social Sciences. In *Simulating Social Phenomena* ed. by R. Conte, R., Hegselmann, R. and Terna, P. Lecture Notes in Economics and Mathematical Systems 456, Springer.

Bruun, C and Luna, F. (2000). Endogenous Growth in a Swarm Economy. In Luna and Stefansson (2000).

Corazza, M. and Perrone, A. (2000). Nonlinear Stochastic Dynamics for Supply Counterfeiting in Monopolistic Markets. In Luna and Stefansson (2000).

Erdogmus, H. and Tanir, O. (1999). Developing Frameworks to Support Design Reuse. In Fayad, M.E, Schmidt, D.C., and Johnson, R.E. (1999b).

Eriksson, H.E. and Penker, M. (1998). *UML Toolkit*, Wiley Computer Publishing.

Fayad, M.E., Schmidt, D.C. and Johnson, R.E. (1999a). *Building Application Frameworks - Object-Oriented Foundations of Framework Design.* Wiley Computer Publishing.

Fayad, M.E, Schmidt, D.C. and Johnson, R.E. (1999b). *Implementing Application Frameworks - Object-Oriented Frameworks at Work.* Wiley Computer Publishing.

Gamma, E., Helm, R., Johnson, R. and Vlissides, J. (1995). *Design Patterns: Elements of Reusable Object-Oriented Software.* Addison-Wesley.

Gulyàs, L., Kozsik, T. and Corliss, J.B. (1999). The Multi-Agent Modelling Language and the Model Design Interface. *Journal of Artificial Societies and Social Simulation.* **Vol 2**, No.3, available at `http:/www.soc.surrey.ac.uk/JASSS/2/3/8.html`.

Hjortlund, M. and Zambelli, S. (1998). *On the Constitutional Choice of a Democratic Voting Rule: An experimental approach.* working paper from department of economics, politics and public administration, Aalborg University.

Horling, B. and Lesser, V. (1998). *A Reusable Component Architecture for Agent Construction.* UMass Computer Science Technical Report 98-30.

Huberman, B.A. and Glance, N.S. (1993). Evolutionary Games and Computer Simulations. *Proceedings of the National Academy of Science USA* 90, pp. 7716-7718.

Jares, T.E. (2000). Numerical Modeling, Noise Traders, and the Swarm Simulation System. In Luna and Stefansson (2000).

Keynes, J.M. (1939). Professor Tinbergens Method. *Economic Journal.* **Vol 49** pp. 558-70.

Krumpus, M.A. (2000). *Overview of the Evo Artificial Life Framework,* `http://www.omicrongroup.org/evo/`.

Kutschinski, E., Polani, D. and Uthmann, T.. *A Decentralized Agent-Based Platform for Automated Trade and its Simulation.* Available at `http://nautilus.Informatik.Uni-Mainz.DE/~eri`.

Lane, D.A. (1993). Artificial worlds and economics, part 1 and 2. *Journal of Evolutionary Economics.* **Vol 3** pp.89-107 and pp.177-197.

Lin, F., Strader, T.J. and Shaw, M.J. (2000). Using Swarm for Simulating the Order Fulfillment Frocess in Divergent Assembly Supply Chains. In Luna and Stefansson (2000).

Luna, F. and Perrone, A. (2000). The Coevolution of Human Capital and Firm Structure. In Luna and Stefansson (2000).

Luna, F. and Stefansson, B. (2000). *Economic Simulations in Swarm: Agent-based Modelling and Object Oriented Programming.* Advances in Computational Economics **Vol 14**. Kluwer Academic Publishers.

Miller, G.G., McGregor, J. and Major, M.L. (1999). Capturing Framework Requirements. In Fayad et al. (1999).

Minar, N., Burkhart, R., Langton, C. and Askenazi, M. (1996). *The Swarm Simulation System: A Toolkit for Building Multi-Agent Simulations.* Santa Fe Institute Working Paper 96-04-2.

Mittone, L and Patelli, P. (2000). Imitative Behaviour in Tax Evasion. In Luna and Stefansson (2000).

Möhring,M.(1992). *Social Science Multilevel Simulation with MIMOSE.* University of Koblenz-Landau, Institute of Social Science Informatics.

Sapienza, M.D. (2000). An Experimental Approach to the Study of Banking Intermediation: the BankNet Simulator. In Luna and Stefansson (2000).

Schelling, T.C.(1978). *Micromotives and Macrobehaviour.* W.W.Norton and Company.

Schlueter-Langdon, C., Bruhn, P, Shaw, M.J.: 2000 "Online Supply Chain Modeling and Simulation. In Luna and Stefansson (2000).

Stefansson, B. (1997). Swarm: An Object Oriented Simulation Platform Applied to Markets and Organizations. In *Evolutionary Programming VI* ed. by Angeline, P., Reynolds, R., McDonnell, J. and Eberhart, R. Lecture Notes in Computer Science. **Vol. 1213**, Springer-Verlag.

Stefansson, B. (2000). Simulating Economic Agents in Swarm. In Luna and Stefansson (2000).

Terna, P. (1998). Simulation Tools for Social Scientists: Building Agent Based Models with SWARM. *Journal of Artificial Societies and Social Simulation.* **Vol 1** No. 2, `http://www.soc.surrey.ac.uk/JASSS/1//2/4.html`.

Terna, P. (2000). Economic Experiments with Swarm: a Neural Network Approach to the Self-Development of Consistency in Agents Behavior. In Luna and Stefansson (2000).

II

# NEW TOOLS

Chapter 2

# AUTOMATED TRADING EXPERIMENTS WITH MAML

László Gulyás
*Computer and Automation Research Institute, Hungarian Academy of Sciences, 1518 Budapest, POB 63, Hungary*
laszlo.gulyas@sztaki.hu

Tibor Vincze
*Department of General Computer Sciences, Loránd Eötvös University of Sciences, 1117, Budapest, Pázmány Péter sétány 1/D, Hungary*
gigaw@valerie.inf.elte.hu

**Abstract**

MAML (Multi-Agent Modeling Language) is a macro-language for Swarm. Its aim is to ease the creation of the most common set of agent-based models by providing a couple of high level constructs and structures in the form of specialized keywords. In this paper we introduce the concepts of MAML through an extension of Chris Preist's auction model on automated trading.

The original model proposes a persistent shout double auction setup for automated business-to-business electronic trading in which seller and buyer agents trade with an abstract good on a daily basis, one unit a day. Our version of the model extends the original setup in three ways. First, it relaxes the one-unit-a-day constraint. Secondly, it allows for the fluctuation of the supply and the demand by letting agents to enter and leave the market. Finally, it introduces time pressure on agents by setting a limit by which the agents must buy or sell the intended amount of good.

## 1. Introduction

MAML (Multi-Agent Modeling Language) is a macro-language for Swarm [SDG][MBLA96]. Its aim is to ease the creation of the most common set of agent-based models and simulations by providing a couple of high level constructs and structures in the form of specialized keywords. Besides these keywords, the other parts of a MAML simulation are written in Swarm. Also, the MAML compiler produces pure Swarm code. This setup has the advantage that basically the full functionality of the Swarm libraries (random number generator, graphical and statistical tools, etc. [SDG]) is available for MAML programmers.

In this paper we introduce the concepts of MAML through an extension of Chris Preist's auction model on automated trading [P98]. The original model proposes a persistent shout double auction setup [FR92] for automated business-to-business electronic trading in which seller and buyer agents trade with an abstract good on a daily basis, one unit a day. To reach an agreement the agents continuously adapt their pricing strategy based on a version of the *Widrow-Hoff* learning rule [RHW86].

Our version of the model extends this original setup in three ways. First, it relaxes the one-unit-a-day constraint. Secondly, it allows for the fluctuation of the supply and the demand (by letting agents enter and leave the market). Finally, it introduces time pressure on agents by imposing a deadline by which the agents must buy or sell the intended amount of good.

The paper is organized as follows. Section 2 defines the automated trading model in detail. This is followed by the detailed discussion of MAML's constructs through a step-by-step guide to the implementation of the model in Section 3 The next section gives a discussion of the model's results, while Section 5 summarizes the paper.

## 2. Agents that Negotiate

After the advent of the global computer network the processes of our everyday life are getting adapted to make use of the new communications potential. One of the latest of these adaptations involved trading. The often cited result of this transformation is electronic commerce.

E-commerce, however, does not only mean to make use of the exceptional communication potential, but also involves the automation of the traditional trading process. For this, autonomous software components, or as they are often named, autonomous agents [WJ95] are needed that are capable of acting on behalf of their owner (a person or an organization) in a responsible manner. In [GMM98] Guttman et al. discussed how agents can be used for different aspects of business-to-consumer electronic commerce.

Agents, however, are also used in another domain of the networked market, namely in business-to-business e-commerce, where companies trade with one another over the computer network. As these trades usually involve large number of transactions and are often sensitive to timely reaction, agents have great potential both in automating the processing of the enormous amount of business information and in the execution of routine tasks. That is, agents are appropriate tools for automated trading.

## 2.1. A Simple Model of Automated Trading

Trading agents, however, are not easy to build. The algorithms used for negotiation should be fair (to the agent's owner and to its partners), they must be computationally efficient and also, they are expected to achieve reasonable deals even in the presence of other agents with unknown strategies. Moreover, a system of such agents should also be efficient. That is, the bids and offers issued by the participating agents should converge at a pace similar to, or rather, higher than that produced by human negotiators. To achieve the goals mentioned above, multi-agent simulation is intensively used to test the behavior of artificial societies of trading agents.

In [P98] Preist describes a business-to-business scenario in which economic agents trade with a single abstract commodity. The units of this abstract commodity are uniform and interchangeable (e.g. as in the case of grain, communications bandwidth, etc.). Agents are divided into buyers and sellers. Each agent is given its own limit price: a buyer will never buy at a higher price; while a seller will never sell for less than this. They are free to make any deal subject to this constraint, but, naturally, buyers prefer lower prices, while sellers tend for higher ones. Moreover, the agents prefer to make trades at their limit prices rather than not to trade at all.

Time is divided into 'trading days' and each agent intends to buy or sell a single unit per day. The negotiation is executed as a daily persistent shout double auction [FR92] [P98], which is organized into rounds. In the first round, all agents must give their initial bid or offer. In the subsequent rounds, the agents can modify their current bid/offer if they choose to do so. However, if an agent skips this option, its previous bid/offer will remain valid. All bids/offers are heard by all participants and trading takes place if a bid and offer meet or cross (i.e. the bid is higher than the offer) at the average of the given two prices. If more than one bid and offer cross, then multiple trades take place: the highest bid is matched with the lowest offer, the involved items are deleted and this process is repeated until there is no overlap between bids and offers. The trading day is over when all agents have bought or sold, or when they are no longer willing to change their bid/offer. At this point a new day starts and the agents are reinitialized with the intention to trade another good.

**The Agents' Negotiation Strategy.** In Preist's model the agents try to maximize their profit (the difference between their limit price and the price at which they actually trade). The profit is calculated for a single unit only, that is, no longer-term profitability is taken into account. The agents use a simple learning strategy to adapt to the varying demand and supply on the market. For this, each agent keeps track of the profit it currently hopes to make (i.e., its profit goal). The price an agent is willing to trade for is its current valuation ($Valuation_t^i$). This is calculated from its limit price and its profit goal (see below).

The initial value of the agents' profit goal is assigned randomly. In each round, the agents adjust their profit goal based on the bids, offers and trades in the marketplace in order to maximize their profit. The algorithm the agents use for this adjustment has two phases. First, they determine a target trade price ($Trade^i$) by using a small set of heuristics. Then they apply the *Widrow-Hoff* learning rule [RHW86] to gradually alter the profit goal (and thus the current valuation) towards the target price. An agent that has no more good to trade does not change its current valuation.

The heuristics used in the first phase are the following:

$$Target^{Buyers} = \begin{cases} Bid_{max} + \epsilon, & \text{if } Bid_{max} < Offer_{min} \\ Offer_{min}, & \text{otherwise.} \end{cases} \tag{1}$$

$$Target^{Sellers} = \begin{cases} Offer_{min} - \epsilon, & \text{if } Bid_{max} < Offer_{min} \\ Bid_{max}, & \text{otherwise.} \end{cases} \tag{2}$$

where $Bid_{max}$ and $Offer_{min}$ stands for the highest bid and lowest offer of the day, respectively, while $\epsilon$ denotes an arbitrary small number.

The learning rule the agents use is fairly simple (see (3)). It is parameterized by a *learning rate* ($0 \le \beta \le 1$) that determines the speed of the adjustment. The higher $\beta$ is, the faster the current valuation approaches the target price.

$$Valuation_{t+1}^i = Valuation_t^i + \lfloor \beta(Target - Valuation_t^i) \rfloor \tag{3}$$

where $t$ denotes time (measured in rounds) and $Valuation_t^i$ stands for the current valuation of agent $i$ at round $t$.

## 2.2. An Extended Version of the Model

The model we use in this paper to demonstrate the capabilities of MAML is an extension of the model discussed above. The alterations incorporated in this version follow the guidelines of the original publication [P98] by addressing three of the five issues listed as prerequisites for moving to realistic markets.

Our first extension is to release the one-unit-a-day constraint. That is, our agents are allowed to trade more than a single unit per day, although they must buy/sell them one by one. Second, we allow satisfied agents to leave. In the original model, the population of the agents remained the same all the time, which meant that as time passed by agents got more and more sophisticated, and adapted to one another's behavior.

In our version an agent that has traded the amount assigned may leave the market. In this case, the agent gets replaced by a newcomer, who has to start the learning over. Finally, we introduced time pressure on the agents. Every agent has to complete its task before an individually set deadline.

As a consequence of the last extension, the agents' rule to adjust to the market price must be altered. The speed of adjustment depends on two parameters. On one hand, the value of $\epsilon$ in (1) (2) specifies the amount by which the agents raise/lower their target prices. On the other, the learning rate ($\beta$) controls the pace at which the agents approach their targets, see (3)

In our extension, we decided to control the speed by altering the first parameter. Therefore, we made $\epsilon$ dependent of the time available to trade. Therefore, we used the following equations to determine the values denoted by $\epsilon$ in (1) and (2), respectively:

$$\epsilon^{Buyers} = \frac{LimitPrice^i - Bid_{max}}{TimeToTrade^i} \tag{4}$$

$$\epsilon^{Sellers} = \frac{Offer_{min} - LimitPrice^i}{TimeToTrade^i} \tag{5}$$

where $LimitPrice^i$ denotes the limit price of and $TimeToTrade^i$ the time (rounds) available to trade for agent $i$. In the calculation of this latter value we took into account the time (rounds) left until the deadline specified ($TimeLeft^i$) and also, the number of units remained to trade ($UnitsToTrade^i$) for the agent.

$$TimeToTrade^i = max(TimeLeft^i - UnitsToTrade^i, 1) \tag{6}$$

Note that if the number of rounds until the agent's deadline does not exceed the number of units the agent still has to trade then

$$TimeToTrade^i = 1 \qquad (7)$$

and therefore the appropriate $Target$ value equals to the agent's limit price ($LimitPrice^i$), see (1), (2), (4) and (5). This simple rule provides appropriate results even if only one unit can be traded per day (e.g., due to the trading capacity of the partner agents)[1].

# 3. The Multi-Agent Modeling Language

The Multi-Agent Modeling Language (MAML) provides high level notations and specialized keywords for the users of Swarm [SDG], in order to ease the development of agent-based models and simulations. Besides these structures, the other parts of a MAML simulation are written in Swarm [MBLA96]. Also, the MAML compiler produces pure Swarm code.

The main advantages of this approach are that the modeler is relieved of the burden of thinking in terms of implementation. Rather, she can think in terms of the model domain. Moreover, the code becomes shorter and more compact. This makes the model building process easier and improves the readability of its result. A detailed description of MAML can be found in [GKF99] and at [MAML].

## 3.1. Building the Automated Trading Simulation in MAML

MAML, similarly to Swarm, uses an object-oriented framework to define the model and its agents [MBLA96]. This is justified by the fact that agents are in many ways similar to objects in the object-oriented programming paradigm [G97]. The states of an agent can be expressed as values of instance variables of an object, and its rules of behavior and communication channels can be coded as message handlers. MAML agents, however, can also have schedules to describe their planned activities.

The MAML keyword for agent definition is **@agent**. The keyword is followed by the name of the agent class and the body of the description. All agents belong to the model (or to the observer, see 3.2), so they must be defined within the appropriate structure.1

*Excerpt 1* The skeleton of the model

```
@model AutomatedTrading {
  @agent TraderAgent {
```

```
    ...
  }
}
```

**Defining the agents' behavior.** In MAML agents' states and rules are described as variables (**@var:**) and subroutines (**@sub:**), respectively. For these structures MAML provides all the modifiers that are usually available in object-oriented programming languages. Visibility modifiers (**public**, **protected**, **private**) are supported, and so is single inheritance [ES90]. Agent classes can also have variables and operations, separately from instance ones: the **static** modifier is to be used for this purpose. The default values for the modifiers are chosen in a way that allows unexperienced users to avoid dealing with issues they do not know or understand. Therefore, public visibility is assumed if it is not ordered explicitly otherwise.

In our automated trading model agents belong to two separate classes: they are either buyers or sellers. We'll follow this logical separation and implement the model accordingly. Therefore, we derive two subclasses from our previously defined **TraderAgent** class. (See Excerpt 2 below. Note the $ClassName : ParentClassName$ syntax denoting inheritance.) In **TraderAgent** we declare all the common parameters of the agents (for a detailed explanation see Table 2.1). Buyers also have a variable named **needed** defined that stores the number of units the agent has to gather.

| *Variable name* | *Parameter role* |
|---|---|
| limitPrice | The agent's limit price ($LimitPrice'$) |
| extra | The agent's initial profit level |
| target | The agent's current target price ($Target'$) |
| valuation | The agent's current valuation ($Valuation'$) |
| day | The number of the current day |
| round | The number of the current round within the day |
| timeLeft | The time left until the agent's due time ($TimeLeft'$)) |
| timeLimit | The agent's time limit |
| piece | The number of units the agent currently possess |
| beta | The agent's learning rate ($\beta$) |
| maxBid | Biggest bid heard by the agent ($Bid_{max}$) |
| minOffer | Lowest offer heard by the agent ($Offer_{min}$) |

*Table 2.1.* Common agent parameters

Besides the parameters, Excerpt 2 also shows the definition of a couple of subroutines. **TraderAgent** for instance, contains an initialization routine and the two main activities of a trader agent (**step** and **shout**). It also contains the **getShouts** subroutine that gathers the maximum bid and minimum offer of the given day. In addition to these, the **TraderAgent** class defines a couple of abstract routines that are called by the methods mentioned above. The implementation of these routines differentiates a buyer from a seller, therefore they are overridden [ES90] in the **SellerAgent** and **BuyerAgent** classes. These later classes also contain a subroutine named **addPiece** that helps in counting the units of good remained to trade. Finally, we also define another agent class, **MarketAgent** that represents the market itself (records shouts, matches bids and offers, etc.). The code sample also shows the syntax of comments.

*Excerpt 2* The definition of the agents

```
@model AutomatedTrading {
 ///////////////////////////////////////////////////////////////////////
  // The trader agent class (common root of seller and buyer)
//
 ///////////////////////////////////////////////////////////////////////
  @agent TraderAgent {
    @var :  int limitPrice, extra, target, valuation;   // Trading
info
    @var :  int day, round;                          // Time administration
    @var :  int timeLeft, timeLimit;
    @var :  int piece;                               // No of good units
    @var :  double beta;                             // Learning
coefficient
    @var :  int maxBid, minOffer;                    // Memory of the agent

    @sub:  (void) init {                            // Initializes the
agent
    }
    @sub:  (void) getShouts {                      // Saves min/max in
memory
    }

       // Abstract methods
       @sub:  (int) unitsToTrade {}              // Units remained to
trade
       @sub:  (void) newLoad {}                  // New load to trade
       @sub:  (int) getTarget {}                 // Actual target price
       @sub:  (void) makeABidOrOffer {}          // Finalizes the
bid/offer

    @sub:  (void) step {                 // The main activity of the
agent
    }
    @sub:  (void) shout {                          // Calculates the
shout
    }
```

```
  }

 ///////////////////////////////////////////////////////////////////
  // The seller agent class
//
 ///////////////////////////////////////////////////////////////////
  @agent SellerAgent:TraderAgent {

        // Implementation of TraderAgent's abstract methods
       @sub:  (void) newLoad {...}
       @sub:  (int) unitsToTrade {...}
       @sub:  (int) getTarget {...}
       @sub:  (void) makeABidOrOffer {...}

    @sub:  (void) init {                        // Initializes the
agent
    }
    @sub:  (void) addPiece {        // Helps the market's
administration
    }
  }

 ///////////////////////////////////////////////////////////////////
  // The buyer agent class
//
 ///////////////////////////////////////////////////////////////////
  @agent BuyerAgent:TraderAgent {
    @var :  int needed;                                // Units to
buy

       // Implementation of TraderAgent's abstract methods
       @sub:  (void) newLoad {...}
       @sub:  (int) unitsToTrade {...}
       @sub:  (int) getTarget {...}
       @sub:  (void) makeABidOrOffer {...}

    @sub:  (void) init {                        // Initializes the
agent
    }
    @sub:  (void) addPiece {        // Helps the market's
administration
    }
  }

 ///////////////////////////////////////////////////////////////////
  // The agent class that represents the market mechanism
//
 ///////////////////////////////////////////////////////////////////
  @agent MarketAgent {
     /* ...  */
  }
```

}

The remaining part of the agent's definition lies inside the body of the subroutines. These sections of the MAML model can be written in pure Swarm code. As an example, let's see what goes in between the two braces of the **TraderAgent**'s **init** routine (see Excerpt 3). Note the use of Swarm's default random number generator and that the model's variables are accessed through the **model->*variable*** construct.

*Excerpt 3* The full definition of the TraderAgent's initialization routine

```
    @sub:  (void) init {                          // Initializes the
agent
      extra = [uniformIntRand getIntegerWithMin:  1
                              withMax:
model->maxInitialProfit];
      limitPrice = 0;
      round = 0;
      beta = (double) [uniformIntRand getIntegerWithMin:
model->minBeta
                                      withMax:  model->maxBeta];
      beta /= 100.0;
      day = -1;
      maxBid = -1;
      minOffer = -1;
      timeLimit = model->timeLimit;
      timeLeft = timeLimit;
      piece = 0;
    }
```

**Plans and Schedules.** The final step to complete the agents' definition is to describe their activities. In MAML this is done by the definition of plans and schedules (**@planDef** and **@schedule** keywords). Plans are composed of actions (events from the point of view of the receiver), that are executed in the specified order[2]. On the other hand, schedules bind events and plans to time-steps, that is to certain points on the discrete time scale of the simulation. Events first specify the receiver, which can be (1) an agent (**@to** *Agent*), (2) a collection of agents (**@forEach** *AgentCollection*), or (3) the environment (**@to model**). This is followed by the name of the subroutine called.

Plans and schedules can be assigned to (defined in) the specific agent classes or the model as a whole. In our model we chose the latter option, see Excerpt 4. Our schedule contains five activities that are repeatedly executed in each time-step as shown by the **cyclic(1)** modifier. The first activity calls the **isNewDay** subroutine of the **market** agent (an instance of the **MarketAgent** class, see below) that initializes the market if a new day has started. The third event scheduled activates the **step** subroutine on all the trader agents. This is done through the

**groupOfTraderAgent** collection. (The **groupOf<*AgentClassName*>** collections are automatically generated by MAML for all defined agent classes and they hold all the members of the given class.) To prepare for this call, the second activity of the schedule calls the model's **shuffleAgentList** method. (Note that the schedule is defined in the model's body, therefore **self** refers to the model.) This method shuffles the **groupOfTraderAgent** collection, in order to randomize the execution order of the agents. (This is not an automatically generated method, so we'll need to implement it later.) After this, the **getShouts** routine is called on all instances of the **TraderAgent** class. As it was discussed in Section 3.1, this method gathers the maximum bid and minimum offer of the given day. Finally, the last activity scheduled addresses the agent **market** (of class **MarketAgent**) to match bids and offers.

*Excerpt 4* The model's schedule

```
@schedule cyclic(1) {
  0:  @to market isNewDay;                    // Clears market if
needed
  0:  @to self shuffleAgentList;              // Shuffles the list
  0:  @forEach groupOfTraderAgent step;       // Let the agents shout
  0:  @forEach groupOfTraderAgent getShouts;  // Let the agents
remember
  0:  @to market trade;                       // Matches bids and
offers
}
```

**Completing the Definition of the Model.** In addition to agents, plans and schedules, one can also declare variables and subroutines within the **@model** structure: these describe the environment of the model. For instance, the agent **market** (an instance of the **MarketAgent** class) addressed above (see Excerpt 4) was a variable of the model. Moreover, the parameters of the simulation are usually implemented as model variables.

The last step of completing our model is to write the code of initialization that sets the initial values of the variables and creates the agents. For this reason, the **@model** construct contains an **@init**: section at the end of its body, see Excerpt 5.

*Excerpt 5* The initialization of the model

```
@model AutomatedTrading {
  /* ...  */

////////////////////////////////////////////////////////////////////////
// Model initialization
//
////////////////////////////////////////////////////////////////////////
@init :
```

```
  if (minPrice < 0)                                    // Safety
checks
    minPrice = 0;
  if (maxPrice < minPrice)
    maxPrice = minPrice;

  if (minBeta < 0)
    minBeta = 0;
  if (maxBeta > 100)
    maxBeta = 100;
  if (maxBeta < minBeta)
    maxBeta = minBeta;

  @create [numOfSellers:i] SellerAgent sellers {  // Creates the
sellers
    [sellers[i] init];
    sellers[i]->limitPrice = minPrice;
  }
  @create [numOfBuyers:i] BuyerAgent buyers {      // Creates the
buyers
    [buyers[i] init];
    buyers[i]->limitPrice = maxPrice;
  }
  @create MarketAgent market { [market init]; }    // Creates the
market
  /* ...  */
}
```

In general, the **@init:** section contains pure Swarm code, but as in case of all Swarm sections in MAML, a couple of MAML statements are also allowed. One of these is the **@create** construct, whose primarily use is in this part of the model. This statement can be used to create and initialize agents and collections of agents in a fairly compact way.

In our case, the creation of the agent **market** automatically calls the initialization of the agent. In the case of **sellers** (an array of the model), we create **numOfSellers** instances with a single command. Furthermore, for each created agent we execute a few lines of code in which we chose to use the pseudo-variable i to refer to the number of already created agents.

## 3.2. The Observation of the Model

Our model is now complete, but still it is hardly usable. This is due to the fact that it does not have any means to gather input to set its boundary conditions, nor it has ways to report what is going on in the system it represents. That is, it lacks the observer.

MAML, just like Swarm, supports the idea of separating the model and the observer [MBLA96]. However, it extends this concept by the limited use of aspect-oriented programming [KLM97]. The details and background of this approach are explained in [GK99]. For now, it is enough to say that the observational aspect of our simulation is defined in a separate construct, designated with the keyword **@observe**. There are two classes of observers, **gui** and **batch**. Gui observers have an interactive (usually graphical) user interface, while batch observers are used to collect the results of lengthy simulations in the background. Out of them, the first is the default. As shown in Excerpt 6 the observer of our model belongs to this class, too. (Note the specification of the name of the observed model after the keyword.)

*Excerpt 6* The @observe keyword

```
@model AutomatedTrading {
  /* ...  */
}
@observe AutomatedTrading {
  /* ...  */
}
```

The **@observe** construct may contain all kind of components that are allowed in the **@model** construct. The main idea is to implement the observational tools here. To achieve this, access to the observed model's components is needed. To provide this access, the observer is seen as an extension of the observed model in MAML. That is, the components defined in the observed model are accessible from within the body of the observer.

The guiding rule is, however, that the code of the model must not be altered, even if the information to be observed was not originally made public. (The reason for this rule is that the (1) model should always be independent of the observation method, and (2) the alteration of the model is dangerous as it might corrupt the already tested results.)

The mechanism MAML offers to support the adherence to the rule above is called *extension*. (In fact, without this mechanism, the rule would be impossible to respect.) The extension mechanism allows for the definition of new components for agents, plans and schedules in the observer, just like they were defined at the place of the original definition of the given component, in the **@model** construct. That is, at the source level, the definition of the affected agent (or plan, etc.) is divided up into two parts, but during compilation these two parts are concatenated. In this way, new variables, new subroutines and additional plans or schedules (e.g., for the monitoring of the agents' states) can be introduced whenever needed. The keywords for the extension mechanism are **@extendAgent**, **@extendPlan** and **@extendSchedule**.

Excerpt 7 shows the usage of the ideas above in practice. Besides all these constructs, the logic of the observer is typically implemented by usual Swarm tools, such as graphs, raster widgets, etc. For instance, in the observer of our model we use a graph. (Note the keyword **@uses**, which is used here to access Swarm's *analysis* library [JL00].)

*Excerpt 7* The code of the observer

```
////////////////////////////////////////////////////////////////////////
// Observes the Trading Model
//
////////////////////////////////////////////////////////////////////////

@observe AutomatedTrading {
@uses <analysis.h>;

////////////////////////////////////////////////////////////////////////
// Observer extension of the agent classes
//
////////////////////////////////////////////////////////////////////////

@extendAgent SellerAgent {
  @sub: (int) getPrice {     // Active current valuation for the
stats
    if ([self unitsToTrade] > 0)
      return valuation;
    else
      return minOffer;
  }
}

@extendAgent BuyerAgent {
  @sub: (int) getPrice {     // Active current valuation for the
stats
    if ([self unitsToTrade] > 0)
      return valuation;
    else
      return maxBid;
  }
}

////////////////////////////////////////////////////////////////////////
// Observer variables
//
////////////////////////////////////////////////////////////////////////

@var: id priceGraph;
@var: int maxBid, minOffer;

////////////////////////////////////////////////////////////////////////
// Observer subroutines
//
////////////////////////////////////////////////////////////////////////
```

```
@sub: (void) updateVariables {      // Updates the observers
variables
  maxBid = [market getMaxBid];
  minOffer = [market getMinOffer];
}

@sub: (int) getAvgPrice {           // Reads the currer.t average
price
  return avgPrice;
}

///////////////////////////////////////////////////////////////////////
// Observer schedule
//
///////////////////////////////////////////////////////////////////////

@schedule cyclic (1) {
  0: @to model updateVariables;    // Updates the observer's
variables
  0: @to priceGraph step;          // Updates the graph
}

///////////////////////////////////////////////////////////////////////
// Observer initialization
//
///////////////////////////////////////////////////////////////////////

@init:
  /* Setting the parameters' default values */

  @create EZGraph priceGraph {                  // Creates the
graph
    [priceGraph setTitle: "List of prices"];
    [priceGraph setAxisLabelsX: "Rounds" Y: "Price"];
  }

                                       // Creation of the graph's
sequences
  [priceGraph createSequence: "Avg Price"
    withFeedFrom: self
    andSelector: M(getAvgPrice)];
  [priceGraph createMaxSequence: "Max Seller's Offer"
    withFeedFrom: groupOfSellerAgent
    andSelector: M(getPrice)];
  [priceGraph createMinSequence: "Min Buyer's Bid"
    withFeedFrom: groupOfBuyerAgent
    andSelector: M(getPrice)];
}
```

One of the strengths of Swarm is the probing mechanism [JL00], which is intensively used in gui mode observers. MAML supports this also, with the keywords **@probe** and **@buildProbe** (that are only valid in **gui** mode observers). The first construct is used to declare that a variable or subroutine is to be displayed (and is applicable wherever the keyword **@var** is valid). On the other hand, **@buildProbe** actually creates the probes (and is to be issued from within the **@init**: section of the observer). A final call to the model's (automatically defined) **probe** subroutine displays the probe window.

As it must be clear by now, the model and its observer are highly interconnected. Hence, it is hard to tell in general in which order they should be initialized. MAML solves this problem by introducing the **@initModel** statement, which can be issued in the **@init**: section of the observer and executes the initialization of the model. (If not issued explicitly, the model's initialization takes place after that of the observer.)

Using the previously introduced constructs, the observer of our model takes the form shown in Excerpt 8.

*Excerpt 8* MAML supports the probing mechanism of Swarm

```
@observe AutomatedTrading {

  /* Same as above */

@extendAgent MarketAgent {
  @probe:  var "unSold", var "unBought";

  /* Same as above */
}

///////////////////////////////////////////////////////////////////////
// Parameter display (probes)
//
///////////////////////////////////////////////////////////////////////

@probe:  var "maxBid", var "minOffer";

@probe:  var "unS", var "unB",
        var "day", var "lastPrice",
        var "numOfSellers", var "numOfBuyers",
        var "minPrice", var "maxPrice",
        var "minBeta", var "maxBeta",
        var "maxInitialProfit",
        var "maxPieceSell", var "maxPieceBuy",
        var "timeLimit", var "newAgents";

///////////////////////////////////////////////////////////////////////
// Observer initialization
//
///////////////////////////////////////////////////////////////////////
@init:
  /* Setting the parameters' default values */
```

```
  @buildProbes;                                       // Creates
and
  [model probe];                                 // Displays the probe
window
  [controlPanel setStateStopped];              // Stops the simulation to
let
                                               // the user set the
parameters
  @initModel;

  /* Creation of the graph as above */
}
```

## 3.3. Other Constructs of MAML

Besides the tools discussed so far, MAML has a couple of other constructs that remain unused in our demonstration model. Most of them are connected to dynamic scheduling (see [B97] and [JL00] for details) and are of use in models in which agents alter their schedules in response to specific events. This dynamism is supported by the keywords @addToSchedule and @addToPlan.

Furthermore, MAML also has keywords (**@createBegin**, **@createEnd**) to support the two-phase creation of agents that is common in Swarm [B95] [JL00]. The other tools of the language are of lower importance.

# 4. Preliminary Results

After finishing the implementation of our model, let's have a look at its execution. The first thing to note is that the outlook of our simulation is just the same as in the case of ordinary Swarm models. (See Figure 2.1.) This is fairly natural, as our MAML code was compiled to Swarm. As this is the normal process, once the MAML simulation is up and running, it is a full Swarm application.

After noting this, let's have a look at the model's behavior. First, we check whether our model produces the results reported in [P98]. For this we turn off two of our extensions (by setting the number of units traded by the agents to 1 and by not allowing the agents to leave or join the market) and select an appropriately soft time pressure value. Figure 2.2 shows the results of the model if run with the default parameters summarized in Table 2.2. (The lines of the graph represent, from the top down, the maximum offer, the average market price and the minimum bid, respectively.) It is visible that if we have equal number of buyers and sellers, the prices converge to the theoretical equilibrium. Moreover, Figure 2.3 shows that the equilibrium is shifted in the asymmetric case (when we have more buyers than sellers) as expected[3].

| *Role* | *Name* | *Default value* |
|---|---|---|
| Number of Sellers | $numOfSellers$ | 10 |
| Number of Buyers | $numOfBuyers$ | 10 |
| Sellers' limit price ($LimitPrice^{Sellers}$) | $minPrice$ | 500 |
| Buyers' limit price ($LimitPrice^{Buyers}$) | $maxPrice$ | 1500 |
| Minimum value of $\beta$ | $minBeta$ (percentage) | 10 |
| Maximum value of $\beta$ | $maxBeta$ (percentage) | 20 |
| Maximum initial profit level | $maxInitialProfit$ | 1200 |
| Maximum number of units a seller wants to sell | $maxPieceSell$ | 1 |
| Maximum number of units a buyer wants to buy | $maxPieceBuy$ | 1 |
| Maximum value of time limit | $timeLimit$ | 100 |
| Whether new agents are allowed to join the market | $newAgents$ [0=no, 1=yes] | 0 |

*Table 2.2.* Default parameter values

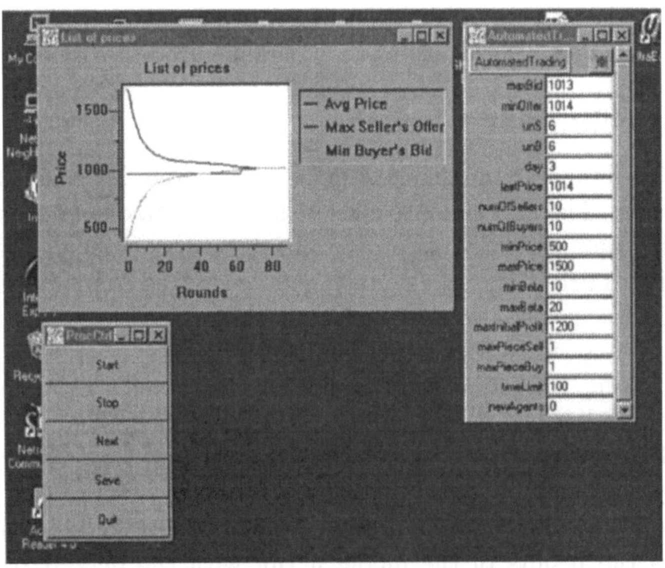


*Figure 2.1.* The outlook of a MAML simulation is the same as ordinary Swarm models

(The parameters are as shown in Table 2.2, except that $numOfBuyers = 100$).

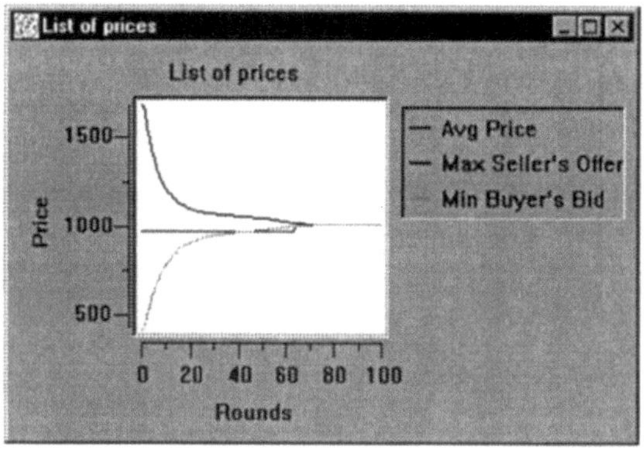


*Figure 2.2.* Convergence to the equilibrium.

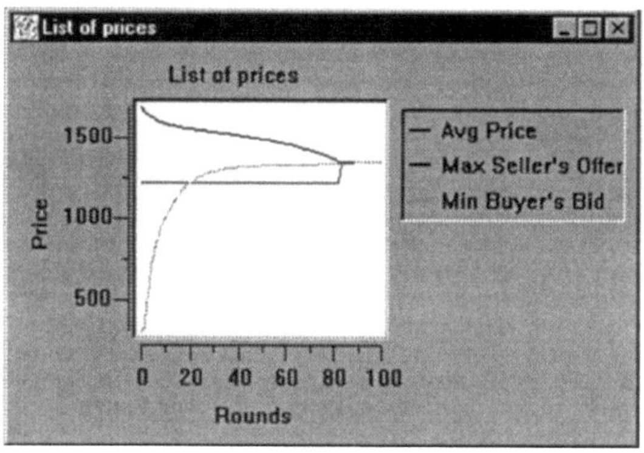


*Figure 2.3.* Shift in the equilibrium price.

After checking the consistency of our replica, let's have a quick look at the effect of some of our extensions. (A detailed discussion of these results will be reported elsewhere.) The effect of time pressure is shown in Figure 2.4 and Figure 2.5. These are the results of two simulation runs with the same parameter set, except the values of the agents' time limits. These were assigned randomly, in the first case from $[0, 50]$, while in the latter from $[0, 10]$. It is clear that in the latter case prices converge faster.

Finally, let's check the effect of agents leaving and joining the market, that is, the possibility of newcomers. It is visible from Figure 2.6 that the system converges to the equilibrium as the agents learn, but the arrivals of new agents destroy this. (The same parameter set was used

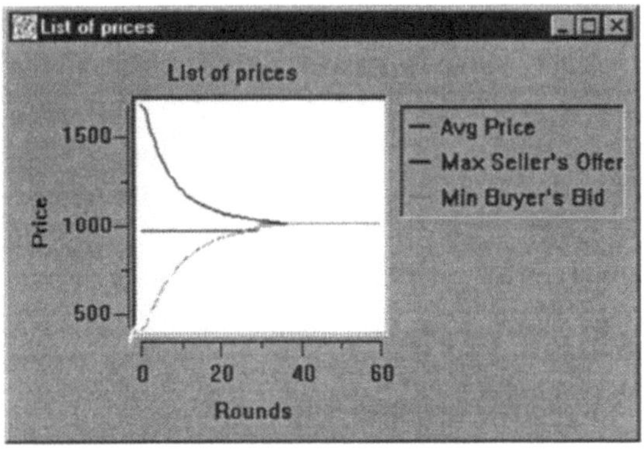


*Figure 2.4.* Soft time pressure

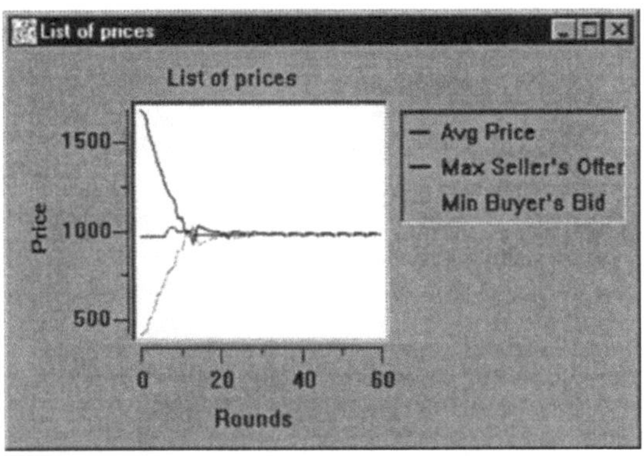


*Figure 2.5.* Hard time pressure

as shown in Table 2.2, except that $newAgents = 1$. Note that minimum and maximum values are displayed, therefore the arrival of a single new agent may have a dramatic effect.)

## 5. Summary

In this paper we have introduced the main constructs of the Multi-Agent Modeling Language (MAML)[4] through an extended version of Christ Preist's model of trading agents [P98]. Even though it is a relatively simple model, its implementation is not a trivial task. With the use of MAML, however, the model's structure is easily mapped into standard programming constructs and thus the implementation becomes tractable. Although only the main logic of the program was discussed,

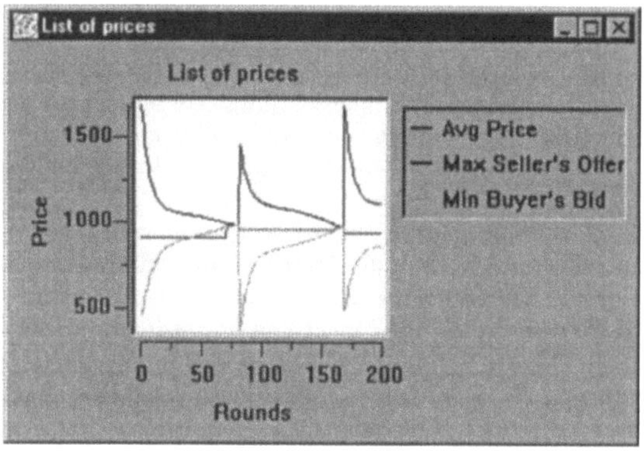


*Figure 2.6.* The effect of newcomers

the remaining parts consist of fairly straightforward algorithms. The full version of the model is available at [GHP] and at [SDG].

The implementation of the same model in pure Swarm would have taken two or three times more lines and, what is more important, much more experience in the low-level details of Objective-C programming. We believe that the main benefit of MAML is this, i.e. that it helps producing more compact simulations in shorter time. Moreover, MAML is easier to learn than Swarm, therefore it makes one's introduction to agent-based computational simulations smoother than Swarm does. A certain amount of Swarm knowledge, however, is still necessary for all MAML modelers as Swarm's libraries (analysis, collections, etc.) are intensively used. Therefore we believe that the two environments will mutually benefit from the presence of each other.

## Acknowledgments

The first version Multi-Agent Modeling Language and that of its compiler was developed at the Complex Adaptive Systems Laboratory, Central European University, Budapest. Currently, MAML is maintained and further developed under the supervision of one of the authors of this paper, a former MAML developer at CEU. The current developments of MAML are supported by Agent-Lab Ltd, Hungary.

# Notes

1. Note that theoretically this solution does not guarantee that the agents finish trading before their due time since the value of their learning rate may prevent them from reaching the targeted price in time. This simple rule, however, is good enough to ensure that the agents do not miss their deadline by too much. In practice, the agents using this rule usually close the trades well before their due time.

2. Theoretically, the execution order can be sequential, concurrent or randomized. The version of Swarm on which MAML is built, however, supports sequential execution only.

3. Note that *AvgPrice* represents the average market price at which tradeswere actually made. Therefore, if offers and bids don't meet and no trade ismade for a certain period, it may stay below the *Min Buyer's Bid*until offers and bids finally converge.

4. The current version of the MAML compiler (xmc) is freely available from [MAML]. It supports the Objective-C version of Swarm.

# References


[B95] Burkhart, R.: Create-phase Protocols for Object Customization, *Object-Oriented Programming Systems, Languages, and Applications (OOPSLA) '95 Adaptable and Adaptive Software Workshop*, October 1995. http://www.santafe.edu/ rmb/oopsla95.html

[B97] Burkhart, R.: Schedules of Activity in the Swarm Simulation System, *Object-Oriented Programming Systems, Languages, and Applications (OOPSLA) '97 Workshop on OO Behavioral Semantics 1997*, 1997. http://www.santafe.edu/ rmb/oopsla97.ps

[ES90] Ellis, M. A., Stroustrup, B.: *The Annotated C++ Reference Manual*, Addison-Wesley, Reading, Mass., 1990

[FR92] Friedman and Rust (eds.): *The Double Auction Market: Institutions, Theories and Evidence*, Addison-Wesley 1992.

[G97] Gulyás, L.: Using Object-Oriented Techniques to Develop Multi-Agent Simulations. *Proceedings of the 1st International Conference of PhD Students*, University of Miskolc, Hungary, 1997, pp. 63-69.

[GHP] Homepage of László Gulyás, http://www.sztaki.hu/~gulyas/

[GK99] Gulyás, L., Kozsik, T.: Aspect-Oriented Programming in Scientific Simulations. *Proceedings of The Sixth Fenno-Ugric Symposium on Software Technology*, Estonia 1999, http://www.syslab.ceu.hu/maml/papers/aopss.ps

[GKF99] Gulyás, L., Kozsik, T., Fazekas, S.: The Multi-Agent Modeling Language, *Proceedings of the 4th International Conference on Applied Informatics*, Eger-Noszvaj, Hungary, 1999

[GMM98] Guttman, R., Moukas, A., Maes, P.: Agent Mediated Electronic Commerce: A Survey, *Knowledge Engineering Review*, June 1998.

[JL00] Johnson, P., Lancaster, A.: Swarm User Guide, *Swarm Documentation*, Swarm Development Group, 2000. http://www.santafe.edu/projects/swarm/swarmdocs/userbook/userbook.html

[KLM97] Kinczales, G., Lamping J., Mendhekar A., Maeda C., Lopes C., Loingtier J-M., Irwin J.: Aspect-Oriented Programming. *Xerox Palo Alto Research Center*,

http://www.parc.xerox.com/spl/groups/eca/pubs/-complete.html#Kiczales-ECOOP97

[MAML] The MAML Homepage, http://www.syslab.ceu.hu/maml/

[MBLA96] Minar, N., Burkhart, R., Langton, C., Askenazi, M.: The Swarm Simulation System: A Toolkit for Building Multi-agent Simulations, *SFI Working Paper 96-06-042*, 1996. http://www.santafe.edu/projects/swarm/overview/overview.html

[P98] Preist, C.: Economic Agents for Automated Trading, HP Laboratories Bristol, *Technical Report 98-77*

[RHW86] Rumelhart, D., Hinton, G., Williams, R.: Learning internal representations by error propagation, In D. Rumelhart, J. McClelland, *Parallel Distributed Processing*, Vol 1: Foundations, MIT Press 1986.

[SDG] The Swarm Development Group Homepage, http://www.swarm.org/

[WJ95] Wooldridge, M., Jennings, N. R.: Agent Theories, Architectures and Languages: A Survey. *Intelligent Agents ECAI-94 Worshop Proceedings, Lecture Notes in Artificial Intelligence 890*, Springer-Verlag, Berlin, 1995, pp. 1-39.

# Chapter 3

# VSB - VISUAL SWARM BUILDER - A VISUAL TOOL FOR SWARM AGENT BASED ENVIRONMENT

Alessandro Perrone
*Department of Economics*
*University of Venice*
Alex@unive.it

Marco Tenuti
*Software Engineer*
*Tencas*
Marco@tencas.com

**Abstract** In some sciences, especially in the study of complex systems, computer programs play an important role as scientific equipment. In the case of computer simulations, the programs under use, can be seen as experimental devices built in software.
We don't, however, forget that Social scientists are not computer scientists, but their skills in the field will have to improve to cope with the growing subject of social simulation and agent based modelling techniques.
The Swarm project can be viewed as an aid to researchers to create a standard tool to build simulations.
But there's a problem. Programming with Swarm is not easy, the scientist have to spend a few hours (50 hours, in Pietro Terna's Opinion) to learn the philosophy of the package, how to use the libraries, how to call the graphic routines, how to call data to plot, etc. etc, and how to program in objective-c. Actually, there's also a java version of Swarm and the learning time may be decreased a bit, because it is very easy to find a java programmer, but the problem of learning the use and the philosophy of Swarm still remains.

For this reason we have thought and programmed a package named VSB (Visual Swarm Builder). It can be viewed as the first visual Rapid Application Development (RAD) tool designed exclusively for the Swarm Simulation toolkit. It is a complete development environment that provides the researcher with a rich set of tools already coded and components necessary to develop and deploy high-performance simulations.

This chapter is divided into 3 main sections: we start from a short overview of the package, we then present a little manual which describes its functionalities, and we conclude with a tutorial containing a wide range of simulations, from the simple implementation of classical simulations, to complex graphical demos.

## 1. Introduction

In some sciences, especially in the study of complex systems, computer programs play an important role as scientific equipment. In the case of computer simulations, the programs can be seen as experimental devices built in software. While computer models provide many advantages over traditional experimental methods, they also raise several problems. In particular, the process of software development is a complicated technical task with high potential for errors, especially when it is carried out by scientists holding their expertise in fields other than computer science.

Early in the development of a scientific field scientists typically construct their own experimental equipment: grinding their own lenses, wiring-up their own particle detectors, even building their own computers. Researchers in new fields have to be adept engineers, machinists, and electricians in addition to being scientists. Once a field begins to mature, collaborations between scientists and engineers lead to the development of standardized, reliable equipment (e.g., commercially produced microscopes or centrifuges), thereby allowing scientists to focus on research rather than on tool building. The use of standardized scientific apparati is not only a convenience: it allows one to "divide through" by the common equipment, thereby aiding the production of repeatable, comparable research results. Unfortunately, computer modeling frequently turns good scientists into bad programmers. Most scientists are not trained as software engineers. As a consequence, many home-grown computational experimental tools are (from a software engineering perspective) poorly designed. The results gained from the use of such tools can be difficult to compare with other research data and difficult for others to reproduce because of the quirks and unknown design decisions in the specific software apparatus. Furthermore, writing software is typically not a good use of a highly specialized scientist's time. In many cases, the same functional capacities are being rebuilt time and time again by different research groups, a tremendous duplication of effort.

A subtler problem with custom-built computer models is that the final software tends to be very specific, a dense tangle of code that is understandable only to the people who wrote it. Typical simulation software contains a large number of implicit assumptions, accidents of the way the particular code was written that have nothing to do with the actual model. And with only low-level source code it is very difficult to understand the high-level design and essential components of the model itself. Such software is useful to the people who built it, but makes it difficult for other scientists to evaluate and reproduce results.

In order for computer modeling to mature there is a need for a standardized set of well-engineered software tools usable on a wide variety of systems. The Swarm project aims to produce such tools through a collaboration between scientists and software engineers. Swarm is an efficient, reliable, reusable software apparatus for experimentation. If successful, Swarm will help scientists focus on research rather than on tool building by giving them a standardized suite of software libraries that provide a well equipped software laboratory.

Swarm is a multi-agent software platform for the simulation of complex adaptive systems. It provides object oriented libraries of reusable components for building models and analyzing, displaying, and controlling experiments on those models. The whole idea of Swarm is to provide an execution context within which a large number of objects can "live their lives" and interact with one another in a distributed, concurrent manner.

But there's a problem. Programming with Swarm is not easy, the scientist have to spend a few hours (50 hours, in Pietro Terna's opinion) to learn the philosophy of the package, how to use the libraries, how to call the graphic routines, how to call data to plot, etc. etc, and how to program in objective-c. Actually there's also a java version of Swarm and the learning time may be decreased a bit, because it is very easy to find a java programmer, but the problem of learning Swarm's use and its philosophy still remains.

VSB (Visual Swarm Builder) is a software engineering environment, built to ease the design and implementation of simulations in Swarm by offering a visual means for describing models.

VSB provides a visual environment, which will allow you to develop and deploy simulations rapidly without writing one line of code.

## 2. The Visual Swarm Builder - A Short Overview

A visual building tool can be considered a useful extension to any programming environment, from the most famous (c, Pascal) to the less known (Python, Oberon, or any other agent based environment). This is especially true with Swarm, a very large and complex simulation environment.

During the design of VSB we always had the idea to build a tool who anyone, from the expert programmer to the "lay" man, could use without difficulty. The graphical interface makes the knowledge of the Swarm sintax unnecessary.

Once the user has built the general simulation, the program itself generates the code, and then the "user" can compile it on his favourite platform. Of course, if the user is able to modify the Swarm code, s/he can do it without problem, because every routine generated by VSB can be easily edited and modified.

With VSB you can create your own simulation with clicks of the mouse. The package is provided with several examples of simple simulations that the reader will enjoy.

Nothing is required of the user if s/he wants to use the built-in examples or if s/he uses ONLY the Visual mode to build the simulations. If s/he wants to modify directly the code, s/he has to know the basics of Swarm programming and objective-c programming language.

VSB is a complete tool for creating simulations using Swarm libraries. It is a visual-based designer and source code editor, together in one package. You can use the program to create all types of content; from basic simulation to complex ones containing several objects (theoretically there's no limit to the objects you can create).
The package comes with a complete set of documentation and an extensive online help system, covering all the procedures for building Swarm Objects.

VSB does not contain a compiler, so you cannot compile or "run" the simulation you develop with the package. Once the code has been generated you must transfer the directory on your favourite Swarm environment and then compile it.

### 2.1. Hardware and software requirements

Actually (at the time of writing this paper) VSB runs only on Macintosh platform. We chose to start this project on this system because the authors have been programming on the Macintosh environment for 10 years and they considered this platform ideal to begin such project.

The system should match the following requirements to run VSB:

- Apple Power Macintosh
- Operating System version 8.1 with Carbon Lib or higher
- At least 3 MB of free RAM
- At least 6 MB of free HD space

## 2.2. VSB's components

The VSB package is composed of:

1 ) an executable file (Visual Swarm Builder);

2 ) a documentation folder, which contains a Swarm Tutorial written by the initiators of the Swarm Project and a manual of VSB;

3 ) a folder containing VSB examples that range from the simple implementation of classical simulations to complex graphical demos;

4 ) a README file containing a brief description of the original idea and of the VSB programmers

5 ) a VSB History file, containing all the bugs corrected and new features of the package

6 ) a About VSB file containing a short description of the product.

When the installation of Visual Swarm Builder is completed, the program opens the VSB folder to launch the program. As soon as the user launches the application, s/he can begin developing a simulation.

# 3. Working with VSB

Before beginning this tutorial, the reader should have already installed VSB in her/his computing environment. Instruction on how to do this can be found on the "Software and Hardware requirement" section of this article. This tutorial assumes that the reader is familiar with the standard Macintosh environment.

In this tutorial the most commonly used parts of the package will be introduced, and in the next section, the reader will be guided to the programming of simple Swarm simulations (without writing any lines of code) to a fairly complex financial simulation.

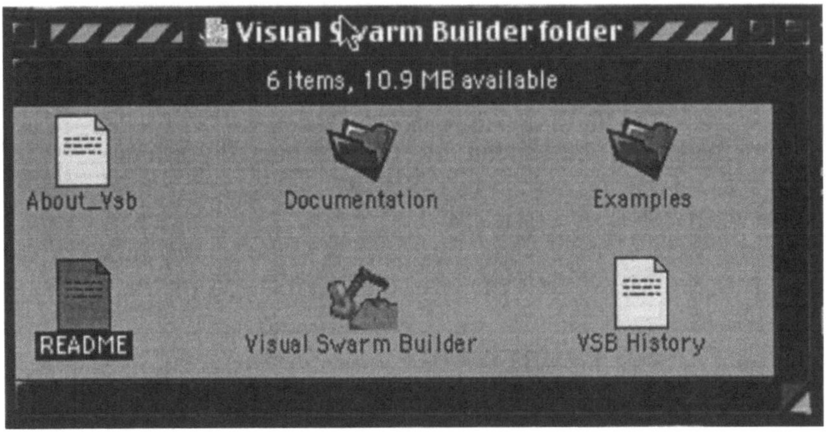


*Figure 3.1.* First Overview of VSB Project

## 3.1. Getting Started

VSB is a package for building full, functioning, visual simulation using Swarm libraries. Although VSB does not compile applications (it generates only the code), it gets a lot of the hard stuff out of the way. To get started, first click on the VSB icon in the Finder. When the application opens, you will see several windows. Once the application is started, you should see the screen as in figure 3.2, which is composed of

- a Menu bar with the program items;
- a Project Window, that is the collection of items that make up the particular simulation you are developing. The project window displays a list of these elements to give you easy access to them. In a standard simulation project we have, for example, the main, the ModelSwarm, and the ObserverSwarm objects. In the project you can insert as many objects as you want;
- a Controls Window (**Swarms** one) that displays a group of various UI objects that can be used to build an interface/simulation.

These UI objects use the "drag and drop tecnique", so, to use one of these, simply click on it, and drag it to the UI in project window. The control will be added to your main window, and specifically to the relative object.

Now let's analyze all the three parts of the VSB package.

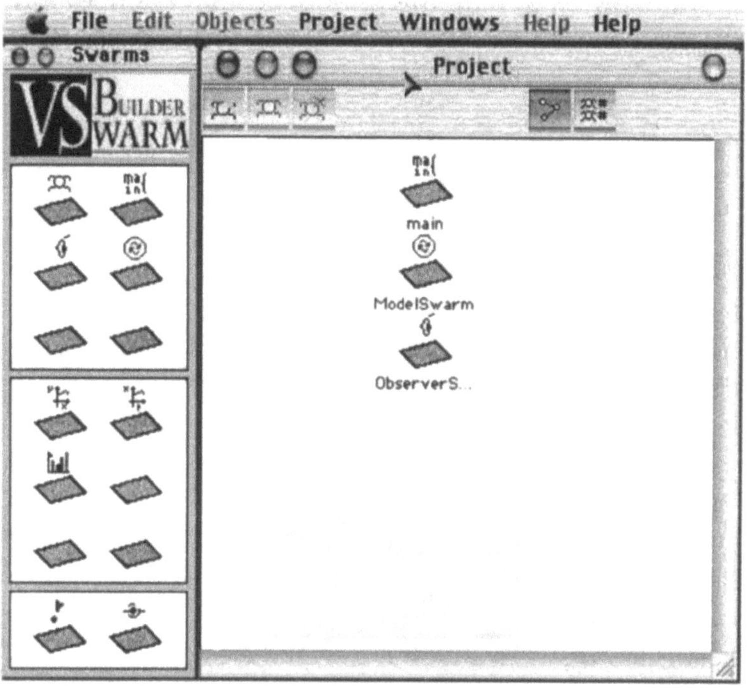


*Figure 3.2.* Initial screen of VSB

## 3.2. Working with Menus

A short descriptions of every menu item follows: the reader can have an idea of VSB's potentiality.

**About menu.** This is the standard Apple menu which shows the VSB logo, and provides authorship and contact information for the package. For further info about the Apple Menu, please refer to the Macintosh Manual.

**File Menu.**

**New** Create a new, empty VSB project. The system will prompt you to create a new project. If you have not saved an existing project, select Cancel and then save it. Otherwise, select OK.

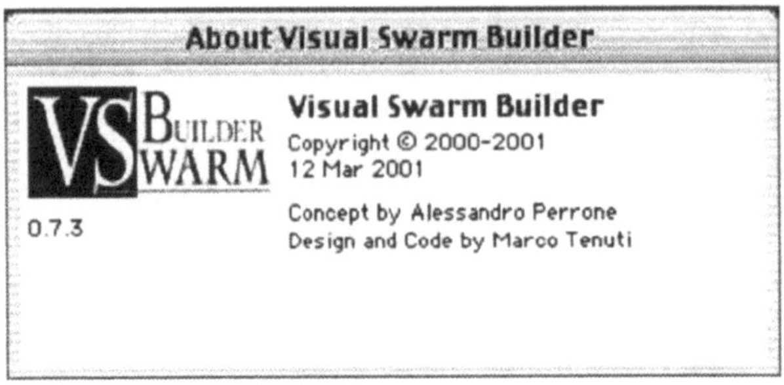


*Figure 3.3.* The "About VSB" dialog.

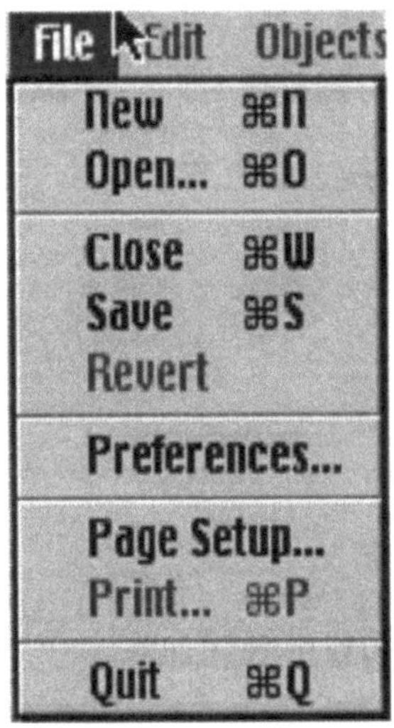


*Figure 3.4.* File Menu Items

**Open** Open an existing VSB project. A new project window will appear with all its defined objects, so the user can add objects to the simulation, can remove some of them, or can change some parameters' value.

**Close** Close your project. If you have never saved your project, a dialog will appear and will ask to save the work before closing the project.

**Preferences** Preferences can be used to store initial parameters to the program. If you choose the preferences item, a dialog like figure 3.5 appears

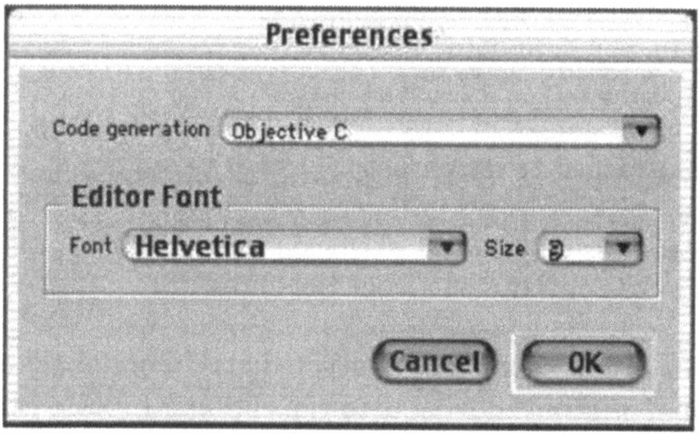


*Figure 3.5.* Preferences Dialog.

Using this dialog, the programmer can choose the language for the simulation, and the default font the system will use to display information about the objects.
If you change the notation, this will not show immediately. You have to close the Preferences dialog, and the changes will be available when the project window simulation is opened again. Actually only objective-c language has been coded, but at the time of SwarmFest, the Javaswarm language will also be available.

**Quit** Exit VSB and return to the standard Macintosh system environment.

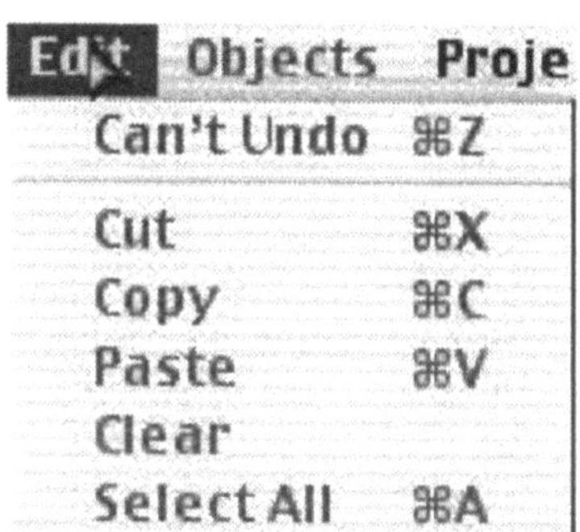


*Figure 3.6.* Edit Menu Items

**Edit Menu.**

**Cut** This command will remove an object from the project window and place it on the clipboard.

**Copy** This command will copy an object to the clipboard. The original one remains attached to its parent.

**Paste** If an object currently exists on the clipboard, this command will allow you to copy the one from the clipboard

**Clear** If an object is currently selected, this command will delete it from its parent without moving it to the clipboard. Note that Select All and Undo/Cannot Undo items are not yet supported in this version of VSB. We inserted to the Edit Menu to preserve the "Macintosh Style of programming" and we will to implement them as soon as possible.

## 3.3. Objects Menu

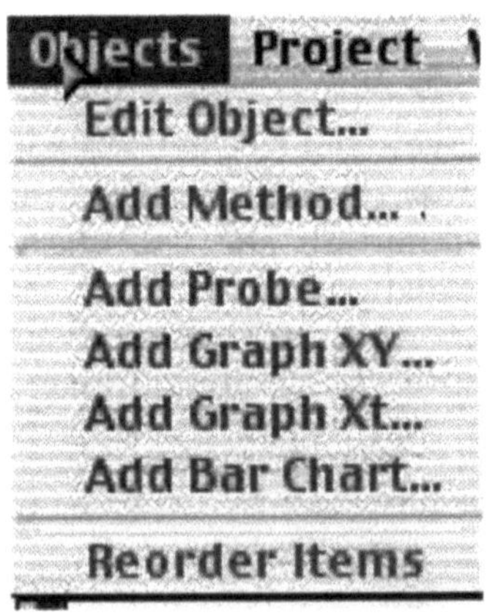


*Figure 3.7.* Object Menu Items

This menu contains items regarding the "drag & drop" objects needed to build a simulation. For a full explanation of these items, please, refer to the part relative to the "Palette component" of this article.

## 3.4. Project Menu

**Run** Once this button has been pressed, a short preview of all the object of the simulation appear on the screen.

**Stop** It permits to exit from the preview mode

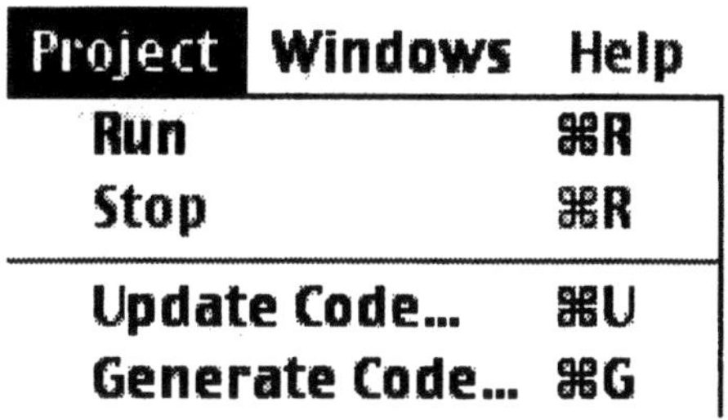


*Figure 3.8.* Project Menu Items

**Update Code** It update the code on every object

**Generate Code** The VSB can generate, at every moment, objective-c or java Code, based on the information in the Project Window. If objective-c is selected, each class will generate two files, a source code (.m) and an include file (.h). The name of the generated files will be "class name.m" and "class name.h".

If the generated class name is longer than 31 characters, the name of the created files will be truncated. The first 25 characters of the field name will always be equal to the first 25 characters in the class name.

When generating code, by selecting the Generate Code command, the dialog as in figure 3.9 appears where you are expected to select the folder where the generated files are to be stored.

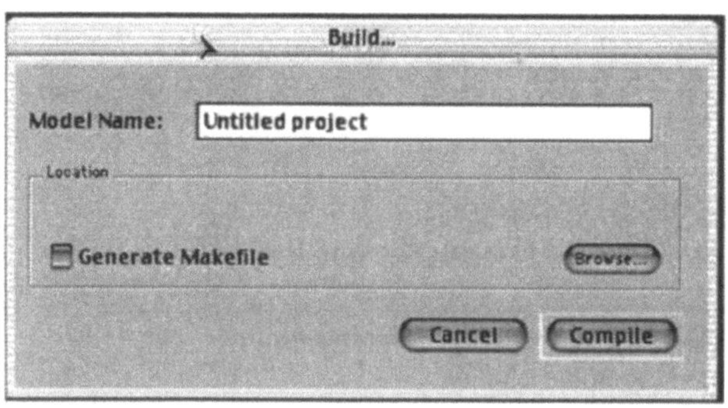


*Figure 3.9.* "Generating Code" Dialog.

The generated files will be stored in the folder you select in the dialog using the browse button, and the model will have the name chosen in "model Name" field.

Once the code is generated, you can compile the source on your favourite

Swarm platform.
For further information on how to compile a Swarm simulation, refer to the Swarm Web Site or Perrone's Swarm Web Page.

## 3.5. Window Menu

*Figure 3.10.* Window Menu Items

This item contains the list of all the project windows that are open at the moment. To select a project window which is not the "front one" simply select the relative item on the menu, and VSB will open the active project window.

## 3.6. Help Menu

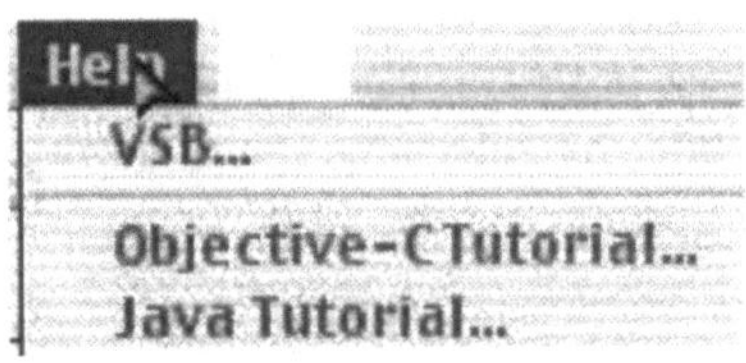


*Figure 3.11.* Help Menu Items

This menu item contains a series of documentation in Apple Help Viewer format.
The goal of this item is to access a quick view of the Swarm Tutorial.

## 3.7. Working with projects

All of the windows, probes, objects, graphs and their programming code that make up a single simulation are stored in a Project window. Projects simply give you a convenient way to organize the objects that make up you application.

Projects can contain any of the following items

- main object
- ModelSwarm

- ObserverSwarm
- SwarmObject
- Other kinds of objects

VSB permits to insert into a simulation, with the drag&drop technique, the following items

- graphs XY
- graphs X vs time
- bar charts
- probes
- new methods

Double-clicking on an item in the principal project window or in the subproject window, will either display the item or open it for editing.

**Creating a new project.** When you open VSB by double-clicking on the VSB Icon, a new empty project is created for you automatically. If you have a project open, and wish to begin a new one, simply choose New from the File Menu. If you have modified your project, you'll be given the opportunity to save the project before creating a new one.

**Adding and Removing items.** An item can be added to a project by dragging it from the "control Window" and dropping it into the Project Window. Items can be removed from a project by clicking once on the item in the Project Window to select it, then pressing the Delete Key or by highlighting the item and choosing the Clear from the Edit Menu.

## 3.8. Working with the Palette Window

The palette allows you to pick widgets to be added to your current active VSB project. There are three major modes of operation.

The first mode is the clicking of the UI under the Palette window. In this mode a short help of the UI appear. A dialog like figure 3.12 appears.

It displays the help message on the "generic SwarmObject". The window is divided into two parts: the first one contains a short description of the object, while the other part contains the name of the parameters the author has to fill if s/he wants to insert the object into the project

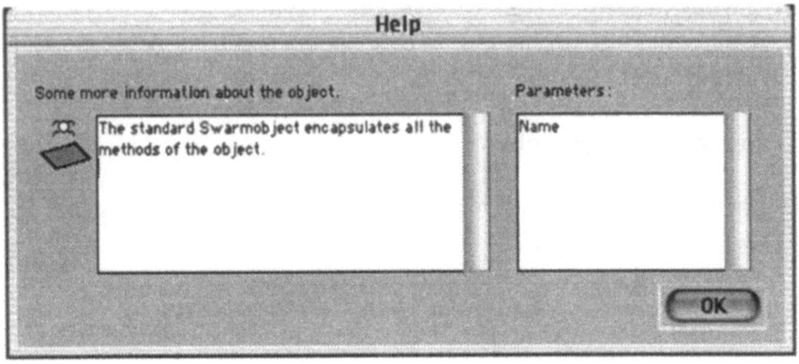


*Figure 3.12.* An example of help dialog

Window.
All the UI in the palette window has its own help.

The second mode of operation is the widget placement. It permits to insert a widget to the project window. To add an element in the Project window, simply select the element in the Palette and drag it into the Project Window near the "master object" the element refers to. Once the element is in the right position, an alert will ask to fill the parameters relative to the element.

The third mode of operation is the click of a widget within the project window. This will cause a dialog box to appear. It contains the parameters of the object and the button "view code" which permits to modify directly the code of the UI selected.
In this mode of operation, the author can change the values of the parameters, or, if s/he wants, s/he can change directly its code.

A list of all widgets supported is provided in figure 3.13.

## 4. TUTORIAL Examples with VSB

In this section we try to build a complex "financial" simulation. We start from a simulation plotting one financial time-series. Next, we build a model in which there are a simple line-graph (X vs time), a XY graph and a bar-chart graph. In the last simulation we demonstrate how to change direcly the code VSB generates.

**How to build our first simulation in Swarm Using VSB.** This section provides a quick tutorial which takes you along the steps required to create the simple application shown in figure 3.14. As you follow the step-by-step instructions in the tutorial, you'll be introduced to some of the major features of VSB.

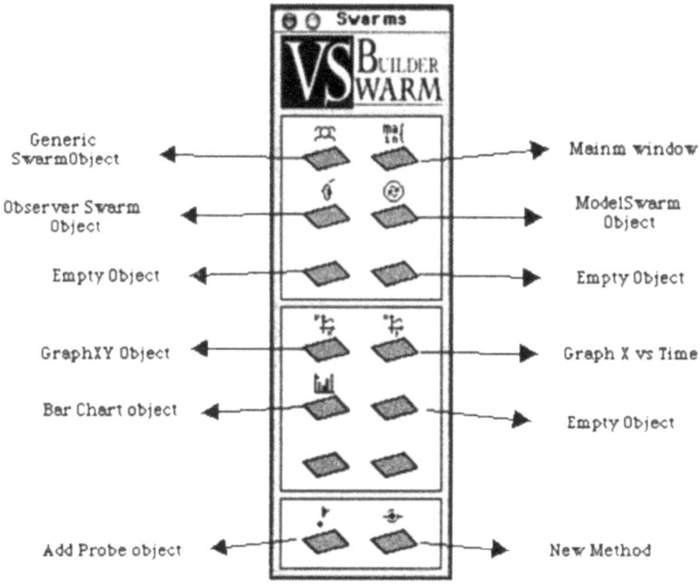


*Figure 3.13.* The widgets supported in the palette Window

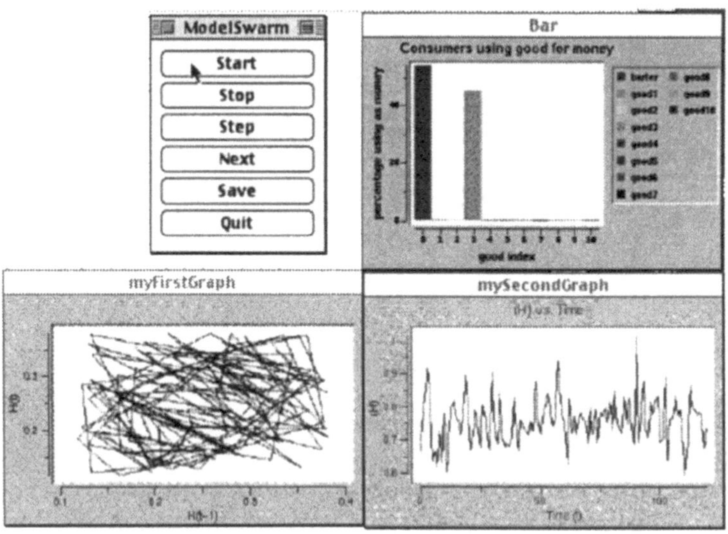


*Figure 3.14.* Output of a model

Here are the steps

1 Create a New project by double clicking on VSB Icon in Macintosh Environment (for further details refer to Maintosh manuals or README file in this package) or, if you are alread in VSB IDE, choose New command from File Menu.

2 Try to replicate the following structures on the project window

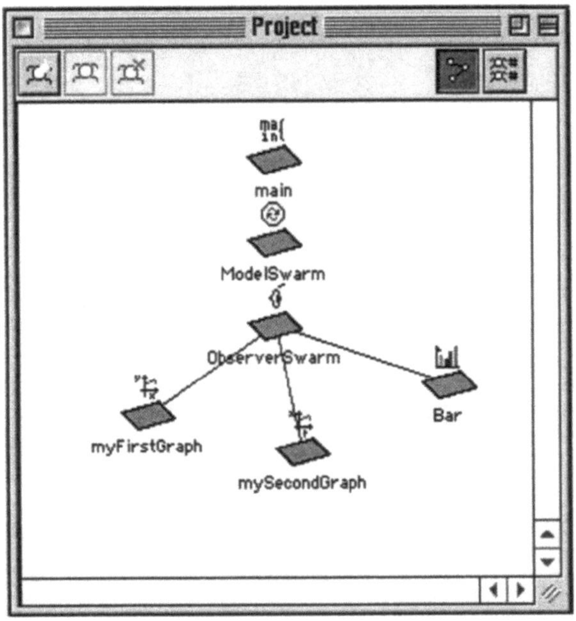


*Figure 3.15.* First experiment

3 Run the project using the Run command from Project Menu

4 Generate the code relative to your simulation

5 Compile and run your first simulation on your favourite Swarm environment.

## 4.1. From Scratch to a simple financial simulation with Swarm using VSB

In this section we'll develop, step by step a real simulation, using a few tools of the VSB, such as the code – editor inside every created object.

This part will be divided into four simulations. In the first one, we start from a simple model written without typing any lines of code, then we'll add a very simple "agent based" approach to the first model, and finally, we'll add some financial features to the model.

**The "simple" model.** Here are the steps to follow for the first simulation.

1 open a new project

2 insert a "graph X vs time" object into the project window

3 Build the code, and compile it under your favourite Swarm Platform.

The result of the simulation is the following:

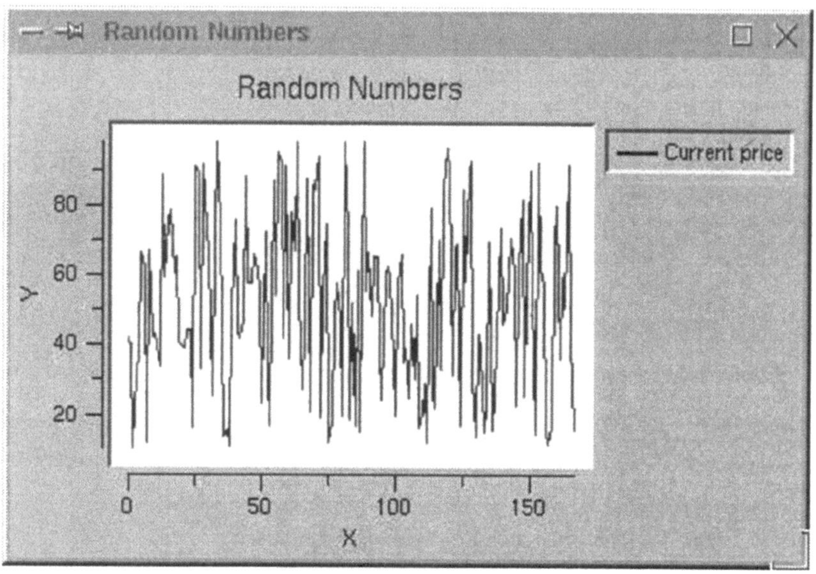


*Figure 3.16.* The output of the simple model

**Simple Model With and Agent.** With this second model we start to build "real" agent based simulations using Swarm. We build an Agent named Nasdaq which contains all the methods inside itself. Here are the steps to follow for the simulation.

1 open a new project

2 insert a "graph X vs time" object into the project window

3 Create an empty object named Nasdaq

4 Click "Update Code" from the menu. Edit the ObserverSwarm by a double click on its icon. The Code editor will appear, and change the following lines of code

| Original Lines | Lines to be substituted |
|---|---|
| `-(float)getValue {`<br>`float valore;`<br>`valore=[uniformDblRand getDouble-`<br>`WithMin: 10 withMax: 100];`<br>`return valore;`<br>`}` | `-(float)getValue {`<br>`float valore;`<br>`valore=[[modelSwarm getNasdaq]`<br>`getMyValue];`<br>`return valore; }` |

5 Build the code, and compile it under your favourite Swarm platform.

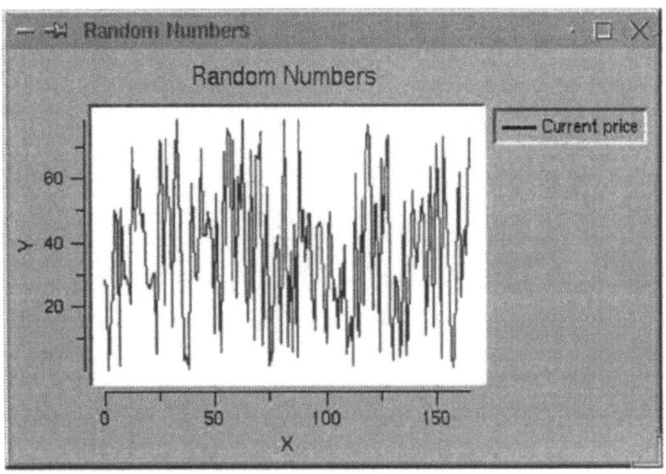


*Figure 3.17.* Result of the first experiment

As you can note, the output is exactly the same as the "simple model": the only difference is that the plotted data, instead of being "taken" from the ObserverSwarm directly, is taken from the object Nasdaq.

**A Real Data Model.** This simulation employes real data. With this further step, we use REAL Nasdaq values to be plotted into our model.
Follow the four steps of the last model and then edit the object Nasdaq and add the following methods

| Original Lines | Lines to be added/substituted |
|---|---|
| `- step {`<br>`value = [uniformDblRand getDouble-`<br>`      WithMin: min withMax: max];`<br>`printf (''Value=\%f\n'', value);`<br>`return self;`<br>` }` | `-initFile {`<br>`char *name = nasdaq.txt;`<br>`nasdaq=fopen(name,r);`<br>`return self;`<br>`         }`<br><br>`-stopFile {`<br>`int i;`<br>`i = fclose(nasdaq);`<br>`return self;`<br>`         }`<br><br>`- step {`<br>`fscanf(nasdaq,''\%f\n'',\&value);`<br>`printf (''Value=\%f\n'', value);`<br>`return self;`<br>`      }` |

As final step, build the code, and compile it under your favourite Swarm Platform.

You'll see a graph like that in figure 3.17

**The financial simulation.** Now we can build the last simulation. In this model we'll show the previous graph along with two other graphs displaying, first, the "trend" of the Index (where trend means the simple average of the latest two values) and, second, its change. This is an example of how to build simple simulations using VSB first to create its front-end and then, after a few changes in the code, the full blown version. The Output will be as figure 3.19

Here are the steps:

1 open a new project

2 insert a "graph X vs time" object into the project window named Nasdaq

3 insert a "graph X vs time" object into the project window named Different

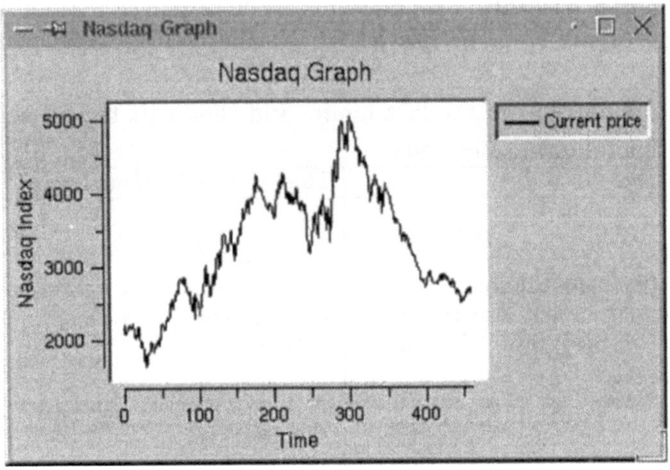


*Figure 3.18.* Output of the Second experiment

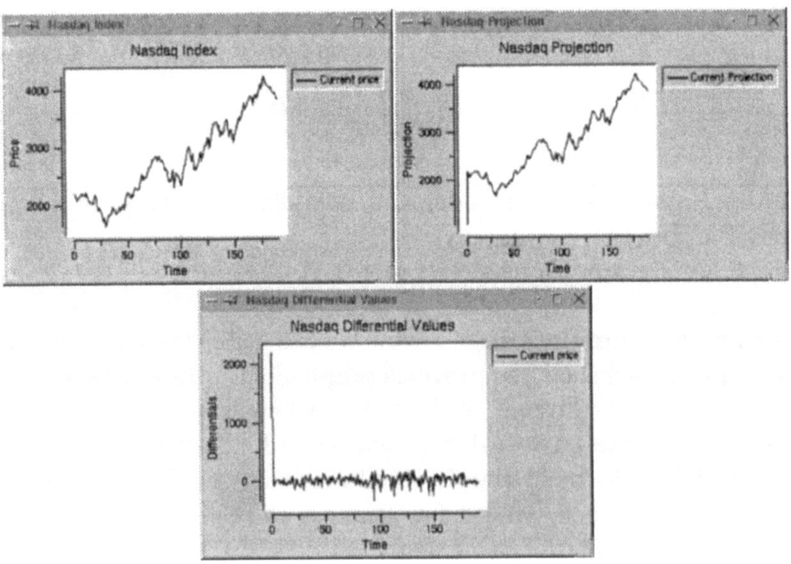


*Figure 3.19.* Output of "Financial Simulation" (all graphs)

4 insert a "graph X vs time" object into the project window named Project

5 Create an empty object named Nasdaq

6 Click "Update Code" from the menu

7 Edit the Nasdaq Object, "patch" it as in 1.3, and add the following line

| Original Lines | Lines to be added/substituted |
|---|---|
| - createEnd {<br>[super createEnd];<br>return self;<br>} | - createEnd {<br>[super createEnd];<br>remind0=0;<br>remind1=0;<br>return self;<br>} |
| - step {<br>fscanf(nasdaq,‘‘%f \n’’,&value);<br>printf (‘‘Value=%f \n’’, value);<br>return self;<br>} | - step {<br>float tmp;<br>tmp=value;<br>fscanf(nasdaq,’’%f \n’’,&value);<br>printf (‘‘Value=%f \n’’,value);<br>remind0=remind1;<br>remind1=value;<br>projection=(remind0+remind1)/2;<br>differential = remind1-remind0<br>printf (‘‘The Projection Value=<br>%f \n’’, projection);<br>return self;<br>}<br><br>-(float) getProjection {<br>return projection;<br>}<br><br>-(float) getDifferential {<br>return projection;<br>} |

8 Edit the ObserverSwarm object and write these changes

| Original Lines | Lines to be added |
|---|---|
| | -(float)getValue1 {<br>float val;<br>val = [[modelSwarm getNasdaq]<br>getProjection];<br>return val;<br>} |

9 Build the code, and compile it under your favourite Swarm Platform.

Now the potential user has all the information to build its own simulation using VSB and Swarm libraries. All the examples can be found into the "Examples" folder in VSB package. We have inserted, also, an evolution of last model, in which there are two stock index (nasdaq and Dj), their projection and their percent variation using not only a single line graph, but also a barchart and a multiple lines graph. This example is a bit hard to explain in a few lines, because we had to "patch" a few objects and several lines have been changed. All the examples are fully explained in every part and before inserting the new lines, the old ones are commented.

## 5. The goal of using a tool like VSB

One of the goals for which we have started programming VSB is to create a Visual tool for Swarm libraries. The way to program, during these years, has changed a lot, because of the availability of VISUAL languages. With simple "clicks of mouse" everyone can build simulatons, even if s/he does not know anything about the language s/he is using. The role of the "pure programmer" is not the same as before, s/he is not an extraterrestrial being, who can, writing a few lines of code, build programs from scratch. One of the advantages of using visual tools, is that the programmer does not have to write always the same boring code, s/he may just input a few parameters, and then the Visual tools will fill the other pieces of code. For example, in Swarm, if the simulator wants to insert a "bar chart" in her/his own program, s/he has to fill only a dialog like 5.20 and, once VSB generates the code, the "compiler" will generate all the code relative to the barchart. As one of our friends has always said, every program is composed of 50% interface, 30% problem analysis, and 20% code typing. VSB let you concentrate on the 30+20% of the program development, while it takes care of the other 50%.

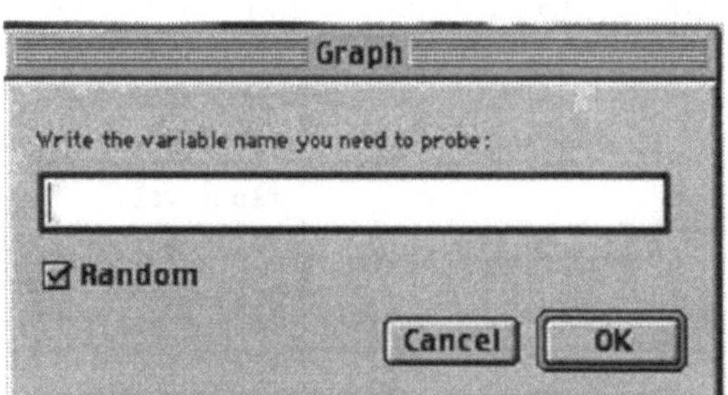


*Figure 3.20.* "Add Bar Chart" dialog

# 6. Future Works

By the time of this book publication, there will be a stable Macintosh version of VSB. During the next Swarmfest we will present a MacOSX version with a full support for both objective-c and java.

A new version of VSB will soon be available with more features, such as the support for Ca2d Objects and Rasters.

VSB is a very dynamic work in progress. For an update on the environment development, to download the latest release or for updated information about the VSB, including sample code, errata and preview of further versions, visit my site (http://pluto.dma.unive.it/~alex/swarm in VSB section)

## References

Luna, F. and Stefansson, B. (eds.), *Economic Simulations in Swarm: Agent-Based Modelling and Object Oriented Programming*, Kluwer Academic Publishers, 2000

Perrone, A. SwarmJournal, available at the following URL http://pluto.dma.unive.it/~alex/swarm

Stefansson, B. (1997). *Swarm: An Object Oriented Simulation Platform Applied to Markets and Organizations*

Terna, P. (1998). *Simulation Tools for Social Scientists: Building Agent Based Models with SWARM. In Journal of Artificial Societies and Social Simulation.*Vol 1 No. 2, available at http://www.soc.surrey.ac.uk/ /JASSS/1/2/4.html

Axtell, R, Epstein, Growing Artificial Societies

Minar, N., Burkhart, R., Langton, C. and Askenazi, M. (1996). *The Swarm Simulation System: A Toolkit for Building Multi-Agent Simulations.* Santa Fe Institute Working Paper 96-04-2.

Minar, N, Roger Bukkart, C. Langton, "Swarm Documentation" (Electronic Document): available at http://www.swarm.org

Tesfatsion, L. (2001). "*Introduction to the special issue on agent-based computational economics.*" Journal of Economic Dynamic and Control, Vol. 25, Issue 3-4, pp.281-293.

Myers B. Hudson S. Pausc, *Past, present and Future of User Interface Software Tools*

Apple Computer Inc. Inside Macintosh, 1985 Addison Wesley

IBM, Visual Age for Java, version 2.0, 1995

Flanagan D, Farley J, Crawford W, Magnusson K, *Java Enterprise in a Nutshell*

L.J. Pinson, Wiener, 1991 "*Objective-C, Object-Oriented Programming Techniques*", Addison Wesley Publishing company

Chapter 4

# SWIEE – A SWARM WEB INTERFACE FOR EXPERIMENTAL ECONOMICS

Riccardo Boero*

*Department of Economics and Quantitative Methods*

*University of Pavia*

*Italy*

boero@econ.unito.it

**Abstract** The goal of this work is to show the advantages of using the Swarm simulation platform as a tool for making Experimental Economics. A complex project, called SWIEE, will be presented. Furthermore, some useful examples will be proposed to spread this approach in the experimenters' community, nowadays accustomed to use closed and proprietary programs. The idea of using Swarm for Experimental Economics derives from the possibility it gives to write simulations in the Java programming language, known to be object oriented and very useful for networked applications. Java allows the design of programs in which an object method can be called by other applications running on computers connected to the Internet, so the RMI (i.e. Remote Method Invocation) standard Java classes are the core of this new usage of Swarm. Furthermore, we illustrate an example (the prisoner's dilemma) and we report some methodological considerations on the possibility of making experiments considering the Internet like a sort of virtual open laboratory. Finally, we display some future developments of the project, in particular those, very interesting, related to the construction of experiments (or better "simulative" experiments) with both human and artificial agents. More information about SWIEE can be obtained from its web pages, http://swiee.econ.unito.it.

*The SWIEE project (http://swiee.econ.unito.it) was born within activities of the GTUS (Gruppo Torinese Utilizzatori Swarm – a Swarm users group at the University of Torino, Italy, supervised by Professor Pietro Terna – http://eco83.econ.unito.it/swarm) and it is supported by the Centre for Cognitive Economics, University of Piemonte Orientale, Alessandria, Italy (http://www.jp.unipmn.it/cenec/index.htm).

# 1. Introduction

Some of the advantages of using Swarm for building Agent Based Models (ABMs) are the possibility to make flexible models that represent numerous real situations, the possibility to reuse the code, the use of an easy way to understand formalization and the possibility to transmit simulations to other researchers who can replicate the experiments. These elements, together with its ever growing diffusion, make Swarm a strong candidate for the standard ABMs simulation platform.

Even in Experimental Economics studies, there is the need for computer programs because the largest part of experiments need a software infrastructure. In particular, programs are necessary to present experimental background, to introduce players to the experimental artificial world, to let many players interact, to store a large amount of data and, finally, to analyze results. The world of experimental laboratory software is composed of many different programs and unfortunately they are generally closed and proprietary. Moreover, most of them are only useful for making specialized experiments[1]: for example it is very difficult to use the same software to conduct an experiment on public goods and one about industrial organizations. The SWIEE project aims to spread the Swarm approach to correct these limitations.

A typical Swarm simulation, furthermore, consists of an artificial world representing a real one, in which artificial agents, that represent real agents, interact with each other. The basic idea of the SWIEE project is to integrate this scheme letting humans directly interact in artificial worlds, with the aim of studying their behavior. This is a typical matter of Experimental Economics, but all experimental social sciences can use SWIEE's concepts and tools.

From a technical point of view, SWIEE is feasible because of the Java programming language. In fact, starting from the 2.0.1 release on, the Swarm simulation system lets users choose the preferred programming language in order to build agent based simulations: the original Objective-C language is now accompanied by Java and therefore many other languages, as was explained by Daniels [Daniels, 1999]. Java is useful for this goal because of its rigorous object oriented architecture and because it is probably the easiest and most complete language for networked applications.

From the point of view of its logical structure, the communication link between humans and artificial Swarm worlds is facilitated by object oriented programming and by considering human players like any other *swarm* ("a collection of agents executing scheduled actions", see [Minar et al., 1996]).

The chapter is structured as follows: Section 2 "SWIEE Basics" presents the basic concepts on which the project is built and the two approaches of which it is composed; Section 3 "The Prisoner's Dilemma" presents an example, inspired by the famous prisoner's dilemma; Section 4 "Making Experiments on the Internet" introduces some considerations on thinking the Internet like a virtual open laboratory; Section 5 "Future Developments" plans future examples and tools of the project.

## 2. SWIEE Basics

The SWIEE project was conceived to show how easy it is to use Swarm for Experimental Economics. In particular the advantages of this choice are:

- SWIEE is an open source project;
- SWIEE is based on Swarm, a largely diffused simulation toolkit;
- SWIEE uses the Java programming language;
- SWIEE uses TCP/IP protocols for client-server communication;
- SWIEE allows for the setting up of any experiment even with some artificial agents interacting, if needed;
- SWIEE can be used to implement laboratory and Internet experiments.

Researchers commonly use Swarm to build models composed of artificial agents that act in artificial worlds. Researchers of Experimental Economics use some software to let human agents act in artificial worlds. Swarm can be a suitable software to run experiments, since it is possible to let humans choose the action that their artificial representations "bring" to the simulated world. With respect to the model structure, there is only one difference between standard Swarm simulations (composed only of artificial agents) and experimental ones: the link between model agents and human players.

### 2.1. SWIEE Framework

The SWIEE project is composed of experiment examples and software tools and it follows two guidelines: to build simple experiments, as much as possible close to Swarm simulations (so as to maintain the typical Swarm structure); to develop a complete toolkit. To reach these partially divergent aims, it is necessary to develop two approaches:

1 To maintain a standard and simple Swarm structure, only one difference has to be introduced between simulations and experiments: the link between model agents and human players (see Figure 4.1). The first software release of the project follows this approach (called **simple**), for example the prisoner's dilemma game illustrated in Section 3.

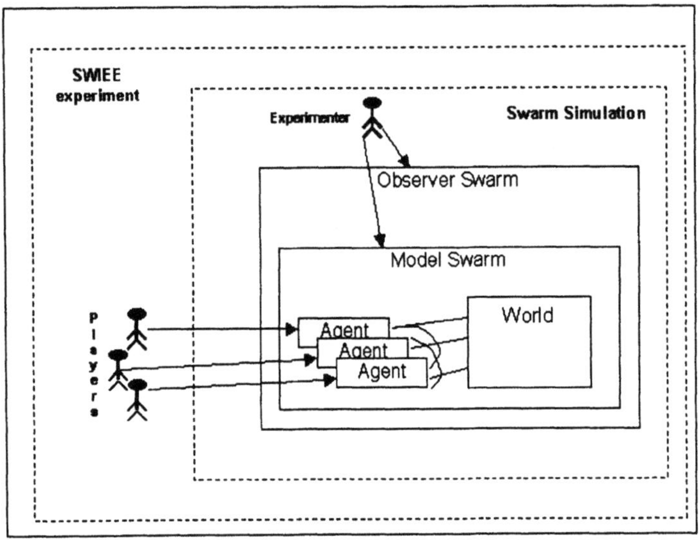


*Figure 4.1.* The simple SWIEE framework.

2 The second approach (the **complex** one) will be developed using more complex tools that let the experimenter manage and automate all tasks. To do so it will be necessary to manage the interaction between Swarm simulations and web servers, using Java servlets and Java database connectivity. Therefore, the new framework (Figure 4.2) will be based on two layers, one for authentication and one for execution, management and access to the experiment.

## 2.2. Java RMI Classes

To setup a remote link between two applications (the client one, with which human players interact, and the server one, the Swarm simulation), it is easier to use Swarm written in Java (rather than the Objective-C version), and Internet as the communication medium, since it is a widespread, versatile and cheap instrument.

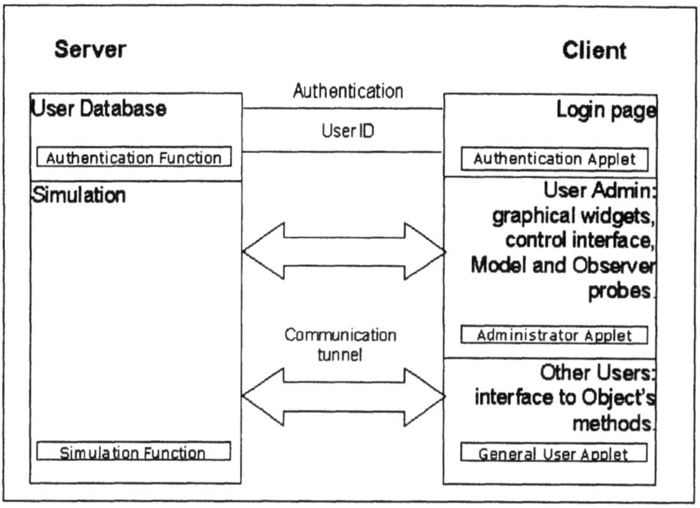


*Figure 4.2.* The complex SWIEE framework.

As a matter of fact, Java has a lot of easy and built-in functions for managing TCP/IP protocols and communications. Moreover, Java permits to prepare particular programs called "applets" that run on the Java virtual machine of the client browser. Hence it is not necessary to download any networked programs: only a client computer is needed, connected with the Internet or with a LAN based on TCP/IP protocols.

The key classes to use Swarm for Experimental Economics are the RMI (Remote Method Invocation) ones. They were introduced in Java 1.1, and are supported by all recent Internet browsers.

To make this concept clearer, it is necessary to remember a fundamental characteristic of Java: programs aren't compiled in machine language but in a byte-code executable by Java Virtual Machines (JVMs – interpreters of Java byte-code available for any platform and integrated in any Internet browser). Therefore, with RMI classes it is possible to establish a communication between objects running on different JVMs. As Seshadri [Seshadri, 2000] states:

> A primary goal for the RMI designers was to allow programmers to develop distributed Java programs with the same syntax and semantics used for non-distributed programs. To do this, they had to carefully map how Java classes and objects work in a single Java Virtual Machine (JVM) to a new model of how classes and objects would work in a distributed (multiple JVM) computing environment ... the RMI architects tried to make the use of distributed Java objects similar to using local Java objects.

**The RMI Architecture.** The RMI architecture creates a distributed object model that integrates naturally into the Java programming language and into the local object model. The core aspect of the architecture is represented by a very important principle: interface and implementation of the distributed services are separated. Clients access only the interface, while the implementation stays beneath the server (see Figure 4.3).

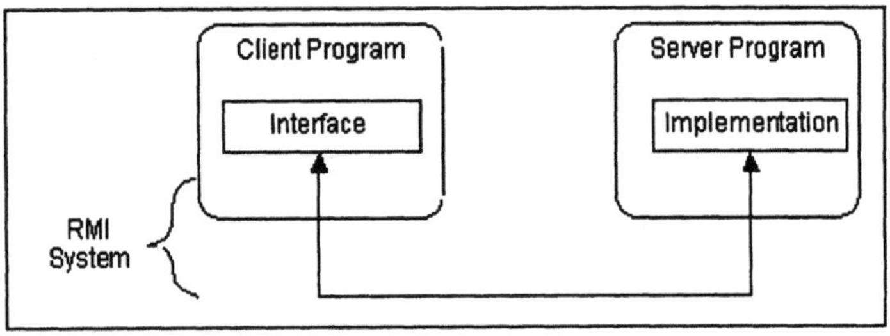


*Figure 4.3.* RMI – separation of interface and implementation.

*Source: Fundamentals of RMI [Seshadri, 2000].*

In other words, we can say that, considering the RMI technology, the interface represents the definition of a remote service, while the implementation of the service is coded in remote classes.

But the RMI architecture has one more very important aspect. The interface of the remote service has to be known by client objects, so it is necessary to have, on the client side, an interface proxy (see Figure 4.4).

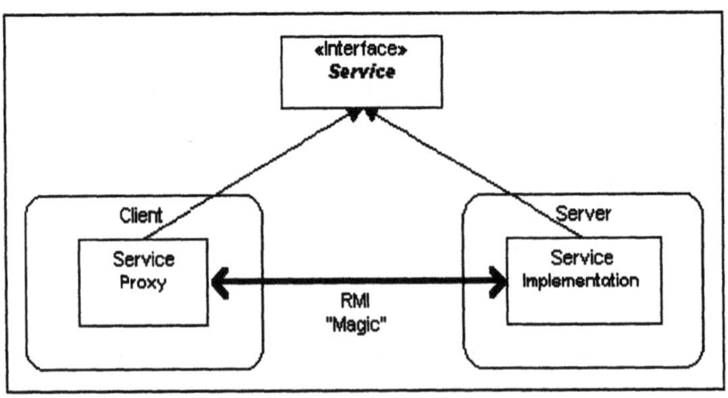


*Figure 4.4.* RMI – the interface proxy.

*Source: Fundamentals of RMI [Seshadri, 2000].*

**The RMI Layers.** To implement such architecture it is necessary to use several "virtual" layers of communication between client and server.

By using a layered architecture, each of the layers could be enhanced or replaced without affecting the rest of the system. For example, the transport layer could be replaced by a UDP/IP layer without the need to change upper layers. In real terms only the lowest layer will be a communication layer, based on TCP/IP connections.

There are, on the whole, three layers. The first one (see Figure 4.5) is composed of Stubs and Skeletons, classes that represent the proxies of the remote service present both in client and in server machines. This layer intercepts calls to the remote service and passes them to the implementation of the service.

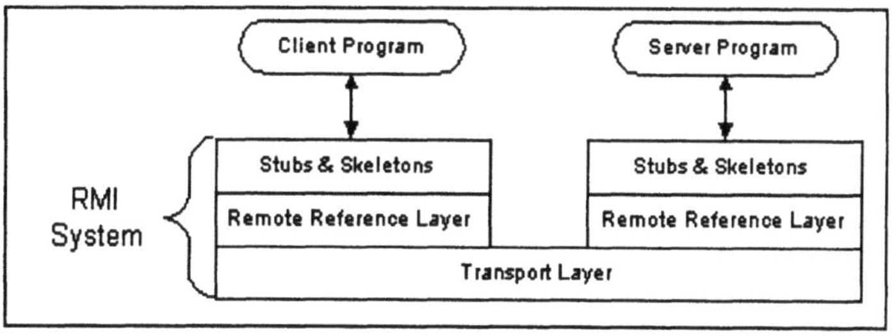


*Figure 4.5.* RMI – communication layers.

*Source: Fundamentals of RMI [Seshadri, 2000].*

The next layer is the Remote Reference Layer, which understands the invocation semantics and manages the RMI connection. Starting from Java 2 SDK on, it supports also the remote activation of services (a function useful for SWIEE "complex approach").

The last layer is the Transport Layer, based on TCP/IP protocols. It manages the connection, the informations transport and has also some useful strategies for bypassing firewalls.

**Naming Remote Objects.** A naming service is necessary for the system to function because it finds remote services for client applications. In other words clients find remote services using a naming service. RMI can use many different naming and directory services (for example the Java Naming and Directory Service – JNDS) but it is simpler to use the small RMI integrated service, the so called RMI Registry, `rmiregistry`. The RMI Registry runs on every machine that hosts remote service objects and accepts queries for services, by default on port 1099. As Seshadri [Seshadri, 2000] noted:

> On a host machine, a server program creates a remote service by first creating a local object that implements that service. Next, it exports that object to RMI. When the object is exported, RMI creates a listening service that waits for clients to connect and request the service. After

exporting, the server registers the object in the RMI Registry under a public name.

On the client side, the RMI Registry is accessed through the static class Naming. It provides the method lookup() that a client uses to query a registry. The method lookup() accepts a URL that specifies the server host name and the name of the desired service. The method returns a remote reference to the service object. The URL takes the form: **rmi://<host-name>[:<name-service-port>]/<service-name>** where the host-name is a name recognized on the local area network (LAN) or a DNS name on the Internet. The name-service-port needs to be specified only if the naming service is running on a different port from the default 1099.

Summarizing, the RMI architecture can be represented by Figure 4.6, in which the RMI registry can be outlined.

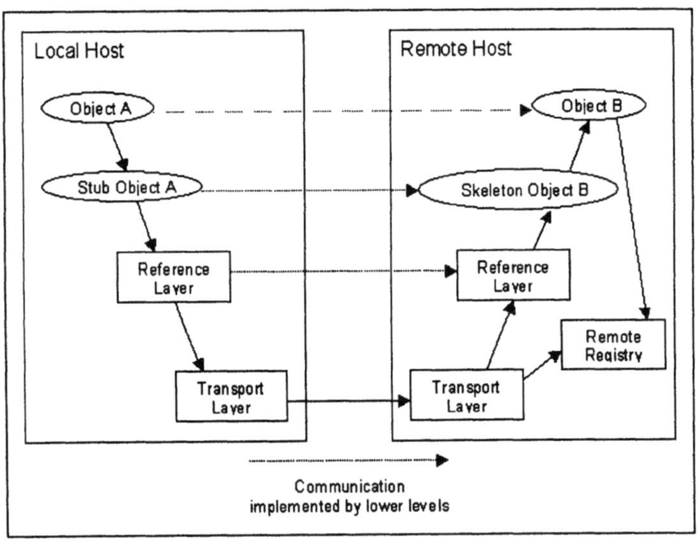


*Figure 4.6.* The RMI scheme.

Finally, a working RMI system is composed of several parts, enumerated in the following list.

- Interface definitions for the remote services.
- Implementations of the remote services.
- Stub and Skeleton files.
- A server to host the remote services.
- An RMI Naming service that allows clients to find the remote services.

- A client program that needs the remote services.
- In case, if one doesn't want to install programs on client machines, an HTTP server (a web server).

After the designing step of the RMI system, there are generally many further steps to make the system work.

1 Write Java code for a remote service host program.

2 Write Java code for interfaces.

3 Write Java code for implementation classes.

4 Compile all codes.

5 Generate Stub and Skeleton class files from implementation classes, using the RMI compiler (`rmic implementation-class`, without file extensions).

6 Develop Java code for RMI client program.

7 Compile the client program, install and run RMI system.

## 3. The Prisoner's Dilemma

In this section, an example of an Experimental Economics game is presented. The game is an implementation of the prisoner's dilemma[2], and follows the SWIEE simple approach.

The prisoner's dilemma was chosen because it is a fundamental game and because it is deeply studied and it has been implemented in many experimental software. Hence, it is easy to make comparisons between them and the SWIEE implementation.

The developing process was very simple and had the following structure.

1 We built a Swarm standard simulation, comprehensive of objects (with all needed methods) representing human players, collected and interacting within couples.

2 We added remote service classes to manage the RMI server side.

3 We prepared the applet for human players' interaction.

## 3.1. The Game

There are a lot of formalizations of the prisoner's dilemma game. We followed Tucker [Tucker, 1950] considering a symmetric payoff matrix, but it is very easy to modify the code to support an asymmetric one[3]. The payoff matrix is the following, with $b$ ¿ $a$ ¿ $c$ ¿ $d$:

| | confess | not confess |
|---|---|---|
| confess | $c,c$ | $b,d$ |
| not confess | $d,b$ | $a,a$ |

As Roth [Roth, 1995] noted:

> The "dilemma", of course is that it is a dominant strategy for each prisoner to confess, since $c$ ¿ $d$ and $b$ ¿ $a$, but that both of them would be better off if neither confessed, since $a$ ¿ $c$. So the only equilibrium of this game is the dominant strategy equilibrium at which both prisoners confess and receive the (non-Pareto optimal) payoff of $c$ each. (In much of the literature the strategy "not confess" is called "cooperate", and "confess" is called "defect".)

The game is played by players matched pairwise and runs for finite or indefinite number of cycles[4]. This SWIEE implementation of the game lets the experimenter choose which information will be displayed to the players.

## 3.2. The Implementation Structure

In addition to the standard Swarm simulation, built with a variable number of objects called "Player", it is necessary to implement the "RemoteServer" class that is the core of the RMI service. This class is activated by the ModelSwarm one:

```
....
// server class to manage RMI - Remote Method Invocation
remoteServer = new RemoteServer(playerArray, timer);
....
```

RemoteServer manages the activation and the registration in the RMI-registry of services:

```
....
try {
    RemoteGt1 c = new RemoteGt1Impl(playerArray, timer);
    // Pay attention to the IP of your host and to the port:
    // default port of RMIRegistry is 1099
    Naming.rebind("//YOUR_IP_ADDRESS:1098/RemoteGt1", c);
    System.out.println("RemoteServer is registered.");
```

```
   } catch (Exception e) {
       System.out.println("Trouble in get RemoteGt1: " + e);
   }
   ....
```

These services are coded in two distinct classes, an interface and its implementation, as was explained in paragraph 2.2. The class called RemoteGt1 contains the definition of services:

```
import java.rmi.*;

// Interface to Remote Methods
public interface RemoteGt1 extends Remote {
    public void setChoice(int i, int v)
      throws RemoteException;
    public void setExpectation(int i, int v)
      throws RemoteException;
    public int getOtherChoice(int i) throws RemoteException;
    ....
```

The RemoteGt1Impl class is, on the contrary, the implementation of remote services:

```
import java.rmi.*;
import java.rmi.server.*;

// Implementation of Remote Methods.
public class RemoteGt1Impl extends UnicastRemoteObject
    implements RemoteGt1 {
    public Player[] playerArray;
    public Timer timer;
    public RemoteGt1Impl(Player[] pl, Timer t)
      throws RemoteException {
        super();
        playerArray = pl;
        timer = t;
    }
    public void setChoice(int i, int v)
      throws RemoteException {
        int id = i, value = v;
        playerArray[id].setChoice(value);
    }
    public void setExpectation(int i, int v)
      throws RemoteException {
```

```
        int id = i, value = v;
        playerArray[id].setExpectation(value);
    }
    public int getOtherChoice(int i) throws RemoteException {
        int id = i;
        int value = playerArray[id].getOtherChoice();
        return value;
    }
    ....
```

Moreover it is necessary to add another key class: "Timer". The aim of this class is to administrate some counters necessary for the synchronization of the applet (the player web interface) and the Player object. Players' choices aren't synchronous and, moreover, each player has to access results of the last round of the game. To obtain this, it is necessary to manage carefully the interaction and to synchronize applets and Player objects functions.

The structure so modified is represented in Figure 4.7, inspired by some slides of Stefansson's Tutorial on Swarm [Stefansson, 1999].

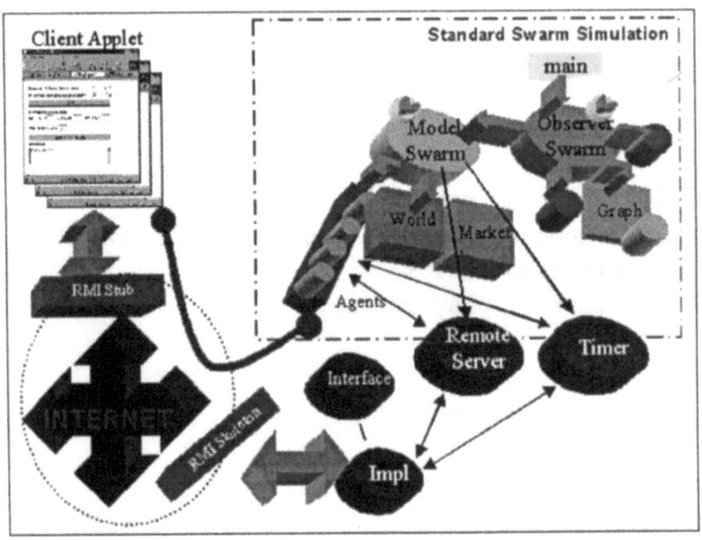


*Figure 4.7.* The prisoner's dilemma – simple structure.

The last piece of code added allows the researcher to save data: this code writes game information on file. it is a buffered writer, so it writes effectively data on disk only on each cycle of the game, and not every time a player chooses an action. Therefore it doesn't weight down the server during game runs.

Once completed the server side of the experiment, it is necessary to build the client applet. Applets are particular Java classes loadable on web browsers and easy to customize. In this case applets represent a sort of human interface to game choices. The class Gt1Client is loaded by an HTML tag, written in a web page. Moreover, it passes to the game the identification parameter of the player:

```
<applet codebase="http://IP_ADDRESS_AND_PATH/gt1"
code="Gt1Client.class" width=364 height=370>
<param name=identification value="7">
</applet>
```

The client class is composed of a part useful to connect the remote server and of a part where remote services are invoked, for example:

```
try {
  URL hostURL = getCodeBase();
  String host = hostURL.getHost();
  // Change the port number if necessary
  server = (RemoteGt1)Naming.lookup
     ("//"+host+":1098/RemoteGt1");
} catch (Exception ex) {
  textArea1.setText(ex.toString());
}

try  {
  a = server.getParameterA();
  b = server.getParameterB();
  c = server.getParameterC();
  d = server.getParameterD();
} catch (Exception ex) {
  textArea1.setText(ex.toString());
}
```

Finally, it is necessary to compile all classes, making sure that the directory with the source codes is in the path of the server machine (this is important for `javac`[5], the Java compiler) and in a document directory of the web server (so to be loaded remotely by players). Then compile RMI stub and skeletons, using the command `rmic implementation-class -name` (this last without file extensions).

To run a simulation on server, standard Java commands can be used, like `java main-game-class` with which the experimenter can access the standard Swarm control panel.

## 3.3. Running the Game

The following paragraphs present the three main steps of a run of the current release of the prisoner's dilemma game (GT1).

**Starting the Game.** When the experimenter starts the simulation (with the instruction `java StartGt1`), he can set some game parameters via the "ModelSwarm" probes (Figure 4.8): the number of players (always an even number); the number of game cycles; the value of payoffs; the file name (and its path) for saving data.

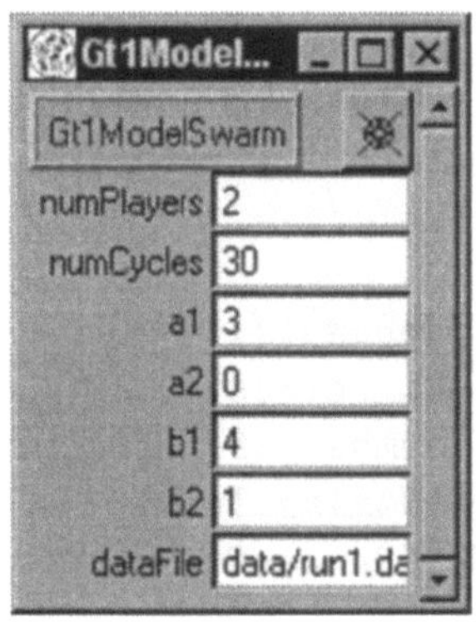


*Figure 4.8.* The prisoner's dilemma – setting game parameters.

Payoff values correspond to the ones proposed in Tucker's payoff matrix, in particular b2 = $a$, a2 = $b$, a1 = $c$ and b1 = $d$.

The output data file is a simple text file, with fields separated by one single blank; it is possible to choose any file name and any file extension depending on the naming constraints of the platform. The first row of the data file presents headers for different data, the first column presents player's identifiers. This file can be easily loaded in many useful applications for data managing.

**Playing the Game.** After the experimenter pushes the "Start" button, players can load their HTML pages with the Java applet (like the one in Figure 4.9) and then interact with the game. HTML pages have to be prepared by the experimenter in advance; these pages are necessary to identify each player.

With this applet, players can make choices and read information about past rounds. The experimenter can choose whether to ask the player's expectation on the opponent's choice: this can be considered a control on each player's consistency.

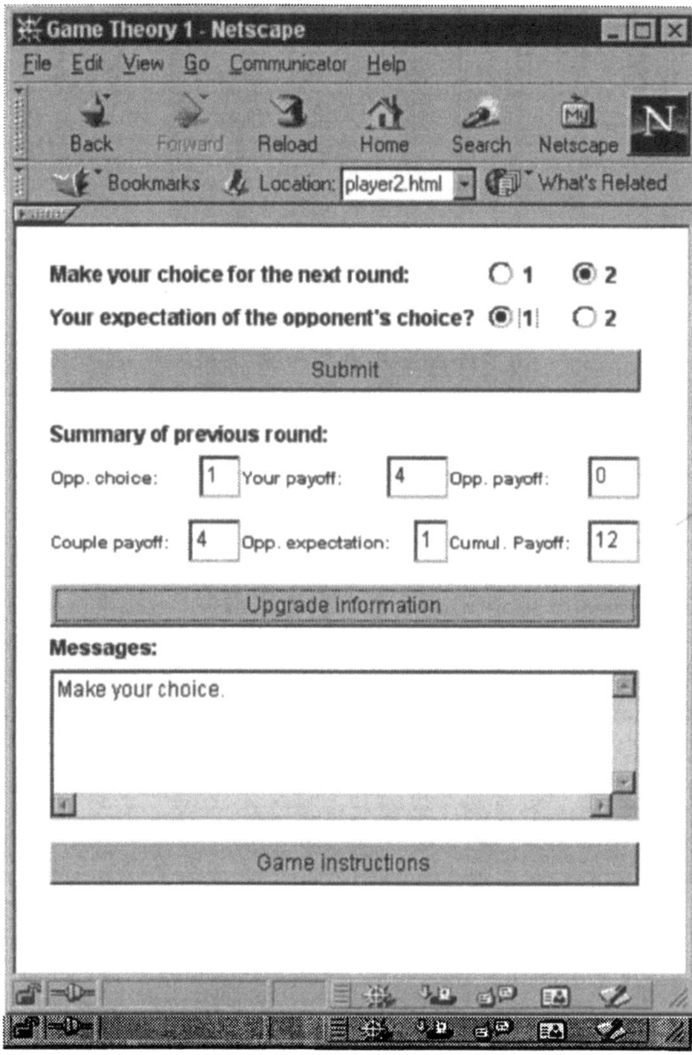


*Figure 4.9.* The prisoner's dilemma – player's applet.

In the "Messages" area they can read information on the steps to follow; clicking on the "Game instructions" button the instructions window appears (Figure 4.10), where players can read a description of the game and where they can see the payoff matrix. Every access to this window is recorded and saved in the last column of the data output file: this is realized using a special window, a Java Dialog object, that forces players to close it if they want to continue playing.

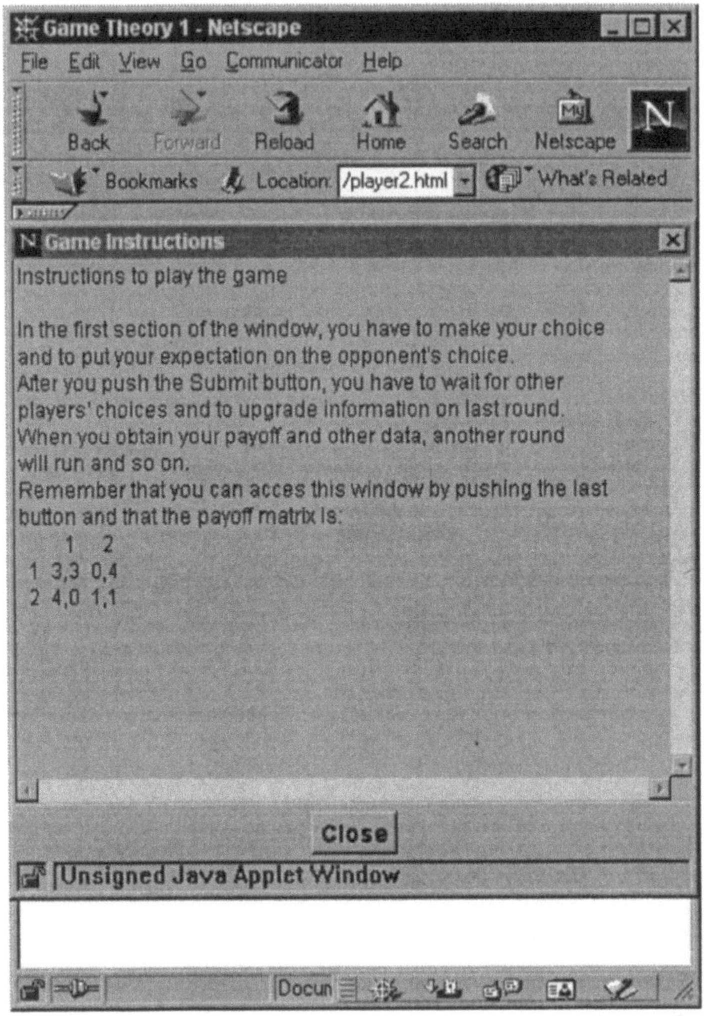


*Figure 4.10.* The prisoner's dilemma – game instructions window.

**Analyzing Game Results.** When all cycles are completed, the experimenter can access the ValueGraph (Figure 4.11) of players' performance. Obviously this graph is customizable, and all game data can be represented. Moreover, one could exploit other Swarm built-in analyzing tools, but saving data to a storage file also allows the use of other applications.

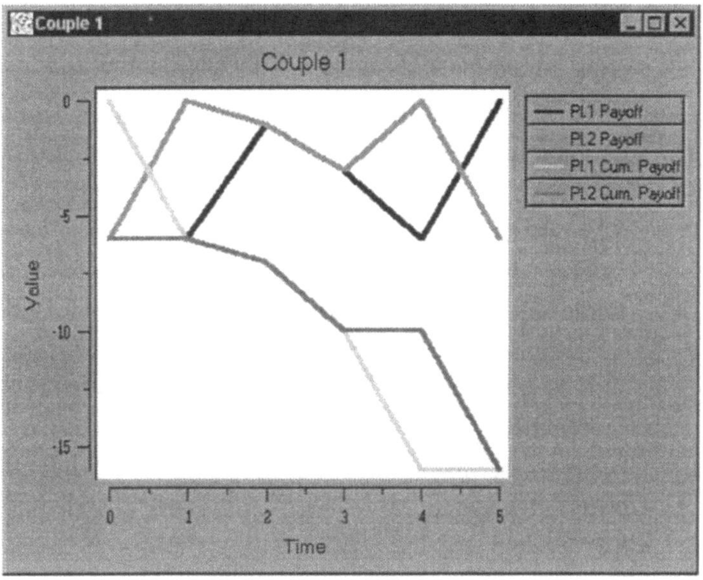


*Figure 4.11.* The prisoner's dilemma – payoffs of a couple of players.

# 4. Making Experiments on the Internet

The SWIEE project uses Internet technologies like TCP/IP protocols to make connections between clients and server. All software is prepared to be managed in a laboratory classroom, where environment variables are controllable. But it is also possible to think of the Internet as an excellent medium to extend the laboratory classroom to the whole world. This choice can have some advantages but also some disadvantages.

- Advantages
  - It can strongly extend the subject universe.
  - Ecological validity of experiments can be higher because of the immediate access to experiment (some filters and psychological barriers typical of classroom experiments are not present).
  - There isn't any limitation to opening times; players' participation is more comfortable and cheaper.
  - It can be easier to attract demographically different groups.
  - Participation in experiment can be easily extended with minor costs.
  - Experiment management will be cheaper.

- Disadvantages
  - Subject universe is however deeply segmented and focused on particular age and income classes.
  - The experiment environment is difficult to control, in particular:
    * access to information cannot be checked as easily as in laboratory experiments,
    * identity can be difficult to verify with absolute certainty,
    * there is a strong selection related to the medium, so that it is normal that a lot of subjects abandon during the experiment.
  - There are stronger negative effects of Computer Mediated Communication (CMC - see [Rocco and Warglien,1996]) on cooperation.

Therefore, the key topic on Internet experiments is the control of environment variables, but as Schmidt and Jacobsen [Schmidt and Jacobsen, 1999] noted:

> Internet experiments can be conducted in a more or less controlled environment. There are experiments conducted close to the standards of laboratory experiments or Internet experiments that are field experiments, yet, all variations between these both extremes are possible.

Schmidt and Jacobsen also reported that, in making a comparison between Internet experiments and laboratory ones, there are always differences, even if minor. Therefore, it is necessary to underline that the choice of making Internet experiments forces the experimenter to consider a lot of methodological matters and to develop carefully a complex project aiming to fix the disadvantages of this approach. This often implies developing big software infrastructures, possibly creating a "web realistic" environment: for example if you want to study a particular good market, you have to build a platform as similar as possible to e-commerce standard web sites.

For this purpose, SWIEE can be very useful. In the first step one needs to follow the complex approach of SWIEE, then he has to develop particular interfaces related to the experiment. In this case the Java base of the SWIEE project is very useful because almost all technologies for web interaction can be managed and integrated by Java.

Finally, we can say that a complete Internet experiment needs a larger starting investment than a laboratory one, but these approaches are also very different: Internet and laboratory experiments appear to be complements not substitutes. Moreover, Internet seems to be very useful and easier to use for the economic surveys needed in the experiment projecting step, see for example the Berkeley Internet Virtual Laboratory, http://elsa.berkeley.edu/ivlab/.

# 5. Future Developments

The SWIEE project is very recent, it dates the beginning of year 2000. In the future we schedule an improvement of the prisoner's dilemma documentation and the release of tutorials. Then, new experiments will be developed following the simple approach. Moreover, we will develop the software infrastructure needed for applications of the SWIEE complex approach. In fact, after the development of authentication and administration functions, we will release the general Game Theory application. This aims to completely automate remote administration of these experiments.

## 5.1. "Simulative" Experiments

The SWIEE project can allow a step forward in making economic experiments. Swarm allows to build agents with Artificial Intelligence or based on simpler algorithms. Therefore, it is normal to use the SWIEE project to build experiments with both artificial and human agents interacting.

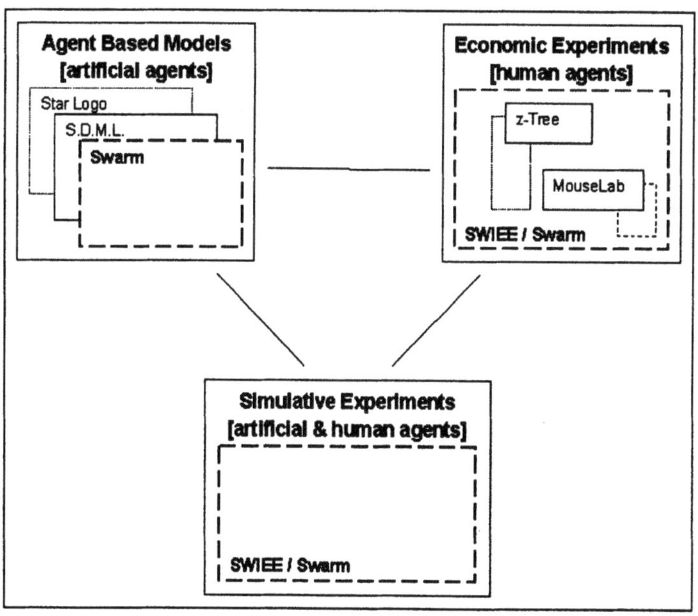


*Figure 4.12.* Simulative Experiments and software tools.

This concept (*simulative experiment* = a mix between a simulation and an experiment) can be ever more useful for simulating contemporary markets, for example the financial ones, but also to render the artificial environment, in which humans interact, more realistic. Moreover, it can be used to prepare experiments in which human players interact with artificial agents that use some algorithms. Summarizing, advantages of simulative experiments could be:

- big but cheap experiments can be made using artificial agents;
- it is possible to simulate better, in a more realistic and more dynamic way, the artificial world in which humans interact;
- human behaviour and beliefs can be studied deeply, putting players in "critical" but realistic situations;
- the possibility to obtain a macro emergence from experiments, maybe representing organizational behaviour.

Finally, examples of these particular experiments will be the ones related to financial markets making of speculative bubbles, or revised Game Theory experiments based on the work of Axelrod [Axelrod, 1984] with some artificial agents following a "tit for tat" strategy, or variations of Roth and Erev [Roth and Erev, 1995] coordination experiment.

## Notes

1. One of the most versatile tool is the "Extensive Form Game" of Carnegie Mellon University, http://www.cmu.edu/comlabgames/, born to execute extensive form iterated games.
2. On the SWIEE web site it is possible to download the last release of the game, also called GT1 (Game Theory 1).
3. The reader is referred to other texts for a complete explanation of the game
4. In the current release of the dilemma, the experimenter has to choose the number of cycles of the game, but, to obtain an indefinite game, it is easy to include a probability $p$ such that at each round the game will continue with probability $p$.
5. For further help on installation and compiling matters, refer to the SWIEE site or to any web site related to Java and to your platform.

## References

Axelrod, R. (1984). *The evolution of cooperation.* Basic Books, New York

Daniels, M. (1999). *Integrating Simulation Technologies with Swarm.* Swarm Development Group.

Hagel, J. H. and Alvin Roth (1995). *The Handbook of Experimental Economics* Princeton University Press

Minar N, Buckhart R., and Langton C. and Askenazi M. (1996) *The Swarm Simulation System: a Toolkit for Building Multi-agent Simulations* Santa Fe Institute. Http://www.swarm.org

Rocco E. and Warglien M. (1996). *Computer Mediated Communication and the Emergence of "Electronic Oportunism"* CEEL - Computable and Experimental Economics Lab - University of Trento. http://www-ceel.gelso.unitn.it

Roth A. E. (1995). *Introduction to Experimental Economics* The Handbook of Experimental Economics

Roth and Erev. (1995) Learning in extensive-form games: Experimental data and simple dynamic models in the immediate term

Schmidt and Jacobsen. (1999) Moving Experimental Economics to the Internet. In *2nd Berlin Internet Economics Workshop*, 8:164-212.

Seshadri, G. (2000). Fundamentals of RMI. Java Developers Connection – JGuru. http://developer.java.sun.com

Stefansson B. (1999). Swarmfest '99 Tutorial. Swarm Development Group. http://www.swarm.org

Tucker A. W. *A two-person dilemma.* Mimeo, Stanford University. Published under the heading On Jargon: The Prisoner's dilemma, UMAP Journal, 1 (1980)

III

# FINANCIAL APPLICATIONS

# Chapter 5

# CONTAGION OF FINANCIAL CRISES UNDER LOCAL AND GLOBAL NETWORKS

Alessandra Cassar
*International Economics,*
*University of California*
*Santa Cruz*
cassar@cats.ucsc.edu

Nigel Duffy
*Department of Computer Science,*
*University of California*
*Santa Cruz*
nigeduff@cse.ucsc.edu

**Abstract** As the world economy becomes increasingly global, will the financial sector become more stable or fragile? In this paper we study how the pattern of relations linking financial institutions - the network - affects the diffusion of a financial crisis. We analyze two such networks with a computational model: the local network, in which each bank is allowed to interact only with the most immediate neighbors, and the global network, in which each bank is allowed to interact with banks located anywhere in the system.

We find that the network matters both for the amount of illiquidity in the system and for the spread of bankruptcy. When interactions are local, bankruptcy spreads slower but illiquidity hits harder. When interactions are global, bankruptcy spreads faster, but illiquidity presents fewer problems. We conclude that a global system, in which financial institutions are not restricted to interact only with close neighbors, is more efficient in collecting and allocating funds, but is more vulnerable to contagion of bankruptcy crises.

# 1. Introduction

As the economy becomes increasingly global, will it be more or less vulnerable to financial crises? The traditional answer is unclear: while a global economy offers diversification against shocks, leading to an increasing stability in the system, new risks arise that might not balance across agents or regions, leading to an increasing instability. In this paper we address this question by analyzing the effect of local interactions and geographically dispersed interactions during financial crises. As in Friedman (1998), we concentrate on one channel of contagion that has not been studied much by economists: the pattern of overlapping claims that financial institutions hold on each other - the network structure.

Since we are interested in isolating the effect of different networks, we do not consider two other important channels of contagion that might play a relevant role during a crisis. The first relates to the idea that bank runs are self-fulfilling prophecies, so that a crisis originating in one region of the economy may create a self-fulfilling expectation of crisis elsewhere, Kindleberger (1978), Diamond and Dybvig (1983), Chang and Velasco (1999). The second is the propagation mechanism via the international currency markets in which financial crises spread from one country to the other, Calvo (1994), Eichengreen (1996), Chang (1998), Chang and Velasco (1998).

In our model we exclude such channels, so that a crisis in one region can spread to another region only through the web of overlapping financial assets that banks hold on each other. This channel of contagion may have different effects depending on the particular network architecture, i.e. the pattern of claims linking financial institutions. We are interested in analyzing how financial crises spread under two such networks: the local network, when financial institutions are allowed to interact only with their most immediate neighbors, and the global network, when financial institutions can be linked to any other institution in the system. We employ a computational model based on Friedman's (1998) model, in which the fragility of the financial market arises from contagion between neighboring financial institutions. Internal forces and random events can push a normal functioning financial system towards a critical insolvent state. Here, an insolvency avalanche can engulf a large connected subset of banks.

Once a specific network takes the place of a degenerate one, the resulting systems behave in ways still not completely understood, Page (1999). On non-trivial architectures, like a lattice or a torus, exact solutions are difficult to find with traditional mathematical tools. For this reason, we use a computational model of an artificial world simulating a financial crisis. For this class of problems, agent-based computations are a good way to look at network interactions which have not been fully explored by economists.

We find that the network structure matters for contagion of both insolvency and illiquidity. In particular, under the system with local interactions, insolvency spreads more slowly, but illiquidity hits harder. Under the random network, the reverse is the case. This result may explain why the banking sector has historically been interested in developing an extensive network of relations. The idea that the architecture of these interconnections can be a source of financial distress has a very long tradition. Even before appearing in the economic literature, this concept is already present in Florence during the Renaissance with its banking system (the origin of mercantile capitalism). The Medici bank had a geographically wide organizational structure, and much thought was given to the system regulating the complex and extensive relations among branches, debtors and creditors, Goldwhite (1987), McLean and Padgett (1997), De Roover (1970). More than four centuries later, in the United States, the National Bank Act of 1864 prohibited national banks from branching, either within a state or across states. The McFadden Act of 1927, and the Banking Act of 1933, finally permitted national banks to branch within a state, but not beyond.

Because of the importance of the real effect on output and growth, financial crises have long been of major concern to economists, Agenor, Aizenman, and Hoffmaister (1999). Only recently however has the pattern of interconnectedness as a channel for contagion come under scrutiny.

Eisenberg (1995), studying the propagation of a bank run, analyzes how increasing the connectivity of the bank system affects the speed of default when the network of inter-bank relations is random. When bankruptcy propagation is fast relative to the maturity of the obligations, the bankruptcy propagation over the network can be less extensive than when bankruptcy propagation is slower. However, when bankruptcy propagation is slower the network tends to reach a complete shutdown. Therefore, shortening the maturity of the obligations increases the extent and speed of the propagation. The network studied by Eisenberg is random. He argues that it is a reasonable and less specific assumption to model the network as random since traders usually cannot predict their trades, especially in the foreign exchange market, and, with secondary markets in debt issues, holders of a bank's obligations do tend to be random.

Allen and Gale (2000) argue, instead, that the network should be local, since banks usually specialize in particular areas of business or have closer connections with banks that operate in the same geographical or political unit. Thus claims may tend to be concentrated in neighboring banks. They analyze how contagion depends on the pattern of interconnectedness generated by the cross-holdings of deposits. Allen and Gale find that when the inter-bank market is complete, i.e. when each region has banks connected with banks in all the other regions, the initial impact of a financial crisis might be either limited to the troubled region, or a small loss might be spread across regions through contagion. When, however, the market is incomplete, in that each region has banks connected only with banks in a small number of other regions, the feature of contagion depends critically on the degree of connectedness (i.e. whether or not any two regions are connected not directly but by a chain of overlapping bank liabilities). With incomplete but connected markets, the initial impact of a financial crisis may be felt very strongly by the neighboring regions and progressively extend to all the system. Only if the degree of connectedness is low, as in the case of disconnected market structure in which certain regions remain isolated, is there no contagion.

In the next section we present the framework for the computational model. The behavior of the model under different networks is presented in section three. Section four reports the results of the simulation and section five the conclusions.

## 2. The Bank Avalanche Model

In real-world financial crises, the mechanism for contagion may entail several channels, including defaults in international payments or self-fulfillment of crisis expectations. Here, however, following Friedman (1998), we consider a single channel of contagion only, the overlapping of claims that banks hold on each other. In this model, events such as public default on loans, and internal forces like the pattern of inter-linkages among banks, can push the financial system towards a critical insolvent state. At such a point, an insolvency avalanche may start, causing a large number of connected banks to default. Increasing individual rationality does not necessarily help when the crisis happens through this channel, and appropriate simple interventions are not immediately apparent.

We employ a computational model with the intention of analyzing whether the network of interlinks between banks affects how financial crises spread. In particular, we will analyze the affects of two such architectures: the local and the global network. In the local networks the interactions among banks are restricted to geographically close neighbors. In the global network banks are free to be connected with banks anywhere in the system.

The computational model has been implemented on the assumptions presented in the following three subsections: Connection Types (which discusses the financial claims available), Behavior Rules (which presents the rules followed by banks and non-financial transactors), and Network Structures (which explains the alternative pattern of ties linking financial institutions).

## 2.1. Connection Types (or States of the Agents)

Consider a finite network with exogenously specified nodes and inter-node connections. Some of these nodes represent banks, some others represent non-financial transactors (NFT), which can be considered to be households or business firms. The inter-node connections are constituted by financial claims, which therefore define the "neighboring" relations. Each bank is assumed to classify its financial claims into five different types.

- $D$ = Deposits: number of deposits that non-financial transactors have at a given bank. The events which cause increase and decrease in deposits are initiated by the NFT according to the rules described below.

- $L$ = Loans: number of loans that a given bank issues to non-financial transactors. The events which cause increase and decrease in loans are initiated by the NFT according to the rules described below.

- $ED$ = EuroDeposits: number of Eurodollar deposits that the given bank accepts from its connected banks. Neighboring banks initiate the events of increase and decrease of EuroDeposits subject to the rules listed below.

- $EL$ = EuroLoans: number of EuroDollar deposits that the given bank places at (i.e. loans to) neighboring banks. The given bank initiates the events of increase and decrease of EuroLoans subject to the rule listed below, which is the same rule that governs EuroDeposits.

- $Reserve$ = balance on the reserve account. These claims are on the issuer of safe assets, like the national central bank. However, since that issuer plays no active role in the analysis, at least in this paper, it is not represented by an explicit node.

## 2.2. Behavior Rules (or Methods)

The rules governing banks' behavior are based on the consideration that banks are profit-oriented, and therefore seek net interest revenue. In particular we make the following assumptions on the structure of the interest rates. The cost of funds is the expected return on EuroDeposits. Neglecting the small transaction costs for EuroDollar, we may presume that the interest rates on EuroDeposits and EuroLoans is equal. We assume that the yields on reserve and deposits are lower than the interest rate on EuroDeposits, while the (expected) return on loans is higher. Market conditions may shift the entire yield structure up and down while preserving the ordering. Every time a bank accepts new deposits and agrees on new loans its net interest revenue increases, and therefore it will always conclude these financial transactions whenever possible. Following the same reasoning, the bank loses net interest revenue when it holds excess reserves, so it will try to keep them as low as possible, after considering liquidity issues. In the model implementation, we simplify by omitting an explicit representation of these returns. Nevertheless each bank will operate with respect to the assumed interest structure.

**Bank's Rules.** Banks are assumed to obey the following rules:

- $B1$: The bank's immediate accommodation to any deposit or loan event is via its reserve account. Thus the immediate impact of $[D \to D+1]$, $[ED \to ED+1]$, $[L \to L-1]$ or $[EL \to EL-1]$ is $[R \to R+1]$; the immediate impact of $[D \to D-1]$, $[ED \to ED-1]$, $[L \to L+1]$ or $[EL \to EL+1]$ is $[R \to R-1]$.
- $B2$: Banks actively manage their reserves, with a target balance assumed here to be $R = 1$. When $R$ is pushed above the target, the preferred use of funds are (in order of preference): accommodating loans, EuroLoans, and refunding EuroDeposits, deposits. We assume that a bank's normal contractual obligations preclude refunding its EuroDeposits or its deposits from NFTs without being asked. Thus the events $[D \to D+1]$ etc. trigger event $[L \to L+1]$ when there happens to be a loan applicant not yet accommodated; typically those events trigger $[EL \to EL+1]$.
- $B3$: The preferred sources of funds to restore $R$ when it is below target are: accepting deposits, EuroDeposits, and calling in EuroLoans and loans. We assume that a bank can call in its EuroLoans (i.e. withdraw its EuroDeposits with a neighbor bank) but not its loans to NFTs. Thus the events $[D \to D-1]$ etc. trigger the event $[D \to D+1]$ or $[ED \to ED+1]$ when there

happens to be a depositor not yet accommodated; typically those events trigger $[EL \to EL - 1]$.

- $B4$: If $R$ falls to 0 and can't immediately be restored to target then the bank is illiquid. In this state it is unable to accept requests to increment $L$ or to decrease $D$. It will still accept decreases (repayments) in $L$ and increases in $D$ and $ED$ , and use them to increment $R$, thus restoring itself to the normal liquid state.

- $B5$: Net worth or capital is $K = L + EL + R - D - ED$ . We start each node at $R = 1$ and the other four gross claims at $L = EL = D = ED = 0$. All the events described so far preserve $K$. Loans defaults, as specified in $NFT3$ below, decrease $K$. In our model it is assumed that $K$ never increases - however, if retained, net interest revenues would gradually increase $K$. In this model we do not account for claims on $K$, i.e. the stock holders; we assume implicitly that these claimants receive all the net interest revenue.

- $B6$: If $K < 0$ then the bank is bankrupt. In this state all its assets ($L$, $EL$ and $R$) are liquidated, and with these funds some of the liabilities are met. Seniority is assigned first to deposits then to the EuroDeposits. The bank cannot do anything but default on the remaining part and become insolvent. Once a bank is insolvent, it is out of the game. Note that liquidating EuroLoans and loans has consequences for neighboring banks and $NFT$s.

**Non-financial Transactors' (NFTs) Rules.** Non-financial transactors are assumed to obey the following rules.

- $NFT1$: New deposit and loan events at a given bank $[D \to D+1]$ and $[L \to L+1]$ are initiated by $NFT$s randomly with probability $p_D > 0$ and $p_L > 0$ per time period.

- $NFT2$: Withdrawal and repayment events at a given bank $[D \to D - 1]$ and $[L \to L - 1]$ are initiated by $NFT$s randomly with probability $p_D > 0$ and $p_L > 0$ per time period.

- $NFT3$: With probability $p_{DEFAULT} \geq 0$ per unit of time per unit of L there is loan default, causing $[L \to L - 1]$, which induces $[K \to K - 1]$, but no change in $R$.

## 2.3. Network Architectures

We implemented the framework defined above on three alternative systems of interactions on a torus (a lattice where the sides wrap around).

- *No interactions.* First, any sort of interactions between banks is assumed away. Even if this cannot be considered a proper network, since its nodes, the banks, are not connected, it will be very useful as a benchmark comparison.

- *Local interactions.* Each bank now has the possibility to interact with the four spatially most immediate neighbors.

- *Global interactions.* Finally, each bank is allowed to interact with four other banks located anywhere on the torus. This network is a particular case of a random graph in which the number of edges, i.e. links, for each bank is constrained to be exactly four, instead of an average of four. We adopt this particular kind of random network in order to make it comparable with the local network. In fact, in both networks banks start with exactly four neighbors; should systematic differences arise we interpret them in terms of the two different network architectures only. This avoids the need to separate the network effect from the effect due to differences in the bank dimensions, as represented by the number of neighbors.

The major concern of this paper is the extent to which changing the architecture of the interactions produces different results in terms of diffusion of illiquidity and insolvency. We discuss the behavior of the model under these alternative networks in the following sections.

## 3. Financial Crises on Networks

The social interactions we have defined induce a network structure on the banking system. Such network structures can be analyzed using tools from graph theory which, while seldom used by economists, give us considerable intuition about the behavior of the systems in which we are interested. We employ two concepts from graph theory namely: the $i^{th}$-neighborhood of a node and the characteristic path length.

The size of the i$^{th}$-neighborhood of a node measures the number of nodes reachable in exactly $i$ steps. Thus, in our model, the $i^{th}$-neighborhood measures the maximum number of other banks that a bank can interact with through exactly $i$ intermediaries. This quantity will be larger for a node when the $(i-1)^{th}$-neighbors are not connected to each other. This number is higher in our global network than in the local network. A trivial calculation shows that the $i^{th}$-neighborhood for the local model is of size $4 \times i$ while for the global network it is of size $4^i$ (on an infinite lattice). For example, if we allow a bank's neighbors to contact their neighbors, and we allow these $2^{nd}$ neighbors to do the same, a bank on the local network can reach $4+4\times2+4\times3=24$ other banks each time-step, while a bank on the global network can reach $4 + 4^2 + 4^3 = 84$. When applied to our model, this number should be treated with caution, first because our lattice is not infinite, and second when banks become insolvent their connections disappear changing the neighborhood structure of the network. However, qualitatively this characterization should be correct. We will see in the next subsection how this impacts on contagion.

The characteristic path length is the median of the means of the shortest path lengths connecting each node to all other nodes. In our model, it represents a measure of the average minimum number of links that must be traversed to get between a pair of banks. The characteristic path length is higher in a local network than in a random network, Watts (1999)[1]. Informally, consider again the size of the $i^{th}$-neighborhood. The proportion of banks reachable in $i$ steps is larger for the global network than for the local network. As a result, the average number of steps required to reach a node from any other is larger in the local network than in the random network. Summarizing, for the networks we consider:

| | | Size of $i^{th}$ Neighborhood | |
|---|---|---|---|
| | | Small | Big |
| Path Length | Short | | Global Network |
| | Long | Local Network | |

## 3.1. Local Network

Assume that $N$ banks are arranged on a torus, and have relations with four other banks and with a single non financial transactor (NFT) not represented on the torus for simplicity. In the case of a local network, each bank $i_0$ is connected with the North-neighbor $i_1$, the East-neighbor $i_2$, the South-neighbor $i_3$, and the West-neighbor $i_4$:

Local Network

| | | | | |
|---|---|---|---|---|
| | | | | |
| | | $i_1$ | | |
| | $i_4$ | $i_0$ | $i_2$ | |
| | | $i_3$ | | |
| | | | | |

The normal functioning of financial intermediation is insured every time *NFT*s initiate a deposit, say at bank $i_4$ and a loan at bank $i_1$ (or $i_3$ and $i_2$). Bank $i_4$ reacts increasing its EuroDeposits, or accommodating a requested EuroLoan at the neighboring bank $i_0$. Similarly bank $i_1$ reacts withdrawing a EuroDeposit, or requesting a EuroLoan, at bank $i_0$. A random event, like a loan request or deposit or EuroDeposit withdrawal from a bank that does not have enough liquidity (as when $i_0$ does not receive the EuroDeposit from $i_4$ while still receiving the EuroLoan request from $i_1$), is able to push the financial system towards a critical state in which illiquidity can spread throughout the connected subset of banks.

The dynamics of an insolvency crisis are similar to the dynamics of a liquidity crisis, although the details are rather different. Again there are internal forces that push the financial system towards a sub-critical solvency state, as when a bank, say $i_4$, receives an NFT default on its loan. A second random event, such as a second default from an NFT or from a neighboring bank, can push the system to a critical state ( $i_4$ defaults on $i_0$). At that point, assuming away central bank intervention, an avalanche might start with a large subset of banks involved sequentially through a chain of defaults.

When interactions are local, a bank's neighbors are not directly connected, but these neighbors have neighbors in common. For example, two of the neighbors of $i_0$, $i_1$and $i_4$, have one other neighbor in common beside $i_0$: the North-neighbor of $i_4$ which coincides with the West-neighbor of $i_1$. Following our previous reasoning the number of banks reachable in $j$ or fewer steps is the sum of the size of the $i^{th}$-neighborhoods for $i < j$, implying that, in $j$ steps, the actual number of banks that a bank can reach is smaller in a local network than in a global network. The effect of reaching a lower number of banks means that the pool of available reserves, from which loan requests may be satisfied, is smaller, making the local system more vulnerable to illiquidity.

While constituting a barrier to obtaining funds in case of need, a smaller neighborhood and a longer distance between banks decreases the spread of insolvency. The high degree of overlap between neighbors implies that the spread of bankruptcy may eventually die off in an isolated region, while the long path length implies that a longer chain of defaults is required to reach geographically distant banks.

In conclusion, we expect the local system to be more vulnerable to illiquidity, but less vulnerable to bankruptcy than the global system.

## 3.2. Global Network

Assume again that $N$ banks are arranged on a torus, but this time we allow them to have relations with four other banks located randomly:

Global Network

| | | | | |
|---|---|---|---|---|
| | | | $i_1$ | |
| | $i_4$ | | | |
| | | $i_0$ | | $i_2$ |
| | | | | |
| $i_3$ | | | | |

Bank $i_0$ has now its four neighbors, $i_1$, $i_2$, $i_3$ and $i_4$, some located in regions far away. Considering the size of the $i^{th}$-neighborhood, it is now highly unlikely that neighbors' neighbors overlap as much as in the local case. As a result, in this global network, in the same number of steps each bank can now contact many more banks, increasing the probability of obtaining EuroLoans in case of need, or allocating EuroDeposits in case of excess reserve. This should result in more efficient collection and allocation of funds, with the beneficial effect of reducing illiquidity.

At the same time, however, each bank can now be reached by any other in a small number of steps, making each bank almost immediately vulnerable to defaults originated anywhere in the network.

Within the confines of the model thus far, it seems that while globalization improves the efficiency of the system in terms of collecting and allocating funds, such financial integration increases the possibility of bankruptcy contagion.

Given the difficulty of finding an analytical solution to illiquidity and insolvency for each model, we analyze them using an agent-based simulation implemented in Swarm.

## 4. Model Implementation in Swarm

Our results were obtained using an agent-based computational model implemented using the Swarm package, developed and maintained by the Santa Fe' Institute. The most fundamental elements (agents) in our simulation are *banks* which interact with each other through *banking relationships* (or simply *relationships*). Ideally in such a simulation the banks act autonomously and are not centrally coordinated. This is precisely the form of an agent-based simulation and is ideal for implementation in an intuitive, bottom-up manner using Swarm.

All banks in our simulation have the same repertoire of available actions, however, their choice of action is motivated by their current state. This fits perfectly with the Object Oriented Programming (OOP) paradigm embodied in such languages as Java, Objective C and C++. In this paradigm *classes* are defined which share a common behavior. This behavior need only be defined or implemented once, for all *objects* belonging to the class. In our simulation, each bank is an object in the bank class, therefore we only need to implement *bank* behavior once. Each object which instantiates a class may also hold additional state information, which is specific to that object. Each bank in our simulation has state which describes its current assets and relationships with other banks. The OOP paradigm is extremely intuitive and efficient for agent-based simulations since it allows one to define agents in terms of their interactions with the environment.

In our implementation, the two most important classes are banks and relationships. Each bank maintains a list of relationships through which they interact with each other. Banks have access to generic actions on these relationships, such as: request loan, offer loan, demand deposit, default on loan. Relationship objects maintain the current state of a relationship between two banks, they are responsible for coordinating the offers and requests of the two parties. In addition, the relationship objects coordinate and control the activities of banks upon completion of a transaction. Embodying a banking relationship as an object has several conceptual advantages. First, it trivially allows different banks to have different numbers of relationships. Second, it removes the need to arbitrate transactions centrally as this is now done by the relationship object itself. Third, it allows banks to trade or exchange relationships easily.

Once the central players or agents in an agent-based simulation are defined, one needs to coordinate their activities and the events in the environment. This is the primary way in which we took advantage of Swarm. Swarm consists of a set of Objective C and Java libraries designed to ease the implementation of agent-based simulations. Swarm provides a range of useful tools, including pre-defined environments and agents. For our simulation we used the Swarm facilities for constructing user interfaces, but more importantly we used the event management facilities. The event management facilities are the means by which one may simulate autonomous behavior. In Swarm, one defines a schedule of events or actions and the Swarm libraries handle the details of carrying out the actions for each agent. One may control the schedule of activities to make them appear simultaneous, occurring in discrete time steps or one may easily implement asynchronous behavior. Our simulation takes advantage of both facilities. The actions of non-financial transactors are synchronized such that all banks appear to receive deposits or withdrawal requests simultaneously. The banks then act asynchronously and autonomously to resolve these requests and negotiate inter-bank transactions. The event management facilities provided by Swarm would be difficult to replicate from scratch in Java or C and greatly simplified the implementation of our simulation.

## 5. Results

We start with results where banks are not allowed to interact. We then introduce inter-bank claims and compare the system with local interactions to the one with global interactions. We ran the simulation on each of the 3 models with 4900 banks on a $70 \times 70$ torus and report results averaged over 10 independent runs. The means across runs of the variables Illiquidity (percentage of illiquid banks[2] and Insolvency (percentage of insolvent banks[3]) were calculated for each time-step, for each model.

In addition to the dimension of the torus (which represents the total number of banks), the parameters of the model are: $p_{Default}$ , $p_D$ and $p_L$ and $CountMax$, where:

- $p_{Default}$ is the probability per unit of time per unit of $L$ with which a bank gets a default on its loans. The results we report are obtained keeping this probability constant and equal to $p_{Default} = 0.01$. Increasing $p_{Default}$ speeds up the process toward the final state of total insolvency.

- $p_D$ and $p_L$ are the probabilities per unit of time with which a bank gets a unitary increase or decrease in its deposits or loans. These probabilities are assumed $p_D > 0$, $p_L > 0$ , and for simplicity are set identical and equal to $p_D = p_L = 0.1$.

- $CountMax$ is the maximum number of times that a bank can negotiate with each neighbor per unit of time. Effectively it is the maximum number of intermediaries that can be involved in the fulfillment of a request or an offer for an inter-bank loan. For the model with no interactions we set $CountMax = 0$, for the models with interactions we set $CountMax = 3$. Values of $CountMax$ greater than 1 mean that when a bank makes a request to its neighbors for an inter-bank loan (or an offer of an inter-bank deposit), that cannot be accommodated, these neighbors can ask their neighbors, and so on for $CountMax$ steps. $CountMax > 1$ therefore, means that each bank can actually reach a number of banks higher than its immediate neighbors, a concept closely related to the sum of the size of the $i^{th}$-neighborhood (see above). Increasing $CountMax$ implies that, for each unit of time, a higher number of banks can be reached. Since our network is finite, increasing $CountMax$ (up until the point where all banks can be contacted in a unit of time) has the effect of decreasing the differences among the local and the global network.

Next we report the results of the simulations. At first the possibility of interactions is assumed away, then the rule for neighbor relations is activated, and we observe whether the network actually matters for the spread of financial crises.

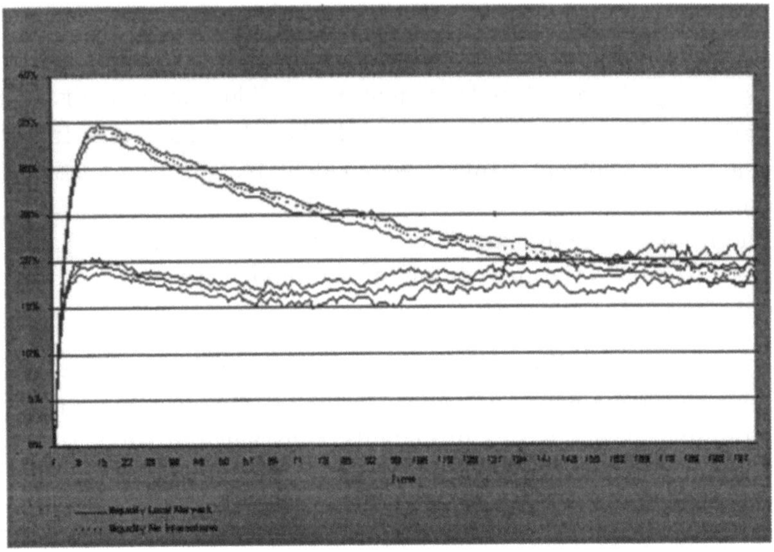

*Figure 5.1.* Illiquidity crises on local networks vs no interac.

## 5.1. Illiquidity Crises

Here we analyze the behavior of illiquidity in the three alternative models, see Figure 5.1 and Figure 5.2 (for each model we plot the mean values and standard deviations of illiquidity).

When interactions between financial institutions are not permitted, banks become illiquid if unable to accommodate a loan request from NFTs through their reserves. Reserves, in the no interactions model, can increase only through unsolicited NFT deposits. Since it takes time for the banks to accumulate enough reserve, illiquidity appears very soon, it reaches its peak after a few periods, after which it begins a steady decline. The continuous decline of illiquidity is due to a positive bias between the rate of growth of deposits and the rate of growth of loans (loan requests or deposit withdrawals can be satisfied only after the accumulation of deposits).

We proceed by allowing banks to accept EuroDeposits and EuroLoans from neighboring institutions (by increasing *CountMax* from 0 to 3). The behavior of the local and global systems are presented in Figure 5.1 and Figure 5.2. Allowing banks to initiate and accept EuroDeposits and EuroLoans, no matter which network is considered, leads to a drastic reduction in illiquidity. Once inter-bank relations are possible, banks

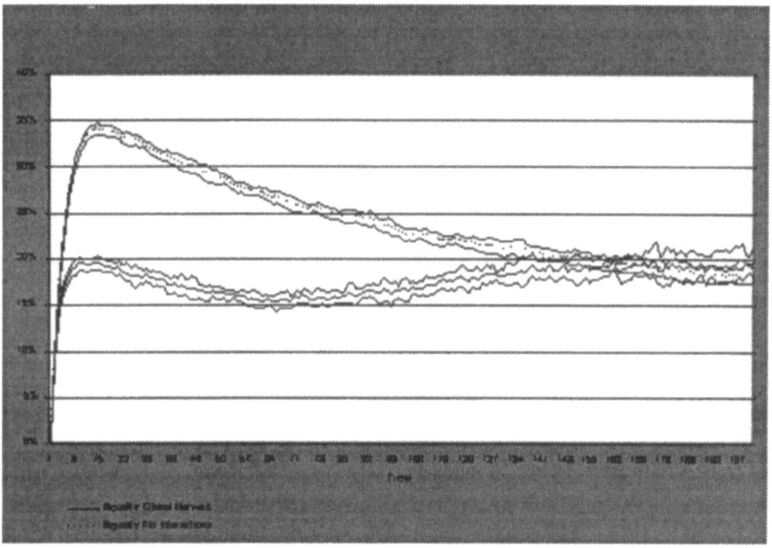

*Figure 5.2.* Illiquidity crises on global networks vs no interac.

can accommodate more financial requests, either from NFTs or from other institutions. This improves the liquidity of the system.

In both the local and global network, the percentage of illiquid banks becomes indistinguishable from the no interaction case after approximately 150 periods. In fact, when roughly 80% of the banks are insolvent (see Figure 5.4 and Figure 5.5) enough links are broken that the system behaves as if there were no interactions remaining.

The comparison of illiquidity between the local network and the global network is presented in Figure 5.3, which reports the difference between the means of illiquidity between the local and the global network. This difference is positive until about period 120. Tests for the statistical significance of this difference in terms of parameter values and empirical distribution functions, are summarized Table 1. Since we cannot exclude correlation in the behavior of illiquidity from one time-step to the next, we averaged the variables of interest over periods of 15 time-steps. Taking a conservative approach we ran the Wilcoxon test and the Kolmogorov-Smirnov test on the 15 time-step means. As a result, the reported P-values overestimate the correct ones. The difference between the two systems is only around 1%, but even with these conservative tests, we can reject the hypothesis of equal behavior between the local and global system for the central periods.

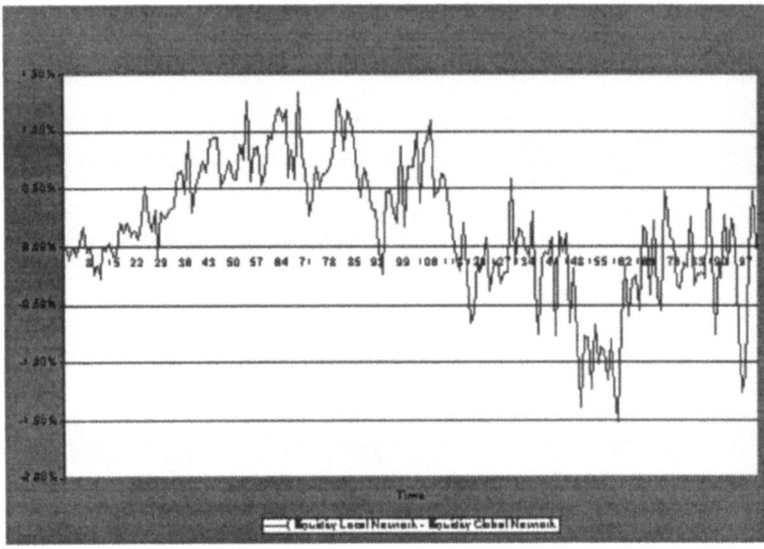

*Figure 5.3.* Comparison of illiquidity crises between local network and global network

| Time Period | 0-14 | 15-29 | 30-44 | 45-59 | 60-74 | 75-89 | 90-104 |
|---|---|---|---|---|---|---|---|
| Period-Mean % Illiquidity Local | 16.5 | 18.7 | 17.7 | 16.8 | 16.4 | 16.7 | 17.0 |
| Period-Mean % Illiquidity Global | 16.6 | 18.5 | 17.1 | 16.1 | 15.6 | 15.9 | 16.6 |
| P (Local=Global) Parameter[4] | 0.62 | 0.68 | 0.05 | 0.02 | 0.04 | 0.04 | 0.38 |
| P (Local=Global) Distribution[5] | 0.40 | 0.76 | 0.16 | 0.05 | 0.16 | 0.16 | 0.76 |

| Time Period | 105-119 | 120-134 | 135-149 | 150-164 | 165-179 | 180-200 |
|---|---|---|---|---|---|---|
| Period-Mean % Illiquidity Local | 17.7 | 18.2 | 18.6 | 18.2 | 19.2 | 19.1 |
| Period-Mean % Illiquidity Global | 15.5 | 18.3 | 18.9 | 19.1 | 19.3 | 19.3 |
| P (Local=Global) Parameter[6] | 0.27 | 1.00 | 0.38 | 0.38 | 0.73 | 0.68 |
| P (Local=Global) Distribution[7] | 0.16 | 0.99 | 0.40 | 0.16 | 0.40 | 0.99 |

Table1: Illiquidity

For the initial periods, the difference in illiquidity is insignificant, because both networks require time for banks to establish relationships with their neighbors. After 50%-60% of the banks are insolvent, again the difference is not significant because the remaining connection structure is too sparse to make a difference between the two networks.

In conclusion, the global network seems more successful in reducing the systems illiquidity, as expected from our previous discussion.

## 5.2. Insolvency Crises

Let us now turn to the behavior of insolvency. Insolvency hits a bank when its capital goes below 0, and this happens when it receives

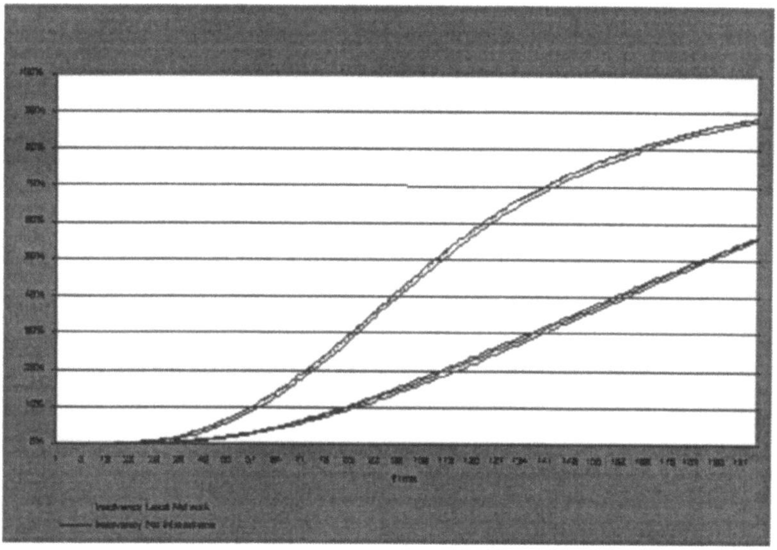

*Figure 5.4.* Insolvency crises on local network vs no interac.

a double default on loans or EuroLoans either from an NFT or from another connected bank. Since we assumed $p_{Default} > 0$, all systems will end up in a complete state of insolvency: we have no replacement rule in the model, so that an insolvent bank can never go back to an alive state.

Once interactions between banks are ruled out, the only event that can trigger a bank's insolvency is a double default on loans from an NFT. Therefore, in a system with no interactions, contagion (as we define it) cannot arise as a means of spreading insolvency. Only when interactions are allowed, can insolvency spread through a chain of defaults on EuroLoans to neighboring institutions. Figure 5.4 and Figure 5.5 show the difference between the number of insolvent banks with $CountMax = 0$ (no interactions case) and $CountMax = 3$ for the local and the global networks (again we plot the mean values and standard deviations for each model). We notice that for either networks insolvency appears sooner and spreads faster with interactions than without. This difference does not only represent the number of bankruptcies caused by neighbors' defaults. In fact, connected systems can accommodate more NFT loan requests, increasing the probability of receiving NFT defaults. Even if the difference in insolvency between $CountMax = 3$ and $CountMax = 0$ does not only estimate contagion, it remains a useful indication of the network effect on insolvency.

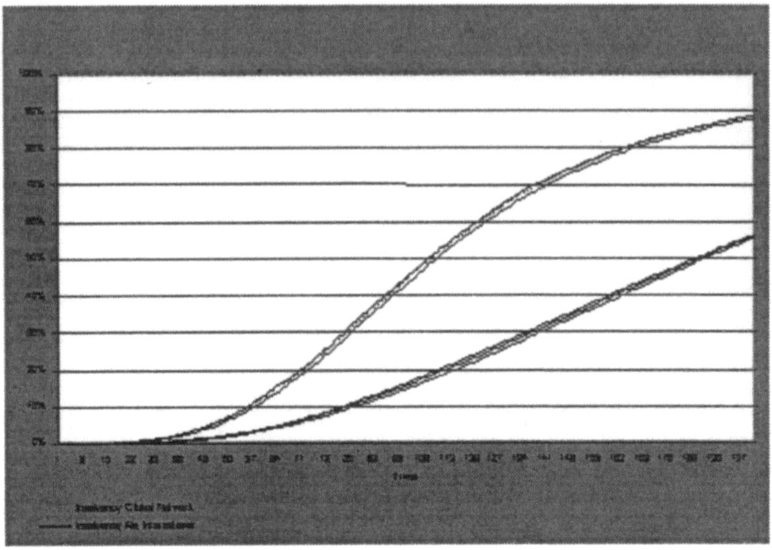

*Figure 5.5.* Insolvency crises on global network vs no interac.

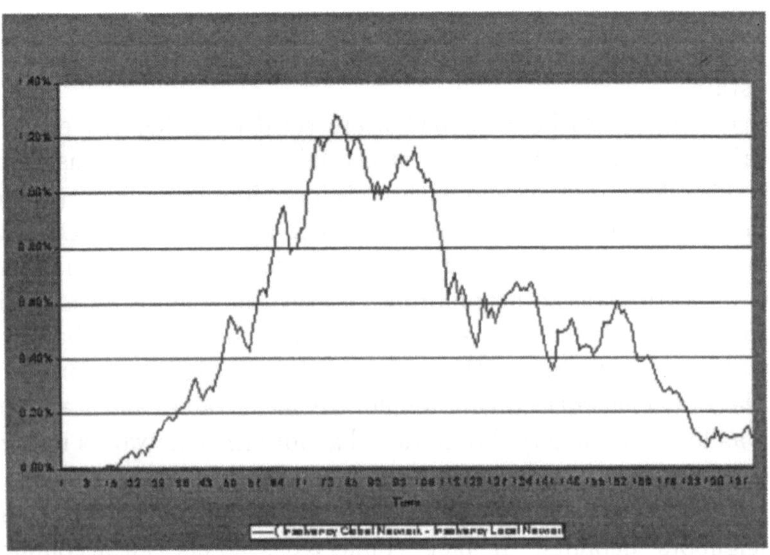

*Figure 5.6.* Comparison of insolvency crises between local and global network

In Figure 5.6 we compare the proportion of insolvent banks between the two networks. We find that the global network constantly suffers more bankruptcies than the local network. As in the case of illiquidity, this difference is only around 1%, but it is statistically significant for the central periods, as we can see from Table 2. Again, the reported P-values are overestimated because the tests have been conducted on the 15-period means. Once more, after 60% of the banks are insolvent, the difference between the two networks is no longer significant.

| Time Period | 0-14 | 15-29 | 30-44 | 45-59 | 60-74 | 75-89 | 90-104 |
|---|---|---|---|---|---|---|---|
| Period-Mean % Insolvency Local | 0.0 | 0.5 | 2.8 | 8.1 | 16.6 | 27.8 | 40.5 |
| Period-Mean % Insolvency Global | 0.0 | 0.5 | 3.0 | 8.6 | 17.5 | 29.0 | 41.6 |
| P (Local=Global) Parameter[8] | 0.88 | 0.20 | 0.05 | 0.02 | 0.01 | 0.01 | 0.38 |
| P (Local=Global) Distribution[9] | 0.99 | 0.16 | 0.16 | 0.16 | 0.16 | 0.01 | 0.01 |

| Time Period | 105-119 | 120-134 | 135-149 | 150-164 | 165-179 | 180-200 |
|---|---|---|---|---|---|---|
| Period-Mean % Insolvency Local | 52.6 | 62.9 | 71.0 | 77.2 | 82.0 | 86.3 |
| Period-Mean % Insolvency Global | 53.4 | 63.5 | 71.5 | 77.7 | 82.4 | 86.5 |
| P (Local=Global) Parameter[10] | 0.06 | 0.19 | 0.16 | 0.10 | 0.10 | 0.38 |
| P (Local=Global) Distribution[11] | 0.40 | 0.40 | 0.16 | 0.16 | 0.40 | 0.76 |

Table2: Insolvency

In conclusion, despite our conservative measures, we cannot reject the hypothesis that the global network is more vulnerable to insolvency than the local network.

## 6. Conclusions

In a financial system in which banks are not allowed to interact, available funds are scarce, and bankruptcies cannot spread by contagion. When banks are permitted to hold claims on each other, illiquidity can be greatly reduced by banks via the new access to inter-bank assets. However, these linkages with other institutions cause problems as well, constituting the means through which insolvencies spread and contagion arises as a separate cause of insolvency.

Once we allow for interactions, the particular pattern of inter-bank claims affects how illiquidity and insolvency crises spread. We analyzed, with a computational model, two alternative systems: a local network and a global network. The system with local interactions appears to be more vulnerable to illiquidity, while the system with global interactions suffers more from insolvency. We offer an explanation in terms of two concepts from graph theory: the $i^{th}$-neighborhood size and the characteristic path length. In a global network the number of banks a bank can reach in a specified number of steps (the $i^{th}$-neighborhood size) is higher than in a local network. In addition, in a global network any two banks of the system can be connected through a number of intermediaries lower than in a local network. These characteristics provide an intuition for the reason a global network has fewer difficulties satisfying loan requests but it is less protected against a chain of defaults.

This result may contribute to the explanation of why, since the beginning of mercantile capitalism, the first financial institutions, and the Medici Bank in particular, attempted to move further than local business and develop strategic alliances geographically dispersed around Europe. Beyond historical interest implicit here, this research has an important lesson for contemporary economies as well. In this electronic age, where physical impediments to banking relationships are being removed, the benefits derived from an increasingly efficient allocation of financial assets must be weighed against the accompanying increase in the risk of bankruptcy contagion.

## Notes

1. In fact, this result applies to a different model of random network. However, the same reasoning appears to apply in this case also.
2. Illiquidity= $\frac{\#illiquidbanks}{\#banks - \#insolvent - \#inbankruptcyprocess}\%$
3. Insolvency= $\frac{\#insolventbanks}{\#banks}\%$
4. Wilcoxon Test
5. Kolgomorov-Smirnov Test
6. Wilcoxon Test
7. Kolgomorov-Smirnov Test
8. Wilcoxon Test
9. Kolgomorov-Smirnov Test
10. Wilcoxon Test
11. Kolgomorov-Smirnov Test

## References

Agenor, P. R., Aizenman, J., and Hoffmaister A., 1999, *Contagion, Bank Lending Spreads, and Output Fluctuations*, Working Paper World Bank.

Allen, F. and Gale, D.,2000, *Financial Contagion*, Journal of Political Economy, Vol.108, pp.1-33.

Calvo, G., 1994, *Varieties of Capital Market Crises*,Inter-American Development Bank Working Papers.

Chang, R., 1998, *The Asian Liquidity Crises*, NBER Working Paper No. 6796.

Chang, R. and Velasco, A., 1998, *Financial Fragility and the Exchange Rate Regime*, New York, C.V. Starr Center-Working Papers.

Chang, R. and Velasco, A., 1999, *Liquidity Crises in Emerging Markets: Theory and Policy*, NBER Working Paper No. W7272.

De Roover, R., 1970, *The Rise and Decline of the Medici Bank (1397-1494)*, Harvard University Press.

Diamond, D. and Dybvig, P., 1983, "Bank Runs, Deposit Insurance and Liquidation", Journal of Political Economy, 91, pp.401-419.

Eichengreen, B., 1996, *Contagious Currency Crises*, NBER Working Paper No. 5681.

Eisenberg, L.K., 1995, *Connectivity and Financial Network Shutdown*, Santa Fe Institute Working Papers.

Friedman, D., 1998, *Bank Avalanche Model*, Private Communication.

Goldthwaite, R., 1987, "The Medici Bank and the World of Florentine Capitalism", *Past and Present* 114, p. 3-31.

Kindleberger, C. P., 1978, *Manias, Panics, and Crashes: A History of Financial Crises.* New York: Basic Books, 1978.

McLean, P.D., and Padgett, J. F., 1997, "Was Florence a Perfectly Competitive Market? Transactional Evidence from the Renaissance", *Theory and Society* 26, p. 209-244.

Page, S.,1999, *Network Structure Matters*, Unpublished Manuscript.

Watts, D., 1999, *Small World: the Dynamics of Networks between Order and Randomness*, Princeton University Press.

# Chapter 6

# SIMULATING FRACTAL FINANCIAL MARKETS

Marco CORAZZA
*Department of Applied Mathematics*
*University "Ca'Foscari"*
*Venice (Italy)*
corazza@unive.it

Alessandro PERRONE
*Department of Economics*
*University "Ca'Foscari"*
*Venice (Italy)*
alex@unive.it

**Abstract** In general, the absolute majority of financial market models is based on the stochastic properties of the asset returns, while the properties of the related asset quantities play a minor role. Starting from these remarks, in this paper we propose a system of nonlinear and stochastic difference equations in which the asset price behaviour and the corresponding asset quantity one are jointly taken into account. More precisely, in order effectively to represent the properties of the real asset price variations, we assume that (also on the basis of well known empirical evidences) their dynamics is distinguished by different stochastic processes alternating each other: the "classical" standard Brownian one, the fractional Brownian motion (which is able to represent the dependence among the returns), and the Pareto-Lévy stable one (which is able to represent the the non-Gaussian distributional features). All these processes are characterized by the same "fractal" quantity, the exponent of Hurst, which is properly utilized in the proposed dynamical model in order to represent the different stochastic properties of the asset price changes. Finally, because of the possible "bad" analytical peculiarities of the system itself, we investigate its dynamics by means of an agent-based approach developed in the Swarm software environment .

## 1. Introduction and motivations

Generally, most markets, both in a static time frame and in a dynamical one, are completely specifiable by interactions of two economic "objects": price and quantity. In such a context a remarkable "anomaly" is the one represented by the financial markets in which, as is well known, the majority of the theoretical models is exclusively based on the (stochastic) properties of the price - or rather: the price change -, while the quantity plays a marginal role in some quantitative models and in some operational tools for practitioners (like, for instance, the ones of the technical analysis). Moreover, limiting ourselves to consider this classical approach following which the price variation is the sole "actor", it is likewise well known that there is not a large amount of suitable stochastic processes able to formally represent the dynamics of the price changes in such a way as to ensure desirable properties to the financial markets (like, for example, the existence of some kind of equilibrium), and - not least - in such a way as to be analitically tractable. In particular, in financial economics, a crucial role as quantitative tool for the stochastic modeling of the dynamic processes generating the financial price variations the random walk model (see, for instance, [Campbell *et al.*, 1997] and the references therein); more in details, from a distributional point of view, perhaps the most common characterization of this model consists in assuming that the financial returns are independently and identically log-Normally distributed (i.e. $\ln[P(t+\mathrm{d}t)]-\ln[P(t)] \sim \mathrm{IID}\mathcal{N}(\mu\mathrm{d}t, \sigma^2\mathrm{d}t)$, where $P(\tau)$ is the price at time $\tau$). This is equivalent to assume that the stochastic process generating the financial logged price changes is the standard Brownian (on following: sB) motion.

However, again limiting ourselves to consider this classical frame of reference, the behaviour of real financial markets is characterized by features which (very) often differ from the ones theoretically stated by the sB motion approach for the dynamics of financial returns. In fact, with respect to the independence among price variations (which ensure, in some degree, the informational efficiency of the financial markets)[1], since the mid-Sixties an increasing number of empirical analyses has shown that the price changes are often dependent, and - at the most - simply uncorrelated instead of fully independent. Then, with regard to the assumption of Gaussian identical distribution for the dynamical processes generating the price changes, it seems extremely difficult to assume that, over medium and/or long time periods, the various events occured during these same periods have left completely unchanged the related distributional laws[2]. More precisely, not only it is quite knotty to conjecture that the parameters of the probability distribution for the dynamics of the financial returns are constant over time, but it is also rather heroic to assume that such a probability law remains the same over time; in fact, the empirical distributions of the log price changes of several assets show evidence of non-Gaussian time-varying kurtosis, skewness, and volatility (see, for example, again [Campbell *et al.*, 1997] and the references therein). Finally, now enlarging the frame of references also to the economic "object" which is usually neglected in order to specify a financial markets, that is the quantity, it is necessary to stress the renewed (and increasing) academic interest towards the role played by this object both in some theoretical models (see, for instance, [Lee *et al.*, 2000] and [Lo *et al.*, 2000a]) and in some indicators of professional technical analysis (see, for example, [Lo *et al.*, 2000b]).

Starting from these remarks, it is reasonable to conjecture that, in order fully to describe the dynamical behaviour of financial markets - which is the aim of this paper -, not only it is important to consider the stochastic properties of financial price variations in their time evolution, but also it is essential to take into account the dynamical progress of the corresponding quantities; in fact, as C.M.C. Lee and B. Swaminathan [Lee *et al.*, 2000] write on page 2017, "*Stock returns and trading volume are jointly determined by the same market dynamics, and are inextricably linked in theory...* [although]... *prior empirical studies have generally accorded them separate treatment.*".

Notwithstanding the obvious significance of such burgeoning topics, in the specialized literature there is not - at least to the best of our knowledge - any quantitative model in which the (time-varying) stochastic properties of the asset price changes and the time evolution of the related asset quantities are jointly taken into account in order to formally model the dynamics of the financial markets in a way as close as possible to their observable behaviours[3]. So, to start to fill such a model deficiency, in this paper we propose and study a dynamical system of (simple) nonlinear and stochastic difference equations in which the financial asset price variation behaviours and the corresponding asset quantity ones are jointly thought of. In particular, in order to properly specify this discrete-time model, we preliminary have to deal with, at least, a couple of topics on which the considered dynamical model are based. In fact,

- firstly, we have to properly establish - from a distributional point of view - what are, among the possible ones, the stochastic dynamics which are more able to formally represent in an effective way the properties of the financial asset price changes, both from the "return independence/dependence" standpoint and from the "Gaussian identical distribution/non-Gaussian time-varying distribution" one; section **2** will be devoted to cope with this matter. In that section we shall simply illustrate the "philosophy" of the approach we shall follow in detecting these stochastic dynamics. We shall briefly describe the main distinctive probability features of the relative processes generating the financial asset returns, and we shall explain the way by which we shall take into account the stochastic properties of such a dynamics in order to specify our model;

- secondly, starting from the detected stochastic dynamics, we shall try to settle, at least from a qualitative point of view, the economic relationships existing between the (time-varying) properties of the asset price variations and the properties of the corresponding asset quantities; section **3** will be devoted to develop this subject.

Once such preliminary topics will be dealt with, in section **4** we shall specify our model by formalizing the qualitative relationships previously settled. On this matter we will show that the difference equations of the system defining this model are characterized, although in a simple way, by nonlinearities and stochasticities. In general, tackling such a dynamics might be technically difficult from an analytical point of view as their time evolutions might be marked by "bad" mathematical peculiarities, and as their solutions might not exist in closed form; moreover, it is also important to notice that the model we shall present in section **4** is only a starting proposal in the considered research area. It is quite reasonable to conjecture that its (desirable) future improvements and developments will make the next versions of this model more analytically intractable than the current one. Because of both these features, in order to study the considered system of nonlinear and stochastic difference equations, we shall investigate its dynamical behaviour by means of an agent-based approach. In particular, each of the variables specifying the model, both the ones corresponding to the asset returns and the ones corresponding to the asset quantities, will be thought of as a single actor dynamically interacting with the other ones following prescribed relationships; in section **5** we shall detail such a computational approach and report the results we obtained by its utilization in the numerical investigation of the specified dynamics. Finally, in section **6** we shall present some critical remarks about the considered dynamical model, and shall propose some (simple) ideas in order to possibly improve and develop the model itself.

## 2. Fractal probability laws for financial asset returns

Both academicians and practitioners agree on the fact that real financial asset returns are bell-shaped distributed; in particular, as previously reported, such bell-shaped probability distributions are often characterized by "non-standard" stochastic properties. Because of that, in order to effectively represent from a distributional point of view the dynamics of the asset price variations, we firstly have to specify (at least) one probability law family for each of the different processes generating the distinctive stochastic behaviours their show, that is (as proposed in section **1**)

- the (classical) one in case the financial returns are independently and identically distributed;
- the one in case the financial returns are not independent;
- and the one in case the distributional properties of the financial returns show evidence of non-Gaussian (time-varying) kurtosis, skewness, and volatility[4].

With regard to the first of the listed cases, the decision we take to characterize the changes of the (log) price by means of the independently and identically Normally distributed probability law class is almost "compulsory" due to the fundamental role played in the field of financial economics by the corresponding stochastic process family, the sB motion one, as generator of such price variations. This issue is so well known that we do not need to spend any other word about it. On the contrary, perhaps it is not likewise well known that this same process class is characterized by a parameter, called exponent of Hurst and denoted by $H$, which is related to some of its fractal aspects, like, for instance, the statistical self-similarity[5] or the Hausdorff and the box-counting dimensions of its graphs (see, for more details, [Falconer, 1990] and [Peitgen *et al.*, 1992]). In particular, for the sB motion family the Hurst exponent is $H = 0.5$.

Concerning the second of the (briefly) itemized cases, it is important to state in advance that in the specialized literature there is not a large amount of "sufficiently" well-behaved stochastic process classes able to formally model the dependence present in real time-evolving phenomena. Among these classes, the fractional Brownian (fB) motion is one of the most popular in the field of quantitative finance. It belongs to the Gaussian stochastic process family whose increments are long-term dependent with each-other (see, for example, in the last decade [Lo, 1991], [Cheung *et al.*, 1993], [Kopp, 1995], [Corazza, 1996], [Campbell *et al.*, 1997], [Corazza *et al.*, 1997b], [Rogers, 1997], [Corazza, 1999] and [Willinger *et al.*, 1999]). On this subject it is essential to stress that taking into account only the long-range memory (and not also the short-range one) at the financial returns is not a restrictive approach; in fact, mainly long-run memory based strategies, thanks to their "low" number of transactions and relative costs, may be able to "beat the market" and, consequently, to affect - at least in some degree - its dynamical behaviour. Going into technical details, ...

## 2.1. FB motion

... the fB motion, introduced by B.B. Mandelbrot and J.W. Van Ness [Mandelbrot *et al.*, 1968], is an almost everywhere continuous Gaussian stochastic process of index $H \in (0,1)^6$, $\{B_H(t), t \geq 0\}$, defined by a Weyl stochastic fractional differo-integral operator[7], such that $B_H(0) = 0$ with probability 1 and $B_H(t_2) - B_H(t_1) \sim \mathcal{N}(0, \sigma^{2H}(t_2 - t_1)^{2H})$, with $0 \leq t_1 < t_2 < +\infty$ and $\sigma > 0$ (see, for example, [Falconer, 1990] and [Beran, 1994]). It is to notice that also this stochastic process is statistically self-similar, that is $\{B_H(t), t \geq 0\}$ and $\{a^{-H}B_H(at), t \geq 0\}$, with $a > 0$, have the same distributional law (see, for more details, [Falconer, 1990] and [Peitgen *et al.*, 1992]). In particular, it is possible to prove that, if $H \neq 0.5$, the increments are stationary but not independent with each other and that they show a long-term memory depending on both $H$ and $\Delta t := t_2 - t_1$. This dependence among the variations is negative for $H \in (0, 0.5)$ and positive for $H \in (0.5, 1)$; the case $H = 0.5$ is the sB motion (which has independent changes). Moreover, it is also possible to prove that, again if $H \neq 0.5$, the fB motion is not a semi-martingale and, consequently, that there does not exist an equivalent martingale measure (see, for more details, [Kunimoto, 1993] and [Kopp, 1995]).

Among the various properties characterizing this process, the latter seems to be the one mainly affecting the grounds of actual theory of financial markets. In fact, such a property - or better: such a lack of semi-martingality - it implies some kind of disequilibrium in financial markets and the consequent possibility of arbitraging; moreover, implies the unapplicability of the classical stochastic calculus to the derivative pricing. Also because of that, a few researchers (like, for instance, [Rogers, 1997]) do not consider the fB motion a proper stochastic process for modelling asset price behaviours. Nevertheless, in accordance with [Kopp, 1995], the fact that the quantitative tools at our disposal are not as "powerful" as we would like them to be is, in our opinion, neither a sufficient nor a convincing argument for refusing the tools themselves.

As for the third case listed , since the seminal study of B.B. Mandelbrot [Mandelbrot, 1962] about the distributional properties of real financial asset returns there has been an increasing significative empirical evidence that the stochastic process family generating the price variations of several financial assets were (and are) often non-Gaussian distributed, tipically because of the heavy-tails, the asymmetry, and the "erratic" volatility characterizing the related probability law. Already in that seminal paper, it was conjectured that a suitable stochastic process class (alternative to the Gaussian distributed one) able to formally represent such peculiarities was the Pareto Lévy stable (PLs) one[8]. In the subsequent years, this stochastic process family had an effective large circulation among the financial modelers not only because of the large number of empirical investigations supporting it (see, for more details, the ponderous [Rachev *et al.*, 2000] and the references therein), but also - and, perhaps, mainly - thanks to a theoretical property which is desirable from a financial point of view: the limit in distribution of the summation of infinite independently and identically distributed random variables (like, for instance, $\ln[P(t+1+i)]-\ln[P(t+i)]$, with $i = 0, 1, \ldots$) is a PLs probability law. Going into technical details, ...

## 2.2. PLs motion

... the PLs motion, originally introduced by P. Lévy [Lévy, 1925] as a generalization of the sB motion, is a stochastic process, $\{L_\alpha(t),\, t \geq 0\}$, characterized by a probability law, $S_{\alpha,\beta}(\mu, \sigma)$, depending on four parameters: the so-called characteristic exponent $\alpha \in (0, 2]$[9], the skewness parameter $\beta \in [-1, 1]$, the location parameter $\mu \in (-\infty, +\infty)$, and the scale coefficient $\sigma \in [0, +\infty)$. This stochastic process is such that $L_\alpha(0) = 0$ almost-surely, and its increments $L_\alpha(t_2) - L_\alpha(t_2)$, with $0 \leq t_1 < t_2 < +\infty$, whose distribution is $S_{\alpha,\beta}(0, (t_2 - t_1)^{1/\alpha})$, are independent from each other and stationary. In particular, if $\alpha \in (0, 2)$ then the tails of this process are decaying slower than the fB motion ones, and, if $\alpha = 2$, it is possible to prove that $\{2^{-1/2}L_2(t),\, t \geq 0\} \equiv \{B(t),\, t \geq 0\}$, which is the sB motion. Moreover, it is worth noticeing that, if the distribution $S_{\alpha,\beta}(\mu, \sigma)$ is symmetric - that is $\beta = 0$ -, the corresponding PLs motion is statistically self-similar, that is $\{L_\alpha(t),\, t \geq 0\}$ and $\{a^{-1/\alpha}L_\alpha(at),\, t \geq 0\}$, with $a > 0$, have the same distribution law[10]. In such a case it is possible to prove that $H = 1/\alpha$, where $H$ is (again) the exponent of Hurst (see, for more details, [Taqqu, 1986], [Falconer, 1990], and [Samorodnitsky *et al.*, 1994])[11].

From all what precedes, it should be clear that the probability law families we think of in order to characterize the observed stochastic behaviours of financial asset returns, beyond their specific characteristic functions, density ones and so on, are all marked by the same fractal quantity: the exponent of Hurst $H$. Moreover, as in both the non-standard stochastic process families for financial modeling we take into account $H$ can take values in proper real interval[12], *a priori* there is not any reason why $H$ has to be constant over time, or alternatively there is not any drawback in assuming that $H$ is a function of time, that is $H = H(t)$. By so doing, we specify this fractal quantity as a parameter-savings quantitative tool for representing the various stochastic dynamics of the financial asset price changes considered in this paper. More specifically, recalling that the values $H$ can empirically take in the "PLs motion regime" belong to a real interval which is a subset of the corresponding one in the "fB motion regime", in order to univocally characterize each of the non-standard stochastic process family we introduce a simple (time-varying) switch-like quantity, $D(t)$, for taking into account the independence ($D(t) = 0$) or the dependence ($D(t) = 1$) among the financial returns. Summarizing, each of the process classes generating the distinctive stochastic behaviours of the asset price variations which are listed at the beginning of this section, can be simply modeled[13] by means of the $H(t)$ and $D(t)$ as presented in the following table:

| **stochastic processes** | **Exponent of Hurst** | **D(t)** |
|---|---|---|
| SB motion | $H(t) = 0.5$ | 0 |
| FB motion | $H(t) \in (0, 0.5) \cup (0.5, 1)$ | 1 |
| | $H(t) = 0.5$ | 0 |
| PLs motion | $H(t) \in [0.5, 1)$ | 0 |

Table 2.1 - H(t) and D(t) for some stochastic processes

## 3. Basics for a possible fractal financial economics

In order to represent the time-evolving behaviour of financial markets, as well as the dynamical stochastic properties of the financial asset returns[14], it is necessary to consider the time progress of the related financial asset quantities. As A.W. Lo and J. Wang [Lo *et al.*, 2000a] write on page 257, "*If price and quantity are the fundamental blocks of any theory of market interactions, the importance of trading volume in modeling asset markets is clear.*". Because of that, in order properly to specify our system of nonlinear and stochastic difference equations, it is of primary importance to settle (at least in some degree) the economic relationships existing between the time-varying peculiarities of the asset price changes and the ones of the corresponding asset quantities since by means of such relationships it is possible to represent the "forces" driving the matching between the demand and the supply in the considered markets. In the following of this work we shall assume - also in accordance with the distinctive stochastic behaviours shown by the various process families generating the asset returns - that the dynamics characterizing the financial markets are structured in two different "regimes" which alternate each other. One is linked to the fB motion class, and one linked to the PLs motion family (see, for more details on this approach, [Pancham, 1994] and [Corazza *et al.*, 1997a])[15]. In particular, each of these regimes will be suitably characterized by means of the dynamical interacting between the stochastic properties of the related process family and the properties of the corresponding asset quantity. On this latter subject it would be useful to show the existence of a large number of "measures" of asset quantity[16], each of them properly developed for a specific kind of investigation; in our analysis, recalling that the model we shall specify is only a starting proposal in the considered research area, we shall use a simple measure of asset quantity, that is the aggregate market liquidity (on following simply: liquidity) at time $t$

$$L(t) = \sum_{i=1}^{I} P_i(t)S_i(t) \tag{3.1}$$

where $L(\tau)$ denotes the liquidity at time $\tau$, $I$ shows the number of different assets traded in the considered market, $P_i(\tau)$ indicates the price of the $i$−th asset at time $\tau$, and $S_i(\tau)$ indicates the number of the $i$−th asset traded at time $\tau$.

## 3.1. The "fB motion" regime

This regime is characterized by an exponent of Hurst $H(t) \in (0, 0.5) \cup (0.5, 1)/H(t) = 0.5$, and by a switch-like independence/dependence index $D(t) = 1/D(t) = 0$. Except the "sB motion" case ($H(t) = 0.5$ and $D(t) = 0$), the peculiarities of the volatility - which is the measure of "financial" risk we use - associated to the related probability law family are such to permit a relatively simple matching between the aggregate market demand and the aggregate market supply for, at least, the two following reasons:

- firstly, the statistical self-similarity characterizing the fB motion guarantees, at least in some degree, that the risk related with investments having different horizon lengths, namely $t$ and $at$, with $a > 0$, are evaluated in the same proportional way by the corresponding different-horizon-length investors; in fact, $\{B_H(t), t \geq 0\}$ and $\{a^{-H}B_H(at), t \geq 0\}$, with $a \geq 0$, have the same probability law[17]. Because of that, the demand and the supply of these investors with different horizon lengths can however match and, consequently, ensure a certain liquidity in the considered markets;

- secondly, the long-term memory distinguishing the underlying stochastic process class makes it possible to (partially) forecast the future behaviour of the returns and, consequently, to "manage" - *ex ceteris paribus* - a lower risk than in the (classical) independently and identically log-Normally distributed case. Of course, this is another source of "attractiveness" for investors having whatever horizon length and, consequently, for higher liquidity level than in the "sB motion" case.

In order to propose some explanation for the presence of this long-range memory, we can conjecture that the considered markets are characterized by the regular arrival of new information which are "coherent" with the ones previously arrived; of course, that reduces the spread existing between the ability of the economic agents to make optimal decisions and the complexity of decision problems under uncertainty.

## 3.2. The "PLs motion" regime

This regime is characterized by an exponent of Hurst $H(t)$ empirically taking values in $[0.5, 1)$, and by a switch-like independence/dependence index $D(t) = 0$. Except for the "sB motion" case ($H(t) = 0.5$), the peculiarities of the volatility associated to the related probability law family are such to permit again the matching between the aggregate market demand and the aggregate market supply, but to a lower degree than in the previously described regime. In fact, in the "PLs motion" regime there exists a single source of "attractiveness" for investors having whatever horizon length (and, consequently, for a certain liquidity level): the statistical self-similarity. On the contrary, the unpredictability of the future behaviours of the returns (due to the independence among the increments of the related stochastic process) and the fact that the tails of the PLs motion probability laws decay more slowly than the ones of the fB motion probability laws, put this regime in an higher risk class than the "fB motion" one. Of course, it causes a lower participation of investors - and, consequently, a lower liquidity - in the considered regime of the market than in the "fB motion" one.

In order to propose some explanation for the presence of this specific higher risk, we can conjecture that the considered markets are characterized by an irregular arrival of (possibly) exogenously noised information; of course, this makes difficult for the investors to detect whatever well-behaved behaviour in the fundamentals of the economy and, consequently, to make "rational" decisions.

Summarizing, each of the regimes can be sintethically described as presented in the following table:

| Regime | Statistical self-simil. | Fore-castb. | Risk class | Demand and supply match. | Liquid. level |
|---|---|---|---|---|---|
| SB mot. | Yes | No | Middle | Middle | Middle |
| FB mot. | Yes | Yes | Low | High | High |
| PLs mot. | Yes | No | High | Low | Low |

Table 3.1

## 4. The market dynamical model

As previously averred, in order to investigate the time-evolving behaviour of the (simple) system of nonlinear and stochastic difference equations that we shall specify in this section, we shall follow an agent-based approach. In particular, each of the variables specifying the model will be taken into account as a single actor dynamically interacting with the other ones on the ground of prescribed relationships. More precisely, such dynamical relationships can be described - in the corresponding discrete time frame - in the following way:

step 1: one initializes a time counter $t$ to a certain time value $\bar{t}$;

step 2: at time $t$ the exponent of Hurst $H(t)$ and the related switch-like independence/dependence index $D(t)$ (which are both variables concerning the asset return dynamical behaviour) take properly values on the basis of the theoretical framework we defined in section **2**. In particular, recalling that the alternation of the two regimes depends on the "kind" of the economic news which reach on the financial market, it should be clear that both $H(t)$ and $D(t)$ are exogenous to the dynamical model we are developing. In other words, they depend on the general economic context rather than on the specific financial one. Because of that, in order to represent formally such variables, we shall think of $H(t)$ as a suitable continuous random variable taking values in the interval $(0, 1)$, and we shall think of $D(t)$ as follows:

$$D(t) = \begin{cases} 1 \text{ if } H(t) \in (0, 0.5) \\ 0 \text{ if } H(t) = 0.5 \\ \text{suitable discrete random variable taking values} \\ \text{in the set } \{0, 1\} \text{ if } H(t) \in (0.5, 1) \end{cases}; \tag{4.1}$$

step 3: one updates the time counter $t$ to $t + 1$;

step 4: at the updated time $t$ the "financial" risk, denoted by $R(t)$ (which is again a variable related to the asset return dynamical behaviour), reacts both to the economic state of the world - represented by $H(t)$ and $D(t)$ -, and to the financial one - represented by the liquidity $L(t)$ (which is the variable corresponding to the asset quantity dynamical behaviour) -. In particular, with regard to the economic state of the world, in accordance with the fractal-financial-economics frame proposed in section **3** and summarized in Table 3.1, we can sinthetically itemize the behaviour of $R(t)$ in the following way:

- if $H(t) \in (0, 0.5)$ and, consequently, $D(t) = 1$ (that is, if the regime characterizing the financial market is the "fB motion") then $R(t)$ decreases;
- if $H(t) = 0.5$ and, consequently, $D(t) = 0$ (that is, if the regime characterizing the financial market is the "sB motion") then $R(t)$ does not react;
- if $H(t) \in (0, 0.5)$ and $D(t) = 0$ (that is, if the regime characterizing the financial market is the "PLs motion") then $R(t)$ increases;
- if $H(t) \in (0, 0.5)$ and $D(t) = 1$ (that is, if the regime characterizing the financial market is again the "fB motion") then $R(t)$ decreases.

Concerning the financial state of the world, we can simply (and quite reasonably) describe the risk behaviour stating that $R(t)$ decreases/increases as $L(t)$ increases/decreases.
Starting from what precedes, in order to specify formally the time evolution of $R(t)$, we propose, among the possible ones, the following dynamics, which is - at least in our opinion - one of the simplest:

$$\begin{aligned} R(t) &= R(t-1) + a_{1,1}\{E_{R,t}[D(t)] \cdot |E_{R,t}[H(t)] - 0.5| + \\ &\quad \{1 - E_{R,t}[D(t)]\} \cdot \{E_{R,t}[H(t)] - 0.5\}\} + \\ &\quad + a_{1,2}E_{R,t}[L(t) - L(t-1)] \\ &= R(t-1) + a_{1,1}\{D(t-1) \cdot |[H(t-1) - 0.5| + \\ &\quad [1 - D(t-1)] \cdot [H(t-1) - 0.5]\} + \\ &\quad + a_{1,2}[L(t-1) - L(t-2)], \end{aligned} \tag{4.2}$$

with $a_{1,1} < 0$, $a_{1,2} < 0$ (both constant parameters), and where $E_{R,t}[\cdot]$ indicates the expectation operator conditional on relevant information available to the "agent" risk at time $t$ or before[18];

step 5: at the same updated time $t$ the liquidity $L(t)$ reacts both to the economic state of the world and to the financial one. In particular, with regard to the economic state of the world, again in accordance with the fractal-financial-economics frame we proposed in section **3** and summarized in Table 3.1, we can sinthetically itemize the behaviour of $L(t)$ in the following way:

- if $H(t) \in (0, 0.5)$ and, consequently, $D(t) = 1$ (that is, if the regime characterizing the financial market is the "fB motion") then $L(t)$ increases;
- if $H(t) = 0.5$ and, consequently, $D(t) = 0$ (that is, if the regime characterizing the financial market is the "sB motion") then $L(t)$ does not react;
- if $H(t) \in (0, 0.5)$ and $D(t) = 0$ (that is, if the regime characterizing the financial market is the "PLs motion") then $L(t)$ decreases;
- if $H(t) \in (0, 0.5)$ and $D(t) = 1$ (that is, if the regime characterizing the financial market is again the "fB motion") then $R(t)$ increases.

Concerning the financial state of the world, we can simply (and, again, quite reasonably) describe the behaviour of the liquidity stating that $L(t)$ decreases/increases as $R(t)$ increases/decreases. Starting from what precedes, in order to specify formally the time evolution of $L(t)$, we propose, among the possible ones, the following dynamics, which is - at least in our opinion - one of the simplest:

$$\begin{aligned} L(t) &= L(t-1) + a_{2,1}\{E_{R,t}[D(t)] \cdot |E_{R,t}[H(t)] - 0.5| + \\ &\quad \{1 - E_{R,t}[D(t)]\} \cdot \{E_{R,t}[H(t)] - 0.5\}\} + \\ &\quad + a_{2,2}E_{R,t}[R(t) - R(t-1)] \\ &= L(t-1) + a_{2,1}\{D(t-1) \cdot |[H(t-1) - 0.5| + \\ &\quad [1 - D(t-1)] \cdot [H(t-1) - 0.5]\} + \\ &\quad + a_{2,2}[R(t-1) - R(t-2)], \end{aligned} \tag{4.3}$$

with $a_{2,1} > 0$, $a_{2,2} < 0$ (both constant parameters), and where $E_{L,t}[\cdot]$ indicates the expectation operator conditional on relevant information available to the "agent" liquidity at time $t$ or before[19];

step 6: one updates again $t$ to $t + 1$ and goes to step 2.

Concluding, it is simply to notice that, in order to appropriately specify our dynamical model for the considered financial market, the formalized time-evolving behaviour of the "agents" thought of in this section (that is $H(t)$, $D(t)$, $R(t)$, and $L(t)$) has to be jointly taken into account as a system of difference equations.

## 5. The agent-based approach

In general, one of the major drawbacks concerning the quantitative social sciences is caused by the impossibility of carrying out physical-like experiments by which to test the "validity" of proposed theoretical models. Tipically, such a want may be filled by a computational approach (and by the consequent numerical investigation), whose effectiveness, of course, depends on the utilized computer science tools. In fact, in this context a crucial role is played, *ceteris paribus*, by the utilized software development environment, whose "philosophy" has to be close as much as possible to the one of the considered social sciences (in our case: quantitative financial economics). In particular, a software development environment which has shown to be able to suitably conform with the "philosophy" of the quantitative economic doctrine is surely Swarm (see, for instance, [Luna *et al.*, 2000]); in fact, Swarm is a software package mainly addressed to the individual-agents'-interacting simulation by an object-oriented approach. Tipically, a Swarm-based code is structured as a set of individually precoded agents dynamically interacting among them following an own schedule[20]; all that is called "Model Swarm". Moreover, it is also characterized by a suitable interface object, which is called "Observer Swarm", which is the manager both of the numerical simulations and of the user input/output.

With regard to the Swarm code we have developed in order to implement the previously proposed dynamical model, we have defined four "simple" agents (that is agents whose structures are not characterized by means of a set of other predefined sub-agents). They correspond with, respectively, the exponent of Hurst ($H(t)$), the switch-like independence/dependence index ($D(t)$), the "financial" risk ($R(t)$), and the liquidity ($L(t)$). Moreover, we have also implemented some probes in order to monitor in a real-time-like way the dynamical evolution of the investigated financial market.

### 5.1. Numerical investigation: the results

The difference equations of the system we have specified in section **4** are characterized by the presence of nonlinearities and stochastics; tackling such a dynamics might be technically difficult from an analytical standpoint (see, for more details, section **1**). Moreover, this dynamical model is only a starting proposal in the considered research area; so, it is reasonable to conjecture that its future improvements and developments will make the next versions of this dynamics more analytically intractable than the current one. Because of that, in order to study the time-evolving behaviour of the considered model, in this subsection we shall report the results we obtained analyzing this system by means of a numerical-investigation-based approach.

Of course, it should be clear that, at first, we need to specify some (stochastic) dynamical behaviours for both the agents we assume as exogenous to our financial market model, that is $H(t)$ and $D(t)$. More precisely, concerning the exponent of Hurst, we generally think of it in the following way:

$$H(t) = H(\bar{t}) + \varepsilon_H(t), \text{with } t = \bar{t}, \bar{t}+1, \dots, \tag{5.1}$$

where $\varepsilon_H(t)$, with $t = \bar{t}, \bar{t}+1, \dots$, are independently and identically distributed continuous random variables with mean equal to 0; of course, these random variables have to be eventually truncated in such a way as to ensure that $H(t)$ belongs to $(0,1)$ for each $t = \bar{t}, \bar{t}+1, \dots$. As for the switch-like independence/dependence index, we describe in a way fully coherent with (4.1):

$$D(t) = \begin{cases} 1 \text{ if } H(t) \in (0, 0.5) \\ 0 \text{ if } H(t) = 0.5 \\ 0 \text{ if } H(t) \in (0.5, 1) \wedge \varepsilon_D(t) \leq 0, \text{ with } t = \bar{t}, \bar{t}+1, \dots \\ 1 \text{ if } H(t) \in (0.5, 1) \wedge \varepsilon_D(t) > 0, \text{ with } t = \bar{t}, \bar{t}+1, \dots \end{cases}, \tag{5.2}$$

where $\varepsilon_D(t)$, with $t = \bar{t}, \bar{t}+1, \dots$, are independently and identically distributed continuous random variables with mean equal to 0.

In the remainder of this subsection we shall present, among the possible ones, five numerical investigations of the proposed dynamical model, each of them organized in four graphs: "Risk *vs.* Time" to present the behaviour of $R(t)$ as time goes on, "Liquidity *vs.* Time" to report the behaviour of $L(t)$ as time goes on, "Risk($t$) *vs.* Risk($t-1$)" to present the behaviour of $R(t)$ on its one-step-lagged value, and "Liquidity($t$) *vs.* Liquidity($t-1$)" to picture the behaviour of $L(t)$ on its one-step-lagged value. It is also important to point out that, in order to make the various numerical investigations completely comparable among them,

- firstly, in all five simulations we have utilized the same starting values for each of the "endogenous" agents, that is $R(\bar{t}) = 0.5$, $R(\bar{t}+1) = 0.25$, $L(\bar{t}) = 0.75$, and $L(\bar{t}+1) = 0.5$, and we have utilized the same values for each of the constant parameters, that is $a_{1,1} = -0.25$, $a_{1,2} = -0.25$, $a_{2,1} = 0.25$, and $a_{2,2} = -0.25$;
- secondly, we have carried out each of the investigations by taking into account the same number of time steps-ahead, that is $t = \bar{t}, \bar{t}+1, \dots, \bar{t}+120$;

- and thirdly, we have properly standardized the variation ranges both as for the time evolution of $R(t)$ and as for the time evolution of $L(t)$.

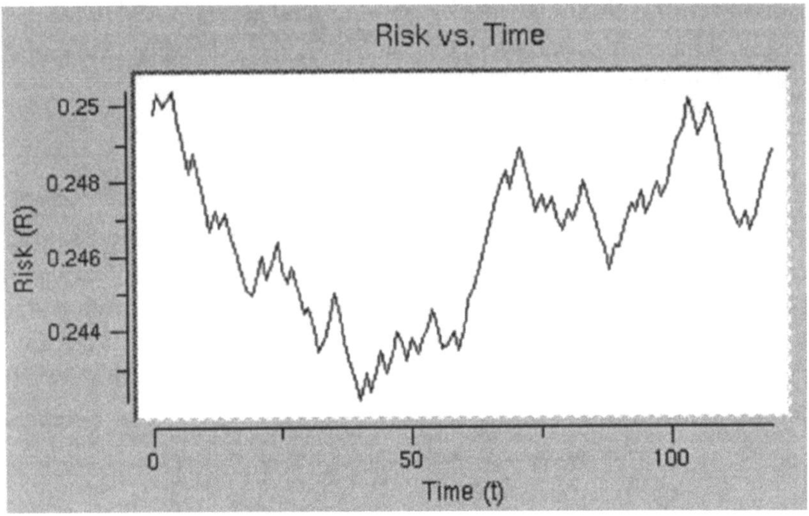


*Figure 6.1.* first investigation (first graph)

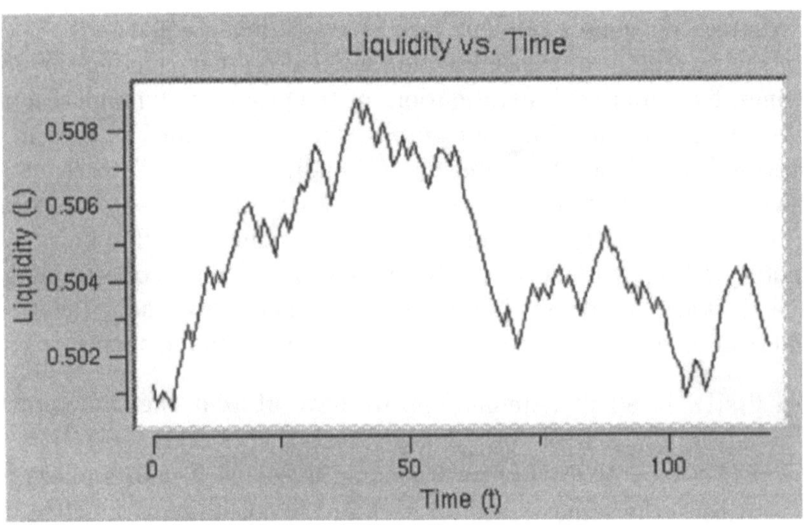


*Figure 6.2.* first investigation (second graph)

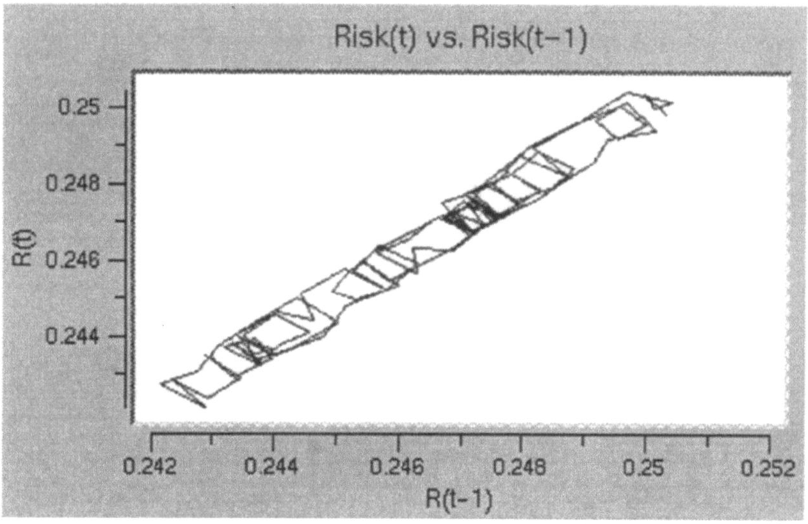


*Figure 6.3.* first investigation (third graph)

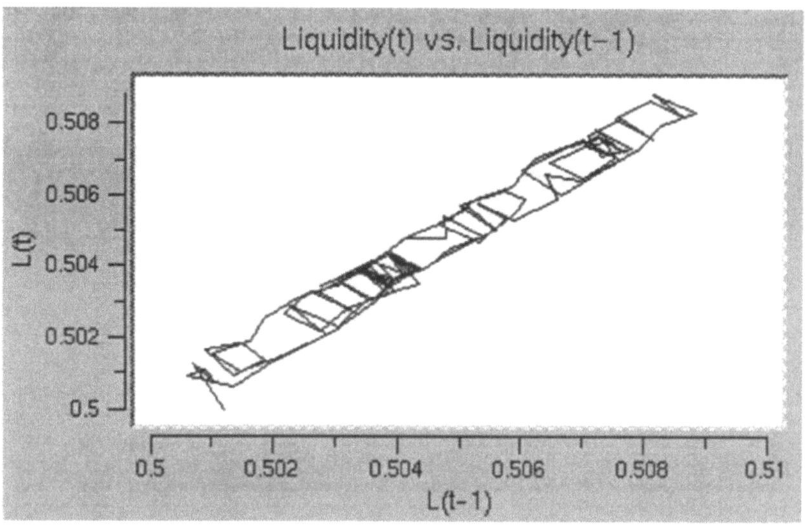


*Figure 6.4.* first investigation (fourth graph)

Obviously, by so doing the characterization of each of the considered numerical simulations mainly depends on the specification of the dynamics for the exponent of Hurst, which is - we briefly recall - the fractal quantity distinguishing the investigated financial market (see, for more

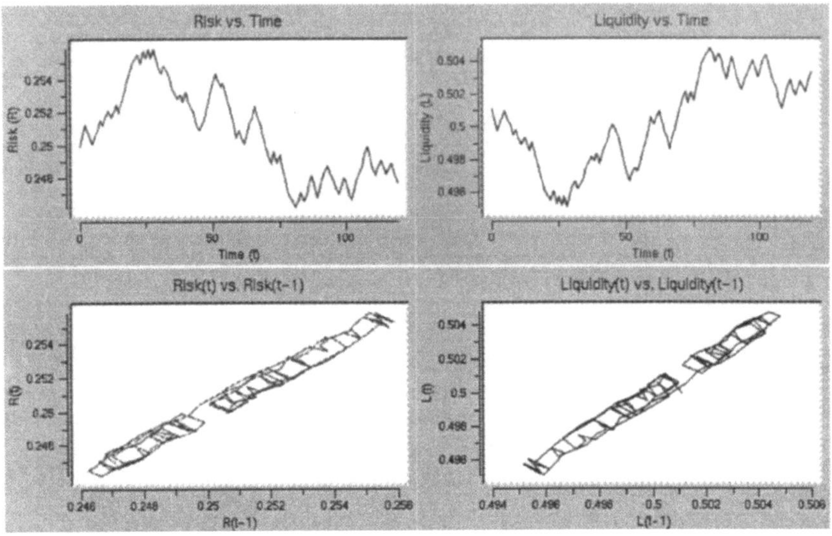


*Figure 6.5.* second investigation (all graphs)

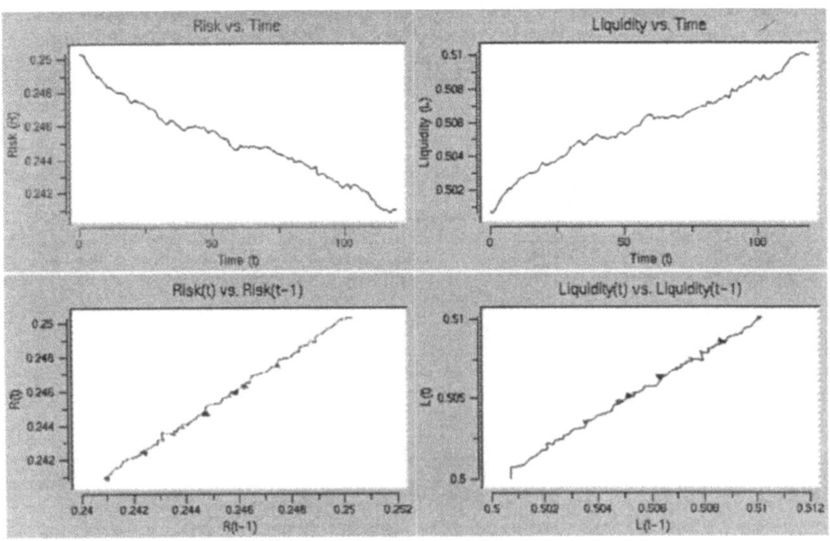


*Figure 6.6.* third investigation (all graphs)

details, sections **2** and **3**). In particular, in the first investigation we presented (see Figures 5.1 to 5.4) we set $H(\bar{t}) = 0.25$ and we consider $\varepsilon_H(t)$, with $t = \bar{t}, \bar{t}+1, \ldots, \bar{t}+120$, as independently and identically truncated-Normally distributed random variables[21]. It is necessary to stress that, in order to provide at least a highly legible numerical investigation, we

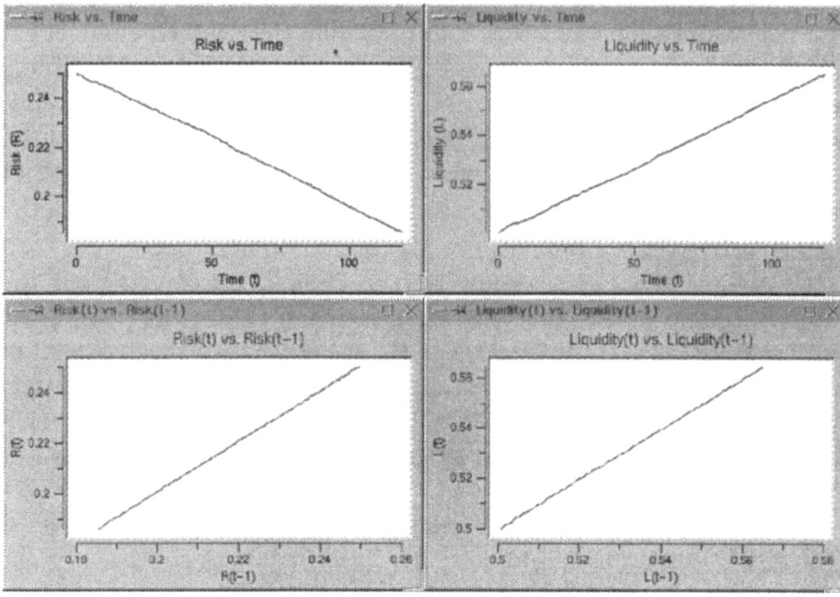


*Figure 6.7.* fourth investigation (all graphs)

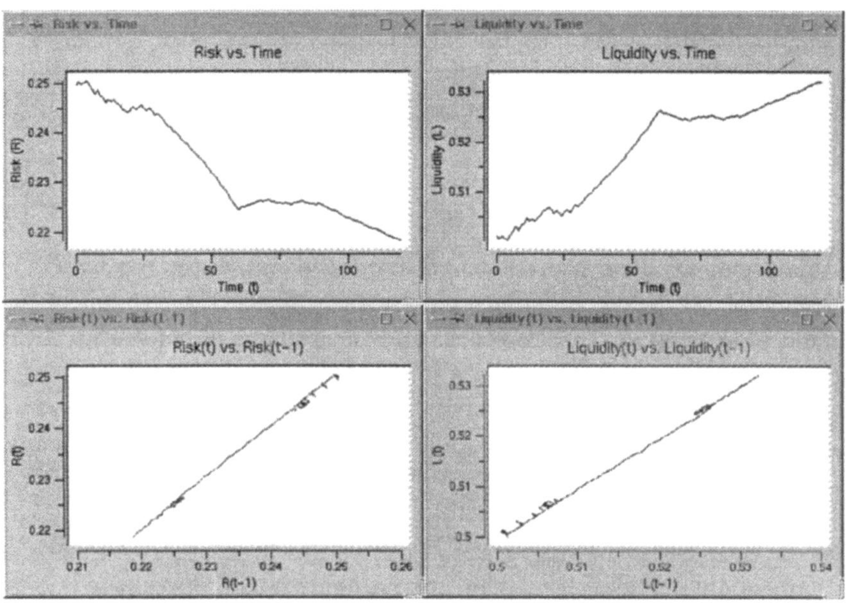


*Figure 6.8.* fifth investigation (all graphs)

intentionally propose the four graphs concerning this first analysis in a larger size than the ones of the graphs regarding the remaining numerical simulations. The second investigation we propose (see Figure 5.5) differs from the previous one in that $\varepsilon_H(t)$, with $t = \bar{t}, \bar{t}+1, \ldots, \bar{t}+120$, are, now, considered as independently and identically Uniformly distributed random variables. The third investigation we report (see Figure 5.6) differs from the first one in $H(\bar{t})$, which, now, is set equal to 0.5; also the fourth investigation we present (see Figure 5.7) differs from the first one in $H(\bar{t})$, which, now, we set equal to 0.75. Finally, in carrying out the fifth investigation (see Figure 5.8) we have taken as starting point some empirical analyses according to which the mean value of the exponent of Hurst (in our case: $H(\bar{t})$) shows a no-costant-over-time behaviour (see, for more details, [Pancham, 1994] and [Corazza *et al.*, 1997a]). Starting from these remarks, the last investigation differs from the first one in $H(\bar{t})$ as follows:

$$H(t) = \begin{cases} 0.2 + \varepsilon_H(t) & \text{if } t = \bar{t}, \ldots, \bar{t}+30 \\ 0.8 + \varepsilon_H(t) & \text{if } t = \bar{t}+31, \ldots, \bar{t}+60 \\ 0.4 + \varepsilon_H(t) & \text{if } t = \bar{t}+61, \ldots, \bar{t}+90 \\ 0.6 + \varepsilon_H(t) & \text{if } t = \bar{t}+91, \ldots, \bar{t}+120 \end{cases} . \tag{5.3}$$

Concluding, with regard to the switch-like independence/dependence index, in all five simulations we have considered $\varepsilon_D(t)$, with $t = \bar{t}, \bar{t}+1, \ldots, \bar{t}+120$, as independently and identically normally distributed random variables.

## 6. Concluding remarks and open questions

In this paper we have proposed and numerically investigated a system of nonlinear stochastic difference equations in which the dynamical behaviour of the financial asset returns and the dynamical behaviour of the corresponding asset quantities are jointly taken into account. This dynamical model is only a starting point in this research area. However we believe it offers evidence for possible developments and improvements, mainly

- by properly generalizing both (4.2) and (4.3) in order to represent formally the time evolution of the financial markets in a way as close as possible to their observable behaviour (of course, this step needs deeper preliminary empirical analyses);
- and by suitably making the fractal agent $H(t)$ endogenous, or - at least - partially endogenous, to the considered system.

# Notes

1. This matter is obviously linked to the research area concerned with the predictability in financial price variations, area in which some of the early contributions appeared in the book edited by P.H. Cootner [Cootner, 1964].

2. In other words, we agree with J.Y. Campbell, A.W. Lo and A.G. MacKinlay [Campbell *et al.*, 1997] when, on pages 32 and 33, they write: "*For example, over the two-hundred-year history of the New York Stock Exchange, there have been countless changes in the economic, social, technological, institutional, and regulatory environment in which stock prices are determined. The assertion that the probability law of daily stock returns has remained the same over this two-hundred-year period is simply implausible.*".

3. On this subject it is essential to stress that the current little agreement on how the dynamics of the financial asset quantities should be correctly considered in the modeling phase is also due to the fact that, generally, suitable quantity data have become available only recently; consequently, only recently the corresponding conjectural and inferential activities (both preliminary to the modeling one) have become possible.

4. Each of the probability law classes we are about to detect can also exhibit more than one of the itemized stochastic property families.

5. The statistical self-similarity implies that the sB motions $\{B(t), t \geq 0\}$ and $\{a^{-1/2}B(at), t \geq 0\}$, with $a > 0$, have the same probability law.

6. This index is the same parameter, the exponent of Hurst, characterizing from a fractal standpoint the sB motion class.

7. See, for more details on fractional differo-integral operators, Miller, K.S. and Ross, B., "*An Introduction to the fractional Calculus and fractional Differential Equation*", John Wiley & Sons, 1993.

8. Of course, this process family was not the unique candidate. Possible alternatives could be obtained from a finite mixture of Normal distributions, or by the Student $t$ distribution, or by the hyperbolic one.

9. If $\alpha \in (0, 1)$ the probability law has not finite mean nor finite variance, if $\alpha \in [1, 2)$ the probability law has only finite mean, and if $\alpha = 2$ the probability law has both finite mean and finite variance.

10. From a financial standpoint it is not restrictive to assume that $\beta = 0$; in fact, the most of the skewness parameter values estimated from return time series, thought different from 0, are quite close to it.

11. Generally, the absolute majority of the characteristic exponent values estimated from financial return time series takes values in the interval $(1, 2]$. Because of it, $H = 1/\alpha$ empirically implies that $H \in [0.5, 1)$.

12. We stress that the standard dynamics for financial modeling, the one for which $H = 0.5$, is comprised in both the non-standard ones as particular case.

13. We shall present this model in section **4**.

14. For example, the volatility, the independence/dependence among the financial asset price variations, ... .

15. Again, we stress that a third possible regime linked to the sB motion class is comprised in both the other ones as a particular case.

16. For example, among the most utilized: the total number of shares traded on a given market, the individual numeraire volume normalized by the aggregate market numeraire volume, the number of trading days per year, ... (see, for more details, [Lo *et al.*, 2000a]).

17. It is noticeable that $a^{-H}$ plays the role of proportionality factor.

18. Clearly the utilization of a single parameter $a_{1,1}$ as factor both for $E_{R,t}[D(t)] \cdot |E_{R,t}[H(t)] - 0.5|$ and for $\{1 - E_{R,t}[D(t)]\} \cdot \{E_{R,t}[H(t)] - 0.5\}$ is due to the will to achieve a dynamical model as simple as possible from an analytical standpoint.

19. As regards the utilization of a single parameter $a_{2,1}$ as factor both for $E_{R,t}[D(t)] \cdot |E_{R,t}[H(t)] - 0.5|$ and for $\{1 - E_{R,t}[D(t)]\} \cdot \{E_{R,t}[H(t)] - 0.5\}$, see the previous footnote.

20. In its turn, the structure of an agent may be characterized by means of a set of other predefined sub-agents, and so on.

21. Going into simple technical details, we developed our Swarm code on an Apple Powerbook G3 computer, by using Linux PPC as operating system, and managing the graphs by the GIMP software package.

## References


Beran, J., "*Statistics for Long-Memory Processes*", Chapman & Hall, 1994.

Campbell, J.Y., Lo, A.W. and MacKinlay, A.C., "*The Econometrics of Financial Markets*", Princeton University Press, 1997.

Cheung, Y.-W., and Lai, K.S., "Do Gold Market Returns Have Long Memory?", *The Financial Review*, 28(2), 181-202, 1993.

Cootner, P.H. (ed.), "*The Random Character of Stock Market Prices*", The M.I.T. Press, 1964.

Corazza, M., "Long-Term Memory Stability in the Italian Stock Market", *Economics & Complexity*, 1(1), 19-28, 1996.

Corazza, M., "Merton-like Theoretical Frame for Fractional Brownian Motion in Finanza", in Canestrelli, E. (ed.), "*Current Topics in Quantitative Finance*", Physica-Verlag, 37-47, 1999.

Corazza, M. and Malliaris, A.G., "Multifractality in Foreign Currency Markets", *Quaderno del Dipartimento di Matematica Applicata e Informatica dell'Università degli Studi di Venezia*, 49/97, 1997a.

Corazza, M., Malliaris, A.G. and Nardelli, G., "Searching for fractal Structure in Agricultural Futures Markets", *The Journal of Futures Markets*, 17(4), 433-473, 1997b.

Falconer, K., "*fractal Geometry*", John Wiley & Sons, 1990.

Lévy, P., "*Calcul des Probabilities*", Gauthier-Villar, 1925.

Lee, C.M.C. and Swaminathan, B., "Price Momentum and Trading Volume", *The Journal of Finance*, 55(5), 2017-2069, 2000.

Lo, A.W., "Long-Term Memory in Stock Market Prices", *Econometrica*, 59(5), 1279-1313, 1991.

Lo, A.W. and Wang, J., "Trading Volume: Definitions, Data Analysis, and Implications of Portfolio Theory", *The Review of Financial Studies*, 13(2), 257-300, 2000a.

Lo, A.W., Mamaysky, H. and Wang, J., "Foundations of Technical Analysis: Computational Algorithms, Statistical Inference, and Empirical Implementation", *The Journal of Finance*, 55(4), 1705-1765, 2000b.

Luna, F. and Stefansson, B. (eds.), "*Economic Simulations in Swarm: Agent-Based Modelling and Object Oriented Programming*", Kluwer Academic Publishers, 2000.

Kopp, E., "Fractional Brownian Motion and Arbitrage", *Mimeo - University of Hull (England)*, 1995.

Kunimoto, N., "Long-Term Memory and Fractional Brownian Motion in financial markets", *Revised version of Discussion Paper at Faculty of Economics - University of Tokyo (Japan)*, 92-F-12, 1993.

Mandelbrot, B.B., "The Variation of Certain Speculative Prices", *IBM Research Report*, NC-87, 1962.

Mandelbrot, B.B. and Van Ness, J.W., "Fractional Brownian Motion, Fractional Noises and Applications", *SIAM Review*, 10(4), 422-437, 1968.

Pancham, S., "Evidence of the Multifractal Market Hypothesis Using Wavelet Transforms", *Mimeo - Florida International University (Florida, U.S.A.)*, 1994.

Peitgen, H.-O., J'urgens, H. and Saupe, D., "*Chaos and fractals. New Frontiers of Science*", Springer-Verlag, 1992.

Rachev, S. and Mittnik, S., "*Stable Paretian Models in Finance*", Wiley, 2000.

Rogers, L.C.G., "Arbitrage with Fractional Brownian Motion", *Mathematical Finance*, 7(1), 95-105, 1997.

Samorodnitsky, G., and Taqqu, M.S., "*Stable Non-Gaussian Random Processes*", Chapman & Hall, 1994.

Taqqu, M.S., "A Bibliographical Guide to Self-Similar Processes and Long-Range Dependence", in Eberlein, E. and Taqqu, M.S. (eds.), "*Dependence in Probability and Statistics*", Birkhauser, 137-162, 1986.

Willinger, W., Taqqu, M.S. and Teverovsky, V., "Stock Market Prices and Long-Range Dependence", *Finance and stochastics*, 3(1), 1-13, 1999.

Chapter 7

# GROWING THEORIES FROM THE "BOTTOM UP". A SIMPLE ENTRY-EXIT MODEL

Domenico Delli Gatti
*ITEMQ, Catholic University, Milan, Italy*
delliga@aixmiced.mi.unicatt.it

Mauro Gallegati
*DSGSS, University of Teramo, Italy*
gallegati@deanovell.unian.it

Roberto Leombruni
*DEA, University of Ancona, Italy*
rleom@rocketmail.com

**Abstract** This paper examines some complex dynamic behaviour emerging in a contestable market. We use nearly zero-intelligence firms: they all sell at a fixed price an equal quantity of the good; they enter and exit according to the lagged profitability of the market. The financial requirements of production are considered, and a spread between creditor and debtor interest rates is introduced. A deterministic case is studied, whose analytical solution shows the presence of infinite equilibria with respect to the number and average capitalisation of the firms. We then proceed in simulating an extended model with the ACE approach, allowing for heterogeneity of firms with respect to their equity, and idiosyncratic shocks on prices. Some other macrobehaviours emerge, among which an asymmetric distribution of firms' equity base, phase transition in the volatility of the equity base time series, out of equilibrium persistence.

## 1. Introduction

In the last decade there has been an emerging attention to models of markets characterized by participants with "zero-intelligence", but whose actions – when ruled by a well defined market structure – give rise to macrobehaviours that tend to replicate those predicted by models with rational and informed agents ([Gode - Sunder, 1993, 1997], [Mirowski, 1998], [Terna, 2000]). We may see this kind of modelling as a "radical wing" of a broader area of studies, the agent-based computational economics (ACE), whose points of departure are individuals with (at most) bounded information and computational capabilities, and whose interaction is studied mainly by means of computer simulations. An approach that has been labelled "generative", whose aims can be synthesised with Epstein's words: "The issue is not how much rationality there is (at the micro level), but *how little is enough* to generate the macroequilibrium"[Epstein, 1999].

Besides the methodological issues that this kind of modelling raises, we must stress the importance of a better understanding of markets with an "arbitrarily small" content of economic theory, since they may constitute a benchmark for evaluating the results of theoretically richer models. Call it a benchmark quest.

This kind of attention is even more crucial when we relax the representative agent hypothesis, and shift the focus on the consequences of introducing heterogeneity and interaction (H&I) among individuals [Kirman, 1992; Gallegati - Kirman, 1999; Delli Gatti et al., 2000]. In a sense, the "bottom up" modelling style of ACE provides the easiest way to tackle the issue of heterogeneity, since the building blocks of ACE models are pieces of software emulating (potentially different) agents interacting with each other. It must be noted, however, that difficulties of interpretation often arise when trying to compare the results of these two polar modelling styles: a formal one, self restrained in its scope by the emphasis on analytical tractability, and a representational one, in which the higher degree of freedom in developing models is achieved at the cost of a greater difficulty in generalising the results.

One way to bridge this communication gap could be to grow artificial societies following Axelrod's "simplicity principle" [Axelrod, 1997], since a clearer design highly facilitates the interpretation of "what's happening" *in machina.* A slightly different way to bridge it, targeting in the meanwhile the benchmark quest, is to extend the "bottom up" modelling style of ACE also to the theoretical content of the model studied, i.e. starting with over simplified artificial worlds for which an analytical solution exists, and extending them step by step to introduce new hypotheses.

This kind of modelling is here adopted to study the rich dynamics emerging in a contestable market, where firms' financial costs are considered. We use nearly zero-intelligence firms: they all sell at an exogenous price an equal quantity of the good; they entry and exit the market comparing the lagged profitability with an exogenous interest rate. Adding to these hypotheses heterogeneity among firms with respect to their capitalisation, and idiosyncratic shocks on prices, a quite rich macro-dynamics emerge, that tend to emulate some patterns observed in real world industrial dynamics. From such benchmark model, then, a hint should be derived that some stylised facts about firms demography – such as asymmetric distribution of firms' size, different growth rates, multiple market structure equilibria – could be explained by the mechanisms of entry exit in the presence of financial constraints.

The paper is organised as follows. In the next section we present the benchmark model. We first derive a qualitative study of the system dynamics, which shows infinite equilibria distributed on a globally stable map and two regimes ruling the motion around it (sect. 2.1). We then study in more detail the dynamics, specifying the entry-exit rules and allowing for heterogeneity (sect. 2.2).

In the third section we cast the model in a stochastic framework, and simulate it using Swarm. The key features of Swarm that drove us to its choice in implementing the simulations are its wide library of pre-written re-usable code tailored specifically to run agent-based simulations, the contextual delivery of a set of "design precepts" for keeping them clear, standardised and reproducible, and the possibility it gives to follow with graphical widgets virtually any aspect of the simulation during the run time. All of these feature revealed to be essential in analysing the dynamics that emerged adding noise to our model. Many of the macro behaviours emerged are widely in accordance with the hints one can derive from the analysis of the deterministic case. They can be seen as a sort of validation of the model, and came with other seemingly unpredictable dynamics which are the specific added value of agent-based simulations: the production of artificial time series in controlled conditions on which to base further theoretical extensions.

As summarised in the conclusions, it should be stressed that these macrobehaviours are due mainly to the mechanisms of entry-exit, and could be considered as a useful benchmark when studying more complex markets with agents following theoretically richer sets of rules.

## 2. The base model

Since Viner [1937], the equilibrium number of firms in a market with free entry is determined comparing the optimal dimension of a representative firm with the position of an exogenous demand for goods. If $q^e$ is the production that minimis variable costs at the level $vc^e$, the market will be in equilibrium with a number of firms such that:

$$N^e = \mathrm{D}(vc^e)/q^e,$$

where $\mathrm{D}(p)$ is demand at price $p$. An expansion of market demand will cause the entry of new firms, a contraction the exit of some active firms.

The efforts of the literature to reconcile this raw portrait with empirics have been mainly directed in two directions: a greater realism of the theoretical assumptions; a greater accordance of the models' results with the stylised facts on firms' demography[1].

As to the first point, a crucial assumption that has been relaxed is the strict concavity of the cost function, in accordance with the observation that for firms there is usually a wide production range for which variable costs are constant [Lucas, 1978, Simon - Bonini 1958]. The relevance of this hypothesis is straightforward: if the production function implies a flat bottom in the variable costs curve the simple mechanism sketched above breaks down, since a change of market demand can be absorbed (at least in part) by the active firms. In this case, therefore, we cannot determine an equilibrium number of firms (at best an equilibrium range can be derived). In addition, the qualitative assessment of market dynamics becomes even looser than in Viner's case.

The debate on the stylised facts on firms' demography, on the other hand, has faced the problem of assessing the overall dynamics of this kind of markets, and developed mostly around the so-called Law of proportionate effects, or Gibrat's Law. Following an "as if" approach, models have been built with "neoclassical" – say, unrealistic – firms, but where the introduction of other hypotheses such as non-homogeneous technical change, scarcity in managerial capacity, local monopoly and so forth, has been sufficient to generate a dynamic behaviour rich enough to be compared with empirical data.

In this section we analyse a simple contestable market where firms have constant variable production costs, and where the costs faced by the firms to finance their production are also taken into account.

The focus is on the dynamics generated by the mechanisms of entry and exit; to isolate their effects we let the model be as simple as possible. In particular, we'll use nearly zero-intelligence firms that hold for exogenous both demand and price. That is, the demand is a "pie" divided among the incumbent firms and sold at a fixed price. The only decision taken by the firms then is "stay" - in (out of) the market, or "go" - out of (into) the market; this decision is driven by the gap between the market profitability and the interest rate, where the former is measured by the aggregate rate of profit – i.e. aggregate profits on aggregate equity base.

Note that if we use a single interest rate – i.e. if there's no spread between creditor and debtor $r$ –, to consider the production financing simply implies higher unitary costs that nevertheless remain constant, and this way the system will still be characterised either by an undetermined market structure of equilibrium (as in Lucas 1978), or by explosive dynamics (when this unitary costs are different from the fixed price).

The simplest way to introduce a spread between creditor and debtor interest rate is to slightly change the behaviour of the agents. It's natural to think of the firms as the only agents that can produce goods. Extend this "exclusive hypothesis", and let the banks be the only agents that can lend money. The "stay or go" decision that each agent-investor must make becomes the decision of being a firm or a bank. When the investor behaves as a firm he can finance production with equity; a negative slack between the equity and the financial requirements will be paid at the prevailing rate of interest, while a positive one won't produce any revenue. If the investor observes that the profit rate is lower than the interest rate, he will change his status and become a bank. Conversely, the banker can be viewed as a potential firm that will eventually enter the market if the profit rate is greater than the interest rate[2].

With these hypotheses the system presents a stable map with infinite equilibria; which of these will prevail depends on the initial conditions of the system and on the other hypotheses one makes to specify the entry-exit rules.

## 2.1. Representative agent

To get started, let us characterise the degenerate dynamics emerging with no spread between creditor and debtor interest rate.

There are $N$ firms with fixed unitary (production) costs $\alpha$. Production is financed by means of the equity base constant $A$, and the negative (positive) slack between equity and the financial requirements of production yields a cost (revenue) of $r$ times the slack.

The market demand $Y$ is exogenous and constant, and is uniformly divided between the $N$ firms at a fixed (unitary) price set to one.

Each firm will then be characterised by the following profit equation:

$$\Pi = (1\text{-}\alpha)\ Y/N - r(\alpha Y/N - A).$$

To study the dynamics of the system we must make some assumptions on the evolution of the equity base and on the mechanisms of entry and exit from the market.

In the following, we'll assume that the firms remunerate their shareholders at the rate $r$[3]; the excess (shortfall) of the profit over the dividend increases (decreases) the equity base. Therefore, the motion equation of the equity will be the following:

$$\Delta A = \Pi - rA = A(\Pi/A - r).$$

We'll assume also that the entry and exit of the firms is cost-free (pure contestable market hypothesis), and is driven by the profitability of the market, i.e. by the spread between the rate of profit and the rate of interest. By now, we let the exact number of firms entering (exiting) the market undetermined; we simply require that the qualitative behaviour of the motion equation for $N$ satisfies the following:

$$\text{sign}(\Delta N) = \text{sign}(\Pi/A - r),$$

We also assume that the firms entering the market have the same equity base as that of the active firms.

With these assumptions, the qualitative dynamics of the system will be ruled just by the spread between $\Pi/A$ and $r$. Remembering the profit equation, we'll have:

$$sign(\Delta A) = sign(\Delta N) = sign[1 - \alpha(1 + r)]. \qquad (2.1)$$

Note that the term $\alpha(1+r)$ represents the unitary cost for a firm when the (opportunity) costs of financing its production are taken into account. If $\alpha(1+r)=1$ the system will be in equilibrium with any value of $A$ and $N$. In the other cases the system will either explode or implode. In other terms, due to the linearity of the profit function, the system will be characterised either by an undetermined equilibrium, or by explosive dynamics. In any case, note that in order to have a positive number of firms at an arbitrary time t, the condition $\alpha(1+r)\leq 1$ must hold; call it the "market profitability condition". In the following, we'll assume it is always verified. When satisfied with the "lower than" operator, we'll say that it is strictly verified.

Allowing for a spread between creditor and debtor interest rate, and setting the former to zero (in accordance with our "exclusive hypothesis"), the dynamics changes as follows.

First of all, observe that at the firm level the condition for the presence of liabilities is that equity be lower than the total production costs, $\alpha(Y/N)$. At the macro level, being all firms equal, this condition yields the following "no liability line":

$$A = \alpha Y/N. \qquad (2.2)$$

If the system lies below this line the firms are demanding money to finance their production, and the qualitative dynamics will still be ruled by equation (2.1) (with a different interpretation of "$r$"). When $\alpha(1+r)=1$ any couple $(A,N)$ will be feasible; when $\alpha(1+r)<1$ the system will move toward the map (both $A$ and $N$ are increasing).

When the system goes over the line, the profit equation will change: the term accounting for the financial revenues will disappear, and equation (2.1) will change. If we rewrite the condition $\Pi/A = r$ using the new profit equation, we arrive at the following equilibrium map:

$$A = Y(1-\alpha)/(rN) \tag{2.3}$$

If the market profitability condition strictly holds, this map will lie strictly over the no liability line (cp. Fig. 7.1).

Hence, all the infinite couples $(A,N)$ along this map are possible equilibria. Which couple will be reached depends on the initial conditions of the system, and on the specification of the motion equation for $N$. Even letting the latter unspecified, however, the following propositions will hold:

Proposition 1: *the map is globally stable*[4];

Proposition 2: *(almost every) a shock to the system will end in a new, different, configuration of equilibrium.*

Proposition 1 states that there is no tendency for the system to converge to a particular couple $(A,N)$ of equilibrium, but nonetheless it will always move toward, and anneal to a point of the equilibrium map. Which of the infinite equilibria will be reached depends on the initial conditions of the system. If, like in figure 7.1, a shock drives the system out of an equilibrium point $E_0$ to $E_1$, in the following periods it will move to the new couple of equilibrium $E_n$[5].

The economic interpretation of the map is straightforward. The market can be in equilibrium with any number of firms, provided that the level of the equity base – given total profits – is such that the rate of profit equals the interest rate. The greater the number of firms, the lower the profit per firm, the lower the level of equity compatible with the no entry-exit condition.

Note that the average dimension of the firms, ex-ante undetermined because of the constancy of unitary costs, is dynamically determined by the initial conditions and by the running in or out of firms to bring the profitability of the market toward the "normal rate" $r$.

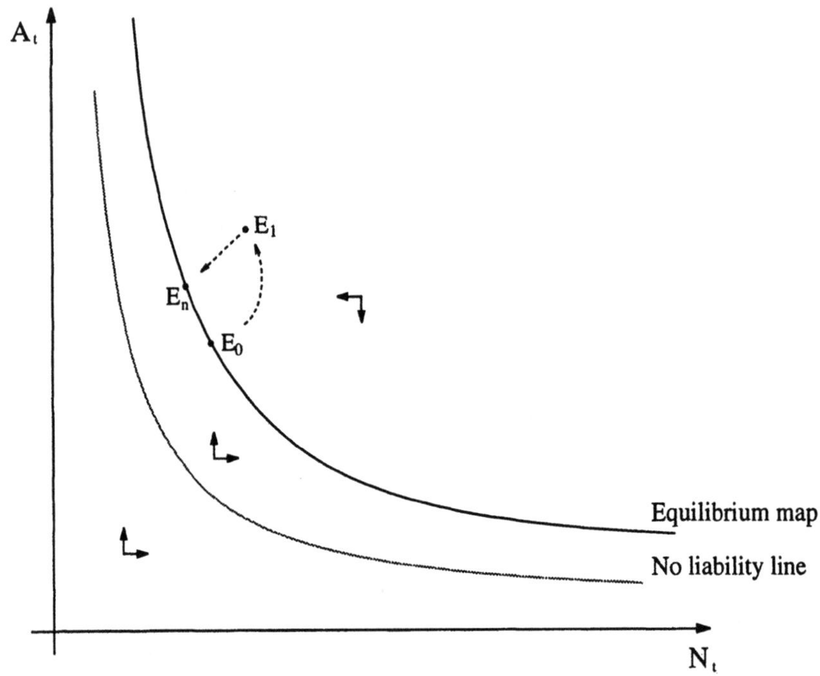


*Figure 7.1.* Qualitative dynamic toward equilibrium map.

**Dynamics around the map.** To study the dynamics around the map, we must specify a motion equation for $N$. The simplest way to do this is to assume that $N$ will vary at a rate proportional to the spread between the rate of profit and the rate of interest. Calling $\beta$ this factor of proportionality:

$$N_{t+1} = N_t + \beta(\Pi/A_t - r)N_t \tag{2.4}$$

Recalling the corresponding equation for $A_{t+1}$ and the two forms of the profit equation, we obtain the system:

$$\begin{aligned} N_{t+1} &= N_t + \beta[1 - \alpha(1+r)]\,Y/A_t \\ A_{t+1} &= A_t + [1 - \alpha(1+r)]\,Y/N_t \end{aligned} \tag{2.5}$$

which describes the dynamics under the no liability line. Above the NLL the following system will hold:

$$N_{t+1} = N_t + \beta(1-\alpha)Y/A_t - \beta r N_t$$
$$A_{t+1} = A_t + (1-\alpha)Y/N_t - rA_t \quad (2.6)$$

By a simple analysis of (5a-b), we can qualify the dynamics around the map by means of the following propositions:

Proposition 3: *the farther the system from the origin, the smaller the rates of adjustment;*

Proposition 4: *passing through the no liability line, the rates of adjustment will increase;*

Proposition 5: *the direction followed by the system approaching the equilibrium map is equal to:*

$$\Delta A/\Delta N = A/\beta N, \quad (2.7)$$

In particular, integrating (2.7), we obtain the following family of continuous trajectories which approximates the path followed by the system:

$$A = kN^{1/\beta} \quad (2.8)$$

where $k = e^C/\beta$ and $C$ is an arbitrary constant (fig. 7.2).

The propositions so far stated, however, aren't sufficient to assess the qualitative behaviour of the system, since there are infinite couples of equilibrium. In other words, we may ask whether there are points on the map that are more "easily" accessed than others. More precisely, we may ask whether introducing some noise on the system the probability distribution of the configurations $(A,N)$ of equilibrium depends only on the initial conditions, or the dynamics is biased toward some zones of the map.

To answer, we must qualify the behaviour of the system in response to various shocks.

Let's first consider shocks that apply to the structural variables $\alpha$, $r$, and $Y$. A permanent change in these variables will cause a shift of the map, and this will cause the system to reach a new couple of equilibrium moving along the trajectory that passes through the initial equilibrium. As a first approximation, we can also say that any *temporary* change in the same variables will result in a *temporary* movement in the $(A,N)$ of equilibrium, while its long run value will not change. This is due to the fact that the trajectories do not depend on variables $\alpha$, $r$ and $Y$ (cp. eq. 6), and hence the system will always move along the same trajectory;

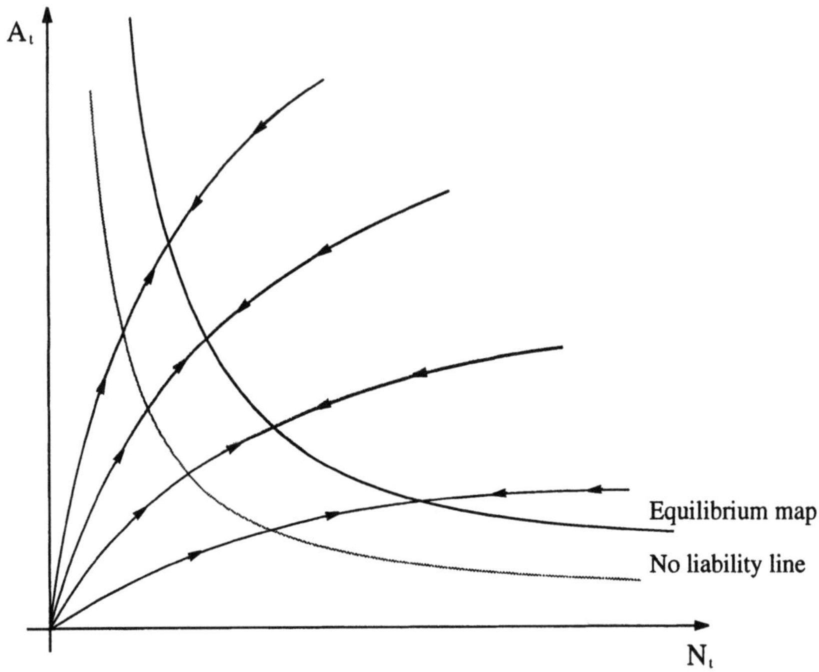


*Figure 7.2.* Trajectories with $\beta > 1$

once the shock is absorbed, then, and the map shifts back to its original position, the system will tend to return to the couple of equilibrium in which it lain before the shock. In fig. 7.3, after the equilibrium map shifts from EM to EM', the continuum case correspond to the movement from equilibrium E to E*, and after the map returns to position EM' the system gets back to the point E moving along the same trajectory.

Anyhow, this is just an approximation, since the trajectories (2.8) have been derived neglecting the discrete nature of the variable $N$. In fact, the exact behaviour of our model in response to this kind of shock is rather complex to assess analytically. First of all, in the discrete case also the trajectories do depend on $\alpha$, $r$, and $Y$. This can be viewed either iterating the motion equations (2.5-2.6) to express $(N_t, A_t)$ in function of the initial conditions, either by means of economic considerations. Let's consider for instance a positive change in $Y$. If the shock is "small", this change won't be a sufficient stimulus to induce a new firm to entry[6], and the trajectory getting out from the map will be vertical – that is, only $A$ will vary. For greater values of the "new" $Y$, instead, the stimulus will be greater and new firms will entry; consequently, the trajectory followed

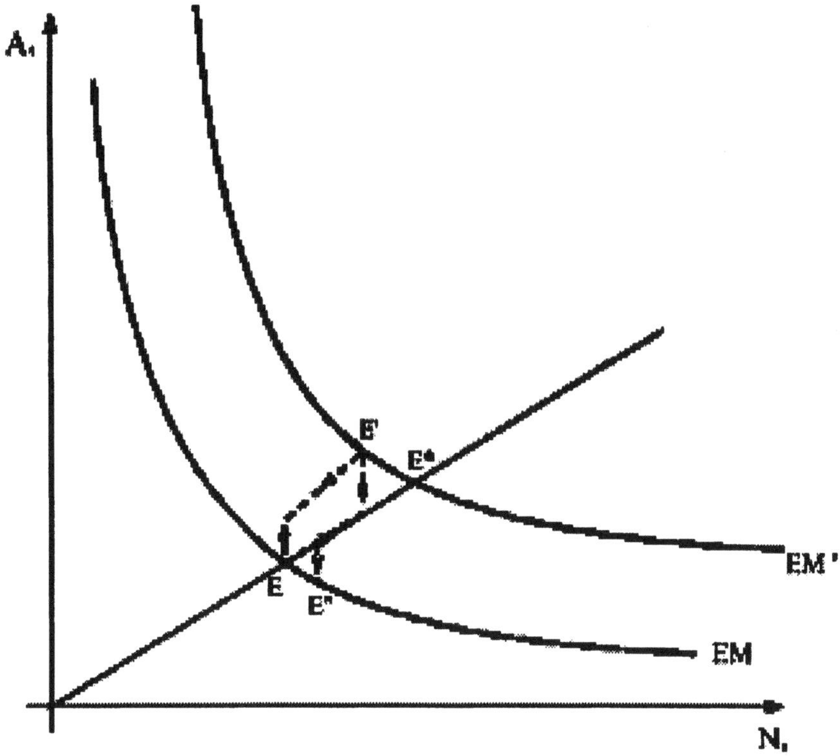


*Figure 7.3.* Discrete trajectories with $\beta = 1$

will have a shape closer to the continuous case defined by equation (2.8). That is, trajectories do depend on the entity of the shock. Moreover, in the case of temporary shocks, also the time span before the shock is absorbed is relevant. The reason stems from the same economic considerations just stated, namely that whenever the system approaches the map it will enter a zone around it in which the trajectories are vertical; then, if the time span is long enough, a new temporary equilibrium will be reached, and the system will face a vertical trajectory two times. In figure 7.3, starting again from the point E, the new equilibrium reached will be E'. Getting back after the counter-shock, the system – as a first approximation – will return to its initial position E. If the time span is short enough, the system will not get too close to the EM', and consequently it will not abandon the continuous-like trajectory. Hence, when the counter shock occurs, it will end in a new point of equilibrium E" different from the initial.

On which is the long run effect of a temporary shock then, we can say the following. A good approximation is the "neutral" conclusions to which one arrives using the equation (2.8). Especially for thick markets, the effect of the discrete change constraint on $N$ can surely be ignored. But if it is the case that one wants to study these effects, however, the best approach is probably the run of simulations in which all the relevant factors can be taken into account. A sketch of this kind of analysis will be presented in next section, to which we postpone a closer look to some "non neutral" effects of these shocks.

Let's consider now shocks that move the system out of the map – i.e. shocks that apply to the system state variables $A$ and $N$ –, and let us focus on the continuum case[7]. In this case, we can single out two "neutrality conditions" that, when violated, introduce a bias toward some zones of the map.

First, using proposition 5, we can better qualify proposition 2:

Proposition 2': *Only the shocks moving the system in a direction equal to (2.7) will end in the same initial configuration of equilibrium.*

This way, we could define as neutral the shocks satisfying Prop. 2', that is, multiplicative shocks with mean one and $\beta$ that apply respectively to $A$ and $N$. When this condition is not verified, we can state the following:

Proposition 6: *It can be shown that when a shock applies in a direction less steep than (2.7), e.g. a shock on the number of firms, the system will tend to "walk" up the map. An opposite shock, e.g. in the equity level, the system will "walk" down the map.*

A somewhat less stringent neutrality condition arises considering "little" additive shocks moving the system in any direction, given they have zero mean and are symmetric in direction.

This gives us a hint when we'll put some noise in the model. Either the noise will result in shocks neutral according to one of the two criteria, or the system will tend to "walk" up or down the map.

## 2.2. Heterogeneity

In a deterministic framework, initial equity base heterogeneity among firms tends to vanish. In fact, the equilibrium map holds also at the firm level: given a certain number of incumbent firms, the equilibrium equity base is unique, and any initial dispersion among the mean will disappear.

The consideration of heterogeneity, however, imposes a better qualification of the mechanisms of entry and exit. In particular, we must define:

1 the characteristics of the new firms;

2 which firms will exit;

3 which is the benchmark profit rate.

About 1), the most neutral choice would be to extract the characteristics of the firms entering the market from the incumbent firms' distribution. Anyway, a more realistic choice would be that of extracting them from the first quantiles (cp. Caves 1998). Both hypotheses will be tested in next paragraph's simulations.

About 2), it may be argued that only low profit firms should exit. Nevertheless, if the point were the profitability of the single firm, the dynamics of the market would degenerate. In fact, if that were the exit criterion, all the quantile of the distribution falling above the equilibrium value of $A$ should exit immediately. That would correspond to wipe out the dynamics above the map. A more interesting approach is to consider the decision of entry-exit as driven by the *market* profitability, i.e. considering this decision as a form of interaction of agents with a statistics defined at the population level. This way, we can grasp two facts: the first one is the presence of limited knowledge for a firm on the performance of its competitors. The second one, nearly correlated, is the presence of information feedbacks between macro- and microlevel qualifying real world decision processes.

The motion equation of $N$, then, should be read as a flow of firms deciding the participation in the market according to its overall profitability, and not to their short-term revenues; i.e. the firms exiting should be randomly extracted from the entire population. Nevertheless, not to ignore completely the actual situation of each incumbent firm, we tested also a restriction on the set of potential exiters, excluding from this firms experiencing high profits.

This leads us to the third point: there are many ways to define the market profitability. Even in our short-term perspective, we must choose whether to calculate an aggregate rate of profit (total profit on total equity base) or to use some mean of the individual's ones. The second choice would make the distribution of the firms relevant also with respect to the definition of the benchmark for the entry-exit. Anyhow, according to preliminary simulations conducted, the different choices don't give rise to significantly different dynamics, and we gave precedence to the less expensive in computational requests – i.e. the aggregate rate of profit.

To conclude this section, it is worth to stress an important case in which heterogeneity can modify qualitatively the behaviour of markets characterised by the same value of $N$ and the same average value of $A$, but a different dispersion of the equity around that average value. It can be shown that, if all the firms lies over the NLL, the trajectories (2.8) are unmodified by heterogeneity; that is, the average value of the equity will follow exactly equation (2.8). But when there is a sufficiently high dispersion around that average value, a not-empty subset of firms will lie under the NLL (fig. 7.4).

When this is the case, equations (2.5-2.6) are no longer an exact aggregation of the firms' level motion equations for $A$ and $N$, and (2.8) will not hold. The aggregate behaviour will compound that of two sets of firms following two different dynamical regimes.

For what concerns the argument of this section, this scenario implies that heterogeneity matters in determining the final equilibrium that will be reached. In the following section, the same condition will switch the system to behaviours quite different from those with low heterogeneity.

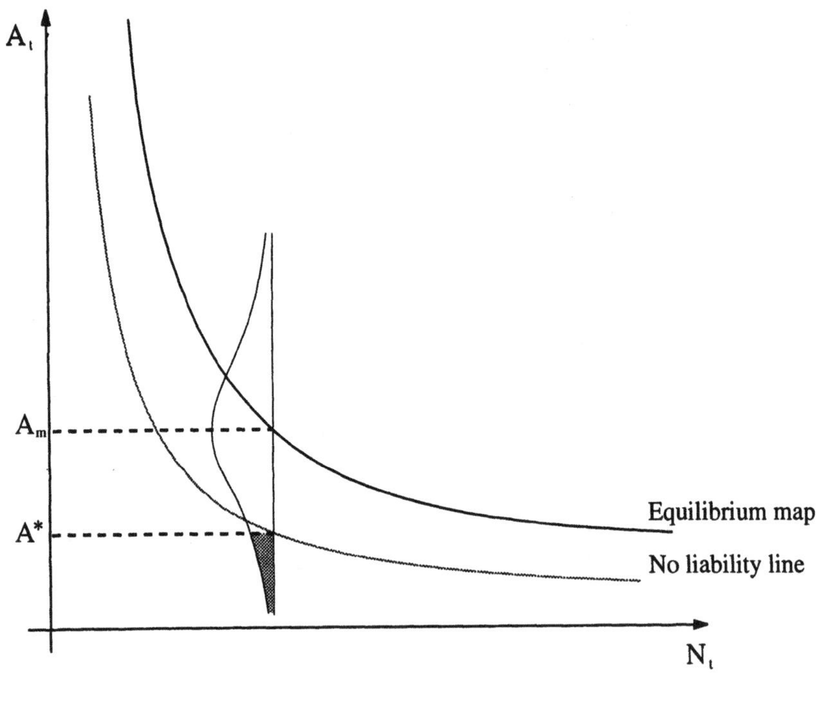


*Figure 7.4.* Distribution of firms' equity bases.

## 3. Simulations

In this section we first report some technical details concerning the simulations conducted. We then proceed to show the outcomes of the simulations, first reproducing the results above derived about the deterministic behaviour of the market, then allowing for idiosyncratic shocks on firms' prices.

## 3.1. Technical details

The simulations have been conducted in Swarm[8], a set of software libraries developed at the Santa Fe Institute in New Mexico – starting from 1995 –, to help simulating complex systems. The underlying programming languages of Swarm are Objective-C and Java, which object-oriented architecture is particularly suited to run agent-based simulations[9]. In a nutshell, to build-up a simulation in Swarm one must specify the behavioural algorithms of the various agents (instance methods), the vector of their state variables (instance variables), and a schedule that contains the ordered list of all the actions each agent will make.

The core of our simulation has been build up with three kinds of agents: firms and households (whose state variables and behaviour are a straightforward translation of the model characteristics described above) and an environment, whose role is to collect and distribute statistics, to co-ordinate entries and exits, and to behave as an interface between the other agents.

Outside the core, there are the two objects typically used in Swarm to coordinate the experiment: an Observer object, that either feeds the graphical widgets to follow the simulation during the run time, or output the artificial time series generated to a file for subsequent analysis; and a Model object, where we defined the schedule of the other agents' actions. Usually in the Model object there are also the routines used to build up the instances of the other agents. To keep the architecture of the messaging simpler, we preferred to delegate this role to the Environment. In fact, during the run time the exit and entry of firms frequently requires to drop or to create Firm instances; in addition, the Firms instances have to be created initialising their equity base in accordance with its statistical distribution in the population. Since both these information and the role of co-ordination have been devolved to the Environment, we implemented in it also the methods for the creation of the households and of the firms.

For every time-step of the simulation, the Model object defines the following schedule:

1. Households: do shopping (method: goShopping);
2. Environment: drives entries and exits (method: killAndCreateFirms);
3. Environment: update statistics (method: updateStateVariables);

Note that we did not schedule any autonomous action for the firms, since they take for exogenous both demand and prices, and do not put forth any optimisation. The only decision they must take is "stay or go", and that is required directly by the environment by sending messages to some set of firms specified below.

During the first step of the schedule, a representative household spends entirely its yearly income. It divides it equally among the incumbent firms, except for a random multiplicative shock on the price they pay to each seller. The shock is extracted from a uniform distribution with mean one; the support of the distribution is a simulation parameter modifiable at start up. The positive or negative slack between yearly income and the actual spending (the latter being influenced by the random extractions) is added to the following period income.

In the second step of the schedule, the environment checks if there have been "hard" bankruptcies, i.e. if any firm's equity base has fallen under a threshold - usually zero. After this check, it tests for the market profitability, comparing the overall rate of profit - the ratio of the sum of all the individual profits to market capitalisation - with the interest rate. From this comparison, the environment will drive new entries and exits, the entity of the flow being determined using either equation (2.4) or a simpler rule, i.e. just one entrant (exiter) if the market is (not) profitable.

If the market is profitable, the environment will create some new firms, building them according to two alternative rules: we tested both the case in which the entrants are extracted from the incumbents' distributions, and the case in which their equity base is centred on the first quantiles.

If the market is not profitable it will communicate it to the firms, and some of these will exit. As stated earlier, we tested two rules with which to choose the potential exiters. In one case, in order to stress the overall profitability of the market as an indicator to drive exits, we randomly extracted them from the entire population. The second rule tested consisted in a restriction on the set of potential exiters, excluding from this set those firms that on average earned positive profits during the latest three periods.

In the third step of the schedule, the environment updates the state variables concerning the entire market (number of firms etc.), and calculates some statistics to feed the graphic widgets of the Observer object and to send them in output for subsequent analysis.

We run the simulations as a norm for about a thousand periods. Since any form of learning in the agents' behaviour is absent, a lower number of periods would have been sufficient for the adjustments toward equilibrium to take place. However, as the model does not present a unique equilibrium, it typically does not anneal on a stable configuration, and its long run behaviour presented a specific interest for what concern the likely presence of zones in the equilibrium map somewhat more probable than others.

This eventuality reveals in several of the simulation conducted, and has also been tested in a first add-on to the raw model here presented. In the base model, the movements out of the equilibrium map are caused by idiosyncratic shocks of firms' prices, and hence the particular equilibrium reached, together with the path described by the system around and along the map, depends on distributional and interaction effects. To test other sources of dynamics, we added two methods to the environment behaviour (sendShock and absorbeShock) to send shocks to the aggregated demand of both entity and periodicity modifiable at start up. This way, it has been possible to better qualify what we stated about the behaviour of the model in response to shocks applying to variables other than $A$ and $N$. The extension of this study to other structural variables as the rate of interest is straightforward.

**Simulation of the base model.** To get started, we simulated the model as described in the third section. With no heterogeneity and with no noise, the market simply anneals to the equilibrium coherent with the initial conditions of the system. As stated, and as shown in figs. 7.5-7.6, starting from different initial conditions the final equilibrium will be different – in the figures, a lower initial value of $N$ (fig. 7.5) implies an higher $A$ of equilibrium.

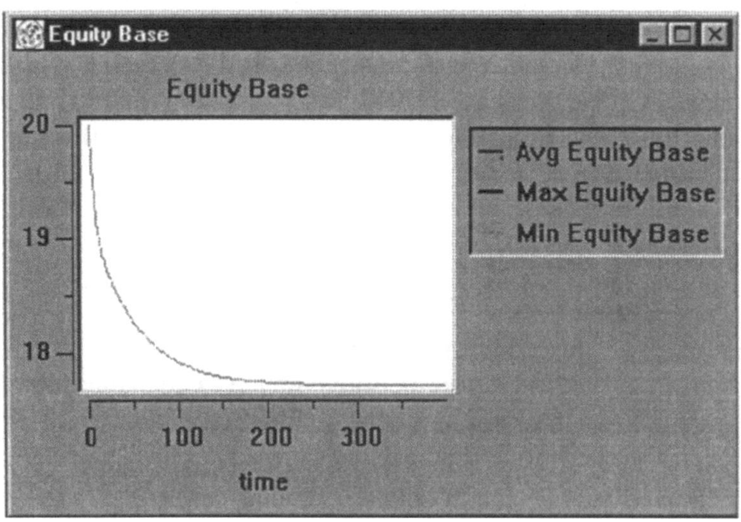


*Figure 7.5.* Path of Equity base towards equilibrium with no heterogeneity, no noise, initial N=400 and A=20

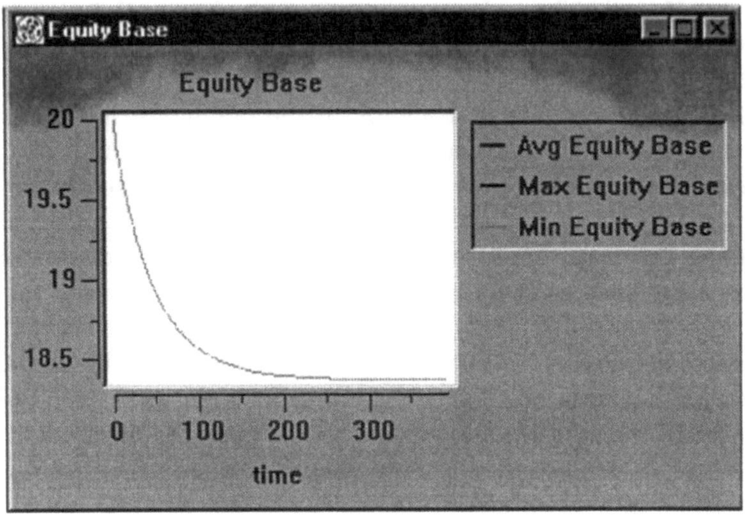


*Figure 7.6.* Path of the equity base towards equilibrium with no heterogeneity, no noise, initial $N$=500 and $A$=20

In figures 7.7-7.8 we allow for initial heterogeneity in firms' equity base. The dynamics of two markets are compared, starting both from the same initial conditions with respect to $N$ and to the average equity base, but having different distributions around that average value. As anticipated in previous section, the distribution can matter in determining the equilibrium reached; *if* every firm lies above the no-liability line – i.e. if no firm faces financial constraints –, the different velocities of adjustment will balance each other and the equilibrium reached will be the same as in the no-heterogeneity case (fig. 7.7). If this condition is not verified, the trajectory followed by the system will no longer be that of equation (2.8). In the case depicted in fig. 7.8, the low profits earned by the firms with positive liability will end in stronger signal to leave the market. The trajectory followed by the system will then be flatter than those depicted in fig. 7.2, and the equilibrium reached will be characterised by an higher value of $A$.

Putting idiosyncratic shocks on prices, we have two main consequences. First, virtually all the points on the equilibrium map can be reached, whichever are the initial conditions. Typically, starting from a point lying out of the map, the system will first go towards it, and then it will "walk" on the map continuously adjusting to the shocks. This behaviour is reproduced in figs. 7.9-7.10, where we report the time series of $N$ and $A$ produced in a simulation run with parameters' values such that all firms can finance production entirely with their equity base[10].

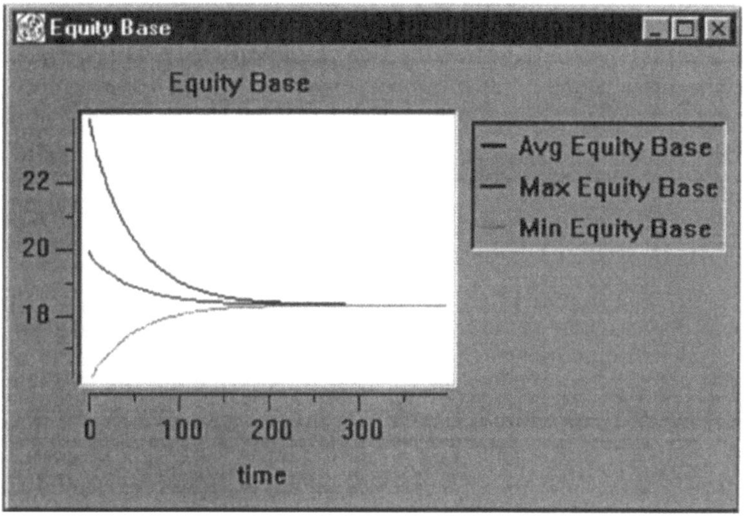


*Figure 7.7.* Path of the equity base toward equilibrium with "low" equity base heterogeneity, no noise, initial $N$=400 and average $A$=20

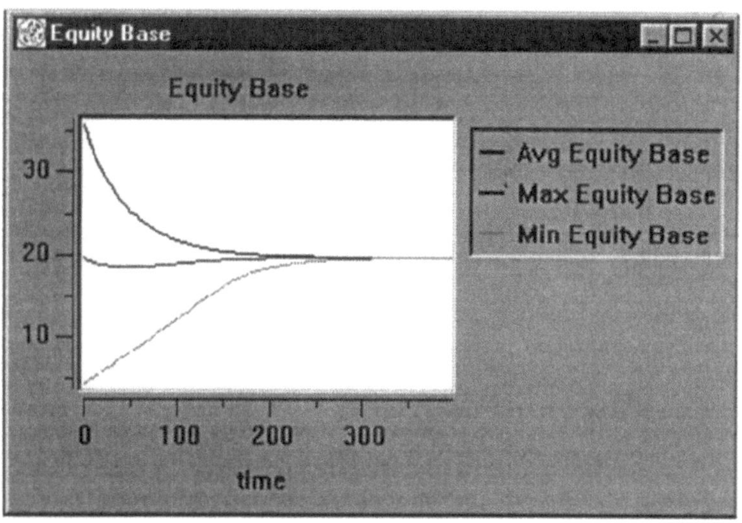


*Figure 7.8.* Path of the equity base toward equilibrium with "high" equity base heterogeneity, no noise, initial $N$=400 and average $A$=20

In fig. 7.11 we put together the two series generated extending the simulation for about three thousands time steps, and draw them against the equilibrium map and the no liability line. In these adjustments around the equilibria the distribution of the equity base among firms remains roughly symmetric.

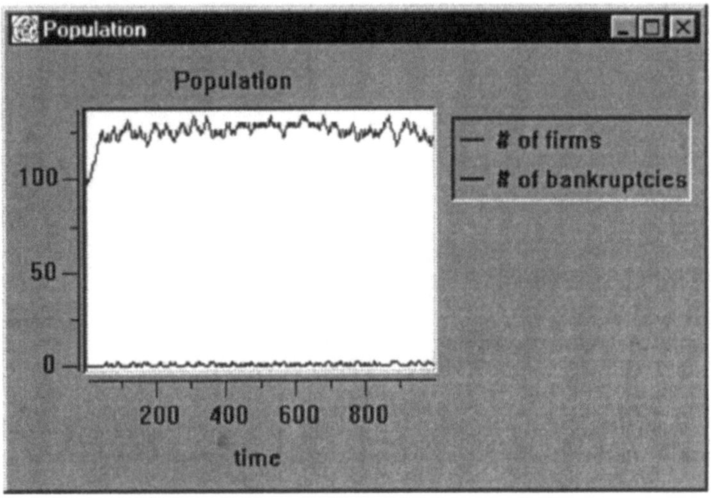


*Figure 7.9.* Number of firms' dynamics.

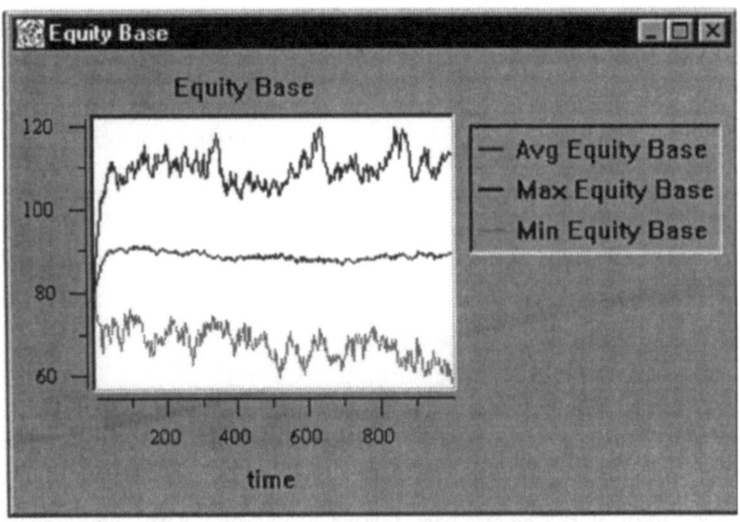


*Figure 7.10.* Firms' equity base dynamics.

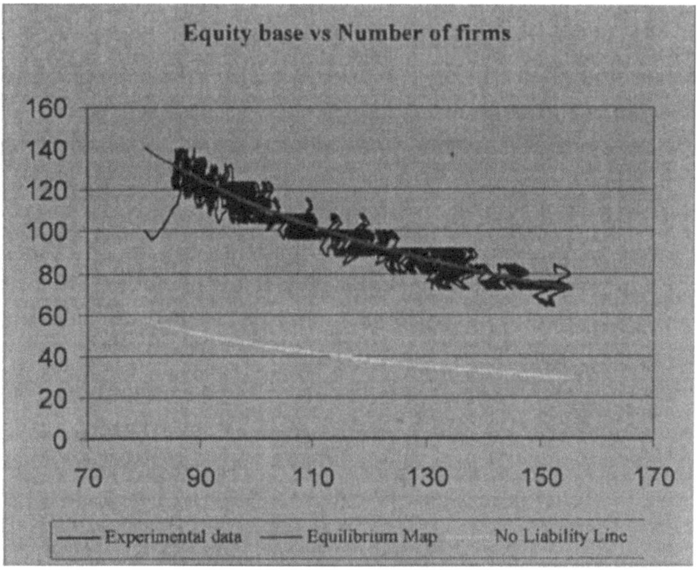


*Figure 7.11.* Equity base vs. number of firms.

The second consequence of introducing idiosyncratic shocks to prices is that, when there is "enough" noise, only a proper subset of the firms will lie "near" the equilibrium map, with a non-empty subset lying under the no liability line. Remembering eq. 5a-b, this implies the presence of two groups of firms moving according to two different dynamic regimes. We saw that in the deterministic case the presence of two regimes made the equity distribution relevant in determining the equilibrium reached from some initial conditions; anyhow, in the long run that heterogeneity wiped out. Now this heterogeneity is kept switched on, and the presence of two regimes gives rise to a dynamic behaviour different from that of figs. 7.8-7.11.

Firstly, we can observe a greater instability, due to the fact that the firms lying under the no liability line face a greater financial fragility. Secondly, $N$ and the average value of $A$ will not converge around the equilibrium map, this latter behaving just as an attractor. Finally, the presence of two dynamic regimes makes the equity distribution asymmetric.

The first two points can be observed in next simulations. We modified the parameters of the previous simulation introducing higher variable costs. The latter change has the effect of nearing the equilibrium map to the no liability line, so that – the equity base dispersion being equal

– a set of firms will fall under the NLL. We also reduced the rates of entry-exit, to soften the instability of the market. This way, the overall dynamics resemble that of figs. 7.8-7.9, except for the wider intervals of $A$ and $N$ spanned during the runs.

When putting together the experimental series of (the average value of) $A$ and $N$, however, we can observe how the equilibrium map behaves just as an attractor (see fig. 7.12). The same map, in fact, doesn't describe any equilibrium for the lower quantiles of the distribution, and the area spanned by the experimental $(A,N)$ pairs is the usual equilibrium map somehow "discounted" for the fraction of the population facing financial constraints.

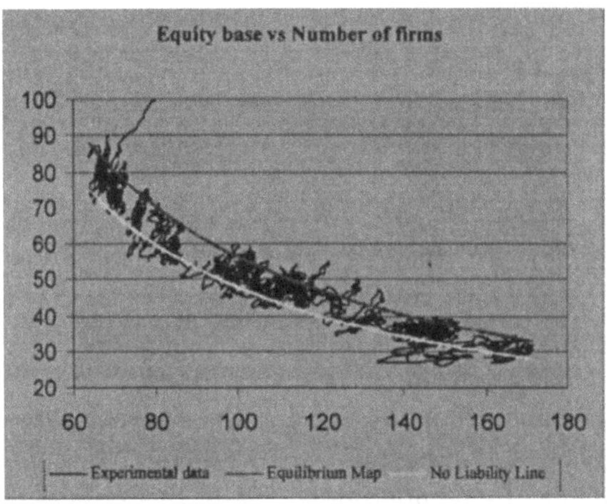


*Figure 7.12.* Equity base vs. number of firms. Two dynamic regimes

It is worth noting that heterogeneity can give rise to two kinds of "instability" in the market. In the first place, the nearer are the values of $(1\text{-}\alpha)$ and $r$, the more erratic will be the dynamics of the firms with positive liability, and accordingly also the overall behaviour of the system will be more unstable. This is an "inner" property of the market, since it derives from the structural parameters by which it is described.

The second type of instability, on the contrary, is linked to the state variables of the system. Keeping the magnitude of the random shocks on prices and the other structural parameters unchanged, a market will face higher flows of entry-exit according to the position on the $(A,N)$ space. In fact, at higher values of $N$, the equilibrium map will be closer to the no liability line, and hence the same dispersion of the equity around its average value will imply a larger share of firms with positive liability.

The more populated is the market, the larger will be the share of firms facing financial fragility, the more vulnerable will be the entire market to the random shocks it faces.

These two situations are represented in figs. 7.13. We run two simulations adding some rigidity in the entry-exit decision – we imposed that the slack between $r$ and the profit rate should exceed a certain threshold –, to concentrate on, say, an instability less constrained to particular realisations of the random sequence. In the first simulation we tested the limit case of $r = (1\text{-}\alpha) = 0.03$, that implies the coincidence of the NLL with the equilibrium map. In this case, the dynamics under the NLL is completely erratic, and is reflected both in the $A$ series, and in that of its minimum and maximum values, signalling a greater variability of the equity distribution (fig. 7.13).

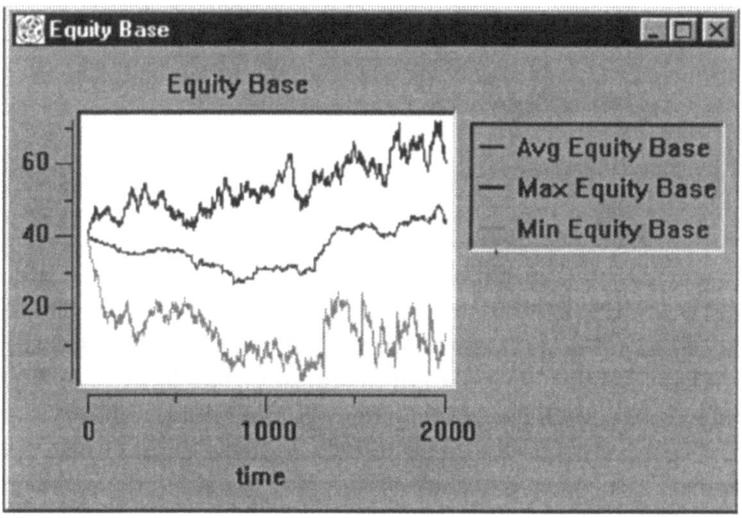


*Figure 7.13.* Firms' equity base dynamic with $r = (1\text{-}\alpha) = 0.03$

We then run a simulation lowering $\alpha$ to 0.96 and leaving all the other parameters unchanged. Starting with initial $N$=$A$=40, the dispersion of the equity isn't enough to bring any firm under the NLL, and the dynamics of $N$ represented in fig. 7.14 is roughly stable for about 1.000 time steps. After that, the system moves towards higher values of $N$, this brings a share of the firms under the NLL, and the entry-exit rates rise significantly. In these cases, we have that heterogeneity remains "inactive" for a while, and the overall dynamics resemble those of the representative agent hypothesis. When $N$ passes a certain threshold, however, the same heterogeneity switches the system to a more unstable behaviour, and the artificial series will tend to span an area lying under that foreseen by the equilibrium map, as in the case of fig. 7.12 above.

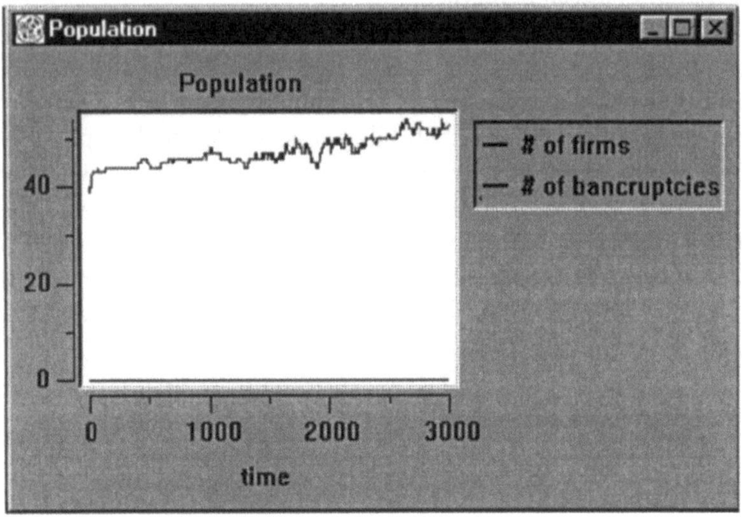


*Figure 7.14.* Firms' equity base dynamic with $r = 0.03$ and $\alpha = 0.96$.

This can be seen in more detail in fig. 7.15, where we reported the series of $A$ and $N$ generated with the same model, run for 13.000 time steps. The simulation starts again with $N$=$A$=40, and, as anticipated, when $N$ gets higher – over an approximate threshold of 90 –, the values generated tend to concentrate under the equilibrium map. It can be noted, also, that at in the final periods of the simulation the situation "normalises", with values concentrating again around the map. This is due to the countervailing tendency, at higher $N$, of the idiosyncratic shocks to cancel each other in their influence on the overall rate of profit.

Finally, the presence of two dynamic regimes makes the equity distribution asymmetric. In the following graph we put together the values of the asymmetry in three of the experiment above conducted, corresponding to figs. 7.11, 7.12 and 7.15. The values are a 12 periods moving average of the first 2.300 time steps of the three simulations. It can be seen how the first and the third simulations present roughly symmetric distributions of the equity base. The average asymmetries in the period considered are respectively -0.004 and -0.025. The second simulation, on the contrary, presents an asymmetry of about -0.5, reflecting the presence of two different regimes for the motion equations of $A$. It should be noted that the symmetric distribution of the third simulation is not at odds with the qualitative analysis presented above; the first 2.300

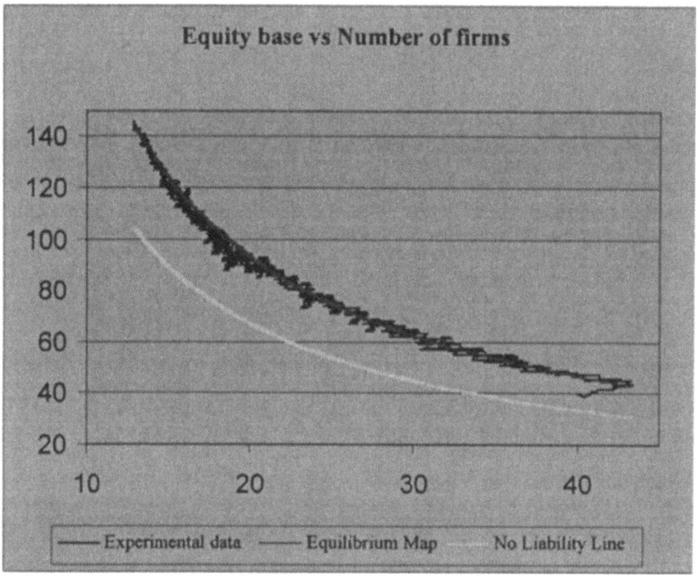


*Figure 7.15.* Equity base vs. number of firms. 13.000 timesteps.

time steps, in fact, correspond to the lower-right part of fig. 7.15, when the series of $A$ and $N$ gathered "normally" around the equilibrium map. The out of equilibrium behaviour depicted there corresponds roughly to time steps between 8.700 and 11.000; in the same period, the asymmetry of the distribution is about -0.2.

Moreover, during the same time span, the liabilities of firms' result higher than the average value, which is near to zero for the rest of the simulation. This is a recurrent fact in all simulations conducted, and is reflected in a positive correlation between asymmetry and average liability.

So far, we have only considered idiosyncratic shocks on prices. In a final battery of simulations, we tested the reaction of the model to shocks applying on the aggregated demand. In paragraph 3 above, we observed that if $N$ were continuous a temporary shock to a structural variable such $Y$ should end in the same position of equilibrium in which the system eventually lain before the shock; in any case, all the adjustments would happen along the same trajectory, this latter remaining unaffected by this kind of shocks.

We also observed that the consideration of the discrete nature of $N$ force us to relax these conclusions, since many other factors become relevant: the entity of the shock, since it influence the shape of the

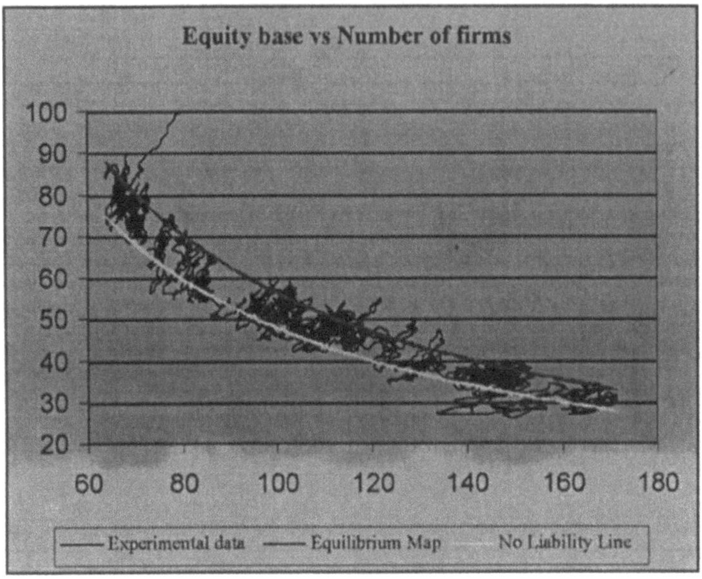


*Figure 7.16.* Asymmetry coefficient.

trajectory followed; the time span before a counter shock, since the entity of the impulse being equal it can select different trajectories in the "way back" to the initial map of equilibrium.

The test of an high number of different typologies of shocks would in any case be both incomplete and irrelevant: generality is in not assessable experimentally. We singled out here just one example which seem to have a methodological relevance. We let the aggregated demand be constituted by a fixed component and a random one:

$$Y_t = Y + \epsilon_t \tag{3.9}$$

with $E[\epsilon_t] = 0$ and $E[\epsilon_t \epsilon_s] = 0$ for $s \neq t$. This way one can "shake" the system without changing the relative competitive position of the firms, and the neutrality conclusion to which we arrived studying the dynamic in the continuous case can be tested. This neutrality conclusion can actually be considered a good approximation of the behaviour of the system, except for a slight tendency to "walk" up the map towards lower $N$ and higher $A$. I must be noted that since the lower are the values of $N$ the worse is the continuous approximation, this mechanism is self-reinforcing; anyhow, this bias towards higher zones of the map is quite weak, and surely not relevant for real markets of the kind emulated here[11]. From a methodological standpoint, however, the conclusion one can derive is that in cases in which some transactions occurs frequently, may be like in financial markets, the discrete nature of a variable can matter, but in directions not exactly forecastable. In our contest, for example, the tendency to "walk" up the map, at least in its strength, is quite sensible to the many other model details tested during the simulations. In these cases, the simulation of a model as close as possible to the rules that actually govern the market emulated seems unavoidable.

## 4. Conclusions

In this paper we studied the dynamic behaviour of a contestable market populated with almost zero-intelligence agents. This limitation on the "cognitive" capabilities of agents has been adopted to keep the focus on the mechanisms of entry-exit, and on the effects of equity base heterogeneity and of agents' interaction with statistics defined at the macrolevel.

The analytical study of the model has shown infinite equilibria for the market structure, dependence on initial conditions, and the possibility of two dynamic regimes ruling the movement of two subsets of the firms.

Casting the model in a stochastic framework and simulating it with an agent-based computational approach, some other features emerged: asymmetric distribution of firms' equity base, phase transition in the volatility of the equity base time series, out of equilibrium persistence. All of these features are strictly related to the presence of a subset of firms facing financial constraints, and hence following the different law of motion derived in the analytical study.

The theoretical relevance of these results stands firstly in their role as a benchmark for more sophisticated models considering firms' demography in presence of heterogeneity and of financial constraints. Secondly, as a raw analytical framework to help interpreting similar research programmes conducted following an ACE approach.

The relevance of these results in aiding the student to understand real world dynamics, would require a deeper consideration of the "zero intelligence" hypothesis imposed on firms, an assumption apparently even more "heroic" than those made when modelling them as intertemporal optimisers.

A complete discussion of this point is beyond the scope of this paper, but it should be stressed that some of the hypotheses adopted reflect more real world information imperfections than a "deeper" inadequacy of the agents. Somehow, they fit quite well with the hayekian idea of bounded knowledge: in large markets with knowledge dispersed between agents and "sedimented" in the market institutions, the only signals a firm can base its behaviour on are prices. Hence, for instance, to drive their entry-exit decision with just a direct comparison between the aggregate rate of profit and the interest rate, rather than implementing the expectations' formation on the discounted value of future profits, can be a way to grasp that idea.

The fact that in our artificial world we adopted other simplifications as an exogenous and constant demand – say, not an unpredictable one –, is from this point of view logically irrelevant. It is not necessary to build an intrinsically unpredictable demand to assume that an agent can not predict it.

## Notes

1. Two bibliographies can be found in [Caves, 1998] and [Brock - Evans, 1989].

2. Later we'll test two rules to determine the size of the new firms, and in the more realistic case we'll extract their size from the lower quantiles. With these hypotheses the smaller firms are also – on average – the younger, and the spread between creditor and debtor interest rate is formally equivalent to assume a borrowing constraint for younger firms, as for instance in [Martinelli, 1997].

3. On this assumption see footnote 6.

4. This proposition will not hold if $\alpha(1+r)=1$. In this case equations (2) and (3) are equal, and all the points of the first quadrant lying below this line are possible equilibria.

5. It can be observed that, mathematically, most of the dynamics here derived stems from the coincidence of the equilibrium conditions for the motion equations of $A$ and $N$: this gives rise to infinite equilibria, and adding "some noise" the rest follows. If one assumed that firms distributed a dividend different from $rA$, the dynamics would have collapsed to a rather simpler one. Anyhow, the theoretical role of this hypothesis was not bound to the choice of a "realistic portrait" of shareholders remuneration. This assumption has been adopted to grasp another point: what it be the proxy chosen to assess the profitability of a market, it seems quite fair to assume that with high (low) profits and no barriers to entry, *both* the number of competitors and the incumbents' equity tend to rise (fall). Hence the coincidence of the equilibrium conditions for $A$ and $N$.

6. It may be useful to stress that the fact that no firms enter the market isn't due to the presence of floors put on the difference between $r$ and the rate of profit, but to the fact that a low difference should imply the entry of just a "fraction" of a firm; as we observed, is a consequence of the discrete domain of $N$.

7. Letting $N$ vary in a discrete domain leads to the same kind of consideration just made. The continuum hypothesis is again a good approximation, but the effective behaviour should be assessed experimentally, as in next section.

8. The graphs presented here have been generated with the release 1.3.1. The code distributed, however, has been ported to the release 2.0.1.

9. For a discussion of the specificities of object-oriented simulations see [Joines - Roberts, 1999]. For economic simulations in Swarm see [Luna - Stefansson, 2000]. Technical details on the Swarm Toolkit can be found at http://www.swarm.org.

10. Namely, we imposed $r=0.04$, $\alpha=0.91$, $Y=5000$. The individual prices are uniformely extracted from the interval [0.9, 1.1).

11. With fluctuations of $Y$ kept under 10% and in a "reasonable" long period – say, no more that some hundred cycles – the equilibrium position do not vary significantly.

## References

Evolutionary Stochastic Dynamics, Multiple Equilibria, and Externalities as Field Effects, Cambridge University Press

William A. Brock - Steven N. Durlauf (2000), *Interaction-Based Models*, forthcoming in *Handbook of Econometrics*, Vol. 5, Elsevier

William A. Brock - David S. Evans (1989), *Small Business Economics*, "Small Business Economics", 1(1), 7-20

Richard E. Caves (1998), *Industrial Organization and New Findings on the Turnover and Mobility of Firms*, "Journal of Economic Literature", 36 (December 1998), pp. 1947-1982.

Rosaria Conte - Rainer Hegselmann - Pietro Terna (Eds.) (1997), *Simulating Social Phenomena*, Springer Verlag

Domenico Delli Gatti - Mauro Gallegati - Alan Kirman (Eds.) (2000), *Interaction and Market Structure: Essays on Heterogeneity in Economics*, Springer Verlag

Joshua M. Epstein (1999), *Agent Based Models and Generative Social Science*, "Complexity", IV (5)

Joshua M. Epstein - Robert L. Axtell (1996), *Growing Artificial Societies - Social Science from the Bottom Up*, Cambridge, MA: MIT Press

Mauro Gallegati - Alan P. Kirman (1999), *Beyond The Representative Agent*, Edward Elgar

Nigel Gilbert - Pietro Terna (2000), *How to Build and Use Agent-Based Models in Social Science*, "Mind & Society", (1) 1, 57-72

Dhananjay K. Gode - Shyam Sunder (1993), *Allocative Efficiency of Markets with Zero-Intelligence Traders*, "Journal of Political Economy", 101(1): 119-137

Dhananjay K. Gode - Shyam Sunder (1997), *What Makes Markets Allocationally Efficient?* "Quarterly Journal of Economics", 112(2): 603-30

Chris Goldspink (2000), *Modelling social systems as complex: Towards a social simulation meta-model*, "JASSS - Journal of Artificial Societies and Social Simulation" vol. 3, n. 2, http://www.soc.surrey.ac.uk/ /JASSS/3/2/1.html. Jeffrey A. Joines - Stephen D. Roberts (1999), *Simulation in an Object-Oriented World*, Proceedings of the 1999 Winter Simulation Conference

Alan P. Kirman (1992), *Whom or What Does The Representative Individual Represent*, "Journal of Economic Perspective", vol. 6, pp 117-136.

Robert E. Lucas, Jr. (1978), *On the Size Distribution of Business Firms*, "Bell Journal of Economics, 9(2), 508-23

Francesco Luna - Benedikt Stefansson (Eds.) (2000), *Economic Simulations in Swarm: Agent-Based Modelling and Object Oriented Programming*, Kluwer Academic Publishers

César Martinelli (1997), *Small firms, borrowing constraints, and reputation*, "Journal of Economic Behavior And Organization", 33 (1), pp. 91-105

Philip Mirowski - Koye Somefun, *Markets as Evolving Computational Entities*, 1998, paper presented at the Third Workshop on Economics with Heterogeneous Interacting Agents (WEHIA), 29-30 May 1998

Herbert A. Simon - Charles B. Bonini, *The Size Distribution of Business Firms*, "American Economic Revue", 48, 607-17

Pietro Terna (1998), *Simulation Tools for Social Scientists: Building Agent Based Models with Swarm*, "JASSS - Journal of Artificial Societies and Social Simulation" vol. 1, n. 2, http://www.soc.surrey.ac.uk//JASSS/1/2/4.html

# Chapter 8

# COGNITIVE AGENTS BEHAVING IN A SIMPLE STOCK MARKET STRUCTURE*

Pietro Terna
*Università di Torino,*
*Dipartimento di Scienze economiche e finanziarie G.Prato,*
*corso Unione Sovietica 218bis, 10134 Torino, Italy*
pietro.terna@unito.it

*Apri la mente a quel ch'io ti paleso*
*e fermalvi entro; ché non fa scïenza,*
*sanza lo ritenere, avere inteso.*

—Dante, *Paradiso, V*

**Abstract** We introduce here the SUM model—the Surprising (Un)realistic Market model—an agent based framework that allows us to deal with the micro-foundations of a stock market. We avoid any artificially simplified solution about price formation, such as to employ an auctioneer to clear the market; on the contrary, our model produces time series of prices continuously evolving, transaction by transaction.

The core of the model is represented by a computational structure that closely reproduces the behavior of the computerized book of a real

*This research has been supported by a grant from the Italian Consiglio Nazionale delle Ricerche, inside the project "Neural Networks for Economic Analysis: Adaptive Agent Models".

stock market. The agents send to the book their buy and sell orders, with the related limit prices.

The more interesting characteristic of this model is represented by the introduction of cognitive learning agents able to develop internally their behavioral rules. We have here the possibility of observing the effects of the presence of this kind of "minded" agents both on their own wealth and on the dynamics of the stock market as a whole.

Swarm represents the correct developing framework for our task: It provides us with a multilayer structure (the model and the observer looking at the model) and offers the computational power needed to run experiments with many agents of several types.

## 1. Introduction

The introductory quotation from Dante (*Paradiso, V*) can be translated as "An open mind is essential to understand novelties". It is introduced here as a premise to discuss the role of an "artificial mind" wired into the agents populating our simulation model, but also the role of the mind (or brain) in the actual behavior of economic agents. There is a little bit of arrogance in this purpose, but I hope that minds are open ... as Dante advocates.

The general idea is that in many cases the complexity of the economic situation is explained by the interaction of simple agents, mainly if behaving in a structured environment (see the random agents and bubbles and crashes in Section 4). So the question is: Are human agents so far from the complexity of the economic system, as ants are from their anthill? We also see here—and this is quite obvious—that only with the presence of "mind" a sort of intelligent behavior, useful to the agents, can emerge. The presence of "minded" agents affects the market, modifying the complexity of its structure: From the external point of view of the social scientist observing actual phenomena is a puzzle difficult to solve! Have we always to search for the effect of agents' rationality ("using" their mind) or can we open our minds and accept Axelrod's (1997) KISS principle[1]?

To discuss these ideas we present, in Subsection 1.1, an overview of the SUM model; in Section 2 the mind/no mind argument; in Section 3 the environment of our artificial experiment; in Section 4 the basic runs with random agents; in Section 5 the runs with other types of agent (market imitating agents in Subsection 5.1, locally imitating agents in Subsection 5.2, "stop loss" agents in Subsection 5.3); in Section 6 we introduce agents that apply estimates of future prices, with Subsection 6.1 describing the forecasting agent that produces those estimates via artificial neural network and Subsection 6.2 reporting the effects of the forecast application into the market; in Section 7 we have a mixed basic case, with stop loss agents and agents applying Section 6 estimates, as a basis for the successive steps; in Section 8 the structure of the cognitive agents is described, (the Cross Target method in Subsection 8.1 and the operating capabilities of this kind of agents in Subsection 8.2); the behavior of cognitive agents is presented in Section 9 with four cases (Subsections 9.1, 9.2, 9.3 and 9.4); finally, in Section 10, the conclusions.

## 1.1. An overview of the SUM model

The core of the Surprising (Un)realistic Market model (SUM) is represented by a computational structure that reproduces closely the behavior of the computerized book of a real stock market. The agents send to the book their buy and sell orders, with the related limit prices. The book executes immediately the orders if a counterpart is found in its log; otherwise, it records separately the buy and sell orders, to match them with future orders. The book is cleared at the beginning of each day.

A complex market emerges from the behavior of very simple random agents that: (i) know only the last executed price, (ii) choose randomly the buy or sell side and (iii) fix their limit price by multiplying the previously executed price times a random coefficient. This structure generates increasing and decreasing price sequences with relevant volatility. Also bubbles and crashes appear in this market, generated within the market structure, without the need of exogenous explanations.

In this framework, we then relax the hypothesis (i) for several groups of agents, in order to investigate the consequences of: (1) the presence of subjects using technical trading rules or continuously trained Artificial Neural Networks (ANNs) to forecast the future market prices; (2) the presence of cognitive agents able to learn from their experience and applying external goals in a CT (Cross Target) scheme, according to the methodology proposed in Terna (2000a). In some way, the groups of agents using ANNs as forecasting tools, or within the CT framework, can correspond to the artificially intelligent agents behaving as econometricians proposed by Sargent (1993).

More generally, within this model we can investigate empirical puzzles that are hard to understand using the traditional representative agent structure. Among these puzzles, the time series predictability and the volatility persistence.

The agents that forecast prices with ANNs, employ those generalized functions as econometric tools, fitting them to price series. The CT cognitive agents hold in input their past behavior and series of prices; they must develop the capability of matching their guesses about actions that have to be taken and about the effects of those actions. They have also to develop the strategic ability of buying, selling or doing nothing, in order to cope with the External Objective (in CT jargon) of increasing their wealth.

So we have here both an *econometrics with neural networks* and an *economics with neural networks.*

Swarm represents here the correct developing framework: It provides a multilayer structure and offers the computational power needed to run the experiments with a large number of agents [2]. Here, the multilayer structure contains: (i) the observer layer, that shows the results, and (ii) the model layer, that runs either the time schedule and the environment, with the stock market book and the multiple groups of agents. The use of ANNs and CT scheme in Swarm is based here upon the bp-ct package introduced by Terna (2000a).

## 2. "Minded" or "no minded" agents in our models

According to Gilbert and Terna (2000):

> Ostrom (1988) proposed that there are three different "symbol systems" available to social scientists: The familiar verbal argumentation and mathematics, but also a third way, computer simulation. Computer simulation, or computational modelling, involves representing a model as a computer program. Computer programs can be used to model either quantitative theories or qualitative ones. They are particularly good at modelling processes and although non-linear relationships can generate some methodological problems, there is no difficulty in representing them within a computer program.
>
> The logic of developing models using computer simulation is not very different from the logic used for the more familiar statistical models. In either case, there is some phenomenon that we as researchers want to understand better. This is the "target". We build a model of the target through a theoretically motivated process of abstraction (this model may be a set of mathematical equations, a statistical equation, such as a regression equation, or a computer program). We then examine the behaviour of the model and compare it with observations of the social world. If the output from the model and the data collected from the social world are sufficiently similar, we use this as evidence in favour of the validity of the model (or use a lack of similarity as evidence for disconfirmation).

The question now is: If our computer simulation model is based upon agents (e.g. built with Swarm, as the models presented here), to what extent must our agents be sophisticated? Should we provide them with a "mind"? The answer ranges from the simplicity principle Axelrod, 1997 to the use of full BDI (Beliefs, Intentions, Desires) cognitive agents.

A possible classification is:

A. "no-minded" agents, that behave in an unstructured environment;

B. learning or "minded" agents, that behave in an unstructured environment;

C. "no minded" agents, operating in a structured environment;

D. learning or "minded" agents, operating in a structured environment.

In Terna (2000b) we discuss different models with rigid "no-minded" agents that behave in an unstructured market generating cycles and chaos, or with learning "minded" agents, that assure some stability to an emerging unstructured market.

Here, in Section 4, 5 and 6.1, we present "no minded" agents operating in a structured stock market (case C), with the sophisticated outcome of bubbles and crashes. In Section 8 we have "minded" agents, operating in a structured environment (case D) with effects both on the individual behavior and the related results on the market as a whole.

No generalized results come from this presentation, but many useful suggestions ...

For a general discussion of agent based models, see Axtell (2000) and the introductory paper Tesfatsion, 2001 on the Journal of Economic Dynamic and Control, vol.24, special issue 3-4.

## 3. The artificial experiment environment

The artificial experiments that we introduce here are based on SUM v,0.65; you can download[3] the package[4] and run it with Swarm 2.1.

The parameters are the following.

- In the Observer (the Swarm side of the program related to the observation of the results) we have two basic parameters (and many technical switches about graphics and files, not reported here).

– *displayFrequency*, the frequency at which the graphic widgets are updated; e.g. if its value is 1000, only one price every 1000 will be reported in the graph; a good choice is to employ the total number of the agents to obtain the last price of each simulated day (each agent does one action per day).

– *stopAtEpochNumber*, the number of simulated days at which the run will stop; a day is the time required to allow all the agents to make an action; any action is a tick of a clock that makes agentNumber (see below) ticks per day.

In the following experiments we have always the following values: displayFrequency = 300 and stopAtEpochNumber = 2000.

- In the Model (the Swarm side of the program related to the execution of the agent based simulation) we have several crucial parameters.

- *agentNumber*: The number of agents present in the model in each day; this value is internally calculated as a sum of the following parameters:

  - *randomAgentNumber*: The number of agents acting in a random way, as described in Section 4;
  - *marketImitatingAgentNumber*: Agents choosing the buy or sell side by imitation, i.e. buying if the market mean price is increasing from day $-2$ to day $-1$ and selling if the price is decreasing; see Subsection 5.1;
  - *locallyImitatingAgentNumber*: Agents choosing the buy or sell side on the basis of the majority of the decisions of the last N agents (here N = 20, see *localHistoryLength*) as in Subsection 5.2;
  - *stopLossAgentNumber*: Agents that sell or buy to stop loss (we can account for the real agent situation, i.e. if it is "long" or "short" on the market following the parameter *checkingIfShortOrLong* reported below) if the current price is decreasing or increasing, at a rate greater or equal to the *maxLossRate* parameter, when compared to the mean price of the day $t - stopLossInterval$; see below and Subsection 5.3;
  - *aNNForecastAppAgentNumber*: Agents that follow the forecasts made by a forecasting agent (see Subsection 6.1), buying or selling in a consistent way with the estimates of futures prices; all the uncovered operations are allowed (selling without shares and buying without cash), as described in Subsection 6.2;
  - *bPCTAgentAEO_EP_0_Number* or *EP_1*, *EP_2*, *EP_3*: these are CT agents[5] of type $A$[6], not used here;
  - *bPCTAgentBEO_EP_0_Number* or *EP_1*, *EP_2*, *EP_3*: these are CT agents of type $B$, introduced in Subsection 8.2. The

cognitive agents used to build our artificial experiment, classified as case D in Section 2 (using a structured environment with "minded" agents).

- Global parameters.

- *asymmetricBuySellProb*: If one of the two imitative strategies described above is adopted, this is the probability $p$ (here 0.9) of buying or selling as the imitative behavior suggests or of doing the opposite $(1 - p)$.

  In absence of an imitative behavior, i.e. in the case of random agents, the probability of choosing the buy or the sell side of the market is 0.5.

- *minCorrectingCoefficient*: The min value (here 0.9) of the random multiplying coefficient $k$ used to fix the price of an agent's buy or sell proposal ('last price' times $k$). This random correction of the buying or selling price to be sent to the book is used by all the types of agents to introduce a little bit of inconsistence or randomness in agents' behavior; it is also the micro source of the price movement in our simulation experiments[7]. Only the stop loss agents, when adopting the stop loss strategy, use directly the last executed price for their proposal.

- *maxCorrectingCoefficient*: The max value (here 1.1) of the previous $k$ coefficient.

- *asymmetricRange*: The correction added to the previous min and max limits to adopt an asymmetric behavior, if any (this parameter is not used in this paper).

- *agentProbToActBeforeOpening*: The probability of placing an order in the opening phase (here 0.05); so a day starts without an empty book, with a realistic effect (anyway, not crucial for the results); all the types of agents reported above use this parameter.

- *floorP*: The floor price (here 0.3, with 1.0 as first price of the simulation) said below; all the types of agents reported above, but the CT agents of type $A$ or $B$, use this parameter and the next one.

- *agentProbToActBelowFloorPrice*: The probability (here 0.5) that an agent would buy if the price falls below floorP.

- *maxOrderQuantity*: The max buying or selling quantity in each order placed by an agent (once a day); the actual quantity $n$ is an integer number chosen randomly in a range from 1 to *maxOrderQuantity*[8]; all the types of agents reported above use this parameter.

- Parameters used by imitating agents (see Subsections 5.1 and 5.2).

- *meanPriceHistoryLength*: The length (here 200) of the vector of mean prices; this parameter is used also by the forecasting agent of Subsection 6.1.

- *localHistoryLength*: The length (here 20) of the vector recording agent actions.

- Parameters used by "stop loss" agents (see Subsection 5.3).

- *maxLossRate*: here 0.10; see above, sub *stopLossAgentNumber*.

- *stopLossInterval*: here 2; see above, sub *stopLossAgentNumber*.

- *checkingIfShortOrLong*: here 1 or *yes*; see above, sub *stopLossAgentNumber*.

- Parameters used by the forecasting agent (see Subsection 6.1).

- *dataWindowLength*: The number of data (here 30), used as inputs of the Artificial Neural Network (ANN); data are return indexes of each daily mean price upon the same value of $-nAheadForecasting$ days before[9].

- *nAheadForecasting*: The output of the ANN is the estimate $\frac{p_n}{p_0}$ (here $n = 10$; see the previous note).

- *forecastingTrainingSetLength*: The number of sequences (here 100) of input data and expected output used to train the ANN; this is a moving training set, which is modified with the internal time of our experiment; note that it must be $meanPriceHistoryLength \geq forecastingTrainingSetLength + nAheadForecasting$ and the artificial neural network training starts only at day $forecastingTrainingSetLength + nAheadForecasting + 1$.

- *epochNumberInEachForecastingTrainingCycle*: The number of the learning epochs (here 100) in each training phase of the ANN; an epoch contains *forecastingTrainingSetLength* training cycles.

- *learningProcessEveryNDays*: Every *NDays* (here 10) we repeat the training of the ANN (here with 10,000 training cycles).

- *cleanForecastingANNEveryMgtemNDays*: Every *M* days (50 in our case; *MgtemN* stays for *M greater than or equal and multiple of N*) the learning process restarts from scratch, with initial random parameters (the ANN weights[10]) to account for major changes in the structure of our input data.

- Parameters used by agents applying ANN forecasts (see Subsection 6.2).

  - *aNNInactivityRange*: The range (here 0.02 or 2%) of the relative forecasted modification of price in which this kind of agent is inactive (doing nothing) even if the following parameter allows it to act.

  - *aNNForecastAppAgentActDailyProb*: The probability (here 0.1) of acting within each day; this parameter is introduced as a realistic characteristic of the agents that operate on the basis of forecasting and so do not modify continuously their behavior.

- Parameters used by CT agents of type *A* or *B* (type *A* is not used here; for type *B*, see Subsection 8.2).

  - *epochNumberInEachBPCTTrainingCycle*: The epoch number (100 in our case) in long term learning, applied every day on a moving data set of the last 10 days[11].

  - *agentAEO_EPDelta*: A parameter used to measure the effect of External Objectives (EO) for CT agents of type *A* (here 0.1, but never used, because we have no type *A* agents in this set of experiments).

  - *agentBEO_EPDelta*: A parameter used to measure the effect of EO for CT agents of type *B* (here 10 as default value, but modified in the experiments reported Section 9).

## 4. Basic runs: random agents only

In this first application of our experimental environment, we are in the case of "no minded" agents, operating in a structured environment (case C of Section 2).

In the runs reported in Figures 8.1 and 8.2, we adopt the hypotheses (i), (ii) and (iii) introduced above (Subsection 1.1). Our random agents[12] know only the last executed price, choose randomly the buy or sell side and fix their limit price by multiplying the previously executed price times a random coefficient (see Section 3 about the parameters used).

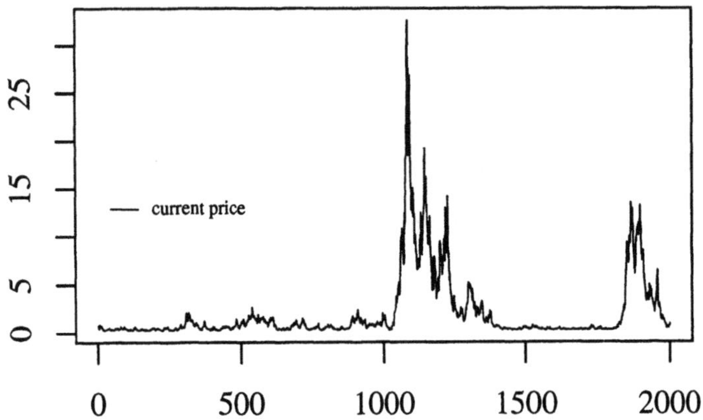


*Figure 8.1.* Random agents: The price sequence of the first basic simulation, with *randomAgentNumber* = 100 and *maxOrderQuantity* = 6.

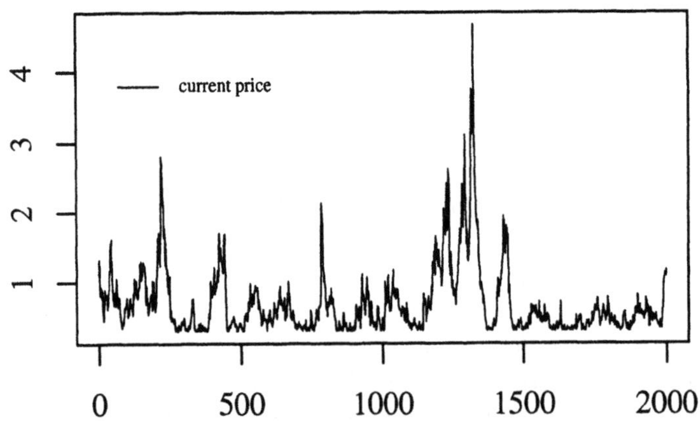


*Figure 8.2.* Random agents: The price sequence of the second basic simulation, with *randomAgentNumber* = 300 and *maxOrderQuantity* = 3.

We introduce also the rule of buying with a fixed probability (here $p = 0.5$) if the price falls below a specific floor.

Bubbles and crashes appearing in this framework are a direct consequence of the structure (the electronic book) of the market.

The emergence of this kind of anomalies in a model of type C is particularly interesting, because it shows the importance of rules (here the technical structure of the market) in influencing the behavior and, mainly, the interaction among agents. So simple agents produce complex results.

Prices are generated transaction by transaction, one per tick (if the agent required to act in a tick does not act, the price is kept unchanged).

As we have seen introducing the *displayFrequency* parameter above in Section 3, we display on the graph only one price every day (the last one).

We are looking here for a basic situation, choosing a number of random agents, and a max quantity of orders for each agent in each day, in order to generate a market with limited bubbles and crashes.

Few agents, with more than one order as max order quantity for each agent and day, can generate a world with huge bubbles and crashes, interesting *per se*, but not easy to be used to investigate the role of different types of agents in the models.

This is the case of Figure 8.1 where we have a run with 100 random agents that can place up to 6 orders per day.

We can also investigate the predictability of the market. Considering the log of the "book" operating in the experiment reported in Figure 8.1, i.e. the number of unmatched buy orders ($b$) and the number of unmatched sell orders ($s$) at the end of each day (as a proxy of the same measures at the exact tick where a bubble or a crash begins), we can simply estimate the $R^2$ coefficient in $pi = c_0 + c_1 b + c_2 s$, where $pi$ is a daily price index calculated upon last prices as $\frac{p_0}{p_{-1}}$, and we obtain $R^2 = 0.35$. The presence of (rare) sequences of actions on the same side of the market is the explanation of huge movements in prices. If we have a lot of random agents with a limited quantity of orders in each tick, the white noise effect prevails and we have a regular market.

In this first basic experiment we consider also the estimates of the prices 10 days ahead (this is a parametric choice) made by a forecasting agent that is looking at the market, but not acting in it. The forecasting agent, based upon an artificial neural network, is introduced in Subsection 6.1.

A simple test about the estimate success is the count of the quota of correct forecasting signs (here 52%).

Besides the interest on bubbles and crashes, our goal here is to obtain a relatively stable market. So we increase the number of random agents, lowering the max quantity of orders in each tick to 3, as in the run reported in Figure 8.2. (The quota of correct forecasting signs is here 48%).

In Figure 8.3 we can also verify the effect of the agents' behavior on their wealth, evaluated as liquidity plus shares at the daily mean price. Initial endowments are zero liquidity and shares; agents can anyway operate doing uncovered operations without limits. We show here our random agents min, max and mean wealth. Being the random agents (r. in the Figure) the unique category of agents in the market (the totality of the agents, in this case) the mean wealth is zero by definition (the

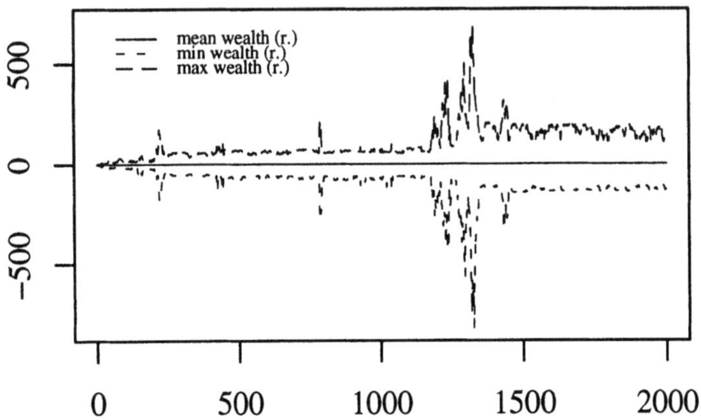


*Figure 8.3.* Random agents: The wealth series of the second basic simulation, with $randomAgentNumber = 300$ (r.) and $maxOrderQuantity = 3$.

exchanges, via the book, are always among agents); min and max shows the possibility of huge gains or losses adopting a random (obviously, on the border lines we have different agents as the time evolves).

## 5. Introducing other types of agents

To evaluate the effects of the presence of phenomena such as imitation and "stop loss" strategies, we introduce now new categories of agents. Our goal is both to explore the effects of the action of these types of artificial subjects and to build a sound framework for the introduction of agents able to apply market forecasts (Section 6) and for the experiments with cognitive or "minded" agents (Section 9).

### 5.1. Market imitating agents

We have here, within the basic structure of Section 4, the presence of market imitating agents[13].

Referring to Subsection 1.1 we relax now the hypotheses (i)—to know only the last executed price—and (ii)—to choose randomly, in a balanced way, the buy or sell side—for a small quota of the agents, in order to investigate the consequences of the presence of subjects imitating the market (general imitation). Their choice—to buy or to sell—will be unbalanced, according to the probability $p = asymmetricBuySellProb$ introduced in Section 3.

The parameter $p$ measures the probability that an agent would choose the buy or sell side as an imitative act of the market as a whole, buying with probability $p$ if the mean price is increasing from day $t-2$ to day

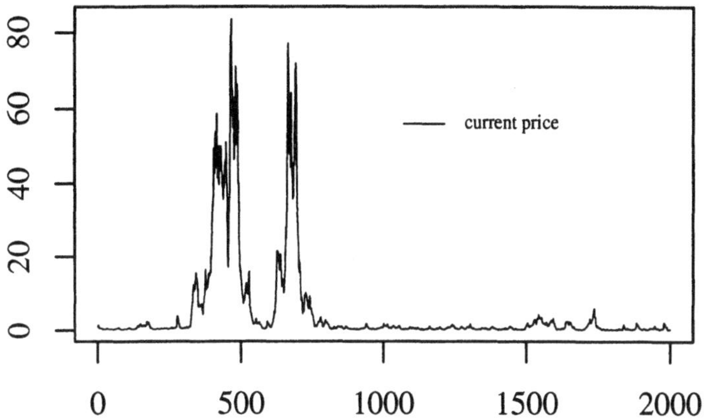


*Figure 8.4.* Market imitating agents: The price sequence of the simulation with *randomAgentNumber* = 285, *marketImitatingAgentNumber* = 15 and *maxOrderQuantity* = 3.

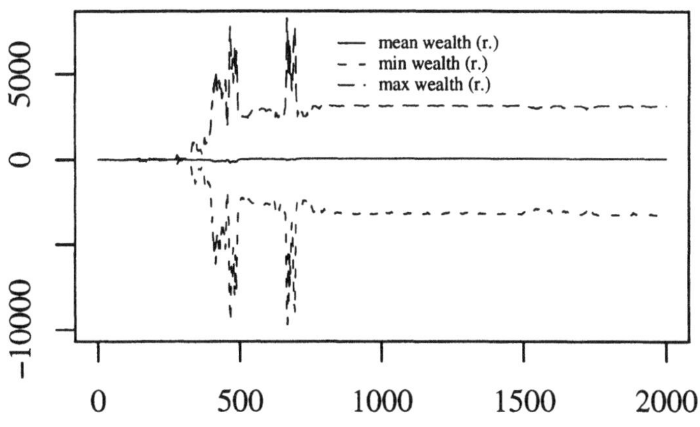


*Figure 8.5.* Market imitating agents: The wealth series simulation with *randomAgentNumber* = 285 (r.), *marketImitatingAgentNumber* = 15 and *maxOrderQuantity* = 3.

$t-1$ and selling with the same probability if the price is decreasing; this is an imitation effect, but also a proxy of the behavior of "chartists" Lo *et al.*, 2000. The presence of this kind of agents—also in a small quota—greatly increases the appearance of bubbles and crashes.

In Figure 8.4 we report the price sequence of a run of the simulation with market imitating agents, with two enormous bubbles. The quota of correct forecasting signs is here 53%.

In Figures 8.5 (random agents) and 8.6 (market imitating agents) we have the effect of the agents' behavior on their wealth[14]. Remembering

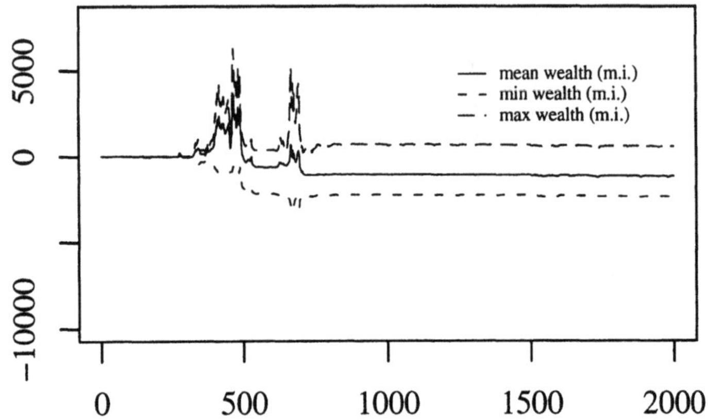


*Figure 8.6.* Market imitating agents: The wealth series simulation with *randomAgentNumber* = 285, *marketImitatingAgentNumber* = 15 (m.i.) and *maxOrderQuantity* = 3.

that on the border lines we have different agents as the time evolves, we can see the enormous consequences of these types of behavior in agents endowments and the special effect of imitation, in limiting losses.

## 5.2. Locally imitating agents

We have here, always within the basic structure of Section 4, the presence of locally imitating agents[15].

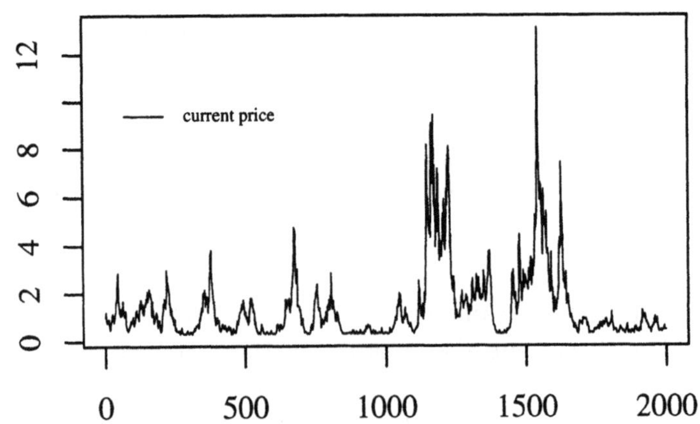


*Figure 8.7.* Locally imitating agents: The price sequence of the simulation with *randomAgentNumber* = 285, *locallyImitatingAgentNumber* = 15 and *maxOrderQuantity* = 3.

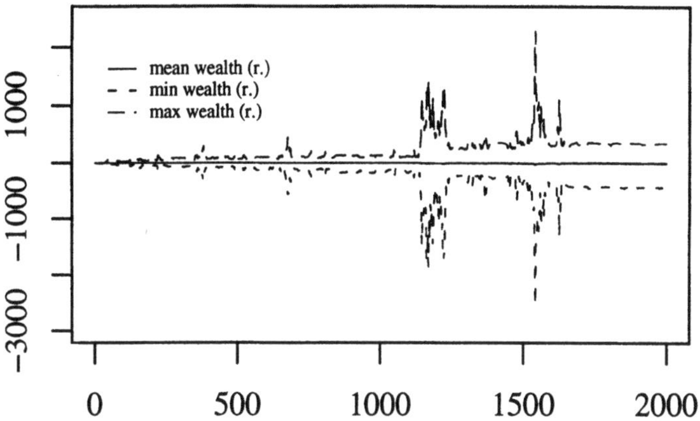


*Figure 8.8.* Locally imitating agents: The wealth series simulation with *randomAgentNumber* = 285 (r.), *locallyImitatingAgentNumber* = 15 and *maxOrderQuantity* = 3.

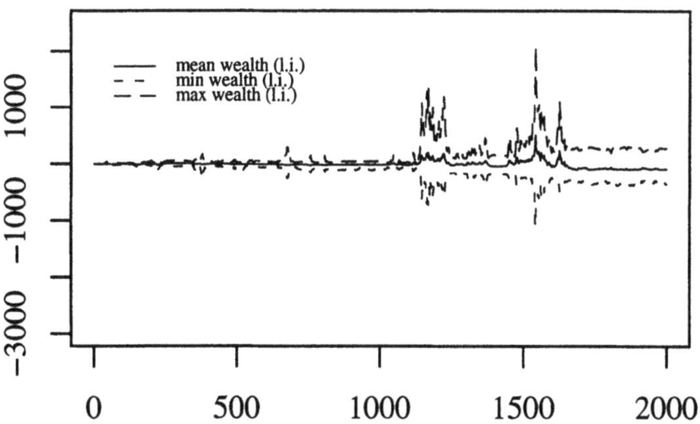


*Figure 8.9.* Locally imitating agents: The wealth series simulation with *randomAgentNumber* = 285, *locallyImitatingAgentNumber* = *15* (l.i.) and *maxOrderQuantity* = 3.

Referring to Subsection 1.1 we again relax the hypotheses (i)—to know only the last executed price—and (ii)—to choose randomly, in a balanced way, the buy or sell side—for a small quota of the agents, in order to investigate the consequences of the presence of subjects locally imitating other agents' behavior (local imitation). Their choice to buy or sell will be unbalanced, according to the probability $p = asymmetricBuySellProb$ introduced in Section 3.

$p$ is the probability of buying or selling following the majority of the last $n = localHistoryLength$ (here $n = 20$) agents' decisions. The "local history" sequence—which is a moving window continuously updated—does not consider idle agents (this is especially important in the opening phase, where only a little quota of the agents is active).

In Figure 8.7 we report the price sequence of a run of the simulation with locally imitating agents, with two bubbles, but not of the dimension of those of the market imitation case. This kind of market structure has a low predictability: The quota of correct forecasting signs is here 47%.

In Figures 8.8 (random agents) and 8.9 (locally imitating agents) we have the effect of the agents' behavior on their wealth[16]. Remembering that on the border lines we have different agents as the time evolves, we can see the relevant effect of these types of behavior on agents endowments and again the special effect of imitation, in limiting losses.

## 5.3. Stop loss behavior

We have here, again within the basic structure of Section 4, the presence of "stop loss" agents[17].

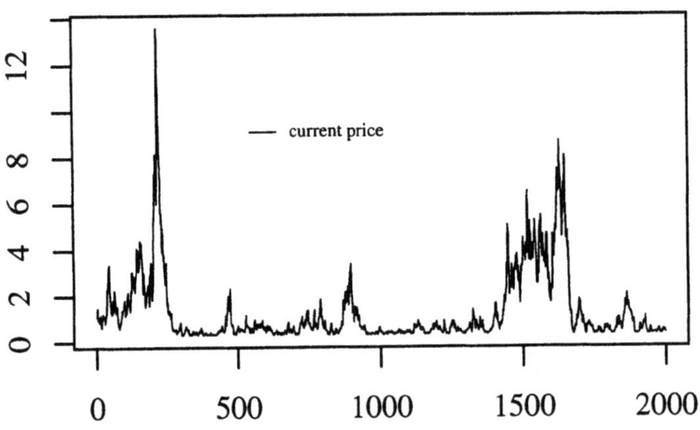


*Figure 8.10.* "Stop loss" agents: The price sequence of the simulation with *randomAgentNumber* = 285, *stopLossAgentNumber* = 15 and *maxOrderQuantity* = 3.

We have here agents that sell or buy to stop a loss[18] if the current price, compared to the mean price of the day $t - stopLossInterval$ (see Section 3), is decreasing or increasing at a rate greater or equal to the *maxLossRate* parameter.

In Figure 8.10 we report a run with stop loss agents (if loss > 10% in two days, agents apply stop loss). The effect of stop loss is to produce reasonable bubbles. The quota of correct forecasting signs is here 54%, so this kind of market appears to have an interesting degree of predictability.

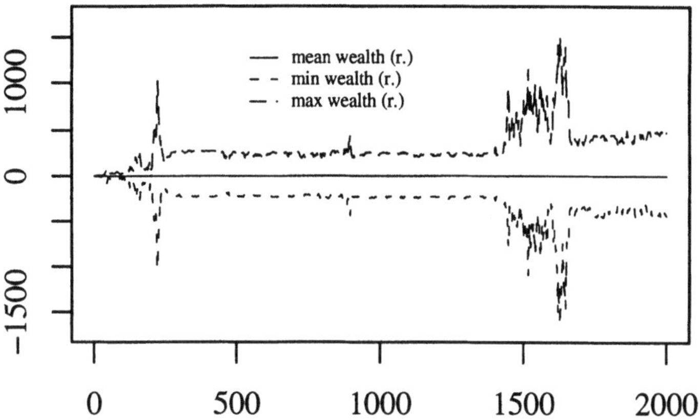


*Figure 8.11.* "Stop loss" agents: The wealth series simulation with *randomAgentNumber* = 285 (r.), *stopLossAgentNumber* = 15 and *maxOrderQuantity* = 3.

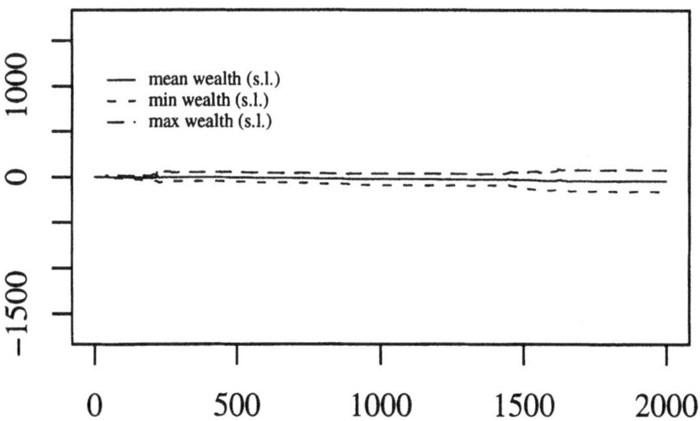


*Figure 8.12.* "Stop loss" agents: The wealth series simulation with *randomAgentNumber* = 285, *stopLossAgentNumber* = 15 (s.l.) and *maxOrderQuantity* = 3.

In Figures 8.11 and 8.12 we have the consequences of the two types of behavior on the wealth of the agents, with—as always—huge gains or losses for the agents (r.) operating by chance, but also with a defensive situation of stop loss agents (s.l.).

## 6. Agents applying ANN estimates of future prices

We introduce now the "applying ANN forecast agents", or more simply "applying forecast agents" (a.f.a.), that follow the estimates of the forecasting agent described below.

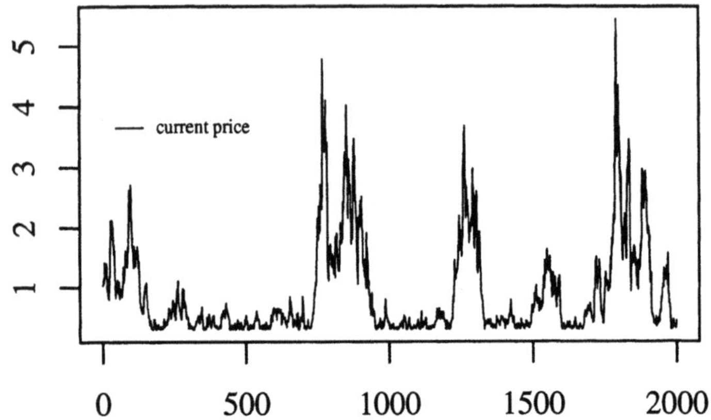


*Figure 8.13.* Applying forecast agents: The price sequence of the simulation with *randomAgentNumber* = 285, *aNNForecastAppAgentNumber* = 15 and *maxOrderQuantity* = 3.

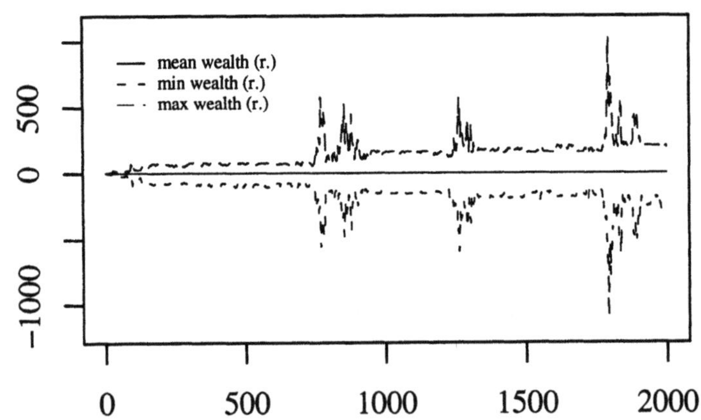


*Figure 8.14.* Applying forecast agents: The wealth series simulation with *randomAgentNumber* = 285 (r.), *aNNForecastAppAgentNumber* = 15 and *maxOrderQuantity* = 3.

We are here near to the field of self-fulfilling prophecies. Our forecaster uses N ANN to produce its estimates and the quality of the estimates is related to the degree of predictability of the market; but as we can see below, if a lot of agents apply those estimates to behave, we have a strong reinforcing feedback to the predictability of the market[19].

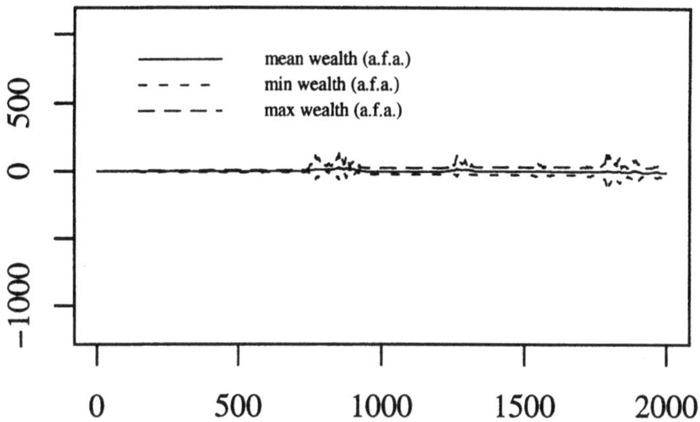


*Figure 8.15.* Applying forecast agents: The wealth series simulation with *randomAgentNumber* = 285, *aNNForecastAppAgentNumber* = 15 (a.f.a.) and *maxOrderQuantity* = 3.

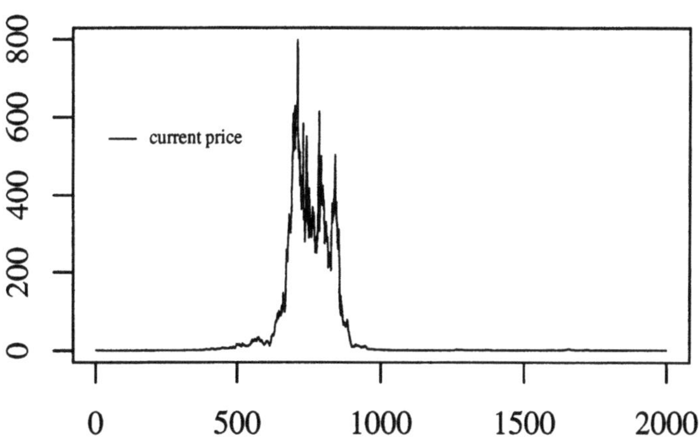


*Figure 8.16.* Applying forecast agents: The price sequence of the simulation with *randomAgentNumber* = 270, *aNNForecastAppAgentNumber* = 30 and *maxOrderQuantity* = 3.

## 6.1. The forecasting agent

We build a new agent, not behaving in the market, that produces in each day a forecast of the stock market price *nAheadForecasting* (here 10) days ahead.

Referring to parameters of Section 3, the forecaster uses an Artificial Neural Network (ANN) with *dataWindowLength* (here 30) data as inputs. Data are return indexes of each daily mean price upon the same value of $-nAheadForecasting$ days before. The output of the ANN is the estimate $\frac{p_n}{p_0}$ (here $n = 10$). *forecastingTrainingSetLength* is the number of sequences (here 100) of input data and expected output used to train the ANN; this is a moving training set, which is modified with the internal time of our experiment. *epochNumberInEachForecastingTrainingCycle* is the number or learning epochs (here 100) in each training phase of the ANN; an epoch contains *forecastingTrainingSetLength* training cycles.

Every *learningProcessEveryNDays* days (here 10) we repeat the training of the ANN (here with 10,000 training cycles). Finally, every *cleanForecastingANNEveryMgtemNDays* days (here 50) the learning process restarts from scratch, with initial random parameters (the ANN weights) to account for major changes in the structure of our input data.

The number of hidden nodes is internally determined as one half the input nodes number; this value can be externally established adding a line with 'hiddenNodeNumber x' into the file `forecasting.setup`.

For a concise introduction to ANN technique, considering multylayer feedforward ANNs trained with the backpropagation technique, see Section 4 in Terna (2000a).

## 6.2. The effects of the forecast application

We have here, always within the basic structure of Section 4, the presence of agents[20] behaving consistently with the estimates of the forecasting agent, acting with uncovered operations in a mechanical way (buying or selling whenever the prediction is respectively greater or less than the current price).

More specifically, agents do not operate if the forecast price index is $> 1 + aNNInactivityRange$ or $< 1 - aNNInactivityRange$. Agents also avoid nonsense situations, not acting if the current price is already over the forecast one.

In Figure 8.13 we report the price sequence of a run of the simulation with a limited number (15) of applying forecast agents, with a reasonable movement in prices and small bubbles. The quota of correct forecasting signs is here 52%.

In Figures 8.14 (random agents) and 8.15 (applying forecast agents) we have the effect of the agents' behavior on their wealth. Remembering that on the border lines we have different agents as the time evolves, we can see the consequences of these types of behavior in agents endowments and the special effect of forecast application, with a limited advantage of gains against losses, while in random behavior losses seem to prevail.

In Figure 8.16 we report the price sequence of a run of the simulation obtained doubling to 30 the number of applying forecast agents, with an "astronomical" bubble. The quota of correct forecasting signs is here 58%, as we are close to a situation of self-fulfilling prophecies.

## 7. A mixed basic case, with stop loss agents and agents applying ANN estimates

This is the key case used in Section 8 to introduce the simulations with the cognitive CT agents of type B.

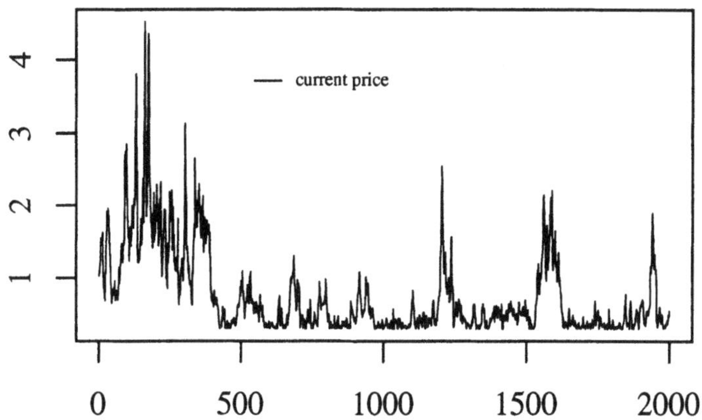


*Figure 8.17.* Mixed basic case: The price sequence of the simulation with *randomAgentNumber* = 275, *aNNForecastAppAgentNumber* = 15, *stopLossAgentNumber* = 10 and *maxOrderQuantity* = 3.

Our goal here is to produce a basic structure with a good level of predictability, without unstable or explosive situations. So we join a limited number of "applying forecast agents" (Subsection 6.2) and of "stop loss" agents (Subsection 5.3) to obtain a market such as the one reported in Figure 8.17, with a quota of correct forecasting signs of 55%. Also the effects on the agents' wealth are bounded in reasonable limits (±300 for the random agents).

## 8. The structure of the CT cognitive agents

We finally introduce "minded" agents in a structured market (case D of the classification reported in Section 2).

We use here the CT scheme Terna, 2000a, which will be briefly explained in Subsection 8.1. This kind of agent uses forecasts as proxies of the true model of the economy; in some way, these are agents applying rational expectations in the Sargent (1993) sense, mentioned in Subsection 1.1.

## 8.1. The CT method

To develop our agent based experiments, we introduce the following general hypothesis (GH): an agent, acting in an economic environment, must develop and adapt her capability of evaluating, in a coherent way, (1) what she has to do in order to obtain a specific result and (2) how to foresee the consequences of her actions. The same is true if the agent is interacting with other agents. Beyond this kind of internal consistency (IC), agents can develop other characteristics, for example the capability of adopting actions (following external proposals, EPs) or evaluations of effects (following external objectives, EOs) suggested from the environment (for example, following rules) or from other agents (for examples, imitating them). Those additional characteristics are useful for a better tuning of the agents in making experiments.

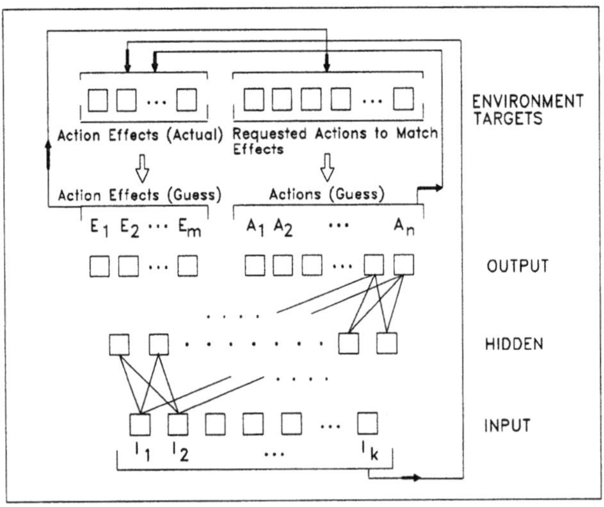


*Figure 8.18.* The Cross-Target (CT) scheme.

The name Cross-Targets (CTs) comes from the technique used to figure out the targets necessary to train the ANNs representing the artificial agents that populate our experiments.

Following the GH, the main characteristic of these agents is that of developing internal consistency between what to do and the related consequences. Always according to the GH, in many (economic) situations, the behavior of agents produces evaluations that can be split in two parts: data quantifying actions (what to do) and forecasts of the outcomes of the actions. So we specify two types of outputs of the ANN and, identically, of the agent: (i) actions to be performed and (ii) guesses about the effects of those actions.

We choose the neural networks approach to develop CT method, mostly as a consequence of the intrinsic adaptive capabilities of neural functions.

Figure 8.18 describes an agent learning and behaving in a CT scheme. The agent has to produce guesses about its own actions and related effects, on the basis of an information set (the input elements are $I_1, ..., I_k$). Remembering the requirement of IC, targets in learning process are: (i) on one side, the actual effects—measured through accounting rules—of the actions made by the simulated subject; (ii) on the other side, the actions needed to match guessed effects. In the last case we have to use inverse rules, even though some problems arise when the inverse is indeterminate. Technical explanations of CT method Beltratti *et al.*, 1996 are reported also in Section 5 in Terna (2000a).

A first remark, about learning and CT: by analyzing the changes of the weights during the process we can show that the matrix of weights linking input elements to hidden ones has little or no changes, while the matrix of weights from hidden to output layer changes in a relevant way. Only hidden-output weight changes determine the continuous adaptation of ANN responses to the environment modifications, as the output values of hidden layer elements stay almost constant. This situation is the consequence both of very small changes in targets (generated by CT method) and of a reduced number of learning cycles.

The resulting network is certainly under trained: consequently, the simulated economic agent develops a local ability to make decisions, but only by adaptations of outputs to the last targets, regardless to input values. This is *short term* learning as opposed to *long term* learning.

Some definitions: we have (i) short term learning, in the acting phase, when agents continuously modify their weights (mainly from the hidden layer to the output one), to adapt to the targets self-generated via CT; (ii) long term learning, ex post, when we effectively map inputs to targets (the same generated in the acting phase) with a large number of learning cycles, producing ANNs able to definitively apply the rules implicitly developed in the acting and learning phase.

A second remark, about both external objectives (EOs) and external proposals (EPs): if used, these values substitute the cross targets in the acting and adapting phase and are consistently included in the data set for ex post learning. Despite the target coming from actions, the guess of an effect can be trained to approximate a value suggested by a simple rule, for example increasing wealth. This is an EO in CT terminology. Its indirect effect, via CT, will modify actions, making them more consistent with the (modified) guesses of effects. Vice versa, the guess about an action to be accomplished can be modified via an EP, affecting indirectly also the corresponding guesses of effects. If EO, EP and IC conflict in determining behavior, complexity may emerge also within agents, but in a bounded rationality perspective, always without the optimization and full rationality apparatus.

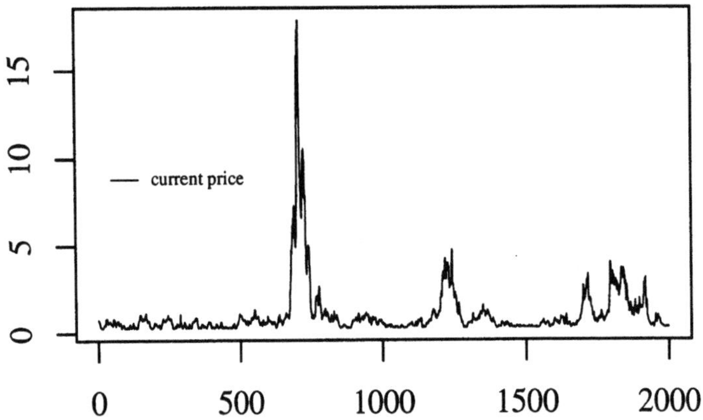


*Figure 8.19.* CT agents: The price sequence of the simulation with *randomAgentNumber* = 270, *aNNForecastAppAgentNumber* = 15, *stopLossAgentNumber* = 10 and *maxOrderQuantity* = 3, *BPCTB* = 5 and *EO* = 2, *d* = 5.

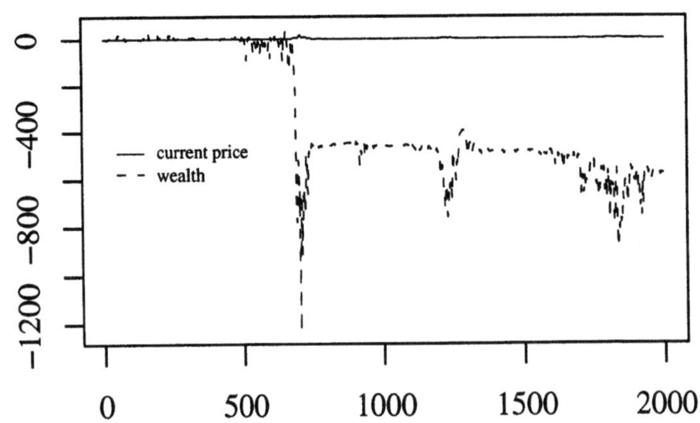


*Figure 8.20.* CT agents: Price and agent wealth series with *randomAgentNumber* = 270, *aNNForecastAppAgentNumber* = 15, *stopLossAgentNumber* = 10 and *maxOrderQuantity* = 3, *BPCTB* = 5 and *EO* = 2, *d* = 5.

Now we may introduce some technical explanations about CTs, with the aid of the general scheme of Figure 8.18, observing that (i) the inputs of the model are mainly data coming from the environment or

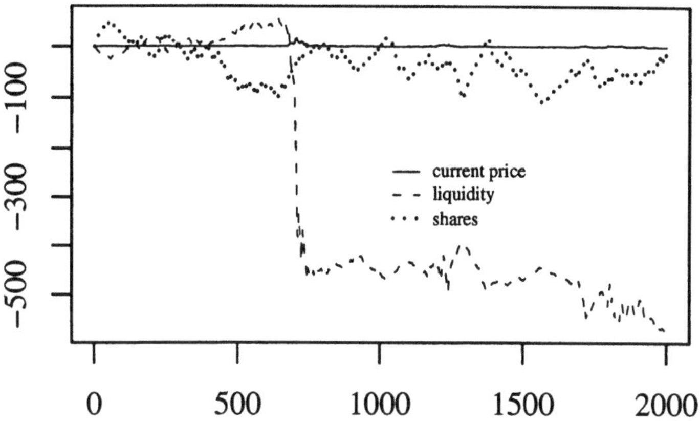


*Figure 8.21.* CT agents: Price, liquidity and shares series with *randomAgentNumber* = 270, *aNNForecastAppAgentNumber* = 15, *stopLossAgentNumber* = 10 and *maxOrderQuantity* = 3, *BPCTB* = 5 and *EO* = 2, *d* = 5.

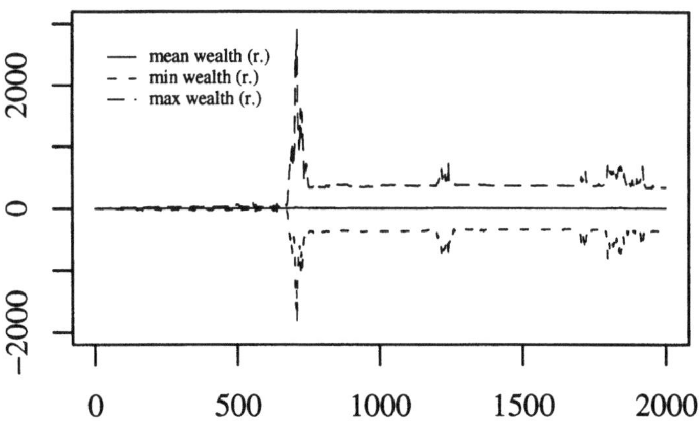


*Figure 8.22.* CT agents: The wealth series with *randomAgentNumber* = 270 (r.), *aNNForecastAppAgentNumber* = 15, *stopLossAgentNumber* = 10 and *maxOrderQuantity* = 3, *BPCTB* = 5 and *EO* = 2, *d* = 5.

from other agents' behavior, (ii) they can be dependent or independent from the previous actions of the simulated artificial subject, (iii) targets are known only when actions take place.

The CT algorithm is a learning and acting one: action is necessary to produce the information by which we can construct targets to train the ANN that simulates the subject.

Learning and acting take place in four steps each "day"; a day is the sum of the four steps required to perform a full cycle of estimation of

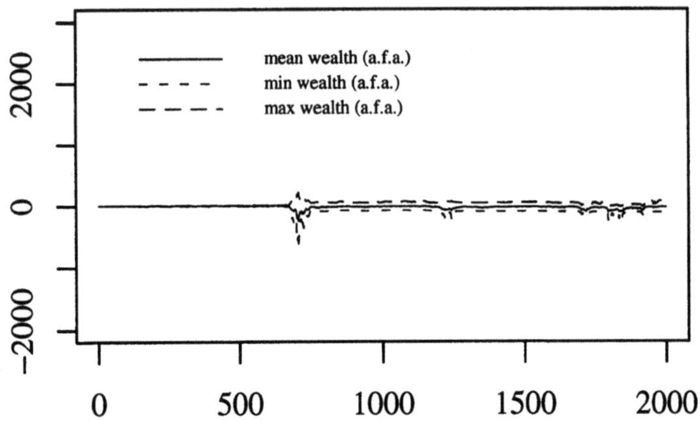


*Figure 8.23.* CT agents: The wealth series with *randomAgentNumber* = 270, *aNNForecastAppAgentNumber* = 15 (a.f.a), *stopLossAgentNumber* = 10 and *maxOrderQuantity* = 3, *BPCTB* = 5 and *EO* = 2, *d* = 5.

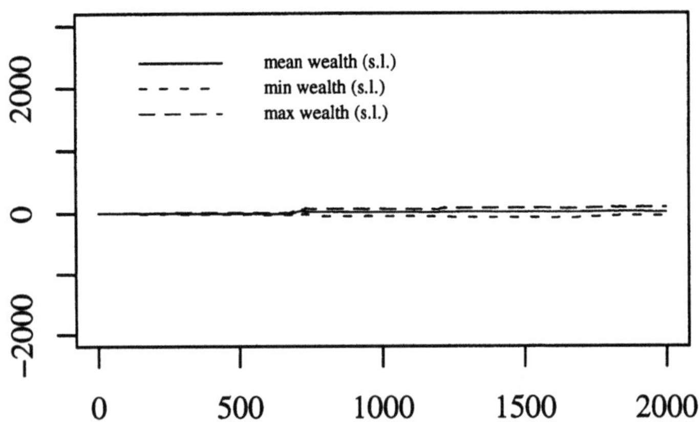


*Figure 8.24.* CT agents: The wealth series with *randomAgentNumber* = 270, *aNNForecastAppAgentNumber* = 15, *stopLossAgentNumber* = 10 (s.l.) and *maxOrderQuantity* = 3, *BPCTB* = 5 and *EO* = 2, *d* = 5.

outputs and of backpropagation of errors, correcting the neural network weights. Initial weights are randomized in a given range.

Looking at Figure 8.18, the four steps can be introduced in the following sequence.

1 Outputs of the ANN: the actions to be accomplished, reported in the right side of Figure 8.18, and the effects of these actions, reported in the left side of the same figure, are guessed following inputs and network weights.

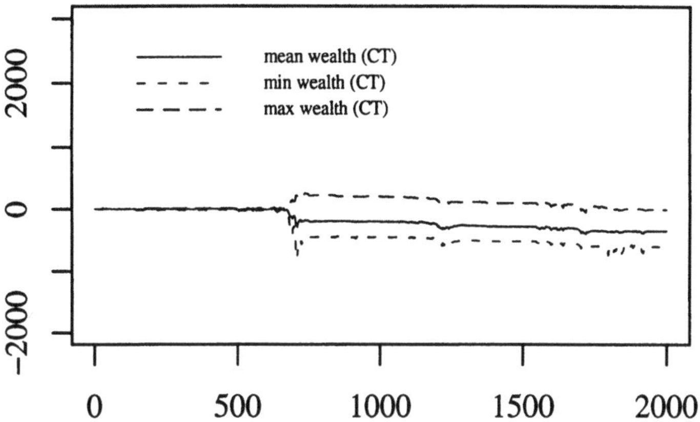


*Figure 8.25.* CT agents: The wealth series with *randomAgentNumber* = 270, *aNNForecastAppAgentNumber* = 15, *stopLossAgentNumber* = 10 and *maxOrderQuantity* = 3, *BPCTB* = 5 (CT) and *EO* = 2, *d* = 5.

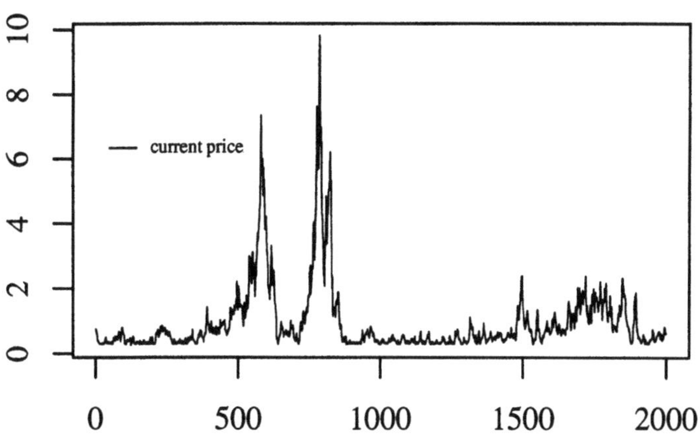


*Figure 8.26.* CT agents: The price sequence of the simulation with *randomAgentNumber* = 270, *aNNForecastAppAgentNumber* = 15, *stopLossAgentNumber* = 10 and *maxOrderQuantity* = 3, *BPCTB* = 5 and *EO* = 2, *d* = 10.

2 Targets for the left side of the network: the targets for the effects supposed to arise from actions, as guessed in the left side of the output layer in Figure 8.18, are figured out by the independently guessed actions. In this way, guesses about effects become more close to the true consequences of actual actions.

3 Targets for the right side of the network: the differences measured in step (2) among targets and ANN outputs on the effect side can be inversely interpreted as starting points for action modifications, to match the guessed effects. So they are used to build the targets

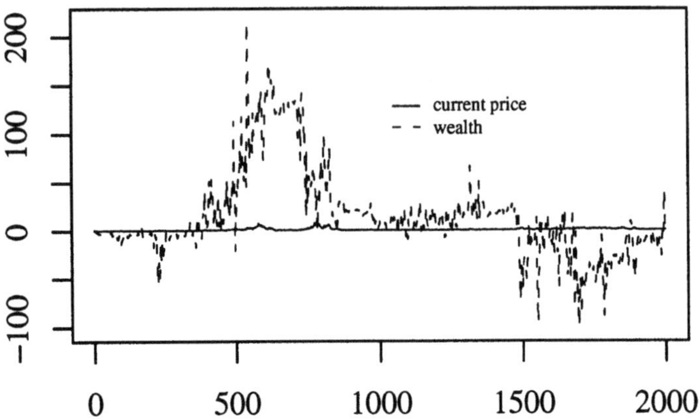


*Figure 8.27.* CT agents: Price and agent wealth series with *randomAgentNumber* = 270, *aNNForecastAppAgentNumber* = 15, *stopLossAgentNumber* = 10 and *maxOrderQuantity* = 3, $BPCTB = 5$ and $EO = 2$, $d = 10$.

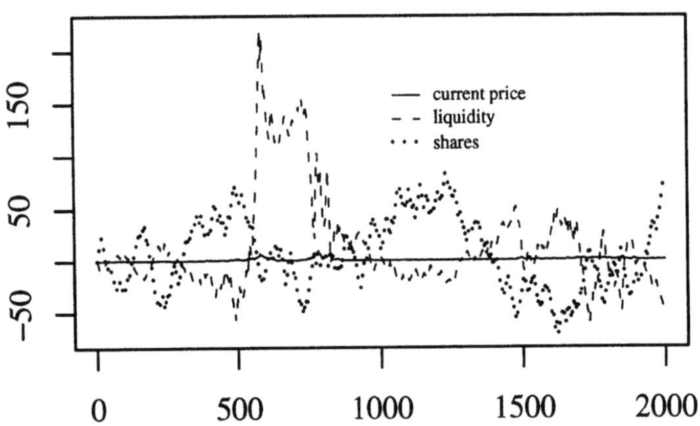


*Figure 8.28.* CT agents: Price, liquidity and shares series with *randomAgentNumber* = 270, *aNNForecastAppAgentNumber* = 15, *stopLossAgentNumber* = 10 and *maxOrderQuantity* = 3, $BPCTB = 5$ and $EO = 2$, $d = 10$.

for the mechanism that guesses the actions. Being the inverses of the formulas shown below often undefined, corrections are shared randomly among all the targets to be constructed; besides, when several corrections concern a target, only the one with the largest module is chosen. In this way, we would like to imitate the actual behavior of a subject requested of obeying to several independent and inconsistent commands: probably the most imperative, here the largest value, will be followed.

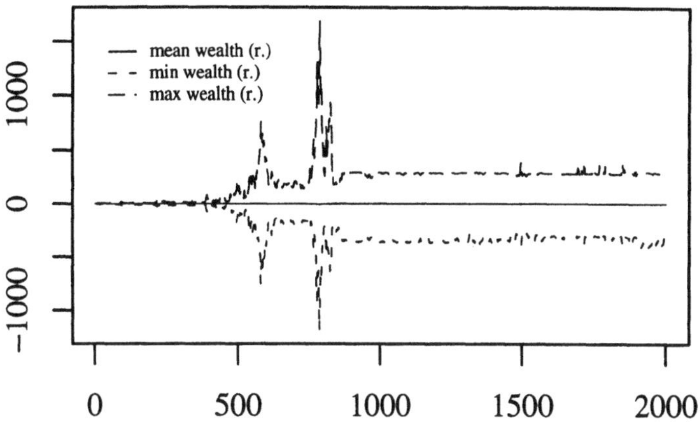


*Figure 8.29.* CT agents: The wealth series with *randomAgentNumber* = 270 (r.), *aNNForecastAppAgentNumber* = 15, *stopLossAgentNumber* = 10 and *maxOrderQuantity* = 3, *BPCTB* = 5 and *EO* = 2, *d* = 10.

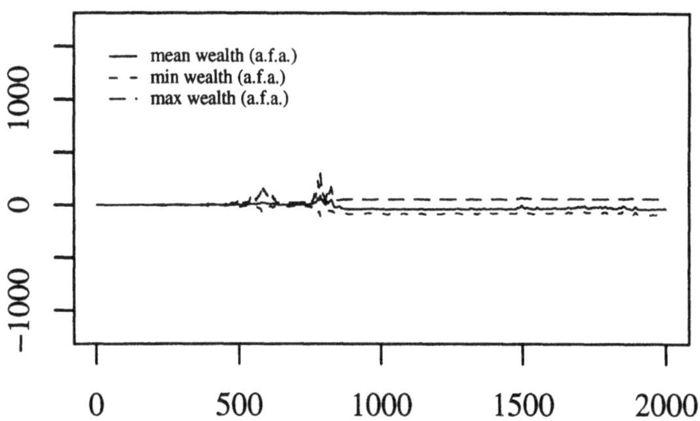


*Figure 8.30.* CT agents: The wealth series with *randomAgentNumber* = 270, *aNNForecastAppAgentNumber* = 15 (a.f.a.), *stopLossAgentNumber* = 10 and *maxOrderQuantity* = 3, *BPCTB* = 5 and *EO* = 2, *d* = 10.

4 Backpropagation: learning takes place, correcting weights in order to obtain guessed effects closer to the consequences of guessed actions, and guessed actions more consistent with guessed effects. Thus, we have two learning processes, both based upon the guesses of the elements of the opposite side of the network.

This double sided process of adaptation, with interaction among the agents and long term learning introduced above, ensures the emergence of non trivial self-developed behavior, from the point of view of time paths of the values generated by the outcomes of the agents.

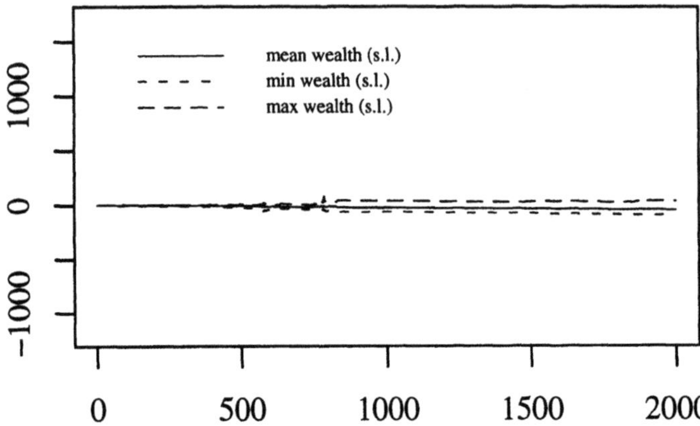


*Figure 8.31.* CT agents: The wealth series with *randomAgentNumber* = 270, *aNNForecastAppAgentNumber* = 15, *stopLossAgentNumber* = 10 (s.l.) and *maxOrderQuantity* = 3, *BPCTB* = 5 and *EO* = 2, *d* = 10.

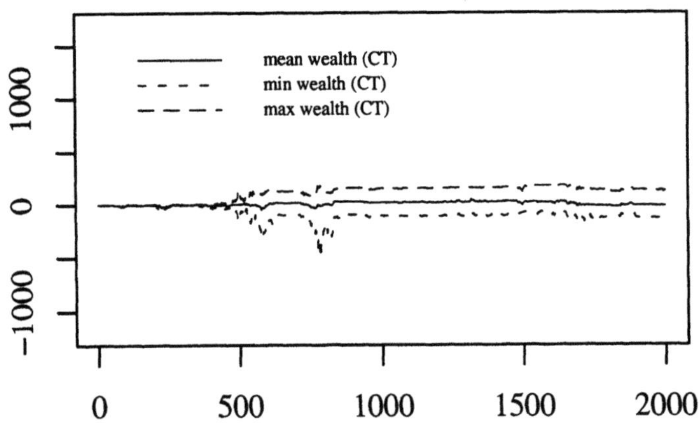


*Figure 8.32.* CT agents: The wealth series with *randomAgentNumber* = 270, *aNNForecastAppAgentNumber* = 15, *stopLossAgentNumber* = 10 and *maxOrderQuantity* = 3, *BPCTB* = 5 (CT) and *EO* = 2, *d* = 10.

## 8.2. The [BP]CT B agent

We introduce now the structure and the behavior of the cognitive agents constituting the core of our agent based simulation. First of all, the name: CT agents or Cross-Target agents of type B, being the SUM package (see Section 3 for the download) able to deal both with simple CT type A agents not used here and with sophisticated type B ones; we use also, mainly internally to the program, the BPCT name (back-propagation CT) referring to the technique used to train the ANN that wires the agents. "bp-ct" is also the name of the general package Terna,

2000a on the CT technique; this package is now included in SUM[21], but it is also useful as a stand alone tool[22].

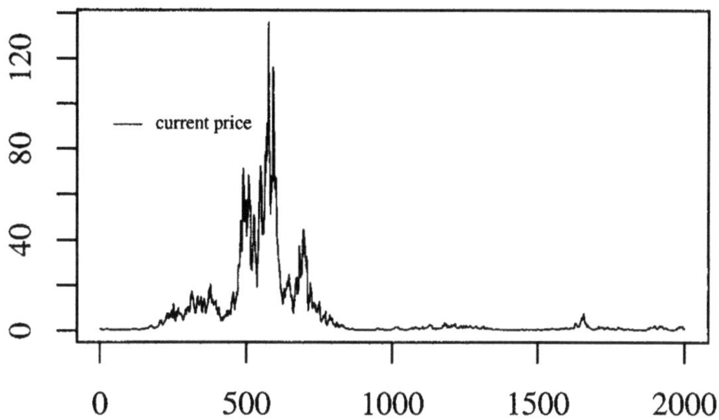


*Figure 8.33.* CT agents: The price sequence of the simulation with *randomAgentNumber* = 270, *aNNForecastAppAgentNumber* = 15, *stopLossAgentNumber* = 10 and *maxOrderQuantity* = 3, *BPCTB* = 5 and *EO* = 2, *d* = 20.

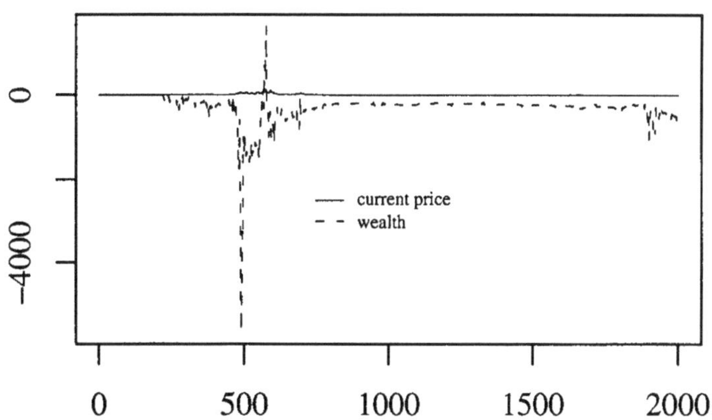


*Figure 8.34.* CT agents: Price and agent wealth series with *randomAgentNumber* = 270, *aNNForecastAppAgentNumber* = 15, *stopLossAgentNumber* = 10 and *maxOrderQuantity* = 3, *BPCTB* = 5 and *EO* = 2, *d* = 20.

The type B agent has eight nodes in input: the mean price from day $t-5$ to day $t-1$ (we are in $t$); the agent's liquidity and share values at the end of day $t-1$ and the estimated price index of day $t+n-1$, with respect to $t-1$ value, where $n = nAheadForecasting$ (see Section 3). The number of hidden nodes is six.

Following the CT scheme, we have four outputs on the *effect* side and one output on the *action* side. Effects (evaluations at the end of day

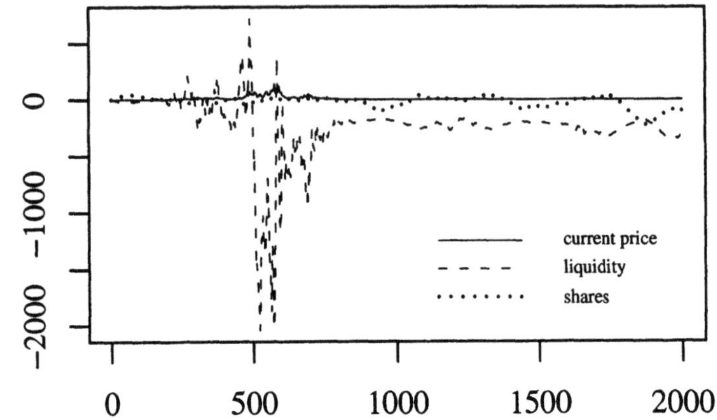


*Figure 8.35.* CT agents: Price, liquidity and shares series with *randomAgentNumber* = 270, *aNNForecastAppAgentNumber* = 15, *stopLossAgentNumber* = 10 and *maxOrderQuantity* = 3, *BPCTB* = 5 and *EO* = 2, *d* = 20.

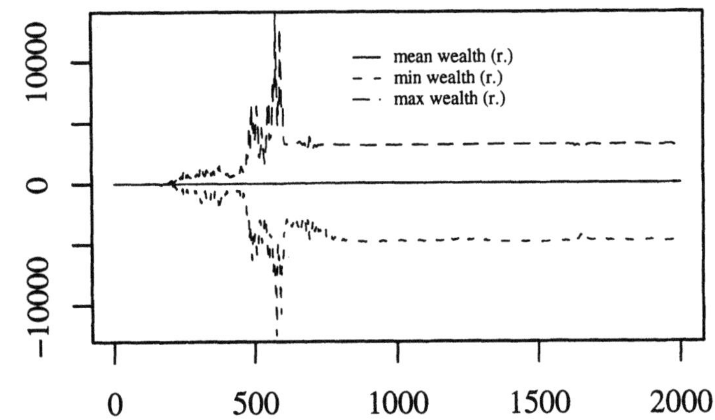


*Figure 8.36.* CT agents: The wealth series with *randomAgentNumber* = 270 (r.), *aNNForecastAppAgentNumber* = 15, *stopLossAgentNumber* = 10 and *maxOrderQuantity* = 3, *BPCTB* = 5 and *EO* = 2, *d* = 20.

$t$): liquidity; share quantity; wealth, using the last daily price; wealth, using the forecast price. Actions: the buy or sell decision.

The buy or sell ($bs$) decision is represented (in external metrics) as a real number in the range $\pm maxOrderQuantity$; if $bs > 0$, the agent is on the buy side; if $bs < 0$, on the sell side; if $bs = 0$ (an absolutely rare case), the agent does nothing; the quantity to be bought or sold (or the number of unitary orders) is determined rounding $|bs|$ to the upper unit.

The EOs are here related to the two wealth effects and are determined[23] adding directly to the wealth internal guesses (those arising from

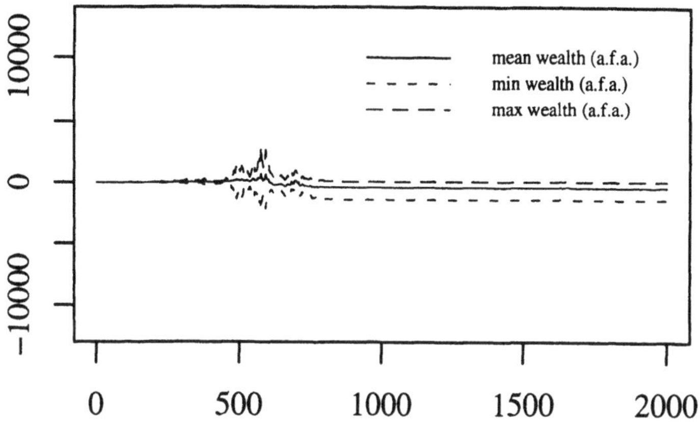


*Figure 8.37.* CT agents: The wealth series with *randomAgentNumber* = 270, *aNN-ForecastAppAgentNumber* = 15 (a.f.a.), *stopLossAgentNumber* = 10 and *maxOrder-Quantity* = 3, *BPCTB* = 5 and *EO* = 2, *d* = 20.

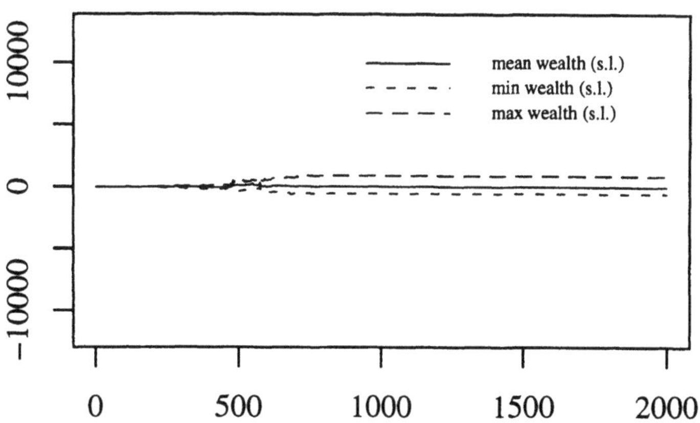


*Figure 8.38.* CT agents: The wealth series with *randomAgentNumber* = 270, *aNN-ForecastAppAgentNumber* = 15, *stopLossAgentNumber* = 10 (s.l.) and *maxOrder-Quantity* = 3, *BPCTB* = 5 and *EO* = 2, *d* = 20.

the development of the IC of the agent) a fixed amount $d$ (measured in wealth metrics). We can have: $EO = 0$ or no EOs; $EO = 1$, i.e. to increase the wealth evaluation based on the closing price; $EO = 2$, i.e. to increase the wealth evaluation based on the forecast price; $EO = 3$ (not used here) as the attempt of increasing both evaluations.

## 9. The behavior of the CT cognitive agents

In the following Subsections we introduce the various experiments with the cognitive CT agents[24], modifying the $d$ value to have light

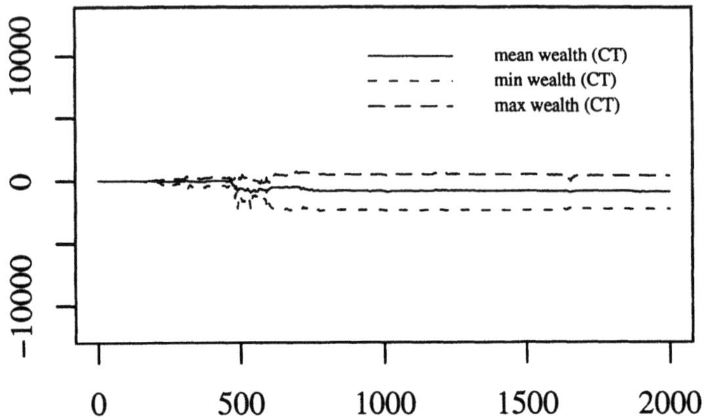


*Figure 8.39.* CT agents: The wealth series with *randomAgentNumber* = 270, *aNNForecastAppAgentNumber* = 15, *stopLossAgentNumber* = 10 and *maxOrderQuantity* = 3, *BPCTB* = 5 (CT) and *EO* = 2, *d* = 20.

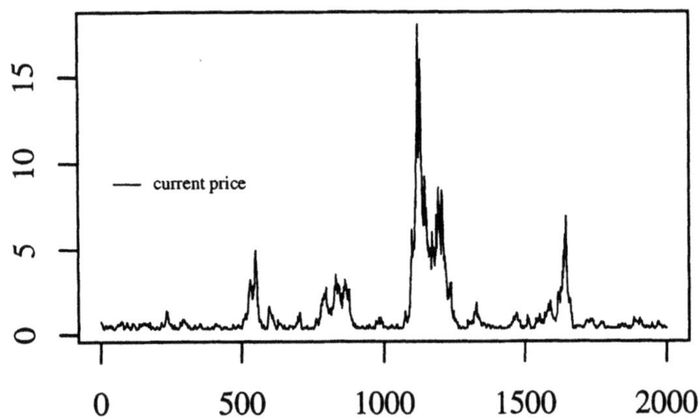


*Figure 8.40.* CT agents: The price sequence of the simulation with *randomAgentNumber = 270*, *aNNForecastAppAgentNumber* = 15, *stopLossAgentNumber* = 10 and *maxOrderQuantity* = 3, *BPCTB* = 5 and *EO* = 1, *d* = 10.

or heavy $EO = 2$ corrections and using also, for comparative reasons, $EO = 1$.

## 9.1. Case 1: EO = 2; d = 5

The first case, with $EO = 2$ (to increase the wealth evaluation based on the forecast price) and $d = 5$ shows (Figure 8.19) a reasonable price sequence, with one relevant bubble. The quota of correct forecasting signs is here 54%, confirming the predictability of the mixed basic case introduced in Section 7.

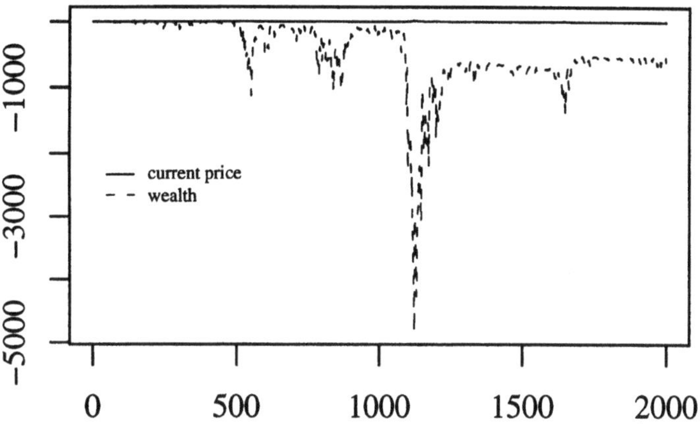


*Figure 8.41.* CT agents: Price and agent wealth series with *randomAgentNumber* = 270, *aNNForecastAppAgentNumber* = 15, *stopLossAgentNumber* = 10 and *maxOrderQuantity* = 3, *BPCTB* = 5 and *EO* = 1, *d* = 10.

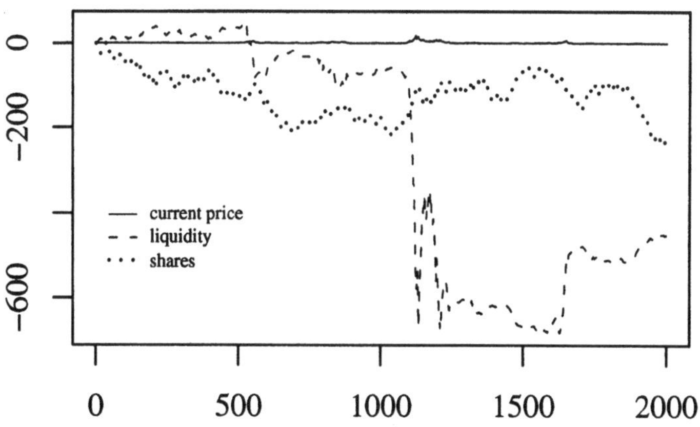


*Figure 8.42.* CT agents: Price, liquidity and shares series with *randomAgentNumber* = 270, *aNNForecastAppAgentNumber* = 15, *stopLossAgentNumber* = 10 and *maxOrderQuantity* = 3, *BPCTB* = 5 and *EO* = 1, *d* = 10.

Analyzing the results of the first of the five CT agents, we see in Figure 8.20 that with this degree of EO correction we have no effect on the agent wealth (evaluated on the forecast price): With the bubble, wealth becomes largely negative and also the significant fluctuation of the share quantity of Figure 8.21 does not change the situation.

Comparing (Figures 8.22, 8.23, 8.24 and 8.25) the min and max wealth situations for the four types of agents involved in the simulation (remembering that on the border lines we have different agents as time evolves),

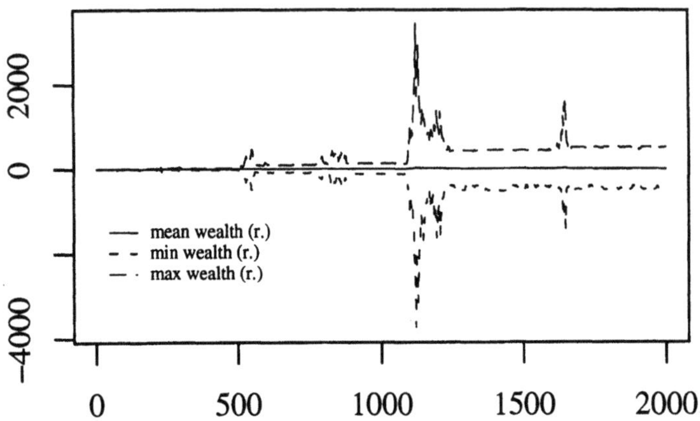


*Figure 8.43.* CT agents: The wealth series with *randomAgentNumber* = 270 (r.), *aNNForecastAppAgentNumber* = 15, *stopLossAgentNumber* = 10 and *maxOrderQuantity* = 3, *BPCTB* = 5 and *EO* = 1, *d* = 10.

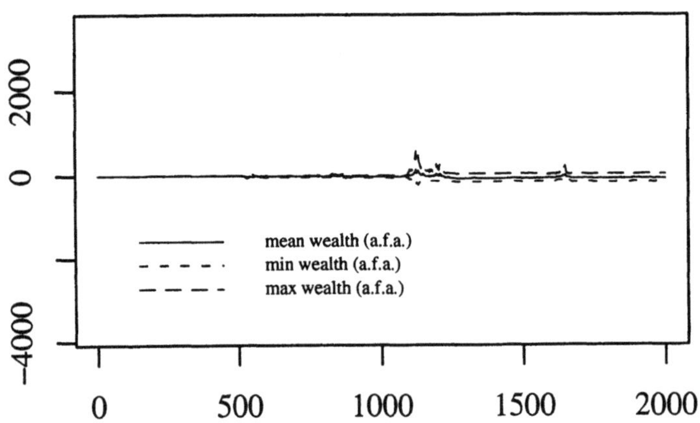


*Figure 8.44.* CT agents: The wealth series with *randomAgentNumber* = 270, *aNNForecastAppAgentNumber* = 15 (a.f.a.), *stopLossAgentNumber* = 10 and *maxOrderQuantity* = 3, *BPCTB* = 5 and *EO* = 1, *d* = 10.

we can see that this light EO presence gives no advantage to our CT agents.

## 9.2. Case 2: EO = 2; d = 10

The second case, with *EO* = 2 and *d* = 10, shows (Figure 8.26) a realistic price sequence with two bubbles of an acceptable dimension in 2,000 days. The quota of correct forecasting signs is here 56%.

In Figure 8.27 we see that now the agent is able to use bubbles to increase in a significant way its wealth, tough in an unstable way. In

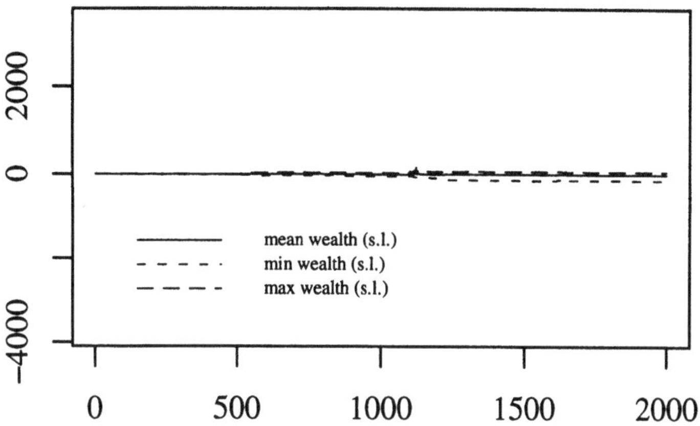


*Figure 8.45.* CT agents: The wealth series with *randomAgentNumber* = 270, *aNNForecastAppAgentNumber* = 15, *stopLossAgentNumber* = 10 (s.l.) and *maxOrderQuantity* = 3, *BPCTB* = 5 and *EO* = 1, *d* = 10.

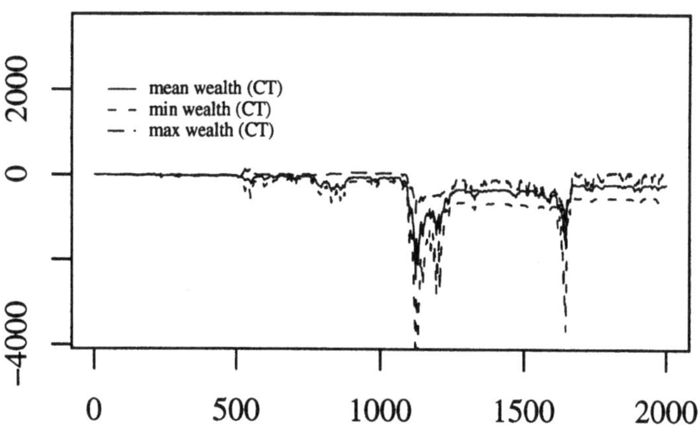


*Figure 8.46.* CT agents: The wealth series with *randomAgentNumber* = 270, *aNNForecastAppAgentNumber* = 15, *stopLossAgentNumber* = 10 and *maxOrderQuantity* = 3, *BPCTB* = 5 (CT) and *EO* = 1, *d* = 10.

Figure 8.28 we can see the "intelligent" use of the share quantity in the presence of the two bubbles; remember that this kind of behavior is self-developed thanks to the CT method and long term learning (see above in Subsection 8.1).

Comparing (Figures 8.29, 8.30, 8.31 and 8.32) the min and max wealth situations for the four types of agents involved in the simulation, we can see that this medium EO gives a significant advantage to the CT agent group.

## 9.3. Case 3: EO = 2; d = 20

The 3rd case, with $EO = 2$ and $d = 20$, shows (Figure 8.33) an unrealistic price sequence with an enormous bubble, as a consequence of the forced behavior of the CT agents in the presence of this heavy EO. The quota of correct forecasting signs is anyway always 56%.

In Figure 8.34 we see that the agent reacts to the losses suffered when the bubble begins and in Figure 8.35 we can investigate the complex behavior adopted.

Comparing (Figures 8.36, 8.37, 8.38 and 8.39) the min and max wealth situations for the four types of agents involved in the simulation, we can see that this heavy EO does not give a significant advantage to the CT agent group.

## 9.4. Case 4: EO = 1; d = 10

The 4th case, with $EO = 1$ (i.e. to increase the wealth evaluation based on the closing price) and $d = 10$, shows (Figure 8.40) a realistic price sequence with a bubble, but the presence of this short term evaluating agents reduces the predictability of the market: The quota of correct forecasting signs is here only 49% (vs. the 55% of the basic mixed situation of Section 7).

In Figures 8.41 and 8.42 we see that the agent is not able to develop a positive strategy, also in the absence of bubbles.

The analysis of the four Figures related to min and max wealth (8.43, 8.44, 8.45 and 8.46) confirms the absolute weakness of this short term EO.

## 10. Conclusions

The following statements may constitute a tentative conclusion:

- first of all we can fully accept Axelrod simplicity principle, since it is easily shown that also very simple agents can generate complex emerging structures;

- external constraints (the "book" of the market) are as strong as a mind proxy (the CT scheme) in determining the emergence of hard to explain patterns, like bubbles in a stock market;

- finally, intelligent behavior can emerge in artificial agents, on a self-developed basis.

So, the (repeated) question is: Are human agents so far from the complexity of the economic system, as ants are from their anthill? But we underline also the result obtained: only with the presence of a (micro) "mind", intelligent behavior—useful to the agents—can emerge.

Future directions of investigation are: the role of the environment and of the agent swarm Bonabeau *et al.*, 1999 in developing intelligence; the micro foundation of behavior, applying econometric techniques to the links existing between individual decision and prices, wealth and forecasting.

This is a "universe" just waiting to be explored!

## Notes

1. Keep It Simple, Stupid; Rosaria Conte in a discussion of ICCS & SS II in Paris last September proposed to reinterpret it as Keep It Simple as Suitable; my counterproposal is: Keep It Sufficiently Simple (to correspond to real life agents.)

2. Swarm is also promising as a common language in agent based simulation, having anyway a look to tools as UML Hunt, 2000 and IMT, the Integrating Modelling Toolkit based upon XML (`<http://flock.cbl.umces.edu/imt/>`).

3. Or obtain it directly from the author.

4. From `<http://eco83.econ.unito.it/~terna/sum/sum.html>`.

5. Cross Targets (CT) are introduced in Subsection 8.1.

6. Agents considering only liquidity and share quantities.

7. This is a realistic microfoundation of price movement also in the real world.

8. A technical detail: The program emulates the different quantities in orders repeating $n$ times—in the same tick—an order of one unit.

9. With $p_i = mean\ price\ of\ day\ i$, $d = dataWindowLength$ and $n = nAheadForecasting$ input data are: $\frac{p_{-d+1}}{p_{-d+1-n}}, \ldots, \frac{p_0}{p_{-n}}$.

10. For a concise introduction to ANN technique, considering multylayer feedforward ANN trained with the backpropagation technique, see Section 4 in Terna (2000a).

11. The length of the training set is defined by the parameter *bPCTPatternNumberIn-TrainingSet* contained in the `bp.setup` file of the package.

12. Background characteristics. Random agents: (a) can operate in the opening phase of the market, (b) can act if the price falls below a specific floor and (c) correct their order prices with a random coefficient.

13. Background characteristics. Market imitating agents: (a) can operate in the opening phase of the market, (b) can act if the price falls below a specific floor and (c) correct their order prices with a random coefficient.

14. The mean wealth of each category is no more constantly zero, since we have exchanges among agents of different categories.

15. Background characteristics. Locally imitating agents: (a) can operate in the opening phase of the market, (b) can act if the price falls below a specific floor and (c) correct their order prices with a random coefficient.

16. We do not recall, here and after, the content of the note about mean wealth, which is anyway always relevant.

17. Background characteristics. "Stop loss" agents: (a) can operate in the opening phase of the market, (b) can act if the price falls below a specific floor and (c) correct their order prices with a random coefficient, but when adopting the stop loss strategy, they use directly the last executed price for their buy or sell proposal.

18. In this experiment we account for the real agent situation ("long" or "short" on the market); see the *checkingIfShortOrLong* parameter in Section 3.

19. A student of mine is substituting the forecaster with an "astrologer" producing its estimates on the basis of random applied rules, with the purpose of simulating various degrees of self-fulfilling prophecies.

20. Background characteristics. Applying forecast agents: (a) can operate in the opening phase of the market, (b) can act if the price falls below a specific floor and (c) correct their order prices with a random coefficient.

21. SUM, as bp-ct, internally uses the ERA scheme Terna, 2000a, with Rule Masters and Rule Makers.

22. It can be obtained directly from the author or dowloaded following the link to the Luna and Stefannson book at <http://www.swarm.org>, or from the "anarchy" Section in the same site (the present version is 1.1).

23. This is an innovation to the methodology used in Terna (2000a).

24. Background characteristics: CT agents (a) can operate in the opening phase of the market, (b) do not care if the price falls below a specific floor and (c) correct their order prices with a random coefficient.

## References


Axtell, R. (2000). "Why agents? On the varied motivations for agent computing in the social sciences." Center on Social and Economic Dynamics, Working Paper No. 17, <http://www.brookings.edu/es/-dynamics/papers/agents/agents.htm>.

Axelrod, R. (1997). "Advancing the Art of Simulation in the Social Sciences." Conte, R., Hegselmann, R. and Terna, P. (eds.), *Simulating Social Phenomena, Lecture Notes in Economics and Mathematical Systems 456*, pp.21-40, Berlin: Springer.

Beltratti, A., Margarita, S., Terna, P. (1996). *Neural Networks for Economic and Financial Modelling.* London: International Thomson Computer Press.

Bonabeau, E., Dorigo, M., Theraulaz, G. (1999). *Swarm Intelligence: From Natural to Artificial Systems.* Santa Fe Institute Studies in the Science of complexity. New York: Oxford University Press.

Gilbert, N. and Terna P. (2000). "How to build and use agent-based models in social science." *Mind & Society*, 1.

Hunt, J. (2000). *The Unified Process for Pratictioners: Object Oriented Design, UML and Java*, Berlin: Springer.

Kirman, A, (1993). "Ants, Rationality, and Recruitement." *Quarterly Journal of Economics*, 1.

Lo, A., Mamaysky, H. and Jiang, W. (2000). "Foundations of technical analysis: computational algorithms, stastical inference, and empirical implementation". *Journal of Finance.*

Ostrom, T. (1988). "Computer simulation: the third symbol system." *Journal of Experimental Social Psychology*, Vol. 24, pp.381-392.

Sargent, T.J. (1993). *Bounded Rationality in Macroeconomics.* Oxford: Clarendon Press.

Terna, P. (2000a). Economic Experiments with Swarm: a Neural Network Approach to the Self-Development of Consistency in Agents' Behavior, F. Luna and B. Stefansson (eds.), *Economic Simulations in Swarm: Agent-Based Modelling and Object Oriented Programming.* Dordrecht and London: Kluwer Academic.

Terna, P. (2000b). "The ≪mind or no mind≫ dilemma in agents behaving in a market." Ballot, G. and Weisbuch, G. (eds.), *Applications of Simulation to Social Sciences.* Paris: Hermes Science Publications.

Tesfatsion, L. (2001). "Introduction to the special issue on agent-based computational economics." *Journal of Economic Dynamic and Control*, Vol. 25, Issue 3-4, pp.281-293.

# IV

# OTHER CONTRIBUTIONS

Chapter 9

# PRODUCTION PARTNERSHIPS FORMATION WITH HETEROGENEOUS AGENTS: A SIMULATION *IN* SWARM

Davide Fiaschi
*Department Scienze Economiche*
*University of Pisa (Italy)*
dfiaschi@ec.unipi.it

Nicolas Garrido
*Department Economia*
*Alcal del Henares (Spain)*
nicolasgarrido@email.com

Pier Mario Pacini
*Department Scienze Economiche*
*University of Pisa (Italy)*
pmpacini@ec.unipi.it

## 1. Introduction

This paper analyzes the organization of an economy where agents with heterogeneous endowments of (human and/or physical) capital and labor can join and form partnerships in order to produce an output[1]. We suppose that the formation of a partnership is the result of a common willingness of a (sub)set of agents to pool and contribute their resources to a production process that takes place within the partnership that has been formed, without any externality onto or from other partnerships. The members of a partnership agree to divide the output among themselves according to an exogenously given distributive rule.

The analogies with non-cooperative coalition formation theory are evident. In this respect the formation of a partnership can be seen as the formation of a coalition and the allocation of agents as a game, where every agent has to decide who s/he wants to coalesce with.

There are two crucial factors affecting individual decisions and therefore the social organization of an economy, i.e. the technological conditions and the distribution of output within any formed partnership. As regards technology we assume that (i) any factor of production is necessary to obtain a positive amount of output and (ii) there are increasing returns to scale. Both these conditions give incentive to aggregation; indeed, if there were no complementarity among inputs then some agents could own factors irrelevant to production and hence they would not be a member of any partnership. On the other hand, the lack of increasing returns to scale could inhibit the aggregation process, as is easily seen when there are constant returns to scale and agents are identical in all respects (see Axtell(1999)).

The other factor affecting individual decisions and the resulting aggregate outcomes is the rule governing the distribution of output within a partnership. In a path-breaking contribution, Farrell and Scotchmer (1988) show that an equal sharing rule can lead agents with heterogeneous endowments not to coalesce in the grand coalition, even if the available technology has increasing returns to scale; this is because in the grand coalition wealthy agents receive less than they could receive in smaller groups in which they interact only with the richest agents. As we will see, such a situation can arise in our model as well; one of the purposes of the paper is precisely to test to what extent the failure in forming the grand coalition (thus exploiting all the advantages of the available technology) depends on the characteristics of the rule governing the distribution of output within a formed partnership. To this end we compare the outcomes of the social aggregation process under different distributive rules that range from the equal-sharing one (see again Farrell and Scotchmer (1988)) to more sophisticated schemes in which a (varying) part of the coalition output is equally shared and the rest is distributed in proportion to what an agent contributes to the partnership of which he is a member.

The other direction in which we move is to test to what extent social results (measured in terms of efficiency and equity) are affected by inequality in the distribution of initial resources, taking the distributive rule as given.

In performing these tests we also analyze the characteristics of the emerging pattern of aggregation. In this respect, this work is similar to Sherstyuk (1998), in which a similar game is considered and people can coalesce to produce and share output; Sherstyuk (1998) characterizes the equilibria of this game and how their features depend on the distribution(s) of endowments and on the distributive rules. However the results depend heavily on the assumed characteristics of the production function, which is separably additive in agents' contributions and factors are perfect complements; here we consider a more general form of the production function. We will see that, ceteris paribus, when the distribution of initial endowments is more unequal, the overall efficiency is lower; we can increase the latter only by setting a distributive rule more favorable to the wealthy agents, thus causing further increase in inequality. This finding seems to be robust to alternative specification of the technology.

In order to shed some light on these problems we take an agent-based simulation approach and construct an artificial society in which a population of boundedly rational agents interact[2] forming and disrupting coalitions; more precisely the interaction takes the form of a signalling process in which all agents send and revise signals indicating who they intend to coalesce with. Time is divided into periods and in every period agents are allowed to change their actions (signals) in reaction to other agents' actions (signals). A situation is taken to be an equilibrium of the process when, given others' signals, no agent has an incentive to revise his/her own signal, in view of the payoff that s/he expects to obtain with it. Both the design and the implementation of this artificial society is performed within the SWARM simulation environment, which allows us to easily test different assumptions about the working of the model and to change the values of different parameters in order to manage different cases.

Summarizing, the paper tries to reconstruct a microstructure of individual interactions in order to find answers to the following questions:

1. under what conditions does the spontaneous allocation of agents in partnerships give rise to a socially efficient outcome?

2. Is there an efficiency-equity trade-off?

3. And finally, can some agent fail in coalescing with some other agent? More precisely, can an agent with only labor endowment remain unemployed?

As already noticed, this paper is related to Farrell and Scotchmer (1988) in so far as the coalition formation game is concerned. We depart from it by assuming that agents can be heterogeneous in two characteristics and taking into account a more general distributive rule. The problem of the relationship between distribution and efficiency has been dealt with in a similar context by Sherstyuk (1998); as already mentioned, we depart from her work by abandoning the restrictive assumptions concerning the production function. In still another context Galor and Zeira (1993) show how growth and inequality can be negatively related if capital markets are imperfect. We find the same type of relationship, but we propose an alternative explanation related to the rule governing the division of output. Finally the paper is close to the literature on bounded rationality and in particular to the contributions using Genetic Algorithms as a means to model the individual decision process (see Arifovic (1996), Holland and Miller (1991)).

The paper is organized as follows: Section 2 describes the basic model; the simulation framework is dealt with in Section 3, while Section 4 illustrates the SWARM implementation. Section 5 reports the results of numerical experiments; Conclusions close the paper. Some technical material is relegated to the Appendix.

## 2. The model

We consider an economy with a population $\Im$ of agents; the number of agents is $I$. Every agent $i$ is endowed with a fixed quantity of capital and labor, $k_i$ and $l_i$ respectively. A subset $S \subseteq \Im$, with $S \neq \emptyset$, is a coalition (or partnership as it will be often termed in the following). A coalition structure is a partition $\sigma = \{S_1, S_2, \ldots, S_k\}$ of the whole population $\Im$. The formation of a coalition corresponds to the formation of a partnership since we assume that the participation of an agent in a group $S$ is tantamount to (i) the conferment of *all* his endowments to the production activity that takes place within $S$ and (ii) the acceptance of the share of output determined by the given distributive rule.

Notice that this definition of coalition structure can be very restrictive in our context, because it implies that an agent cannot use his capital endowments in more than one coalition. This suggests that capital is to be interpreted more as human than physical capital.

### 2.1. Partnership production function

The total amount of the productive factors conferred by the members of a partnership are used to produce the "partnership output" $Y^S$; $y_i$ is the payment that agent $i$ receives out of the total product of the coalition $S$ as determined by the governing distributive rule. Since the partnership output is entirely distributed, we have $\sum_{i \in S} y_i = Y^S$.

The available technology is described by a Cobb-Douglas production function and the output of a partnership $S$ is given by

$$Y^S = \left(\sum_{i \in S} k_i\right)^{\alpha} \cdot \left(\sum_{i \in S} l_i\right)^{\beta}, \tag{2.1}$$

where $\alpha$ and $\beta$ are the elasticity of output to capital and labor respectively. The use of a Cobb-Douglas production function is justified on account of its flexibility and because it allows us to easily incorporate some features that will be crucial in what follows: since our concern is in increasing returns to scale, we always set the parameters $\alpha$ and $\beta$ so as $\alpha + \beta > 1$. To focus on the importance of complementarities in production, we assume that the marginal productivity of each factors is decreasing, i.e. $\alpha, \beta < 1$.

We notice that there are no productive externalities in this setting, i.e. the only relevant factors to the partnership output are the endowments of members of the partnership itself[3].

## 2.2. Distributive rule

The distributive rule crucially affects individual decisions about the formation of partnerships, since it determines the different advantages that an agent receives from entering different coalitions. In the literature there are few contributions on this aspect and particularly for the case in which the heterogeneity of agents is multidimensional (as already noted, a remarkable example is Sherstyuk (1998)). Most works concentrate on the characterization of equilibria when the distributive rule is of the *equal sharing* type, i.e.

$$y_i^E = \frac{Y^S}{|S|} \tag{2.2}$$

where $|S|$ is the cardinality of $S$. This, for example, is the rule used in Farrell and Scotchmer (1988) and it implies that every member in a partnership receives the same share of the partnership output, independently of his/her endowments.

At the other extreme we can imagine a rule assigning to every agent a part of the partnership output in proportion to the endowments s/he confers to the coalition. This is the *proportional sharing rule*, that is formalized as[4]

$$y_i^P = Y^S \cdot \left[ \frac{\alpha}{\alpha + \beta} \cdot \frac{k_i}{\sum_{i \in S} k_i} + \frac{\beta}{\alpha + \beta} \cdot \frac{l_i}{\sum_{i \in S} l_i} \right]. \tag{2.3}$$

In the following we assume that the distributive rule governing the division of the partnership output is a mixture of the two extreme cases (2.2) and (2.3) above. In particular we consider a rule that is a linear combination of the equal and proportional sharing rules and it takes the form

$$y_i = \lambda y_i^P + (1 - \lambda) y_i^E, \quad \lambda \in [0, 1], \tag{2.4}$$

In other words we assume that there is a convention in society by means of which agents agree to equally share a fraction $(1-\lambda)$ of what they produce in the partnership, whereas the remaining part is distributed taking into account the amount of endowments that each agent has conferred to the coalition.

## 2.3. Agents' actions, partnership structure and Nash equilibria

The actions available to an agent are signals by means of which he proposes to a subset of agents the formation of a partnership; more specifically, an action shows an agent's willingness to coalesce with a group of agents and, at the same time, it is a veto to form a partnership with those to whom the proposal was not sent[5]. An action for an agent $i$ is denoted by $\theta_i \in \Theta_i$. Of course, the objective of all agents is to choose an action to maximize the payoff they expect to receive from it, given other agents' actions $\theta_{-i} \in \Theta_{-i} = \prod_{j\in\Im/\{i\}} \Theta_j$. Agents cannot play mixed strategies, i.e. they cannot choose more than one signal and play each of them with a positive probability.

As regards the determination of payoffs, we assume that the utility functions of the agents are identical and *linear* in the payments $y_i$ they receive from participation in a partnership. Therefore, in order to set up the individual choice problem, the relation between a configuration of actions (signals) $\theta = (\theta_i, \theta_{-i})$ and the consequent individual payments $y_i$ must first be detailed. Suppose, for the moment, that there is a deterministic relation between a set of signals $\theta$ and the partnership structure that forms therefrom, i.e. for any $\theta$ let $S(\theta) = \sigma = \{S_1, S_2, \ldots, S_k\}$ be the unique allocation of agents into groups $S_1, \ldots, S_k$ compatible with $\theta$ (the meaning of compatibility will be clarified later in § 3). Then let $S_{\iota(i)}(\theta)$ be the partnership which $i$ belongs to in $S(\theta)$ and denote by $\gamma_i\left(S_{\iota(i)}(\theta)\right)$ the payment $y_i$ that $i$ receives in the partnership $S_{\iota(i)}(\theta)$ s/he belongs to when the profile of actions is $\theta$[6]. In this simple case, the individual choice problem would be

$$\max_{\theta_i\in\Theta_i} \gamma_i\left(S_{\iota(i)}(\theta_i, \theta_{-i})\right)$$

for a given expectation about others' actions $\theta_{-i}$. In general, however, a given set of signals $\theta$ may be compatible with a multiplicity of partnership structures (on this point see again § 3 later); to this end denote by $\sigma^n = S^n(\theta)$ the $n$-th partnership structure compatible with $\theta$, $1 \leq n \leq N$, and by $\gamma_i\left(S^n_{\iota(i)}(\theta)\right)$ the payment that $i$ receives in the partnership s/he belongs to in $\sigma^n$. If $P(S^n(\theta))$ represents the probability with which $S^n(\theta)$ is observed, given $\theta$, the individual choice problem in the general case becomes

$$\max_{\theta_i \in \Theta_i} \sum_{n=1}^{N} \gamma_i \left( S^n_{\iota(i)} \left( \theta_i, \theta_{-i} \right) \right) \cdot P \left( S^n \left( \theta_i, \theta_{-i} \right) \right)$$

or simply

$$\max_{\theta_i \in \Theta_i} E \left[ \gamma_i \left( S_{\iota(i)} \left( \theta_i, \theta_{-i} \right) \right) \right] . \tag{2.5}$$

As already mentioned, we assume that agents are boundedly rational and possess limited computational capabilities; therefore they try to solve the decision problem (2.5), but, precisely on account of their limited capabilities, the best solution they can find is not necessarily the optimal one. The next Section will provide further details on this point.

Finally, notice that a Nash equilibrium (in pure strategies) for this game is defined as a set of signals $\theta^*$ such that

$$\theta_i^* = \arg \max_{\theta_i \in \Theta_i} E \left[ \gamma_i \left( S_{\iota(i)} \left( \theta_i, \theta_{-i} \right) \right) \right] \quad \forall i$$

Clearly the characteristics of these equilibria will depend on the basic parameters of the economy; we will concentrate on the role played (i) by technological factors, as described by the return to scale of the available technology, (ii) by the distribution of the property rights on capital (thus, and for the sake of simplicity, we will assume that agents do not differ as to their labor capacities) and (iii) by the rule governing distribution within formed partnerships. From a general point of view it can be stressed that, independently of technological and distributive factors, agents with lower (or null) endowments of capital always have an incentive to form coalitions with agents with greater capital endowments; this is because such a strategy enables them to exploit production complementarities and returns to scale so as to receive a greater amount of output. However, and this is the crucial aspect of the working of the model, it may be the case that wealthier individuals refuse to coalesce with others because they might consequently be forced by the distributive rule to accept a lower amount of output than they would perhaps receive in a smaller group or even by producing in isolation. Cases may also occur in which individuals with a large amount of capital would be willing to coalesce with labor owners (in order to exploit productive complementarities), but only with a subgroup of labor owners, because the acceptance of a greater number of workers would bias distribution in favor of labor rather than capital; this is the prototype of a situation in which there is a part of the population that remains unemployed, notwithstanding its willingness to enter into a contractual relationship with the capital owners. These points will emerge in commenting on the results of the simulations.

## 3. Simulation framework

In the following we describe the main aspects of the framework within which simulations were performed, with particular attention to agents' decision process and the rule governing the formation of a partnership. The effective implementation in SWARM is the subject of the next Section.

The basic characteristics of a single simulation environment are completely specified by a triple $Q = [T_k, D_h, R_j]$:

- $T_k \in T$ denotes a particular configuration of technological parameters (given (2.1) $T_k$ is a pair of positive numbers summing up to more than one);
- $D_h \in D$ denotes a particular distribution of capital across agents in $\Im$ (therefore $D_h$ is a $I$-tuple of non-negative numbers specifying each agent's endowment of capital); as far as labor endowments are concerned, we assume that each agent has a one unit of labor.
- $R_j \in R$ denotes a particular distributive rule (given (2.4) it is a real number in the interval $[0, 1]$).

Given an environment $Q$, people interact in a sequence of periods indexed by $t$; in each period they form expectations about other agents' actions (signals) and try to solve problem (2.5), thus choosing a signal that maximizes expected payoff. Chosen signals are publicly observable (i.e. they are communicated to everyone) and can be revised in every period. In this respect, this process configures a sort of best reply dynamics and a rest point of the simulation is a situation where no agent can modify the previously chosen signal and thereby improve his/her payoff; this corresponds to a Nash equilibrium of the game (see definition in the previous Section).

**Expectations about other agents' signals.** For the sake of simplicity, we assume that agents form static expectations on other agents' signals; therefore, in period $t$, agent $i$ expects that the other agents will maintain the actions (signals) of period $t-1$. This aspect can be an important source of limitation in our analysis, but it appears to be coherent with our approach where agents are assumed to be not fully rational and unable to perform forward strategic reasoning.

**Choice of signals.** The optimization process is performed by means of Genetic Algorithms (GAs)[7]. The use of GAs to represent individual behavior has been motivated by important contributions from the theory of cognitive processes (see Holland, Holyoak and Thagard (1986), Holland and Miller (1991)) and tends to capture the idea that agents, when called upon to make a choice in a complex environment, do not make explicit optimization, but rather operate on a set of rules that they continuously modify by reacting to the effects of their own behavior. In order to operate, GAs need to assign to every possible signal $\theta_i$ a fitness index which, in our context, is the payoff that an agent expects to receive if s/he adopts that signal.

The problem here comes from the fact that *ex-ante* an agent can be uncertain about which partnership structure will come out of a given set of signals since, in principle, a given profile of signals is compatible with more than one partnership structure[8]. However, we assume that all agents know how a partnership structure will form and will use this knowledge in forming their expectations.

## 3.1. Partnership formation

The procedure by means of which coalition structures are actually formed assumes that a partnership can form if and only if all its members agree to form the partnership. It presumes that there is no first mover, but agents randomly match and, if their signals are compatible, they form a group, otherwise they separate and wait for a newcomer, if any. No one can be forced to join a group if either (i) s/he did not signal willingness to coalesce with all the agents of the group or (ii) some agents in the group did not signal their willingness to coalesce with the agent in (i). A rule satisfying all these prerequisites is what we have termed the *Random Matching* (RM) procedure. It works as follows: initially two agents are randomly drawn from the population and if their messages are compatible they form the first (part of a) partnership, otherwise two singleton groups are formed. Then a new agent is randomly drawn and, if his/her signal is compatible with one of the existing partnerships, s/he joins it, otherwise s/he constitutes the third singleton coalition. Subsequently another agent is randomly drawn and the same test is performed. The procedure stops when all agents are allocated.

As can easily be verified, given a certain set of signals the RM procedure does not give always the same results depending on the order of extraction of the agents[9]. However multiple application of this procedure (always taking the same set of signals) gives a probability distribution over possible partnerships. This probability distribution is used by agents to compute the expected utility of a given signal.

## 4. SWARM implementation

The model described above has been implemented in SWARM. One important feature of SWARM is the possibility of setting an economic environment and, at the same time, an independent representation (model) of it for all agents, so that they act independently on the basis of the knowledge *they have* of the environment in which they live. In the present context and for the sake of simplicity, we have assumed that agents know and use the "true" representation of the world, but more complex environments in which agents behave on the basis of strictly personal (mis)representations of the *reality* could be constructed and analyzed with little modification.

In every description of an agent based simulation it is necessary to describe the entities acting in the simulation and how they interact. When we describe the entities we are interested in showing what their properties are, the tasks assigned and what they have in common. This description constitutes what we will call the *Static Structure* (Class Diagram in Object Oriented Design)[10]. On the other hand, when we are concerned with the explanation of how these entities interact through messages (which can change their properties) or when an entity is called to act, we will make reference to a *Dynamic Structure*. Rather than making an exhaustive description of the Static and Dynamic Structure of the simulation, we will restrict the description to the most relevant points, in order not to overload the text with unimportant details.

### 4.1. Static structure

In designing our framework of partnership formation, we face the problem that, in addition to the agents, we need a meta-agent whose purpose is to make publicly available the signals independently and privately chosen by everyone; we call this meta-agent blackboard (we use this term because it seems to represent rather well the idea of the function performed by this particular object). It knows all the public information generated during the simulation and in every period it retains the current payoffs, signals and partnership structures. As already hinted, the internal representation of each agent is the same as in the *reality*; this means that agents and the blackboard use the same algorithm to compute partnership structures and agents' payoffs.

The following simplified class diagram describes the different classes defined in our framework specifying for each of them the activities (methods) they perform.

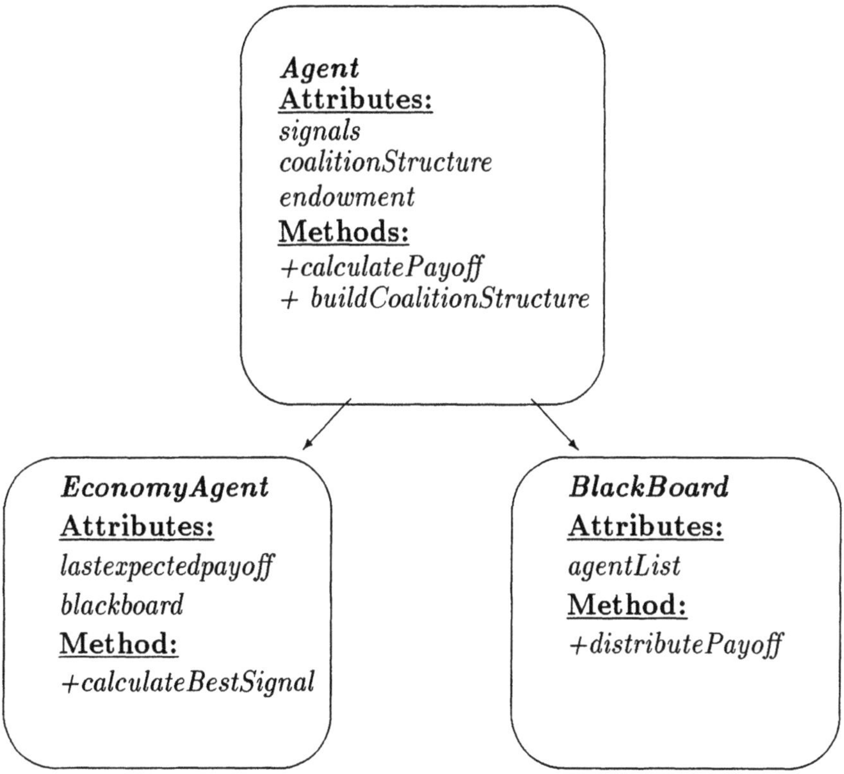


*Figure 9.1.* class diagram

The class *Agent* is an abstract class whose attributes and behaviors are common to the *EconomyAgent* and *Blackboard* classes. In particular, *Agent* has the following attributes: (i) *signals*, where the signals sent by all the agents in the previous period are saved; (ii) *coalitionStructure*, where the partnership structure related to the set of signals is stored and (iii) *endowments*, which keeps track of the capital and labor distribution. This amount of information is common to all entities belonging to the simulation; therefore *Agent* is an abstract class in our structure.

In so far as methods are concerned, *Agent* computes the payoff of a signal using the *calculatePayoff* method. To do this, it has to know which partnership structures can form depending on a given set of signals, including the one under evaluation; for this purpose the RM procedure is implemented in this class in the method *buildCoalitionStructure*. Moreover both *BlackBoard* and *EconomyAgent* use the same methods, but with different intentions; whereas *EconomyAgent* uses it to calculate the expected payoff of a signal, the *BlackBoard* uses it in order to obtain the actual partnership structure and corresponding payoffs distribution once agents have sent their signals.

The *EconomyAgent* class is the abstraction of the agents in our economy. Agents perform the most intensive computational procedures in the simulation, so *EconomyAgent* implements the optimization process used by the agents to look for the best signal. The method *calculateBestSignal* is the interface for the procedure in which, by means of Genetic Algorithms, agents find their best signals.

An agent compares the payoff of the best signal of the current period with the payoff of the signal of the previous period (evaluated at current expectations) and changes his/her signal only if the first one is strictly greater than the second. In order to accomplish this task *EconomyAgent* inherits from *Agent* all its properties and adds the *lastPayoff* attribute. Thus, after the best current signal has been computed (using *calculateBestSignal)*, an instance of the *EconomyAgent* class will compare it with the value in *lastPayoff*. The attribute *blackBoard* allows agents to find out where to collect the set of the previous period signals and to input their new best signals.

Besides making agents' signals publicly available in every period, at the end of the simulation the blackboard class receives the final signals from all the agents and returns a partnership structure and the associated distribution of payoffs to the agents. In order to perform this task the class *BlackBoard* has an *agentList* with the reference to every agent and implements the method *distributePayoff*.

With this static structure in mind, we can describe some advantages of using an Oriented Object environment as SWARM. Should one wish to test our economic environment under a partnership formation rule other than RM, all that needs to be done is simply to change the method *buildCoalitionStructure,* in the *Agent* class and immediately *EconomyAgents* and *BlackBoard* will use the new rule. Similarly, if one were interested in simulating an economy in which agents have different internal representations of the world, then we could add another class inheriting from *EconomyAgent* all the properties and we merely have to redefine the *buildCoalitionStructure* method. Thus, while our agents will use the newly defined formation rule, any instance of the *BlackBoard* class will still use the previously defined method in the *Agent* class.

## 4.2. Dynamic structure

The distribution of activities in SWARM is basically determined by the Scheduler; therefore, by making reference to the latter, it is possible to outline how objects interact. In short, the scheduling of the simulation is the following:

1 Every agent starts with a set of signals that are candidates to being chosen (this set can be different for every agent); then s/he computes the utility s/he expects to receive from each of them, given that s/he expects that the other agents will not change their own signals.

2 Every agent applies GAs to his/her own set of signals and the fitness of every signal is its expected utility. The application of GAs will produce the finally chosen signal, the one with the best fitness. If the expected utility of the chosen signal is not greater than that of the signal currently played (re-evaluated at current expectations), s/he continues playing the old one. This produces profiles of signals, one for every agent.

3 Given all the signals played by the agents, a stopping condition is checked[11]. If the latter fails, the procedure goes back to point 1, with the new configuration of signals replacing the old one. Otherwise simulation ends and, given the set of signals, the RM procedure provides the final coalition structure.

# 5. Numerical experiments

In this Section we show the results of the numerical simulations of the model described in the previous Sections. Our purpose is to investigate and compare the properties of the rest points of the simulations when the environment $Q$ changes, i.e. when the distribution of endowments, the technology and the distributive rule vary. Thus we investigate the results of the simulations in 75 different environments obtained by specifying 3 possible technological configurations (i.e. $|T| = 3$), five possible distributions of endowments (i.e. $|D| = 5$) and five possible distributive rules (i.e. $|R| = 5$). In all experiments the number of agents ($I = 20$) and the parameters of GAs (see Appendix 6 for details) are kept constant. For every possible environment $Q = [T_k, D_h, R_j]$ we ran 20 simulations with different seeds; this was undertaken in order to smooth out the effect of the random components of GAs and RM on the results of the simulation.

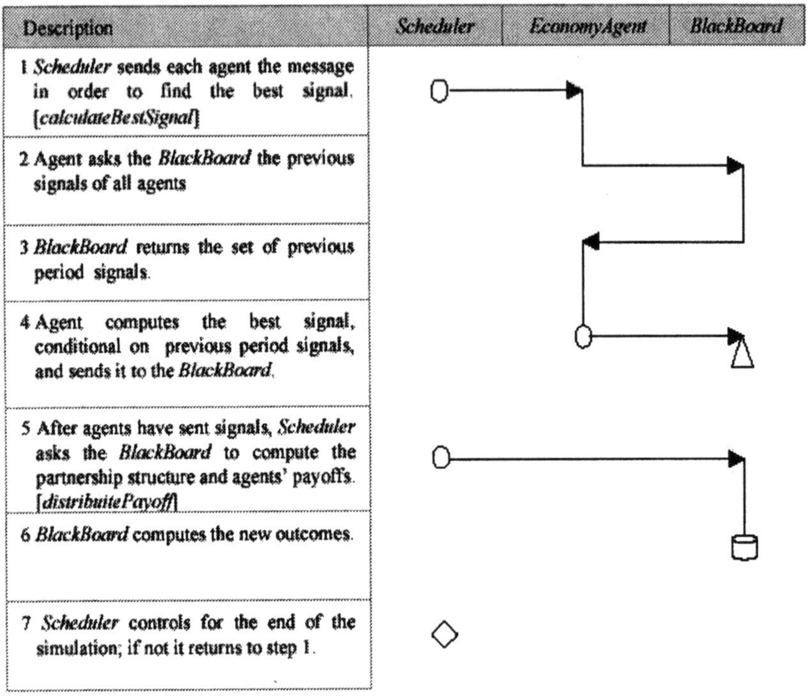


*Figure 9.2.* simulation flow

In the presentation of the results we follow the three questions posed in the Introduction; the next Section then addresses the issue of what conditions are sufficient to obtain an efficient allocation of resources. Subsequently, we endeavor to detect whether there is an efficiency-equity trade-off. Finally, we search for evidence of agents that fail in coalescing with at least one other agent, or, in other words, we verify whether an agent who possesses only labor endowment can remain unemployed.

Before proceeding to in-depth analysis of the results, we describe the details of the different environments $Q$ that have been simulated.

**Distribution of resources.** In so far as the distributions of endowments are concerned, we assume that all agents have 1 unit of labor and their heterogeneity comes only from the fact that they have different property rights on the total capital stock. Thus we assume that the total amount of capital is constant and equal to 20 (this would avoid possible scale effects), and is distributed in the population in one of the ways reported in the following Table:

| | 1 | 2 | 3 | 4 | 5 | 6 | 7 | 8 | 9 | 10 | 11 | 12 | 13 | 14 | 15 | 16 | 17 | 18 | 19 | 20 |
|---|---|---|---|---|---|---|---|---|---|---|---|---|---|---|---|---|---|---|---|---|
| $D_1$ | 1.1 | 1.1 | 1.1 | 1.1 | 1.1 | 1.1 | 1.1 | 1.1 | 1.1 | 1.1 | 0.9 | 0.9 | 0.9 | 0.9 | 0.9 | 0.9 | 0.9 | 0.9 | 0.9 | 0.9 |
| $D_2$ | 1.7 | 1.7 | 1.7 | 1.7 | 1.3 | 1.3 | 1.3 | 1.3 | 1.0 | 1.0 | 1.0 | 1.0 | 0.7 | 0.7 | 0.7 | 0.7 | 0.3 | 0.3 | 0.3 | 0.3 |
| $D_3$ | 2.0 | 2.0 | 2.0 | 2.0 | 2.0 | 2.0 | 2.0 | 2.0 | 2.0 | 2.0 | 0.0 | 0.0 | 0.0 | 0.0 | 0.0 | 0.0 | 0.0 | 0.0 | 0.0 | 0.0 |
| $D_4$ | 6.0 | 4.0 | 3.0 | 2.0 | 1.0 | 1.0 | 0.3 | 0.3 | 0.3 | 0.3 | 0.3 | 0.3 | 0.0 | 0.0 | 0.0 | 0.0 | 0.0 | 0.0 | 0.0 | 0.0 |
| $D_5$ | 20 | 0.0 | 0.0 | 0.0 | 0.0 | 0.0 | 0.0 | 0.0 | 0.0 | 0.0 | 0.0 | 0.0 | 0.0 | 0.0 | 0.0 | 0.0 | 0.0 | 0.0 | 0.0 | 0.0 |

Table1: Distribution of capital endowments.

While $D_1$ is very close to an egalitarian distribution of the total capital stock, $D_5$ concentrates all capital in one agent; $D_2$ is characterized by the presence of five classes of capital owners, while $D_3$ by just two equally numerous classes. Finally $D_4$ is the case closest to a Paretian distribution.

**Technology.** We consider three alternative technological regimes:

| | Elasticity of output to | |
|---|---|---|
| | Capital | Labour |
| $T_1$ | 0.55 | 0.55 |
| $T_2$ | 0.6 | 0.9 |
| $T_3$ | 0.9 | 0.6 |

Table 2: production technologies.

$T_1$ is the case closest to constant returns to scale, while both $T_2$ and $T_3$ show strong increasing returns to scale, but the former implies a greater elasticity of output to labor, while the opposite holds for $T_3$.

**Distributive rule.** Finally we consider five possible distributive rules obtained by changing the value of $\lambda$ in (2.4); namely, the set $R$ is given by:

| | $R_1$ | $R_2$ | $R_3$ | $R_4$ | $R_5$ |
|---|---|---|---|---|---|
| $\lambda$ | 0.0 | 0.25 | 0.5 | 0.75 | 1.0 |

Table 3: alternative distributive rules

$R_5$ ($\lambda = 1$) entails a completely proportional sharing of the partnership output, while $R_1$ ($\lambda = 0$) entails equal sharing of the same output. The other distributive rules are intermediate cases.

## 5.1. Efficiency

The first problem we address concerns the conditions that ensure efficient utilization of resources. To answer this question we take the average payoff as a proxy for the system efficiency and then, given a technology, we analyze how efficiency varies as the rule governing distribution changes. This is done in the following Figures; each one of them corresponds to a technology in $T$ and each line in a graph traces the system efficiency for a particular distribution of resources in $D$ (to be read on the right) when the parameter $\lambda$ (and hence the distributive rule) varies from 0 to 1 (to be read on the horizontal axis):

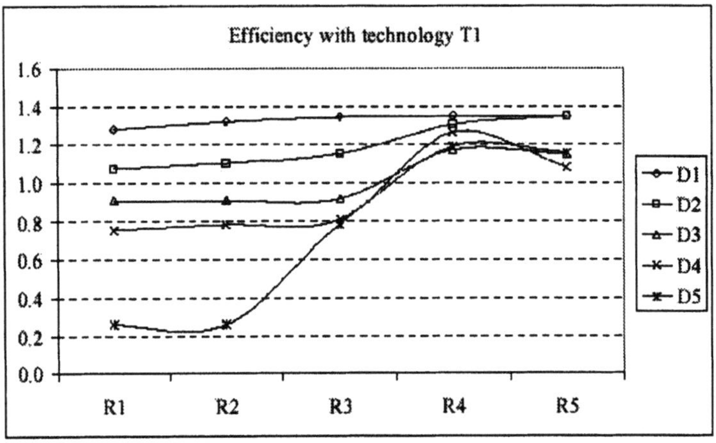


*Figure 9.3a.* efficiency for technology $T_1$

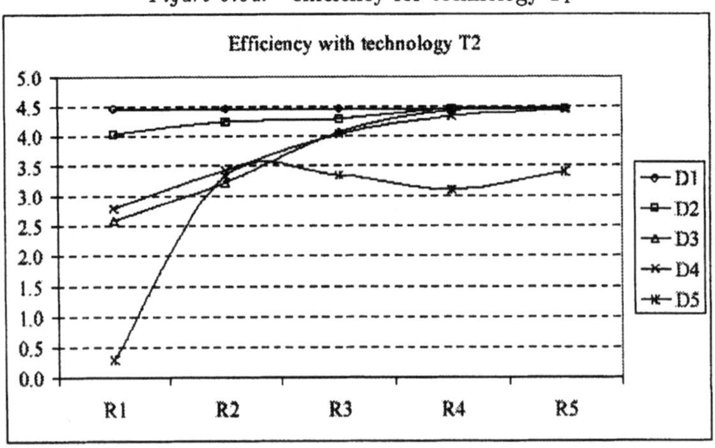


*Figure 9.3b.*efficiency for technology $T_2$

As a general rule, we can observe that, for technologies $T_2$ and $T_3$ and independently of the distribution of endowments, the maximum efficiency is reached when the distributive rule is $R_5$, i.e. the distribution of partnership output is proportional to members' endowments and no

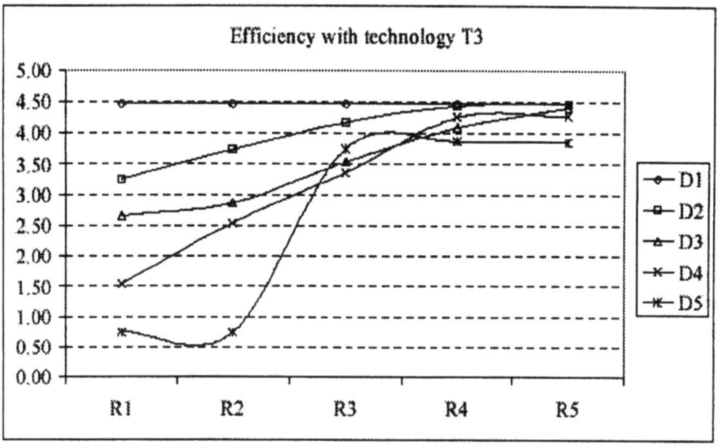


*Figure 9.3c.* efficiency for technology $T_3$

of what they confer. The explanation is highly intuitive and is linked to the fact that under $R_5$ there are strong incentives to social aggregation. Thus when the distributive rule is proportional, wealthier agents are guaranteed to receive a substantial amount of output and the more they can exploit complementarities and returns to scale (by accepting less endowed subjects into their own partnership) the more they receive in terms of payoff. Clearly, poor agents are willing to enter into such a partnership, because it is likely to enable them to obtain more than they will probably achieve by remaining outside. Clearly this incentive to social aggregation is the weaker the greater is the part of the partnership output that is to be put aside and shared equally; in this case it is as if wealthy agents received no acknowledgement of the extent of their conferment in obtaining the partnership output, receiving (at least in part) as much as less endowed members. This fact clearly incentivates wealthy agents to withdraw from the coalition and form smaller partnerships with members that have similar endowments.

When the technology is $T_1$ we obtain a somewhat different result; when the distribution of capital endowments is fairly concentrated (see $D_3$, $D_4$ and especially $D_5$), efficiency is maximized under the distributive rule $R_4$, i.e. when a part of the partnership output is distributed regardless of the individual conferment. Here we observe a rather interesting phenomenon that we explain specifically with reference to case $D_5$. In this case the payoff of the capital owner increases with the cardinality of the partnership of which s/he is a member, but this does not hold for workers: their payoff (under whatever distributive rule with the obvious exception of $R_1$) is a decreasing function of the cardinality of the coalition they are in (provided it includes the capitalist). Therefore each of them prefers to be the only partner of the capital owner, leaving any other agent outside the partnership. However, for those who adopt this line of action, given the working of RM, there is a high probability of failing to enter into any partnership at all; in order to avoid this situation, they increase the number of agents with whom they would be willing to enter into coalition, and send signals accordingly, without however proposing the grand coalition (that is, the situation in which the payoff is minimal), thus giving rise to a sort of mixed strategies Nash equilibrium[12].

**The partnership structure.** To probe more deeply into the analysis of the results let us examine the emerging organization of society in partnerships. This is pictured in the Figures 9.5, 9.6 and 9.7; any block $T_k$ corresponds to a technology and every picture at the cross of row $D_h$ and column $R_j$ shows on the vertical axis the size of the coalition in which an agent expects to find him/herself (vertical bars represent the standard deviations) and on the horizontal axis the agents, maintaining the same order as in Table 1 (i.e. richest to poorest agents from left to right). As an example, an enlargment of a single little box is reported below, showing the common labelling of the $x$ and $y$ axes

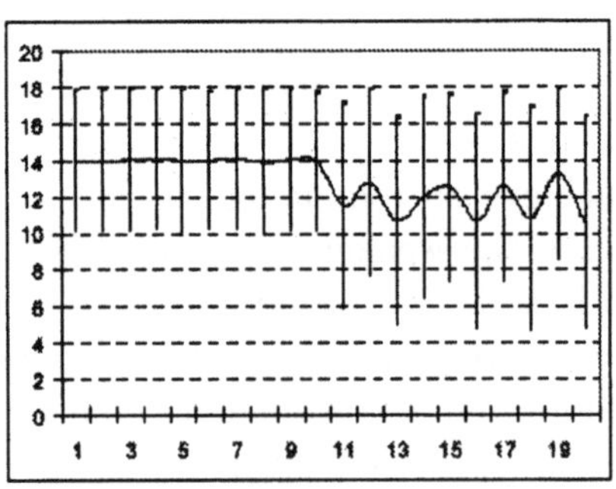


*Figure 9.4.* enlargement of box $(D_1, R_1$

From the previous Figures we see that generally, in passing to distributive rules in which the proportional component is greater (e.g. from $R_1$ to $R_2$) the expected coalition size increases (this is simply the explanation of the previously observed increase in efficiency). The exception to this rule is again $T_1$ for $D_3$, $D_4$ and $D_5$, for the same reasons examined in the previous Section, i.e. a mismatching among the actions of those agents (namely the poorest ones) who would like to exclude some other

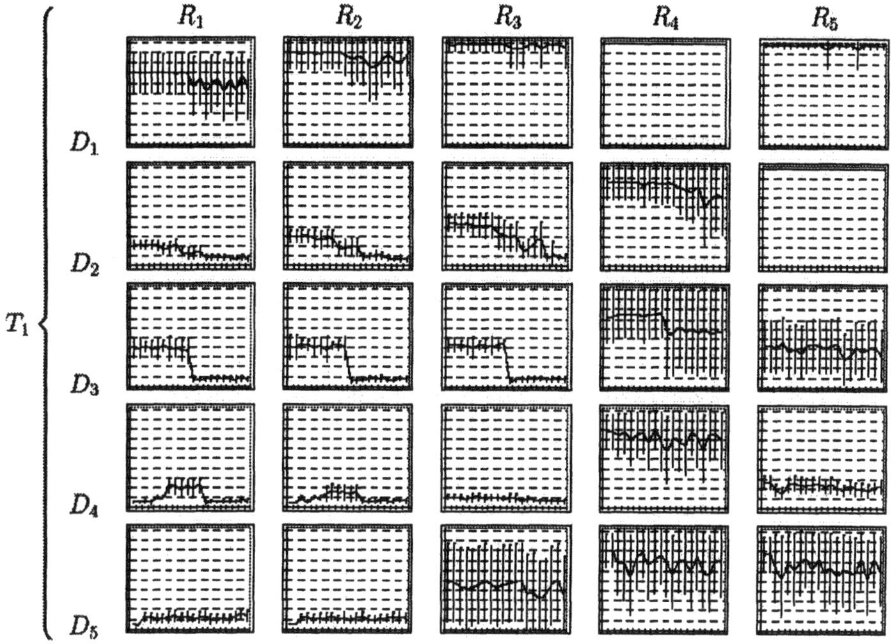


*Figure 9.5.* expected coalition size and standard deviation for $T_1$

agent, without incurring too high a risk of being the excluded one. In contrast, even in these cases, wealthy agents always succeed in coalescing.

This pattern of coalition formation among similar agents holds for every simulation; this confirms the intuitions of Section 2.3 and it is particularly clear when we examine the endowment distribution $D_3$. We can see that when the distributive rule contains a strong component of egalitarianism (as under $R_1$ or $R_2$), the economy partitions into two classes; the first is characterized by agents with positive endowments both of capital and labor, while the second is made up of agents with labor only. Another confirmation of this pattern comes from the analysis of the (rather realistic) distribution $D_4$. Agents in the middle of the distribution (characterized by similar endowments) coalesce even under $R_1$, while the wealthy individuals do not. However, when the distributive rule becomes more proportional, e.g. $R_3$, then some agents belonging to the middle class begin forming partnerships with wealthier agents; at the same time, the other agents belonging to the middle class start coalescing with some poor agents. Therefore we observe that the middle class is split into two subsets, one where agents form aggregations with

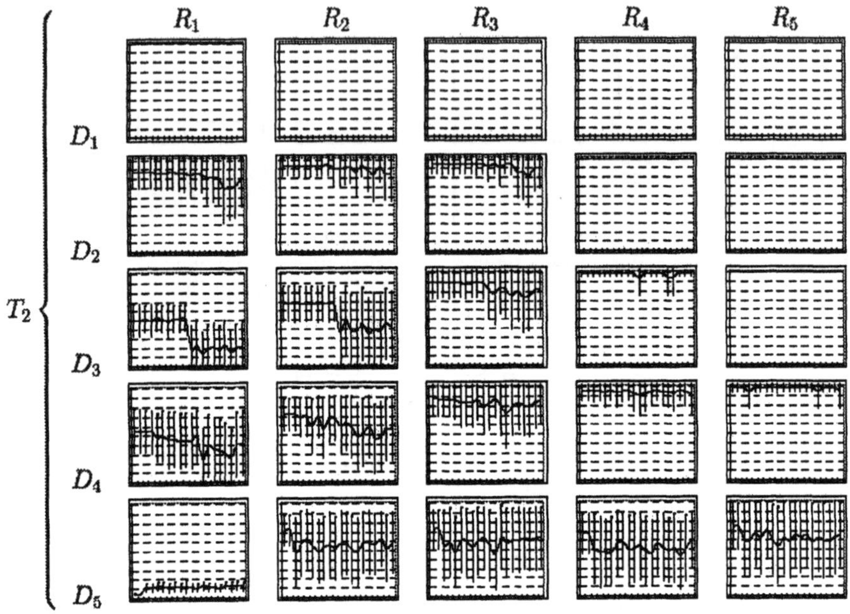


*Figure 9.6.* expected coalition size and standard deviation for $T_2$

wealthier individuals and one where agents coalesce with poorer agents. Again this confirms the intuitions of Section 2.3.

**Which technology?.** With respect to the problem of the efficiency of an economic organization, we can raise yet another problem. Suppose that the economy is in a technological state as in $T_1$ and that an Authority aims to promote a technological improvement: if the rules of the game among the agents are those described here, what kind of technology would be preferable (and hence incentivated)? In other terms, would the system be more efficient with a technology exhibiting higher elasticity of output to labor (i.e. $T_2$) or to capital (i.e. $T_3$)? To answer this question we show in the Figure 9.6 and 9.7 the expected payoffs obtained under each technological regime in $T$, when the distribution of endowments and the distributive rule change (the variables $D_h$ and $R_j$ are to be read on the bottom axes).

Apart from $D_1$ (in this case the technologies with higher returns to scale are equivalent), we can see that $T_2$ is generally more efficient than $T_3$ for every distributive rule, provided the distribution of property rights on the capital stock is not excessively concentrated (this holds for $D_2$, $D_3$ and $D_4$). In contrast $T_3$ is the most efficient technology when the

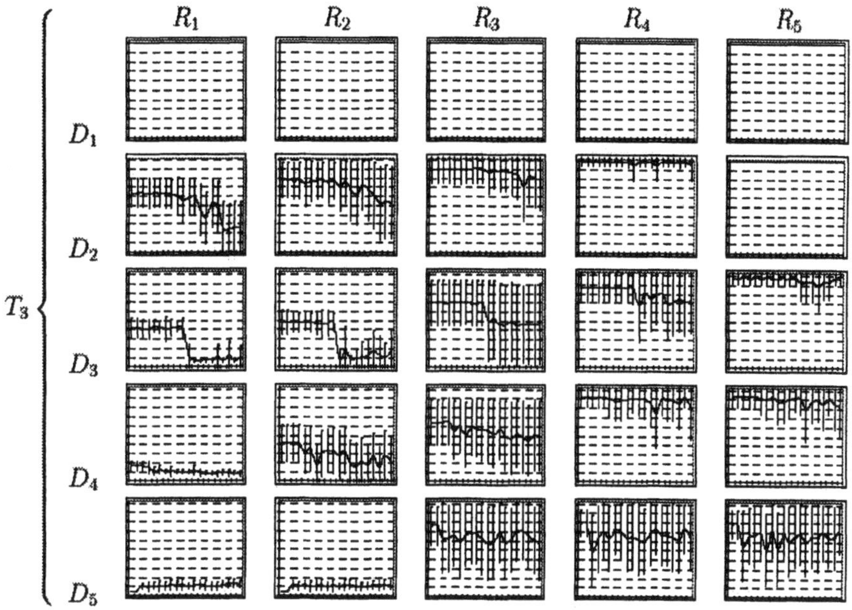


*Figure 9.7.* expected coalition size and standard deviation for $T_3$

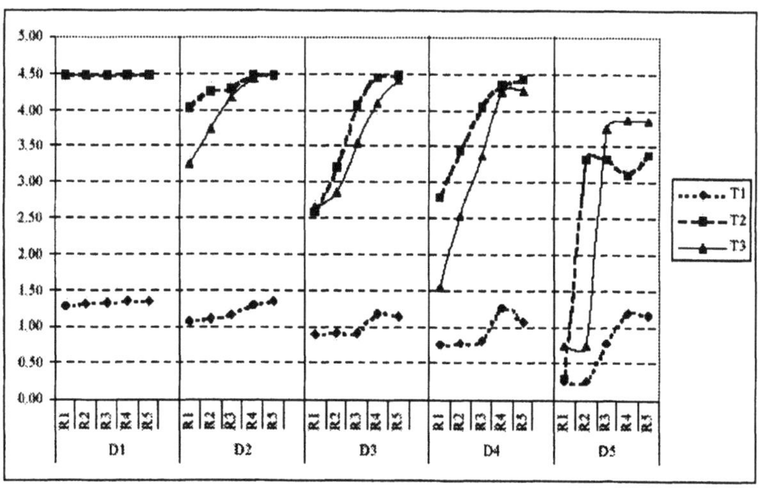


*Figure 9.8.* comparison of alternative technologies

distribution of endowments is highly concentrated ($D_5$) with the single exception of $R_2$. The explanation of these results lies again in the incentives to social aggregation in relation to the distribution of endowments.

Thus it is clear that, when the technology is $T_2$, the most productive factor is the one that all agents possess in equal amounts; therefore the capital owners likewise receive a greater amount of output by accepting workers in their partnership, because this substantially increases the productivity of the capital stock. This in turn implies a greater expected coalition size for every agent and hence greater overall efficiency. On the other hand, $T_3$ does not induce such strong incentives to social aggregation because the privileged input is capital and the productivity of labor is lower than in $T_2$; this increases the incentives for capital owners to aggregate with one another, using the capital stock and labor they own, without opening up the partnership to workers (for the latter would not increase the output sufficiently to enable the capital owners to receive a greater payoff).

$D_5$ is again a special case, because it is characterized by the reluctance of workers to extend the partnership with the capitalist to the grand coalition. In face of the impossibility of aggregating the whole population, the best technology is clearly the one that privileges the factor that is certainly fully employed, i.e. capital, so that $T_3$ proves more efficient.

One might wonder whether a similar reasoning could be applied to determine which technology gives rise to the most equitable distributions of output. To this end, we present below a Figure similar to the one previously examined, but representing the value of an index[13] measuring the degree of equity corresponding to any combination of technology, distribution of endowments and distributive rule. There is no doubt in this case that if the equity of the distribution of output is a value, then the technology that proves to be superior is $T_2$. In such a technological regime, the greater part of output (*especially* when the distributive rule has a proportional component) is distributed to labor, a factor that every agent possesses in equal amount, so that the final distribution is certainly more even than in the other cases ($T_1$ and $T_3$) where capital (the unevenly distributed factor) receives a greater share of output.

## 5.2. The equity-efficiency trade-off

From what we have seen in the previous Section, it appears that a technology like $T_2$ is definitely superior to $T_3$ since it almost always proves more efficient than $T_3$ (the comparison with $T_1$ is useless because the lower strength of return to scale entails a lower output, given the same available amount of resources) and it certainly gives rise to more equitable outcomes. However, even if it comes to be the ruling technological regime, there is still a trade-off between efficiency and equity in

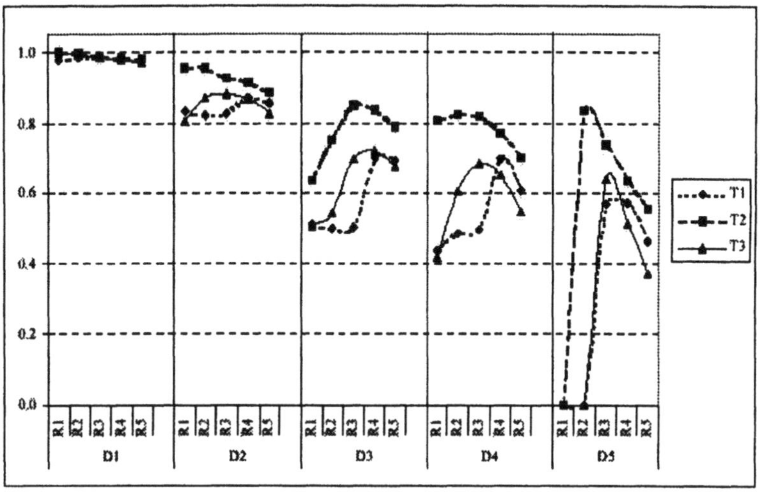


*Figure 9.9.* Equity

the choice of the distributive rule to implement in this economy (here, for the sake of exposition, we examine the case of $T_2$ but the same phenomena occurs under $T_3$). In order to illustrate this point we make reference to Figure 9.9: here, for any distribution of endowments ($D_1 ... D_5$) we plot expected average payoff (on the horizontal axis) versus an equality index of the same distribution of payoffs (on the vertical axis); the pictures in the bottom row of Figure 9.10 are simply the enlargements of the part enclosed in the rectangle in the pictures immediately above.

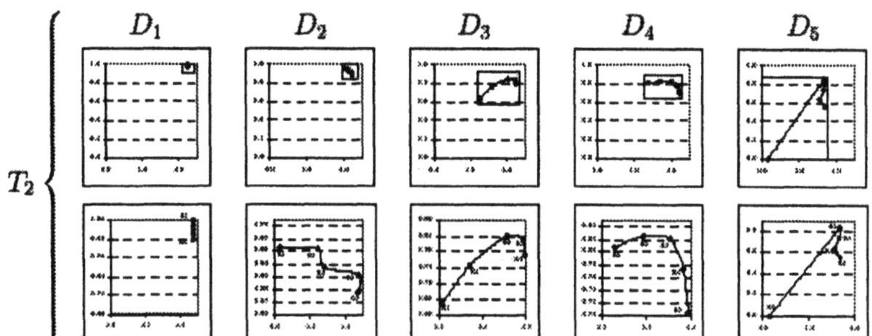


*Figure 9.10.* Pairs equity-efficiency to different distributive rules

In Figure 9.10 we have marked with a dot the pairs equity-efficiency corresponding to the different distributive rules. We notice that a trade-off between equity and efficiency always arises for at least a couple of distributive rules when the proportional component in the distributive rule increases. The explanation for this finding is easy; the more the distributive rule is proportional the more there are incentives to social aggregation, as already seen in Section 2.3. The consequent increase in size of the formed partnerships increases the produced output, thus improving efficiency. However, the fact the proportional component in the distributive rule becomes more important has the effect of amplifying in terms of distributed output the asymmetries among agents already present in the distribution of initial endowments, thereby also increasing the inequality of the distribution.

This can be further exemplified by looking at the distributions of individually expected payoffs for $D_3$ and $D_4$ and the five possible distributive rules, as shown in Figure 9.11 (every picture in the following Figure depicts on the vertical axis the expected payoff -and its variance- for each agent $i$ shown on the horizontal axis -the range is from 1 to 20 as usual- ). When the distributive rule has a strong equitative component, the incentives for aggregation are very low and the poorest subjects may occasionally enter into a contractual relationship with the wealthier agents, while the latter coalesce rather easily. This explains both the fact that the expected payoff is an increasing (and its variance a decreasing) function of the capital endowment an agent possesses. However, when the distributive rule becomes more proportional, the emerging coalitional structure is well defined and the distribution of output is an amplification of the distribution of the capital endowments[14].

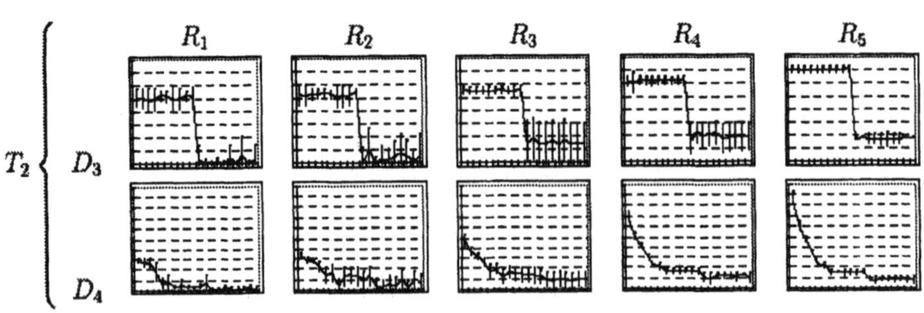


*Figure 9.11.* expencted payoff and its standard deviation for $T_2$

A particularly interesting result is that $R_1$ is almost never efficient or equitable (the only exception is when the distribution of initial endowments is $D_2$). The explanation of this finding is that under $R_1$ the incentives to coalesce for wealthy agents are very low and such agents do not enter into a partnership with subjects lacking capital endowments, so that the latter cannot produce (and consume) any output. When the distributive rule becomes more proportional, the incentives to coalesce increase and therefore even the poorest agents have positive expected payoffs. In short, the gain of the poorest agents, at least when passing from $R_1$ to $R_2$, is proportionally greater than that of the wealthy agents and this explains the increase both in equality and in the average expected payoff.

## 5.3. Can there be unemployment?

In the Introduction we raised the question of whether there could be unemployment in our economy. The intuition was that if the distributive rule is too egalitarian then the poor agents would prefer to coalesce with the wealthy agents, but the latter find it more advantageous either to stay alone or to form a coalition with one another. Therefore, we can state that situations can arise in which full utilization of labor does not occur because of insufficient demand for labor itself (of course, this is conditional on the governing distributive rule). There are many instances of such a phenomenon in our results, but for the sake of exposition we focus on the environment $Q = [T_3, D_5, R_2]$. The following matrix shows the average probabilities with which a player from a row (i.e. the capital owner (1) or one of the laborers $(2 \ldots I)$) signal his willingness to coalesce with one of the players in columns:

| | 1 | $2 \ldots I$ |
|---|---|---|
| 1 | 1 | 0 |
| $2 \ldots I$ | 0.92 | 0.48 |

Table 4: agents' signals for $Q = [T_3, D_5, R_2]$.

Clearly the capitalist rejects any cooperation with the poorest agents (the average probability of the latter receiving a signal of collaboration is 0). On the other hand, agents from 2 to $I$ would be willing to form a partnership with the capitalist (the probability with which on average they signal their willingness to cooperate with the capitalist is 0.92). The outcome is certainly a situation in which the capitalist produces in autarchy and the poorest agents match their willingness with a probability of 0.48, but cannot produce and consume since they do not possess any capital endowment[15].

Now we can further extend the argument and see whether labor is the only factor that is not satisfied in the equilibria of this type of economy, or whether capital may likewise turn out to be partly unequipped, notwithstanding the readiness of its owners to pool with workers. This is the type of phenomenon that has already been hinted at in Section

2.3. Thus in some environments there may be incentives for the capital owners to extend the partnership to agents who are less endowed, but each of the latter would like to be the only one to pool his/her own resources with those of the capitalists and is reluctant to extend the size of the coalition, because this would imply a loss of welfare for himself/herself. In this situation the poorest agents seek to lower the cardinality of the partnership with the capitalist and signal their unwillingness to accept any other individuals in the same situation. Therefore, since a partnership can form only if all its members agree to accept the others, this implies that there are potential candidates who would be willing to coalesce with the capital owner but do not succeed in doing so because other workers veto their access to the partnership, even though the capitalist would be ready to accept the contractual relation. This is a case of under-utilization of capital due to the opposition of the (potential) employees to an enlargement of the partnership. This outcome arises rather frequently in the results of the simulations when the distributive rule is proportional and the ownership of capital is strongly concentrated. Again for the sake of exposition, we show just one case related to the environment $Q' = [T_3, D_5, R_5]$; in this case the matrix of the average probabilities of agents' communicating their willingness to coalesce with others is the following:

| | 1 | $2 \ldots I$ |
|---|---|---|
| 1 | 1 | 0.78 |
| $2 \ldots I$ | 1 | 0.76 |

Table 5: agents signals for $Q' = [T_3, D_5, R_5]$.

The capitalist sends a strong signal (0.78) of his willingness to form a partnership with the less endowed agents; the latter wish to coalesce with the capitalist, but at the same time each of them objects with probability $(1 - 0.76^2)$ to the concept of another agent of his/her group participating in the partnership with the capitalist, so that the total conferment of labor is less than the capitalist would have liked, i.e. capital may be under-utilized.

## 6. Conclusions

In this paper we have set up an artificial society in which a population of heterogeneous, sophisticated, but not fully rational agents interact and form production partnerships. The way in which the output produced is divided among the members of a partnership is not a matter of bargaining; instead the distributive rule is assumed to be a commonly accepted social convention. Given these premises, agents are engaged in a signaling process by means of which they communicate and revise their willingness to coalesce with others on the basis of the advantages they perceive from aggregation. The process that we represent is not dynamic in the strict sense, because there is no accumulation of resources, but rather it is meant to represent a (virtual) signaling process by means of which agents allocate themselves in groups, i.e. production partnerships.

We have analyzed the emerging organization of the population through the lenses of efficiency and equity, to see if and how these quantities are related to the available technology, the distribution of property rights and the rule governing the distribution of the partnership output. We find that the average payoff, a proxy of the efficiency of the system, is positively correlated to the share of the partnership output that is distributed among the members in direct proportion to their conferred amounts of resources. The explanation for this is that even though a more egalitarian distributive rule may award greater protection to the weakest parties in society, it leads the wealthy to refuse to coalesce with the poorest agents, since the wealthy would obtain more either in isolation or by forming a small group among themselves. It is precisely this fact that prevents the aggregation process: hence returns to scale are not exploited. In contrast, a distributive rule that assigns shares of output in proportion to individual endowments protects the wealthiest individuals; such a rule attributes to them a substantial share of what is produced, so that they have incentives to allow other contributors into the production process (at least to the extent that their shares of resources over aggregate conferment entitles them to receive an increasing amount of output). This defines the limit to the aggregation process, so that we may observe poor agents that would like to coalesce with others but are rejected because their entrance would imply a lower payoff for the current members of the partnership. We have interpreted this as a prototype of involuntary unemployment.

On the other hand, given a social convention concerning the distribution of output, the more a productive factor (capital in our case) is unevenly distributed among agents, the more the resulting organization of society is inefficient, at least when the distributive rule prescribes that a part of the partnership output is to be divided equally. The explanation is the same as before; the fact that a share of total output is to be distributed independently of the individual conferment is a protection for the poorest individuals, but induces the wealthier members of society to refrain from coalescing with them; it follows that society is more fragmented (and hence inefficient, given increasing returns to scale) the more the distribution of capital is concentrated.

On the question of equity, similar considerations apply; the less the distributive rule has equitable elements, the more the aggregation process (net of coordination problems) is incentivated; the presence of increasing returns to scale then allows production of a greater amount of output and the poorest agents are likewise entitled to receive a payment that they would not otherwise be able to obtain. When the distribution of property rights is fairly even, this has the effect of reducing inequality, but when there are huge differences in the ownership of one factor of production, this may have the effect of amplifying the differences in what individuals receive, thereby increasing inequality in face of an increase in aggregate social output. This is particularly noticeable when the factor on which people have different property rights is also the one with respect to which output has the greatest elasticity. This explains the presence of the trade-off between equity and efficiency that we have observed in many cases. To the limited extent of our model, we find that the equal sharing distributive rule is never a social optimum.

These welfare considerations and the presence of a possible trade-off between equity and efficiency open the path to intervention policies aimed at either promoting alternative distributive policies or redistributing the ownership of some productive factors according to the objectives deemed to be relevant, i.e. the efficiency or equity of the final organization of society into production partnerships. It goes without saying that the appropriateness and the effects of any such policies is better evaluated in a purely dynamic context composed of a sequence of economies such as the ones analyzed here which are linked by accumulation of the reproducible factors of production, so that a part of the output received by a member of a partnership is saved and invested. This enrichment would link the present model with many issues in the current debate on endogenous growth and distribution; this is precisely the line that will be pursued in the agenda for further research within this project.

## Appendix: Genetic Algorithms

Building on the idea of natural selection, GAs start working on a set of candidate signals (randomly generated and/or inherited from the past) and select the signals with the highest fitness and then "recombine" their single components (building blocks) to produce new ones. The basic engine behind GAs is such as that, if a single component corresponds to a particularly efficient action (and this is measured by the fitness of the signal itself), then it will be more easily reused in the formation of new signals. In the following we briefly describe the working of the GAs procedure.

# 1. Encoding

The first step is to represent the signal in a way that can be handled by GAs. This is done by coding a signal in a binary alphabet as a string of bits of length equal to the number of agents; a 1 in the $j^{th}$ position of the string will indicate the willingness to coalesce with agent $j$, while a 0 means the opposite. For example take an economy with 4 agents; in such a case a possible signal of agent 1 is a string like the following:

| | | | |
|---|---|---|---|
| 1 | 0 | 1 | 1 |

which means that agent 1 is ready to coalesce with agents 3 and 4 (or even only one of them), but excludes agent 2 from any coalition containing 1.

Therefore the set of signals on which the GAs work is a $J \times I$ binary matrix, where $J$ is the number of signals available to the procedure and $I$ is the number of agents.

As is well known, GAs work sequentially and their procedure is made up of three basic steps: (i) selection, (ii) recombination and (iii) mutation.

# 2. Selection

In biological evolution, the greater is the ability of a species to adapt and cope with the environment, the higher is the probability for it to survive and reproduce; similarly GAs privilege those strings (actions, signals) with the highest fitness, giving them the highest chance to survive and reproduce. In order to model this mechanism we assume that $J$ strings are drawn from the available population, where the probability of a string's being drawn is positively correlated to its fitness indexes. In this way the higher is the fitness index the higher is the probability that the corresponding signal will be selected and passed to the next step of the procedure; conversely strategies with a low fitness index are likely to be eliminated rapidly, since they proved inefficient.

There are many types of selection operators; we consider geometric selection, roulette wheel selection and tournament selection and use them randomly. For more details on these types of algorithms see Koza (1993)).

# 3. Cross-over

Mere selection of the signals with the highest fitness serves the purpose of refining the set of current schemas but does not allow for the discovery of better ones. This further step is accomplished by recombining the building blocks of the selected strings, as in the natural process of procreation and consequent exchange of genes. By "mixing" the building blocks (genes) of the fittest signals we obtain new strings with hopefully enhanced capacity of adaptation to the environment; such a mixing is called *cross-over*.

The cross-over operator can be modeled in several ways. We adopt the most commonly used in the literature: first a pair of strings is picked up at random from the set of selected strings (they are candidates to be parents) and, with a certain probability, they mix their genes. The newly generated proposals are substantially different from their parents, although they are "based" on them.

# 4. Mutation

A crucial element in any evolutionary process is chance. The presence of chance in our context is taken into account by adding a further step in the GAs procedure in which every single bit in the set of strings is subjected (with a low probability) to a random mutation of its state. By this trick we avoid the lock-in phenomenon and we assist in the search to escape from local inefficient optima.

## 5. Setting of the parameters in the simulations

In all simulations we set $J$, i.e. the number of strings that every agents considers when applying GAs, equal to 30; the probability of geometric selection, i.e. the probability that the best string is selected, equal to 0.8; the parameter of tournament selection, i.e. the number of strings that are selected and compared to find the best string, equal to 4; the probability of cross-over, i.e. the probability that given two strings they crossover their genes, equal to 0.6; and finally the probability of mutation, i.e. the probability that a bit of a string changes its state, equal to 0.03[16].

## Notes

1. The main difference between a partnership and a firm is the possibility for any agent belonging to a partnership to veto the participation of anyone else, while these are not usually the terms of the contractual relations within a firm.

2. Agents are boundedly rational because (i) they are not far sighted, i.e. they do not engage in any strategic reasoning in order to forecast the consequences of their own actions and mantain static expectations, (ii) they try to find the best responses to the expected configuration of strategies, but the optimization process takes the form of Genetic Algorithms that are good but not perfect at finding optimal responses. On the implementation of Genetic Algorithms as a decision procedure see Holland, Holyoak and Thagard (1986) and Holland and Miller (1991) and the Appendix 6.

3. There are many contributions in the literature studying coalition formation games with externalities (e.g. see Guesnerie and Oddou (1988), Ray and Vohra (1999), Thoron (1998), Yi (1997)). This feature could easily be introduced in our context as well and could arise, for example, if the partnership output were valued by a price, whose level depends on the total quantity of output produced in the economy. To keep things simple, we disregard these situations.

4. As can easily be checked, this proportional scheme is a proper generalization to the case of increasing returns to scale of the standard marginal distributive rule.

5. In this is implicit the idea that no one can be forced to participate in a group if they do not wish to (and hence do not show their willingness) to adhere to it; on the other hand a group can form only if all its members agree to it.

6. This presumes that any agent $i$ knows (a) the production function, (b) the endowments of the other members of $S_{\iota(i)}(\theta)$ and (c) the distributive rule. This assumption will be retained throughout.

7. In the Swarm Community there is a GAs library contributed by J. J. Merelo (*Breeder-2.1*). In this work, however, we have used a completely indipendent procedure that we think better suits our purposes, mainly due to the implementation of different selection and crossover methods.

8. Consider the case in which agent 1 sends a signal {1,2,3}, agent 2 {2,3} and agent 3 {1,2,3}; then the three partnership structures $\sigma^1 = \{\{1\},\{2,3\}\}$, $\sigma^2 = \{\{2\},\{1,3\}\}$ and $\sigma^3 = \{\{3\},\{1,2\}\}$ are compatible with individual signals.

9. To see this point, take the example of the previous footnote and suppose that agents are extracted in the order 1,3,2: the formed partnership structure is $\sigma^2$. On the other hand, if the order of extraction is 3,2,1 the formed partnership structure is $\sigma^1$. If all possible orders of extractions are equally likely, we have $P(\sigma^1) = \frac{1}{4}$, $P(\sigma^2) = \frac{1}{2}$ and $P(\sigma^3) = \frac{1}{4}$, which are the probabilities of § ??.

10. Althought we will only represent the inheritance relation, it is worth noticing that a Class Diagram also shows the aggregation and composition relations.

11. Again for simplicity purposes, the stopping condition is simply that the number of periods does not exceed an exogenously given threshold. This threshold has been chosen heuristically to ensure convergence of the system.

12. This argument holds also for $D_3$ and $D_4$, but the situation is less dramatic for the laborers, thus explaining the fact that the efficiency curves, though downward bending in passing from $R_4$ to $R_5$, do not have the same negative slope as in the case of $D_5$.

13. More precisely this index is equal to 1 minus the Gini index, so that a value of 1 means a uniform distribution, while for 0 we have the maximum concentrated distribution.

14. Notice that the range of vertical axis is from 0 to 8 for $D_3$, while it is from 0 to 20 for $D_4$.

15. Notice that the probability that $k$ agents out of the 19 without capital endowments match their respective signals and form a coalition is the value at $k$ of the binomial distribution with 19 degrees of freedom and a probability of success $p = 0.48^2$. The mean value of the cardinality of a coalition among the poor, computed with these probabilities, is very close to that found in the numerical simulations and shown in Figure 9.6.

16. Heuristically, these values seem sufficient to ensure convergence of agents' sets of signals at the end of every simulation. Changing the basic characteristics, this value should also change; for example it is clear that a greater number of agents would require an increase in the number of periods needed for convergence.

## References

Arifovic, J. (1996). "The Behaviour of the Exchange Rate in the Genetic Algorithm and Experimental Economies". *Journal of Political Economy*, 104(3), 510-541.

Axtell, R. (1999). "The Emergence of Firms in a Population of Agents: Local Increasing Returns, Unstable Nash Equilibria, and Power Law Size Distributions". CSED Working Paper N 3.

Bernheim, B. D., B. Peleg and M. D. Whinston (1987). "Coalition-Proof Nash Equilibria: Concepts". *Journal of Economic Theory*, 42(1), 1-12.

Farrell, J. and S. Scotchmer (1988). "Partnerships". *Quarterly Journal of Economics*, 103(2), 279-97.

Fiaschi, D. and P.M. Pacini (1998). "Endogenous Coalition Formation with Identical Agents". Working paper n *308. Progetto d'Ateneo: L'economia italiana e la sua collocazione internazionale: una redifinizione delle politiche di welfare e dell'occupazione per una piu' efficiente crescita economica*, Dipartimento di Scienze Economiche, Universita' degli Studi di Bologna.

Fiaschi, D. and P.M. Pacini (1999). "Simulation of Coalition Formation with Heterogeneous Agents". Paper presented for the International Workshop "Syntethic Biographies: State of the Art and Developments", 1999 San Miniato, Italy.

Galor O. and J. Zeira (1993). "Income Distribution and Macroeconomics", *Review of Economic Studies*, vol. 60, 35-52.

Guesnerie, R. and C. Oddou (1988). "Increasing Returns to Size and Their Limits." *Scandinavian Journal of Economics*, 90, 259-73.

Holland, J.H., K.J. Holyoak, R.N. and P. Thagard (1986). *Induction: Processes of Inference, Learning and Discovery.* MIT Press, Cambridge Mass.

Holland, J.H. and J.H. Miller (1991). "Artificial Adaptive Agents in Economic Theory". *American Economic Review, Papers and Proceeding*, 81(2), 365-70.

Koza J. R. (1993). *Genetic programming: on the programming of computers by means of natural selection.* London, MIT Press.

Kremer M. (1993). "O-ring theory of economic development". *Quarterly Journal of Economics*, 108, 551-576.

Mailath, G. J. (1998). "Do People Play Nash Equilibrium? Lessons From Evolutionary Game Theory". *Journal of Economic Literature*, Vol. 36, September, 1347-1374.

Ray, D. and R.Vohra (1999). "A Theory of Endogenous Coalition Structures". *Games and Economic Behavior*, 26(2), 286-336.

Sherstyuk K. (1998). "Efficiency in partnership structures". *Journal of Economic Behavior & Organization*, Vol 36, 331-346.

Thoron, S. (1998). "Formation of a Coalition-Proof Stable Cartel". *Canadian Journal of Economics*, 31(1), 63-76.

Yi, S.S. (1997). "Stable Coalition Structures with Externalities". *Games and Economic Behavior* 20(2), 201-37.

Chapter 10

# CASINOWORLD:AN AGENT-BASED MODEL WITH HETEROGENEOUS RISK PREFERENCES AND ADAPTIVE BEHAVIOR

Michael Harrington
*Department of Political Science, UCLA (310)*
michaelharrington@home.com

Darold Higa
*Department of International Relations, USC (626)*
dhiga@vtechmedia.com

**Abstract** One of the central presumptions in general equilibrium models widely used in neoclassical macroeconomics today is that people are pretty much alike, or homogeneous in their preferences. A second presumption, one of mathematical convenience, is that people's preferences are exogenous and fairly fixed over time and thus do not vary or adapt readily to changing circumstances. Lastly, rational actor behavior implies the availability of requisite information and the ability of individuals to process that information accurately. There is a vast class of theories that are consistent with these presumptions but such theories have difficulty in explaining persistent skewed distributional outcomes such as income and wealth inequalities within groups and across societies. Because of these limiting presumptions, the proffered explanations for such skewed distributions necessarily refer back to differences in initial resource endowments. We would restate the inequality question more provocatively by asking: Is poverty deliberate?

The CasinoWorld model presented in this paper uses agent-based simulation modeling in an attempt to overcome the limitations of standard equilibrium models. We use the SWARM programming environment to model agents with heterogeneous risk preferences in an environment of uncertainty and allow them to adapt their gaming strategies to maximize survival by preserving their wealth stakes. In this way SWARM allows us to endogenize heterogeneity and adaptability with regard to agent behavior. The results show that players with initial high risk preferences who are lucky can adapt their gambling strategies to increase their relative wealth. This model provides a rudimentary foundation for demonstrating that natural, rational behavior and luck can form the basis of inequality. We support the assumptions of the model with a discussion of experimental research in economic behavior, decision-making behavior and evolutionary psychology.

# 1. Introduction

The CasinoWorld model presented here is an effort to employ agent-based simulation modeling techniques to study distributional dynamics in a population of autonomous agents. Our two related goals are 1) to develop a basic model to study distributional dynamics and 2) to develop some simple behavioral rules for economic agents that expand upon standard neo-classical assumptions. We believe that the second goal is directly related to the first in that a divergence in natural human behavioral choices may be a significant determinant of distributional outcomes.

We use the object-oriented SWARM programming environment to build the model. Admittedly, in its initial stage it is merely a rudimentary demonstration of distributional dynamics. Most simply, the model is a representation of risk averse agents "gambling" with their wealth in an uncertain, probabilistic "casino" environment. At this preliminary stage there is no interaction among agents, only between agents and the environment. Agent preferences over gaming strategies vary across agents and over time in response to changing individual wealth as well as parameter changes in the environment. In this sense they are heterogeneous and adaptable.

The attempt here is to use simulation modeling to overcome some of the limitations of equilibrium models in examining the puzzle of skewed distributional outcomes. In particular we are interested in the persistence of skewed wealth distributions. While persistent, we do not believe that these skewed distributions represent an equilibrium state, especially when considered in a political and social context. We also suspect that neo-classical explanations of skewed distributions flow partly from the assumptions of equilibrium models and that these explanations have not really borne fruit empirically [Galbraith (2000), Lucas (2000)].

With this model we hope to take the first step to convincingly demonstrate that persistent skewed distributions can partly result from heterogeneous preferences and rational, deliberate survival strategies that perpetuate the effects of good and bad luck. More importantly, these may be the internal behavioral dynamics that partly drive the system. In other words, the distributional outcomes may be endogenous to a population of heterogeneous adaptable agents with rational survival strategies and that this may be a fair representation of the real world. The economic and social policy implications of this possibility are manifest but will not be discussed at great length here.

The paper is organized into several sections. In section 2, following this introduction, we discuss some of the limitations and criticisms of equilibrium models employing the standard economic notion of human behavior. This notion encompasses the set of assumptions often used to describe *homo economicus* and include exogenously determined, homogeneous, fixed preferences and the availability of information by which agents are able to calculate those preferences. The rational maximand is assumed to be utility or profit maximization, depending on whether the calculus applies to consumers or firms. Thus stated, the rational economic agent is "a perfectly informed individual with infinite computing capacity who maximizes a fixed exogenous utility function[1] ."This conceptualization too often bears little relation to actual human beings.

In section 3 we discuss some of the multi-disciplinary approaches to the study of human behavior and decision making. These approaches derive from the disciplines of the natural sciences, sociobiology, cognition, behavioral psychology, anthropology and evolutionary psychology. Our purpose is to draw upon the experimental research in these various fields to expand our notion of *homo economicus* to better approximate *homo sapiens*[2].

In section 4 we present the model and our rationale for the agent decision rules. We explore the dynamics of the play and adaptive strategies. In section 5 we discuss the results, which are suggestive rather than profound, and we also explore our intentions for future developments of the model. The object-oriented Swarm programming language is most useful in allowing us to establish a basic framework in which to increment future changes without having to rewrite all the code. This is an important aspect of computer simulation tools as the initial stages of model building can involve a considerable expenditure of time and effort. In particular we are interested in incorporating agent interaction by introducing trade into the environment and thereby making our proto-society interdependent.

## 2. Standard Economic Models of Human Behavior

There has been considerable discussion in the literature regarding the limits of equilibrium models and their appropriateness and applicability to various real world phenomena. Most of the qualified criticism of equilibrium theory has been addressed to the informational assumptions inherent in the rational calculations of agents as well as the overall endogeneity problems of equilibrium systems. One prominent example is the literature on increasing returns to scale [Kaldor (1985, 1994); Arthur (1994); Buchanan and Yoon (1994)]. Moreover, equilibrium models impose many concepts and structures that predetermine the set of possible actions for individual agents, essentially anticipating the equilibrium outcome [Kochugovindan and Vriend (1998); Vriend (1994)]. Before we suggest the "irrelevance" of equilibrium theory, we should remind ourselves that the intent of equilibrium models has been to find, study and understand equilibrium states. In this respect these tools have been very powerful and their use has virtually defined economic science for most of the past century.

Nevertheless, there are some vitally important puzzles characterized by disequilibria states that have persistently eluded sufficient explanation within the discipline. These puzzles are particularly salient to the "big picture" of life in a market society and include the mechanisms of trade and distribution in a decentralized, self-ordered system [Galbraith (2000)]. In the applied arena, these macroeconomic puzzles have presented difficulties for explaining fluctuations of the business cycle as well as the dynamics of wealth, poverty and underdevelopment [Leijonhufvud (1993); Lucas (2000)]. These are especially critical issues for those who depend upon the discipline for the formulation of economic and social policy.

The specific limitations of equilibrium models that concern us are several. First are the assumptions about information and rational behavior whereby the relevant information is available to agents who then can accurately make complex, probabilistic calculations regarding their own interest. Second are the assumptions of fixed, homogeneous preferences that allow for sets of simultaneous equations with tractable solutions. We argue that the ultimate result of these technical limitations leads to the most obvious explanations—that skewed distributional outcomes result from unequal endowments. These unequal starting points are most typically ascribed to individual or group differences with regard to education, skills, culture and access to productive resources. We hypothesize that this is only part of the story.

We can illustrate our doubts with a counter-factual question. Do we truly believe that could we equalize all endowments in terms of education, physical and financial capital etc., we would essentially achieve the socialist, egalitarian ideal—that of a free and equal society in a stable equilibrium state? Or rather do we observe that the human psyche is constantly striving for inequality through status and that differences in relative risk tolerance or desire, the vagaries of fate and the dominant strategies of survival instincts ultimately determine and reinforce the distribution of economic outcomes?

Our particular focus here is on the dynamics of skewed wealth, as opposed to income, distributions. In considering this problem we expect that equilibrium assumptions are inappropriate and that the behavioral assumptions are probably too constraining or inadequate. Such models based on simultaneous equations result in explanations that must distill to different initial endowments in order to explain different outcomes. Our point is that these explanations likely obscure the endogenous human behavioral components determining distributional outcomes. For our purposes we need to consider the framework suggested for complex adaptive systems whereby individual agents are different, interactive and change as a result of events occurring through the process of interaction.

## 2.1. Sugarscape

This approach was motivated by the Sugarscape model produced by the Brookings—Santa Fe Institute 2050 Project and presented in the book by Epstein and Axtell (1996), *Growing Artificial Societies.* Sugarscape is an agent-based complex adaptive system. In the model's most basic form, agents move around a landscape searching for sugar to consume and accumulate in order to survive. They start with a specified endowment of sugar wealth, some of which they burn with each move. Each agent is assigned an internal state consisting of two variables: vision and metabolism. These are essentially natural skill endowments that favor agents with long distance vision and low rates of metabolism. Agents that fail to replenish and thus burn all their sugar soon expire.

With this simple model, Sugarscape generates skewed distributions of sugar wealth, which naturally derive from the differentiated initial endowments: wealthy agents have good vision and low metabolism or rather, agents with good vision and low metabolism become wealthy. The Gini coefficients of these skewed artificial distributions closely approximate those found in real world developed economies. These results are strongly suggestive of a systemic phenomenon hidden within the dynamic processes of interaction among autonomous agents—the "invisible hand" of complex, adaptive systems. The introduction of a second commodity, spice, and trade among agents with various stocks of sugar and spice seem to amplify the skewedness of the wealth distributions. The authors suggest that this implies a tradeoff between economic equality and economic performance.

We are sympathetic with the Sugarscape design, especially since agent decision-making behavior is autonomous and based solely on local knowledge. But we observe that the outcome is still directly attributable to the distribution of initial endowments—the varying vision and metabolic attributes, which essentially comprise the *deus ex machina* of the model. This is not wholly inconsistent with equilibrium model explanations of skewed distributions that could flow from different starting points or endowments. But we would like to extend the argument and show that distributional outcomes may be determined by heterogeneous *preferences*, unpredictability and adaptability. In other words, the determinant factors on which we focus are rational choices made by agents rather than exogenous endowments. We control for endowments by equalizing initial wealth distributions and differentiating adaptive strategies during the process of agents interacting with the environment. Our question then is: can we generate the same skewedness by equalizing endowments and merely varying behavioral preferences? Could we also introduce uncertainty by introducing an element of luck in determining outcomes and allow agents to adapt their choices according to the dictates of survival? Our reasoning is described in the next section.

## 3. A More Refined Model of Human Behavior

For some time researchers have questioned the abilities of human agents to calculate and act upon their rational self-interest [Kahnemann and Tversky (1979, 1982, 1986, 1991); Coombs (1975); Lopes (1987); Arthur (1991); Thaler (1991, 2000)]. These doubts have been raised through experiments primarily in the fields of psychology and decision making behavior. The results variously suggest that humans display poor intuitive understanding of statistical probabilities and Bayesian updates. They frequently make conflicting, "irrational" choices and change their preferences according to how the choice language is framed or according to their individual frame of reference. Under differing circumstances they seem to be both risk averse and risk seeking. Evolutionary psychologists have also weighed in to claim that many of the psychological experiments are methodologically flawed because humans intuitively understand frequency counts, not probabilities [Cosmides and Tooby (1994, 1996)].

The ubiquitousness of uncertainty in a dynamic world also calls into question the informational assumptions of neo-classical economic models. There is often a distinction made between two elements of uncertainty, the unknown and the unknowable, with the former as a function of the availability and accessibility of information. But from a behavioral perspective this distinction is not really relevant—the fickle finger of Fate or Fortune may be the most determinant factor over life's outcomes. This suggests to us a negative behavioral bias towards risk in everyday decision making, especially economic decisions. The noted socio-biologist and etymologist E.O. Wilson refers to this as the "superordinate heuristic of risk aversion[3]." We suspect that risk sensitivity may be a powerful determinant of behavioral preferences that will ultimately help to explain economic outcomes. To deal with this behavioral bias we are interested in developing a simple set of behavioral rules of behavior for individual agents consistent with the survival imperative.

## 3.1. Risk Aversion in Finance

First, we start with the basic assumption of risk aversion in finance and portfolio theory. This assumption defines absolute risk aversion as when the utility of expected wealth received with certainty is greater than the expected utility of wealth provided by a gamble[4]. The risk premium is the amount of wealth individuals are willing to give up to avoid the gamble. The existence of an insurance industry as well as empirical evidence based on investment portfolios bear out absolute risk aversion in people's behavior[5].

It has proven to be a most useful assumption in explaining financial market behavior as investors seek to minimize risks inherent in changing prices with portfolios of diversified assets. This has led to a comprehensive theory of capital asset markets and asset pricing models. However, outside the realm of financial markets, people have exhibited behavior inconsistent with the assumptions of simple absolute risk aversion. These anomalies have been most thoroughly demonstrated in the experimental studies of Daniel Kahnemann and Amos Tversky.

## 3.2. Cognition and Decision Making

One of the most glaring violations of risk aversion is that, while people tend to be risk-averse in the domain of gains, they also tend to be risk-seeking in the domain of losses. It has been shown that experimental subjects become more risk-seeking, as measured by the variance of expected outcomes, when faced with a probable loss as opposed to a probable gain. Kahnemann and Tversky have labeled this loss aversion, as opposed to pure risk aversion and its relevance depends on the relative endowments of agents. In other words, how you evaluate your survival needs and how much you have to lose. Kahnemann and Tversky argue that subjects weight losses at roughly double the value of gains. Thaler (1991) has suggested a psychological or mental accounting system to explain the apparent bias of loss aversion. The findings of these studies point to the proposition that risk preferences will vary depending on one's level of wealth and preferences will change (*i.e., adapt*) as wealth changes. This is not counter-intuitive when we think about it in terms of survival. Faced with a crippling loss, most people would choose to take a risky gamble to avoid that loss. We can also observe this in people's tendency after suffering a loss to take a previously unacceptable risk just to try to "break even". This establishes what we call a survival or "capital preservation" strategy. We conclude that loss aversion is a most basic rule consistent with the instinct for survival in an uncertain world.

## 3.3. Evolutionary Psychology

The usefulness of a survival strategy is further bolstered by the experimental research in evolutionary psychology [Cosmides and Tooby (1996, 1994b)]. One vein of this research has been based on what is referred to as optimal foraging theory [Rode, et. al (1998)]. Foraging refers to animal behavior in securing adequate food for survival. In the unpredictable natural world, animals consider the mean and variance of available food options. If the mean caloric payoff is above the current need, they choose options with the lower variance. However, they select higher variance options if their need is above the mean outcome. The theory holds that preferences under uncertainty are determined by the mean expected outcome, variance, *and* the minimal survival needs of the agent or organism. The foraging problem faced is qualitatively different from simple expected utility maximization and provides a principled basis for circumstances under which organisms will avoid or prefer uncertain options. The three relevant parameters are mean, variance and need level as opposed to just the expected mean-variance of a decision option. This reinforces our conviction that preferences are a function of economic need.

Another vein of evolutionary psychology takes issue with the conceptual bias of probabilities and the statistical intuition of rational economic agents employed in the cognition research testing. As previously mentioned, many experimental results of cognition studies suggest that humans are notoriously poor at calculating probabilities. Experimental subjects have been shown to make inconsistent choices, underestimate high probabilities, and, in general, violate many of the assumptions of rational behavior. However, counter evidence has been provided by a frequentist conceptualization of framing information to describe choices, as opposed to stating probabilities. Results from frequentist experiments show that when framing problems in terms of frequency counts rather than probabilities, subjects were much more acute in choosing consistent preferences when presented with complex problems [Cosmides and Tooby (1996)]. In addition, these results were most significant within three specific domains: problems characterized by social cheating, threats, and uncertainty. Cosmides and Tooby argue that frequency observations are much more attuned to actual human experience and have attributed domain specificity to instincts fundamental to human survival in a hunter-gatherer society. We further observe that each of all these three domains suggest that humans are more informationally acute and intuitively accurate with *perceived threats to their physical well-being or general survival.*

Given the implied applicability of this experimental research to economic decision making, we have sought to develop some simple rules for agent behavior within our model. We have specified a graduated table of odds ratios from low to high to characterize choices as gambles in expected mean-variance terms. We believe odds ratios, such as 2 to 1 or 10 to 1 are intuitively comprehensible decision choices that adhere to frequentist conceptualizations. The expected payoff and variance are explicitly stated in frequency terms and it appears fairly obvious that a 2 to 1 gamble has a lower mean-variance (less risk, less payoff) than a 6 to 1 gamble (of course, our simple agents have no reasoning ability to make such rational calculations).

Next, we deal with the concept of survival needs or the endowment effect by varying preferences according to the level of the changing wealth endowment. We will discuss these behavioral rules in greater depth in the next section.

## 4. CasinoWorld – The Basic Model

This agent-based simulation model is a simple interaction between individual agents and the environment. The environment is a composed of two look-up tables that determine the risk preference. The first is an odds ratio table where the "odds" or probability of success is the inverse of the payoff: a gamble with a 20% chance of success will command a 5 to 1 payoff while a gamble with a 50% chance of success will command only a 2 to 1 payoff. All return-to-risk ratios are thus equivalent and specified in the casino.odds file[6]. The second lookup table is a table of percentage amounts that determine the proportion of wealth for the agent's gambling stake (betValue = % of stake). These two tables are variable parameters of the Casino environment. In addition, agents receive an equal initial Wealth endowment (initialWealth) and a lower bound subsistence level (subsistLevel). Also, there is a bonus that accrues for player experience as a proxy for skill so after each play the player receives a small incremental bonus to the payoff (experienceScale). These parameters are variable and specified in the casino.setup file.

The two dimensions of risk-taking yield four separate categories of agents (see Table 10.1):

High odds/variance + high stakes = gambler

Low odds/variance + high stakes = investor

High odds/variance + low stakes = lottery player

Low odds/variance + low stakes = subsistence/saver

| | Low Odds (Low var.) | High Odds (High Var.) |
|---|---|---|
| Low | Subsistence /Saver | Lottery Player |
| High Stakes | Investor | Gambler |

Table 10.1: Risk-taking yeld

The initial random assignment of risk preferences are distributed across the Swarm GUI 2-dimensional lattice. The positions and migration of the agents on the Swarm GUI lattice follow this two-by-two matrix.

The graphic representations of agent wealth are tabulated according to agent type. The agent type is a strict partition of the world population into four quadrants that characterize each type as presented in Table 10.1. The partition corresponds to the calculated medians of the population.

## 5. The Play

Play is initiated according to the following rules:

1 The agent is randomly assigned a risk preference consisting of an odds ratio and a stake percentage preference and is placed accordingly on the 2x2 matrix or lattice;

2 Random chance, characterized by the odds ratio probabilities of success and failure with respective payoff structures, determines every player outcome at each iteration;

3 Agents adapt their risk preferences based upon the success and failure of previous gambles reflected in their changing stock of wealth;

- Winners incrementally increase their gambling stakes to reflect their winnings. Simultaneously they incrementally reduce the odds ratio, effectively reducing the variance and payoff of the next gamble. In other words, this strategy allows them to wage higher stakes on less risky gambles;
- Losers incrementally decrease their gambling stakes to reflect their losses and simultaneously incrementally increase their odds ratio to increase the variance and payoff of the next gamble to try to recapture their loss. In other words, they take higher risk gambles with smaller stakes;

4 Playing experience enhances the payoffs of successful gambles. Each play increments the skill level of the agent which provides a small percentage bonus to successful gambles, essentially enhancing the payoff structure;

5 Agents who consistently lose reach a subsistence level of wealth where they are stuck because they no longer have the option of gambling to improve their wealth;

6 There is no interaction among agents at this initial stage of the model as agents only choose gambles and play against the probabilities[7].

For example:
An agent starts with an initial endowment of 50 units of wealth, of which 5 units are necessary to survive and the remainder is available for wagering. Risk preference is randomly assigned before the first round and consists of a preference for an odds payoff ratio (with an implied mean-variance) together with a desired stake amount to wager as a percentage of total wealth. Thus, an aggressive high risk player would have a preference to wager a high percentage stake on a gamble with a high odds ratio. A conservative, subsistence player would wager a small stake on a gamble with a low odds ratio. The assigned risk preference determines the player type and the initial round of player preferences. After a round of play all players wealth endowments will change depending on whether they made winning or losing gambles. In the subsequent round they will adapt their risk preferences accordingly.

## 6. Adaptive Strategies

If an agent "wins" in a round, then the incremental wealth is added to the agent's endowment and the remaining gambling stake is larger in the next round. The agent responds to this good fortune by *increasing* the proportion of *the gambling stake* while *reducing* the variance or *the odds ratio* of the next gamble. This is meant to encourage an effective "capital preservation" strategy while enhancing the chances of increasing wealth. This is demonstrated in the movement to the lower left in the lattice. Thus, as wealth increases from players' success, risk preferences move toward Investor with higher stakes, but lower odds ratios.

If an agent "loses" a round, the loss is subtracted from the agent's endowment. In response to this loss, the agent necessarily reduces the gambling stake but increases the odds ratio, in effect trying to recapture the loss by trying to score big with little money. This results in moving toward the upper right in the lattice until the agent wins a lottery or is slowly driven by small losses to the level of subsistence whereby, due to the loss of a stake, one loses the ability to gamble.

As wealth decreases, risk preferences move toward Lottery Player and ultimately toward Subsistence/Saver with low stakes, high variance gambles and finally no gambles. The experience factor is a small percentage bonus to the payoff that we have varied from 1 percent to 0.001 percent.

## 7. Results

We can observe the outcomes of the model as they develop over repeated iterations of the program. The resulting distributions can be graphically or numerically represented in several ways with raster or lattice images, wealth accumulation graphs, and Gini coefficient graphs.

The raster images, or 2x2 lattices, show the distribution of agents in a 2-dimensional space according to risk preferences, with black squares on a white background (see Figures 10.1, 10.2). The darker squares represent more agents at that specific location. Gambling stakes increase as one moves down vertically, while variances increase as one moves to the right horizontally. The geographical locations on the lattice correspond to the 2x2 Table 10.1. As we might expect, over time agents migrate by moving either left and down or up and to the right. High-risk, high-stakes gamblers exhibit the most rapid movement, moving towards investors if they are lucky or towards lottery players if they are not. In a few isolated cases a lottery player is able to move down and to the left, essentially getting lucky enough to win back enough capital to adopt a preservation strategy. But given the probability distributions this is not a likely event. Most of the agents end up congregating along the two axes, either becoming rich but conservative investors or subsistence savers who can no longer gamble. The general result is a highly skewed

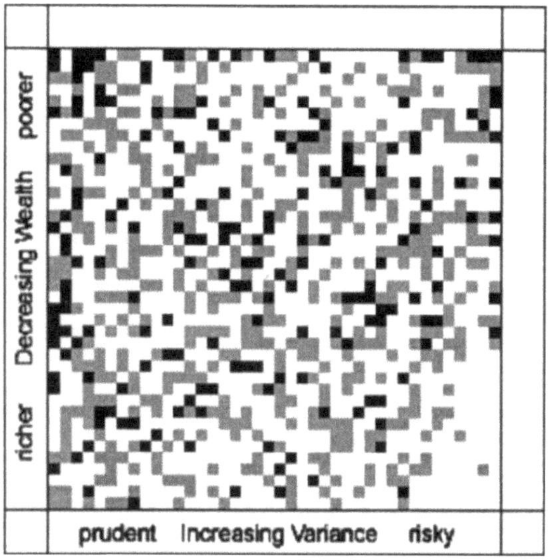


*Figure 10.1.* Initial Preference Distribution of Agents, experienceScale=1000, Time=1

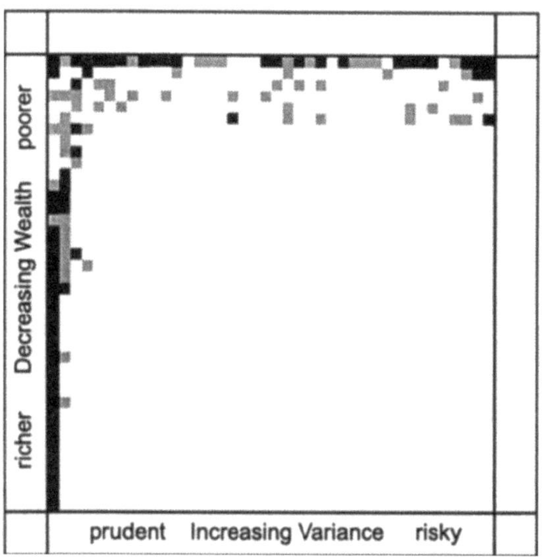


*Figure 10.2.* Preference Distribution of Agents, experienceScale=1000, Time=82

distribution with many subsistence agents with little wealth and a few very wealthy investors.

The wealth accumulation distributions are divided according to the four agent categories. We can observe the rapid accumulation over time of investor wealth and the uniform decline of the other three agent categories in shares of total wealth. (Figures 10.3,10.4,10.5)

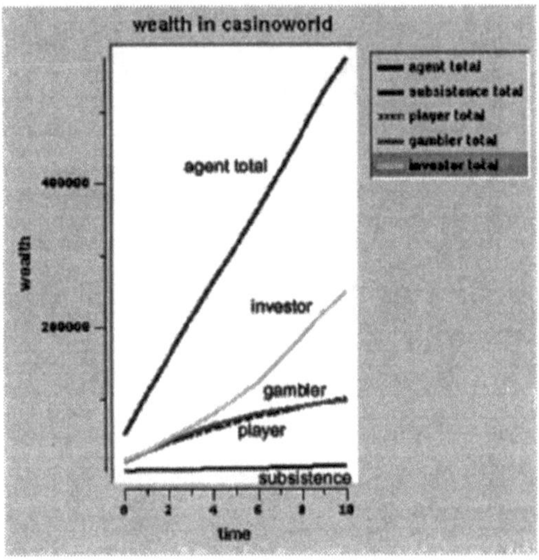


*Figure 10.3.* Wealth Accumulation, experienceScale=1000, Time=10

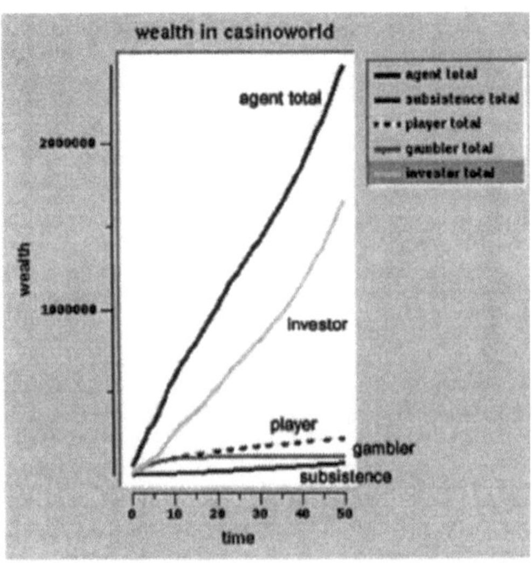


*Figure 10.4.* Wealth Accumulation, experienceScale=1000, Time=50

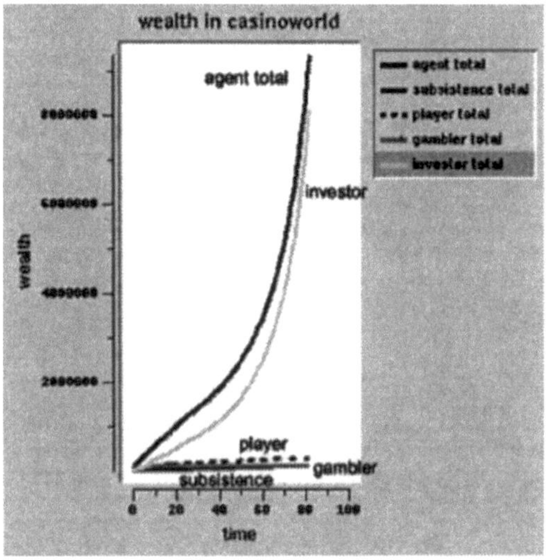


*Figure 10.5.* Wealth Accumulation, experienceScale=1000, Time=82

Gini coefficients representing the relative inequality of these wealth distributions have been calculated and graphed over time. The initial distribution is randomly chosen and has a starting Gini coefficient of.3. The Gini coefficients rapidly increase to very high levels above.9, essentially approaching the asymptote of 1, representing complete inequality. (Figure 10.6)

We might question the weight of the experienceScale factor in determining the skewedness of the distribution results. This is the only parameter variable that we can really tweak at this stage. However, varying the experience parameter does not appear to have a significant effect on the outcome of the distribution, but only the rate of divergence with which the distribution reaches its extreme skewedness. With an experience scale of 1% (experienceScale = 100), investors garner 90% of the total wealth after 32 reiterations. With an experience scale of.1% (experienceScale = 1000) this increases to 82 reiterations (Figure 10.5). At.01% it takes 195 reiterations and at.001% (experienceScale = 100,000) it takes roughly 246 reiterations. Altering this variable, or even dropping it out by rendering it completely meaningless does not change the substantive results of the model.

## 8. Future Developments

The simplistic shortcomings of this model appear glaringly to its creators. Understandably, economic sophistication is wanting but the goal

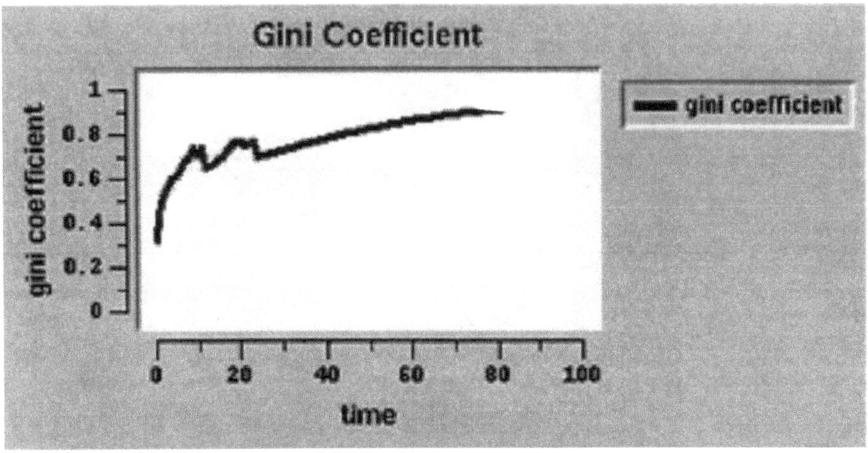


*Figure 10.6.* Gini Coefficient, experienceScle=1000, Time=82

was modest—to establish and demonstrate another, somewhat different foundation for human economic behavior and interaction. In so doing, it appears that the hypothesized dynamics are sufficiently demonstrated, but the important questions must focus on the rules and behavioral assumptions on which the interaction is built.

First, there are some minor items that could use a bit of refinement. Under the present design, the odds eventually catch up with all agents and they are driven to the subsistence level. This is true for even the wealthiest investors as they end up gambling almost all their wealth on small variances, eventually hitting the small probability, with the losses wiping them out. This could be corrected with a low risk-free rate of return that becomes a virtual certainty. At this point there is no long-term adaptability built into the model and thus when the iterations get above 100 the results become less meaningful.

We also intend to incorporate a global parameter in order to gauge the effect of changing levels of uncertainty on agent behavior and distributional outcomes. This reflects a desire to measure the effect of economic or political crises on interactive economic behavior. We hypothesize that changes in global uncertainty would uniformly change the risk preferences and payoff matrices so that overall return-to-risk payoffs would be affected. This change in initial conditions would then lead to greater or lesser levels of divergence or differentiation between category types. The point is to get a better understanding of the sensitivity of various parameter sweeps.

From the standpoint of improving the usefulness of the model, the most important modification would be to incorporate agent interaction through some set of trade rules. Economic transactions in the real world are not conducted with the "house" or the environment but with a multitude of other agents. A more consequential study of the economic effects of skewed wealth distributions would need to explore the basis of exchange between agents and how disparities in wealth affect those exchanges. One possibility may be to require all gambles to be two-sided in terms of matching gambling stakes and risk preferences across the population.

Another shortcoming that may need to be addressed is the lack of a role for prices. Real and financial assets are the most significant components of wealth and thus, asset price adjustments are fundamental to economic change and movements toward equilibrium. To measure wealth accumulation we have only added or subtracted units of wealth rather than try to allow relative values to change. This may be important as wealth changes through price valuations will occur exogenous to individual agent activity.

Despite these shortcomings, we hope to have demonstrated the future usefulness of agent-based simulation modeling for studying particular problems and puzzles that do not lend themselves well to standard equilibrium modeling. At the same time we seek to provoke further explorations into the assumptions of human behavior that drive all social science research.

## Notes

1. Epstein and Axtell (1996), p. 1.

2. See Richard H. Thaler, "From Homo Economicus to Homo Sapiens," *Journal of Economic Perspectives*, 14, 1, pp. 133-41.

3. Edward O. Wilson, *Consilience: the Unity of Knowledge*, NY: Alfred A. Knopf, 1998, p. 207.

4. See Copeland and Weston (1980), pp. 64-88. In general, finance theory assumes underlying normal distributions and characterizes risk according to mean-variance criteria.

5. Friend and Blume (1975).

6. This is analogous to the capital market line in finance theory. See Copeland and Weston (1978). The lookup tables are variable parameters and we have initially set the odds ratio from a high of 64 to 1 to a low of 1.01 to 1. The table is highly skewed towards the lower end so as to more resemble real world investment returns rather than the roulette wheel.

7. However, the set of possible risk-return gambles could imply interaction among agents as well as against the "house" by imagining agents on either side of an odds gamble.

## References


Aaron, Henry. 1994. Public Policy, Values, and Consciousness. *Journal of Economic Perspectives,* 8, no. 2: pp. 3-21.

Alchian, Armen A. 1950. Uncertainty, Evolution, and Economic Theory. *Journal of Political Economy,* 58, no. 3: pp. 211-21.

Arrow, Kenneth J. 1988. Behavior Under Uncertainty and Its Implications for Policy. in *Decision Making.* David E. Bell, Howard Raiffa, and Amos Tversky, eds., pp. 497-507. Cambridge: Cambridge University Press.

Arthur, W. Brian. 1991. Designing Economic Agents That Act Like Human Agents: A Behavioral Approach to Bounded Rationality. *American Economic Review,* 81, no. 2: pp. 353-59.

Axelrod, Robert. 1984. *The Evolution of Cooperation.* NY: Basic Books.

Bernstein, Peter L. 1996. *Against the Gods: the Remarkable Story of Risk.* NY: John Wiley & Sons.

Buchanan, James M., and Yong J. Yoon. 1994. *The Return to Increasing Returns.* Ann Arbor, MI: Univ. of Michigan Press.

Casti, John L. 1997 *Would-Be Worlds.* New York: John Wiley & Sons.

Cederman, Lars-Erik 1997, *Emergent Actors in World Politics.* Princeton: Princeton University Press.

Cosmides, Leda, and John Tooby. 1996. Are Humans Good Intuitive Statisticians After All? Rethinking Some Conclusions From the Literature on Judgment Under Uncertainty. *Cognition,* 58, no. 1: pp. 1-73.

Epstein, Joshua M., and Robert Axtell. 1996. *Growing Artificial Societies.* Washington, D.C.: Brookings Institution Press.

Friend, I. And M. Blume, "The Demand for Risky Assets," *The American economic Review,* December 1975, pp. 900-922.

Galbraith, James K. 2000. "How the Economists Got It Wrong," *The American Prospect,* 11, 7, February 14, 2000.

Hirshleifer, Jack, and John G. Riley. 1992. *The Analytics of Uncertainty and Information.* Cambridge: Cambridge Univ. Press.

Holland, John H. 1998. *Emergence: From Chaos to Order.* Cambridge, MA: Perseus Books.

Holland, John H., and John H. Miller. 1991. Artificial Adaptive Agents in Economic Theory. *American Economic Review,* 81, no. 2: pp. 365-70.

Kahneman, Daniel, and Amos Tversky. 1992. Advances in Prospect Theory: Cumulative Representation of Uncertainty. *Journal of Risk and Uncertainty,* 5, no. 4: pp. 297-323.

Kaldor, Nicholas. 1985. *Economics Without Equilibrium.* Armonk, NY: M.E. Sharpe, Inc.

Kaldor, Nicholas. 1994. The Irrelevance of Equilibrium Economics. in *The Return to Increasing Returns.* James Buchanan, and Yong J. Yoon, eds., pp. 85-106. Ann Arbor, MI: University of Michigan Press.

Knight, Frank H. 1921. *Risk, Uncertainty and Profit.* 7th ed. Boston: Houghton Mifflin.

Kochugovindan, Sreekala, and Nicolaas J. Vriend. 1998. Is the Study of Complex Adaptive Systems Going to Solve the Mystery of Adam Smith's Invisible Hand? *The Independent Review,* 3, no. 1: pp. 53-66.

Leijonhufvud, Axel. 1993. Towards a Not-Too-Rational Macroeconomics. *Southern Economic Journal,* 60: pp. 1-13.

Lopes, Lola L. 1987. Between Hope and Fear: The Psychology of Risk. *Advances in Experimental Psychology,* 20: pp. 255-95.

Lucas Jr., Robert E. 2000. Some Macroeconomics for the 21st Century. *Journal of Economic Perspectives,* 14, no. 1: pp. 159-68.

Mandel, Michael J. 1996. *The High-Risk Society.* NY: Random House.

Rode, Catrin, Leda Cosmides, Wolfgang Hell, and John Tooby. 1998. When and Why Do People Avoid Unknown Probabilities in Decisions Under Uncertainty? Testing Some Predictions From Optimal Foraging Theory. Working Paper.

Slovic, Paul, Baruch Fischoff, and Sarah Lichtenstein. 1982. Facts Versus Fears: Understanding Perceived Risk. in *Judgement Under Uncertainty: Heuristics and Biases.* Daniel

Kahneman, Paul Slovic, and Amos Tversky, eds., pp. 463-89. Cambridge: Cambridge University Press.

Thaler, Richard H. 2000. From Homo Economicus to Homo Sapiens. *Journal of Economic Perspectives,* 14, no. 1: pp. 133-41.

Tversky, Amos. 1990. The Psychology of Risk. in *Quantifying the Market Risk Premium Phenomenon for Investment Decision Making.* William F. Sharpe, and Katrina F. Sherrerd, eds., pp. 73-77. NY: Institute of Chartered Financial Analysts.

Tversky, Amos, and Daniel Kahnemann. 1986. The Framing of Decisions and the Psychology of Choice. in *Rational Choice.* Jon Elster, ed., pp. 123-41. NY: NYU Press.

Tversky, Amos, and Peter Wakker. 1995. Risk Attitudes and Decision Weights. *Econometrica,* 63, no. 6: pp. 1255-80.

Vriend, Nicolaas J. 1994. A New Perspective on Decentralized Trade. *Economie Appliquee,* 47: pp. 5-22.

Waldorp, M. Mitchell. 1992. *Complexity: the Emerging Science at the Edge of Order and Chaos.* New York: Touchstone. Wilson, Edward O. 1998. *Consilience: The Unity of Knowledge.* NY: Alfred A. Knopf.

Chapter 11

# SEARCH IN ARTIFICIAL LABOUR MAKETS: A SIMULATION STUDY

Massimo Daniele Sapienza
*University of Rome - Tor Vergata (Italy)*
sapienza@economia.uniroma2.it

Magda Fontana*
*University of Turin (Italy)*
fontana@master.de.unito.it

**Abstract** Job search theory involves perfectly rational, maximising actors that make decisions under imperfect information. In this paper we simulate a labour market which works differently: heterogeneous firms and workers interact following rules that place only bounded demand on their computational capacities. We stress the relevance of heterogeneity, formal education, and training on the job in determining employment and skill mismatch phenomena by comparing the ACE model with a more traditional competitive model. Results are interesting from both the theoretical and the empirical point of view.

## 1. Introduction

Job search theory involves perfectly rational, maximising actors which make decisions under imperfect information. As long as the benefits from searching exceed costs, workers will refuse any job offer which is lower than their reservation wage. Of course, the logic is Neoclassical and, therefore, unemployment is voluntary.

In this paper, we simulate a labour market which works differently. In Epstein's words: "*Certain social systems, such as trade networks (mar-*

*I acknowledge financial support of MURST. We wish to thank Francesco Busato, Bruno Contini, Pietro Terna, and Davide Vannoni for useful comments. The usual disclaimer applies.

*kets), are essentially computational architectures. They are distributed, asynchronous, and decentralised and have endogenous dynamic connections. [ ... ] when economists say the market arrives at equilibrium, they are asserting that this type of dynamic "social neural net" has executed a computation - it has computed P*, an equilibrium price vector -. No individual has tried to compute this, but the society of agents does so nonetheless. [ ... ] it is clear that the efficiency – indeed, the very feasibility – of a social computation may depend on the way in which agents are connected. After all, information in society [ ... ] is collected and processed at the agent level and transmitted through interaction structures that are endogenous*" (Epstein 1999, p. 46). Of course, the idea is not new. From Adam Smith to the Scottish philosophers, and to the Austrian economists the attempt at understanding the way in which given regularities emerge from decentralised interaction of autonomous and heterogeneous agents has been central to social sciences. The absence of appropriate tools to explore such complex structures has led, on the one side, to the Neoclassical simplification in the name of analytical treatment feasibility, and to the absence of rigorous applicable heterodox theory, on the other. The methodology we apply in this essay, the so called Agent-based Computational Economics (hereafter ACE), seems to help avoid both the excessive simplification of Neoclassical models, and the lack of rigour of the competing heterodox theories.

ACE investigates, by means of computer simulations, economic structures and group behaviour as emerging from the interaction of the individuals operating in artificial environment under rules that place only bounded demands on each agent's information and computational capacities. This methodology has a long lineage, from Von Neumann to Schelling, but it is only in the last decade that advances in computing have made Agent-based modelling practical (Epstein – Axtell 1996).

In brief, the underlying philosophy can be summarised in Epstein and Axtell's words: "*We view artificial societies as laboratories, where we attempt to 'grow' certain social structure in the computer - or in silico – the aim being to discover fundamental local or micro mechanisms that are sufficient to generate the macroscopic social structures and collective behaviours of interest*" (Epstein – Axtell 1996, p.4).

In this paper, we implement an ACE model in which workers and firms interact on the basis of decentralised bilateral matches.

In adopting the ACE framework, we underline the relevance of non linear effects of interaction in the dynamics of the market together with the importance of heterogeneity of agents in determining its setting and evolution. Moreover, we can observe the evolution of the market and its dis-equilibrium spells.

## 2. An overview of the literature: building blocks

When markets are characterised by imperfect information, it is rational for the individual market participants to engage in some form of information-gathering or search exercise. Clearly, there are both costs and benefits involved in the pursuit of such activity, search theory considers the ways in which firms and workers balance one against the other in the design of an optimal search strategy.

Roughly speaking, literature has developed following two lines. The first one, tracing back to Stigler (1962), is based on the so-called *fixed sample size rule (Stigler rule)*. The worker, before starting her search, fixes an optimal number of firms[1] to canvass and, at the end of the search process, chooses the highest observed wage. The second one, known as *sequential search rule*, was born to overcome a criticism to the fixed sample rule. In fact, it was argued, it is unlikely that the worker continues applying for jobs when she comes across a sufficiently high wage offer. Sequential search models pivots around the concept of reservation wage. This is a minimum acceptable wage, which indirectly determines the duration of search. In fact, the worker keeps on searching until she receives a wage offer which is equal or greater than her reservation wage.

As compared to Walrasian market, the market depicted in search theory is decentralised since workers do not face a unique wage offer but receive, and have to choose among, different offers. Moreover, there is no auctioneer. However, the market participant, even in the lack of complete information, still maximises in order to find the most suitable search strategy. Literature on search in the labour market is large and still growing. Developments of the sequential search approach cover the issues of dynamic reservation wage (adaptive search and finite horizon models), random job offers and the effect of discount rate on reservation wage.

These latter models give a number of interesting predictions that have generated a large body of empirical works. Search theory has shed considerable light on the factors which determine the time it takes for a frictionally unemployed worker to find an acceptable job offer. Many economists have analysed the increase in unemployment in the 70s' and the 80s' in terms of search behaviour.

Results underpin the well-known propositions about the displacing influence of unemployment benefits. Moreover, empirical tests of search theories seem to confirm that the increase in the duration of unemployment spells that many industrialised countries have experienced seems to depend more on a decrease in the probability of finding a job than on the influence of the reservation wage.

Another explanation of the raise in unemployment that has interested especially the European Community is that of skill mismatch. The shift from traditional heavy manufacturing to high technology industries has relegated unskilled workers to unemployment since new jobs are typically in sectors requiring skilled workers. Empirical evidence on the relevance of such mismatch is somewhat confused, so that it cannot be interpreted as a primary cause of the increased unemployment.

Our model amends job search theory by relaxing some of the most common assumptions, such as identical workers, homogeneous jobs, and, above all, maximising behaviour. Moreover, it includes skill and training considerations.

The essay is a first step of a wider research that, in our purposes, should provide a general framework for agent based computational labour economics. We have at hand a sort of machinery that can simulate a neoclassical competitive labour market and its main deviations, and whose explanatory power we aim at exploiting in further researches.

## 3. An artificial labour market: Labour Sim

A typical agent-based model consists of units (the agents), sets of data (internal states of agents) and methods (rules that update data), that are the behavioural rules of agents.

In Labour Sim, agents are boundedly rational, heterogeneous adaptive workers and firms interacting through bilateral relationships.

## 4. The model

The following is a sequential search model in which search is carried out by workers. Search is adaptive and therefore reservation wage varies in time. The latter is determined according to individual features such as wealth and skill and evolves according to their changes. Wages offered by firms and a worker's reservation wage depend, respectively, on required/owned skills. We assume that firms (more precisely industries) which require a more educated labour force are willing to pay higher wages and that workers that are more skilled have higher reservation wages.

This allows us to analyse conjointly the process of search and the possibility of skill mismatch phenomena.

We first introduce a benchmark version of the model, in which there are neither limits to the number of firms that may be contacted nor explicit search costs. We then introduce different informative sets and skill dynamics (random learning on the job, systematic training investment, etc.). At this stage of the research, we are mainly interested in testing the assumptions of traditional models against the effect of decentralisation and interaction.

Agents have few crucial variables. Workers behave on the basis of *wealth*, *skill*, and the resulting *reservation wage*. Firms' states depend on *required skill* and *offered wage*. In Labour Sim, time is discrete. Agents' actions take place according to a schedule which is repeated for as many cycles as desired. Rules that modify the agents' state are fixed rules of thumb, which are applied without evolution at each step of the simulation. The schedule of the model is the following:

- **Labour force**: workers must decide whether to enter the labour market or to be enrolled in formal instruction programs to acquire skill. This choice is made by comparing reservation wage by unit of skill with the mean offered wage per unit of skill required by firms.
- **Vacancy**: firms decide whether to hire a worker.
- **Matching**: workers contact firms by means of work links.

Firms are randomly chosen. If the worker reservation wage and skill are compatible - respectively, lower and higher - with those required by the firm, then the vacancy is closed. If the worker is already employed, she checks whether compatibility is still there. If it so, the contract continues for three periods, otherwise the search process starts anew. The bargaining structure is very simple, however it is empirically relevant, at least for low skill positions, "*Ring up Mc Donald and ask what their starting wage is: they will give you an answer (sometimes)*" (Manning 1998).

The worker's search process consists in establishing successive work links with firms. The number of these opportunities is a proxy for information. If the number of allowed work links is lower than the number of firms, then information is limited or imperfect. On the contrary, if the worker can contact all the firms on the market information is complete. In what follows we explore both hypotheses. We first allow the worker to establish a number of links equal to the number of the firms on the market. This only approximates perfect information: since links are randomly established, it could happen that a worker contacts the same firm more than one time. It is worth noting that, even under perfect information, the worker has a satisficing attitude, that is to say, she stops searching as soon as she finds a match that respects the above-cited conditions. To sum up, Labour Sim models multi-period bilateral contracts with a preferential link for workers that already cover a position within a firm.

- **Production.** Firms produce if they have hired at least one worker.
- **Selection of workers.** Workers that do not find an open vacancy or a match leave the market when their wealth becomes negative.

At the end of each cycle, agents' variables are updated and the corresponding output produced.
We observe activity and unemployment rate, skill and wage dynamics of employed and unemployed workers and firms, wealth accumulation and wages differentials. In what follows we will describe in more detail the structure of the agents and their decision-making rules. We start with a competitive model to use as a benchmark, and then we introduce deviations and frictions.

## 5. The Benchmark

We refer to Competitive Labour Sim as the version of the model which is closest to the traditional view of the labour market. Frictions are almost absent in that workers can, in principle, acquire complete information about the firms in the market and agents have infinite life. Nevertheless, agents are not maximisers. Workers are heterogeneous in wealth, and initial skill. Firms are heterogeneous in technology and, consequently, in productivity and skill requirements. More precisely, a worker initial state is so determined:

- Initial Skill ($S_{w0}$), which is randomly assigned under a uniform distribution on the computable reals interval [0.0, 1.0]. It is assumed to be observable and measurable by a continuous variable. Skill is homogeneous and general. Skill dynamics when the agent is not part of the labour force is:

$$S_{wt} = S_{wt-1}(1 + sch) \tag{5.1}$$

$$0 \leq S_w \leq 1$$

Where: *sch* is the rate of skill's growth due to formal education, which is equal for all agents.

- Wealth($R_{w0}$), which is sampled from a normal distribution with [100, 50].
- Reservation wage $(w_{wt})^2$ of workers that are not part of the labour force is:

$$w_{wt} = \beta log(R_{wt} S_{wt}) \tag{5.2}$$

Where: $w_{wt}$ is the worker's reservation wage at time t, $R_{wt}$ is the worker's wealth at time t, and $S_{wt}$ is the worker's skill in a given point in time. $\beta$ is a scale parameter. As the worker enters the labour market, her reservation wage also responds to experience:

$$w_{wt} = (R_{wt}S_{wt}) + \psi(w_{wt-1} - \overline{w}_{it})$$

Where $\psi$ is the speed of adaptation and $w_{it}$ is the mean wage offered by firms.

Firms' initial state is so defined:

- Skill ($S_{io}$), which is sampled from a normal distribution with [0.5, 0.1];
- Offered wage ($w_i$) which depends on marginal productivity of labour, as determined by the following production function:

$$Y = a(\overline{S}_{wt}L) \tag{5.3}$$

where $a$ is a scale factor and $S_{wt}$ is the mean skill of employed workers at time t, and L is the number of employees in a given cycle. $S_{wt}$ is updated every $n$ cycle according to [5.7]. It is assumed that there are positive spillovers from labour force to firms: as workers increase their skill so do firms' technology and productivity.

$$w_{it} = \partial Y/\partial L \tag{5.4}$$

According to the schedule these states and variables determine the behaviour of agents and, by virtue of interaction, the properties of the labour market. At each cycle all workers and firms, sequentially perform all the steps of the schedule.

Let us consider **Labour force** (LF) as a dummy variable which assumes the values of zero if the worker is not seeking an employment and one in the opposite case. In order to decide whether to enter the labour force, each worker compares his own reservation wage and skill with the mean wage paid on the market ($w_{it}$) and with the mean skill required by firms ($S_{it}$):

$$LF = 1 if w_{wt} \leq [(\overline{w}_{it}/\overline{S}_{it})S_{wt}] or S_{wt} = 1 \tag{5.5}$$

In other word, the worker compares her personal skill price [$w_{wt}/S_{wt}$] with market average skill price [$w_{it}/S_{it}$ ] and decide to "sell" her skill on the labour market if market price for skill is greater or equal than her own price.

If LF= 0 worker's skill are going to increase according to [11.1] while her wealth is going to decrease according to:

$$R_{wt} = (1 - c)R_{wt-1} - z \tag{5.6}$$

where c is marginal propensity to consume and z is autonomous expenditure. For all workers with LF=0 there are no actions left to execute until next cycle. For the others, it is time to look for a job. All firms which expect profits greater or equal than zero open a **Vacancy** with a corresponding wage and skill. Wage is determined according to [11.4] while skill evolve according to workers' skill improvement:

$$S_{it} = S_{it-1} + (\overline{S}e_{wt}/\kappa) \tag{5.7}$$

Where $Se_{wt}$ is the mean skill of employed workers and $\kappa$ is a parameter that drives the speed of adjustment. Notice that the firm increases its skill with a given frequency and only if the mean skill of employed workers is higher than $S_{it-1}$.

In the **Matching** phase, each worker that is in the labour force can establish a number of links which is equal to the number of firms. In the competitive setting this stands for complete information, notice however that the only information concerning the market that the agent has before contacting a firm is the mean market wage and skill. Moreover, there are no costs connected directly with searching. The match is concluded if a condition analogous to [5.4] holds. In this case, however, wage and skill are specific to the contacted firm. A worker is employed if

$$w_{wt} \leq w_{it} \quad and \quad S_{wt} \geq S_{it} \tag{5.8}$$

Worker and firms that are already matched verify the same condition. If the matching does not hold, the mechanism re-starts.

If the matching is concluded the firm produces and the workers is paid a wage. It follows that a worker's wealth will be:

$$R_{wt} = (1 - c)(R_{w_{t-1}} + w_{it}) - z \tag{5.9}$$

If the worker remains unemployed, her wealth will be:

$$R_{wt} = (1 - c)R_{wt-1} - z \tag{5.10}$$

Notice that consumption implies the presence of implicit search costs. If the workers were infinitely rich they could explore the market for a potentially infinite time. Workers with low skill and few resources are more sensitive to skill decay and more likely to fall below the survival threshold. If wealth becomes negative we make two different hypotheses:

- a strict evolutionary interpretation of the market according to which the unfit worker leaves the market;
- a more realistic interpretation of the market mechanism according to which long term unemployed workers does not exit the labour force.

As for the skill, unemployed workers are subject to skill decay:

$$S_{wt} = S_{wt-1}(1-d) \tag{5.11}$$

where $d$ is the skill's decay rate that is equal across agents. For what concerns employed workers' skill, we have devised various paths. The simplest one is no dynamics:

$$S_t = S_{j-1} \tag{5.12}$$

This assumption is quite unrealistic; however it meets the need of implementing a simple competitive model. More interesting dynamics, which will be considered, are learning by doing and stochastic learning. Respectively, they are modelled as follows:

$$S_{wt} = S_{wt-1} + (S_{wit-1}/\lambda) \tag{5.13}$$

Where $\lambda$ is a fraction of the technology of the firm in which the worker is employed. A different context with non-systematic learning by doing could be modelled by means of a stochastic increase of skill on the job:

$$S_{wt} = S_{wt-1} + \xi_t \tag{5.14}$$

with $\xi_t$ is a white noise random process.

In what follows we will stress the relevance of the different hypotheses to the dynamics of the simulated system.

**Production** takes place only in firms which have hired at least one worker. Notice that there are no limits to the number of employees in each firm. It is assumed that firms sell all the produced goods at a price equal to unity. It follows that profits $\pi$ are equal to:

$$\pi_t = Y_t - w_i L \tag{5.15}$$

Where $L_t$ is the number of worker employed by a given firm.

The **selection of workers** expels workers with wealth lower than a survival threshold ($d$).

## 6. The Labour Net as an artificial labour market

Labour Sim's core characteristic is the search process implemented in the model. The artificial environment in which market transactions take place, the Labour Net, is modelled as a network of one to one links (WorkLinks) between workers and firms. At the basis of the code for the simulation there is the DiGraph library by Manor Askenazi[3]. Thanks to this library we can easily represent relationships between interacting agents and, at the same time, observe the evolution of the network with a fine graphical interface (using the DiGraph object). Each link is an object (DiGraphLink) carrying fundamentally one piece of information and one method: the key information contained is the list objects linked by the link-object, the key method is the drawing method, that enables the link to move within the population of agents.

Depending on the informational characteristics of the modelled environment, each link could be specialised in order to carry simulation-specific information or it could be used as a pure networking device as in Labour Net.

In Labour Sim, the Labour Net (which inherits from the graphic class Digraph) is built by the model Swarm before the generation of the population of agents (workers and firms):

```
theLabourNet = [LabourNet createBegin: [self getZone]];
[theLabourNet setCanvas: graphCanvas];
theLabourNet=[theLabourNet createEnd];
```

The next step generates the population of workers and firms and includes it within the Net:

```
     for (y = 0 ;  y < workerN ;  y++) {
          aName=xmalloc(10) ;
          sprintf (aName,"WO%d ",y) ;
..........................................
[theLabour Net addNode: tmp]; }
```

Once this set-up phase is completed, the network is updated by means of methods coded within workers. To explore their matching opportunities workers relies basically on two methods: makeWorkLinkTo and TransferWorkLinkTo.

```
- makeWorkLinkTo: aFirm {
  workLink = [[[[WLink createBegin: [self getZone]]
                    setCanvas: canvas]
                   setFrom: self To: aFirm]
                  createEnd];
 return self;
 }

-TransferWorkLinkTo: aFirm {
[workLink drop];
[self  makeWorkLinkTo: aFirm];
return self ;
}
```

makeWorkLinkTo generates an instance of workLink from the Class Wlink which inherits its features from DiGrahLink. A workLink connects an agent running the method with a firm. TransferWorkLinkTo dynamically adjusts the matching relationships between workers and firms, dropping the previous workLink and generating a new relationship with the same origin (the worker ) and a new firm.

Matching is the method coding the essence of Labour Sim search process. The matching mechanism is coded to implement a quite general representation of labour contracts. Workers and firms can commit themselves for a variable number of periods with contracts of different lengths.

```
-Matching {
...................
if (period>0)   {
  [[workLink getTo] setFil: 1];
  [[workLink getTo] addToEmpl: 1];
  empl = 1 ;
....... }
```

The workLink is the medium through which the variables of the firm linked to a worker by an effective labour contract (period>0), are updated. The Vacancy of the firm is closed (setFil 1) and the Laborforce of the firm is increased of one unit (addToEmpl 1). When the contract ceases its effects, worker and firm "re-negotiate" exchanging information through the workLink.

.........

```
if ( [[workLink getTo] getSkillf] <=  skillw
&&  [[workLink getTo] getWagef]>=wagew
&& laborForce==1 && [[workLink getTo] getVacancy]==1 ) {
.........
```

Finally, if the negotiation does not ends in a new contract the worker starts to look for other employers. The length of this search period is a parameter that the experimenter has to set in accordance with the goals of the chosen informational context:

```
for (y = 1 ;  y <= firms;  y++) {
 if  (laborForce==1) {
  someone = [model getRandomFirm] ;
  [self  TransferWorkLinkTo : someone] ; }
       if ( [[workLink getTo] getSkillf] <=  skillw
       &&[[workLink getTo] getWagef]>=wagew
       &&   laborForce==1
       && [[workLink getTo] getVacancy]==1 ) {
  empl = 1 ;
.........}
else
..........
empl = 0;
...........
return self; }
```

The search period is coded by a loop which in each iteration simulates the random matching between the worker and firm (*someone = [model getRandomFirm] ;)*, the establishment of a relationship (*[self TransferWorkLinkTo : someone] ;* }, and the "negotiation" phase according to the matching rule *(if ( [[workLink getTo] getSkillf] <= skillw &&[[workLink getTo] getWagef]>=wagew && laborForce==1 && [[workLink getTo] getVacancy]==1 ) {)*.

## 7. Simulations

Simulation consists in running the schedule for 2000 cycles. The choice of the length of the simulation is driven by the criterion of variability. The simulation should stop when the model settles on a stable pattern in which case continuing the run would not produce significant changes in the observed variables. Different runs of the simulation, the so called experiments, test the relevance or put under stress the assumptions of job search theory, whereas the output must be compared with their predictions.

Job search theory is extremely rich in predictions. In the basic version of traditional search models the optimal value of the reservation wage and the expected duration of search are inversely related to the magnitude of search costs. Thus, theory predicts that, *ceteris paribus*, the lower the cost of search, the higher the reservation wage and the expected duration of search. In such models, the reservation wage is positively related to the probability of receiving a job offer in a given period.

These simulations aim at exploring the properties of the chosen assumptions and testing their economic plausibility. Thus, in what follows, we limit ourselves to the description of the output of the various runs. Statistic and econometric analysis will be conducted in a further work. The experiments consist in comparing the competitive benchmark with elements that pertain more closely to search models. Even in this preliminary phase, Labour Sim provides extremely interesting insights. Firstly, we observe the coexistence of structural unemployment (derived from skill mismatch and informational problems) together with frictional unemployment. Consistently with empirical literature (Bean 1994), in Labour Sim, we observe both workers which change job with a high turnover, and workers that are hired only after long periods of training.

Secondly, the skill's decay rate of unemployed produces interesting effects. As shown by Pissarides (1992), the decay rate not only greatly affects the steady state level of the unemployment rate but also, the convergence rate and the moments of the generated time series. As the skill decay rate increases, the mean unemployment and the variance of the time series also increase.

However, the most interesting outputs regard the effect of different policies performed by the firm. These will be analysed in a separate paragraph.

## 7.1. The benchmark

This setting represents a frictionless world in which workers with infinite life undertake an unbounded search activity at no cost. Moreover, we assume that there is no learning during employment, but, at any point in time, workers can leave the labour force to join a re-training program. Unrealistic as it may seem, this version helps us obtain an unfettered labour market that mimics the traditional competitive approach.

As figure 11.1 shows, the competitive model with evolutionary pressure generates a labour market in which all agents participate to the labour force and find a job, due to the absence of any barrier to search and training programs. The labour market experiences an initial period of high unemployment and a very smooth activity rate. As the graphics show, heterogeneity of workers collapses into a sort of representative agent whose characteristics approach the mean values of the market variables. Figure 11. 2 shows the setting without selection. The unemployment rate rises dramatically while the activity rate decreases. The scenario tells us that low-skill workers, in spite of the low reservation wage, are unable to find a suitable match. This result is very interesting to us. In the previous setting, the possibility of expunging unfit/poor workers was responsible for the efficient outcome of the market process. That is to say that our search mechanism is not enough to assure competitive equilibrium. Firstly, agents choose firms randomly. Even if there are firms that in principle require their characteristics, workers may complete the search process without contacting one of them. Furthermore long periods of unemployment reduce the possibility of finding a job due to skill decay. Secondly, our benchmark heavily relies on information that is gathered and processed at the individual level. In the absence of an auctioneer, prices and their adjustment will follow the experience of the single worker and firm without any guarantee that the direction of change will meet the evolution of market variables. This raises a series of crucial issues. Many criticisms to traditional equilibrium models are grounded on the lack of an explanation of the way in which equilibrium is actually attained. The idea that competitive market is a process that translates the action of different agents into an order in the absence of a central planner does not find a consistent development in traditional models. Individuals listen to the *prix criés au hazard* and then trade at the equilibrium price. The presence of the auctioneer drives out all the issues concerning decentralisation, information gathering, information processing, and out of equilibrium trade. When, in line with the concepts of ACE, we abandon this line of thought, we find that actual decentralisation of interaction matters to economics results. Since market conditions are continually changing and individual information is partial, it is extremely unlikely that the individual agent is able to respond to changes in ways that trigger the dovetailing mechanism.

Still referring to traditional models, we would like to stress that the bounded abilities of agents are crucial to our results. We will cope with this aspect in paragraph devoted to informational constraints. Moreover, we analyse full employment equilibrium attainment when agents face a resource constraint. Attributing finite wealth to agents amounts to introduce indirect search costs that limit the number of attempts available to them. Let us see this point in more detail.

Table 11.1 shows response of unemployment rate and unemployed skill and wage to changes in initial average wealth. Recall that our model links reservation wage to wealth and skill and that being wealthier implies having a higher initial reservation wage. This, in turn, for given technology of firms, leads to a higher skill when entering the labour force and therefore to a lower sensitivity to skill decay.

As initial wealth increases unemployment rate decreases and long term unemployed turn to frictional unemployment. This is shown by the unemployed reservation wage and skill that remain lower than those of employed workers until scenario 3 showing, *ceteris paribus,* a longer period of search. From scenario 4 onwards the nature of unemployment is frictional with full employment reached in around 500 rounds. It is worth noting that in case 4 unemployed workers are more skilled than the employed ones.

| **Scenario** | **Wealth** | **Activity** Rate | **Unempl.** Rate | **Unempl.** Skill | **Unempl.** Wage |
|---|---|---|---|---|---|
| 1 | 1500 | 0.8 | 0.22 | 0.6 | 58 |
| 2 | 3000 | 0.87 | 0.13 | 0.6 | 68 |
| 3 | 6000 | 0.95 | 0.05 | 0.65 | 80 |
| 4 | 12000 | 1 | 0 | 0.79 | 87 |

Table 11.1 - Link between indirect search costs
and unemployment rate without selection

This depends on perfect mobility between education and labour. When the market wage for unit of skill is not high enough to satisfy the agents aspiration level the only other available chance is to enter formal training to increase skill. We assume that the marginal productivity is constant over the workers life. This assumption introduces some additional flexibility in the model. This higher degree of flexibility is evident in the variability of the activity rate time series. Some restriction on formal training productivity decay will cause, as expected, a reduction in the participation rate of older workers in formal training. The wealthiest workers enter the labour market with such a lag, or stay in the formal training for such a long period, that their skill becomes higher than those of employed workers. The negative relation between wealth and unemployment, however, does not hold indefinitely. For very high values of initial wealth the model becomes too rigid to adjust. We already know that higher wealth implies higher reservation wages and, ceteris paribus, a more skilled labour force. Since we assume that firms benefit form skill positive spillovers only from employed workers, a more educated labour force does not positively affect productivity (and wage) and therefore does not permit to over skilled workers to be hired. Before complicating the model let us briefly reflect on the choice of parameters, and namely, on the number of agents. Results change considerably when few agents

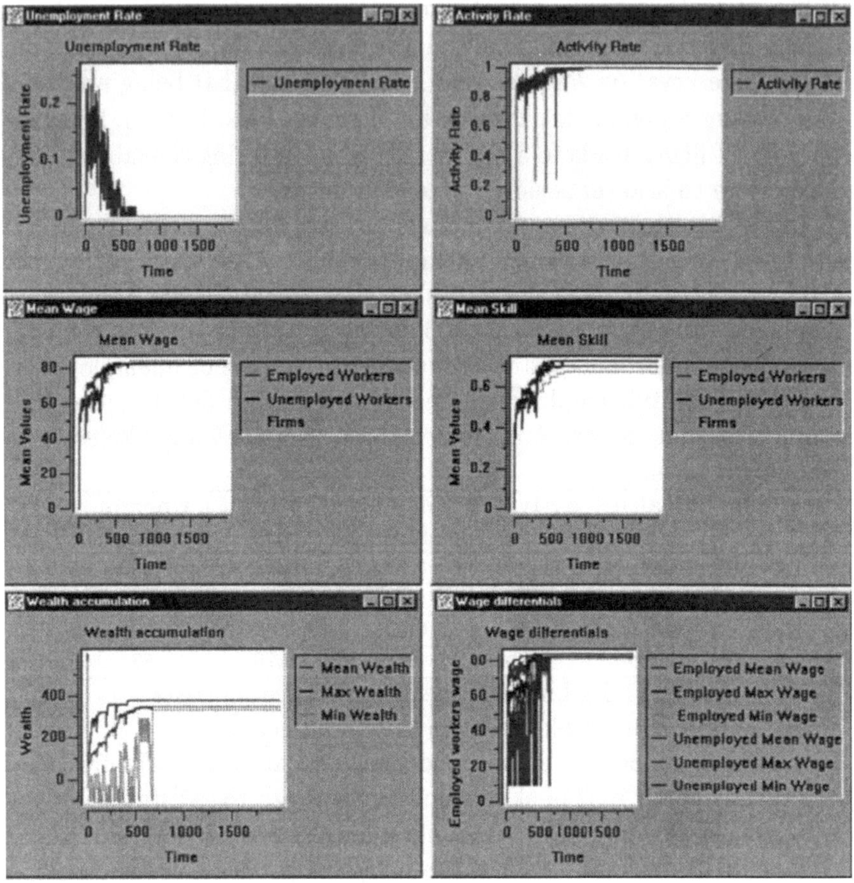


*Figure 11.1.* Competitive Labour Market

are used. In the setting without selection, when firms are few, unemployment is equal to 100% and the activity rate amount to 60%. This is quite reasonable since few firms render a match less probable than in the case with numerous firms , given the hypothesis of mono technological firms. When workers are few, on the other hand, the distribution of skill (see 4) among workers does not satisfies firms requirements and causes ubiquitous mismatch with unemployment that reaches 80%. From a theoretical standpoint, we interpret such phenomenon as the absence of market order due to the lack of redundancy (Sugden 1997). The latter is a feature of spontaneous orders referring to their insensitivity to the malfunctioning of some of their elements and to their inter-changeability. Within a redundant order, relationships among agents compose a dense network of interconnections. In a competitive market, a network sim-

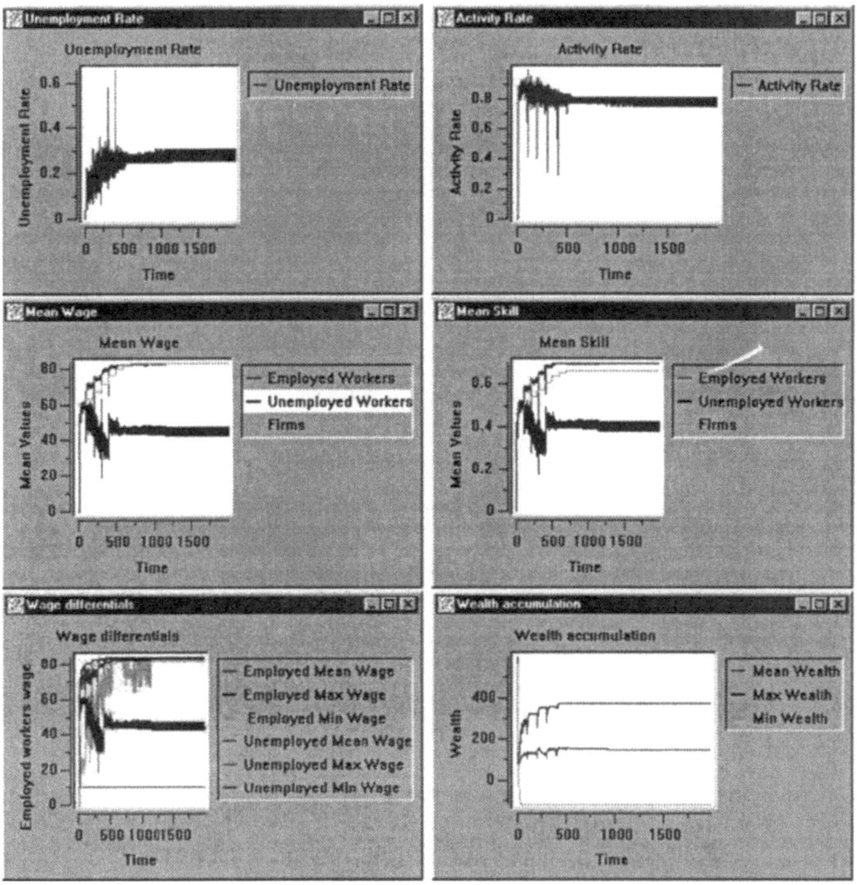


*Figure 11.2.* The Competitive Labour Market without Selection

ilarly connects buyers and sellers of labour but a minimum number of participants is required.

## 7.2. Informational Bounds

The lack of information is a founding block of job search theory. Here the wideness of market information is represented by the maximum number of firms that the worker can contact. In the previous version this was equal to the number of firms, that is to say that the worker was able to canvass the entire demand side. The number of possible links must not be confused with the Stigler rule which fixes the optimal sample of firms to contact given a certain amount of search costs. In this case the informational constraint is fixed a priori, is equal for all agents.

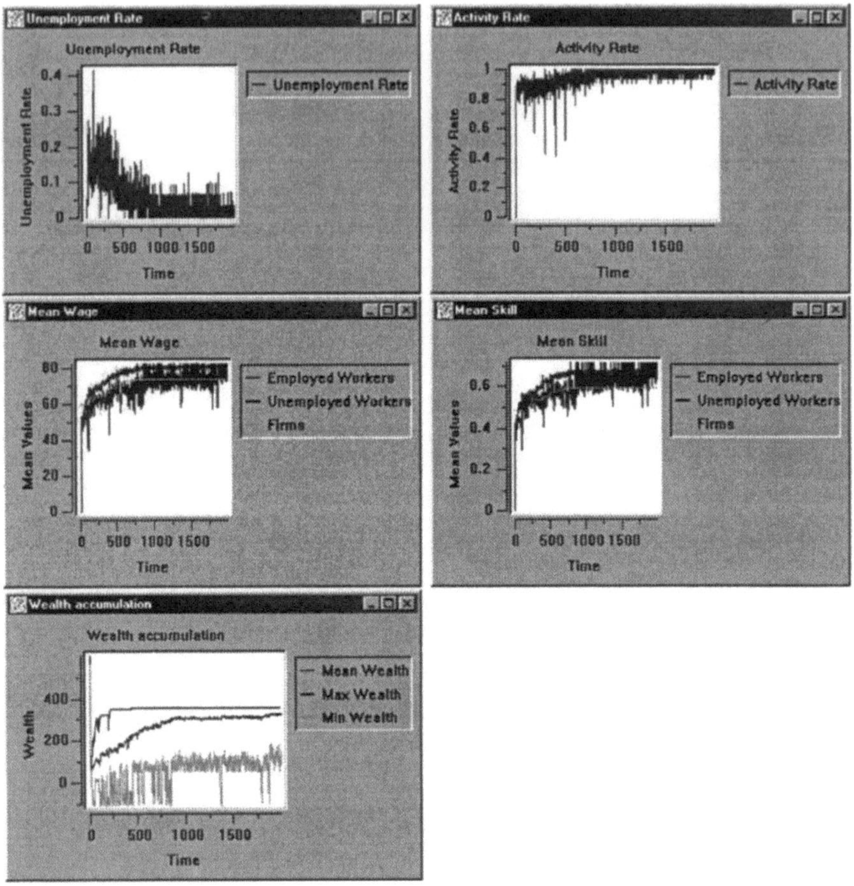


*Figure 11.3.* Informational Bounds (50 firm)

As information decreases unemployment increases. In the setting with selection (figure 11.3) the main effect is that of generating frictional unemployment. With respect to the full information output, the difficulties in finding a suitable match appears in the increased variability of the workers mean wage and in the emergence of significant differences in the accumulation of wealth. In the setting without selection (figure 11. 4), unemployment rises dramatically in response to the lack of information. The unemployed mean wage signals that finding a job is more difficult and costly, whereas, at the aggregate level wealth is influenced only by the presence of unemployment.

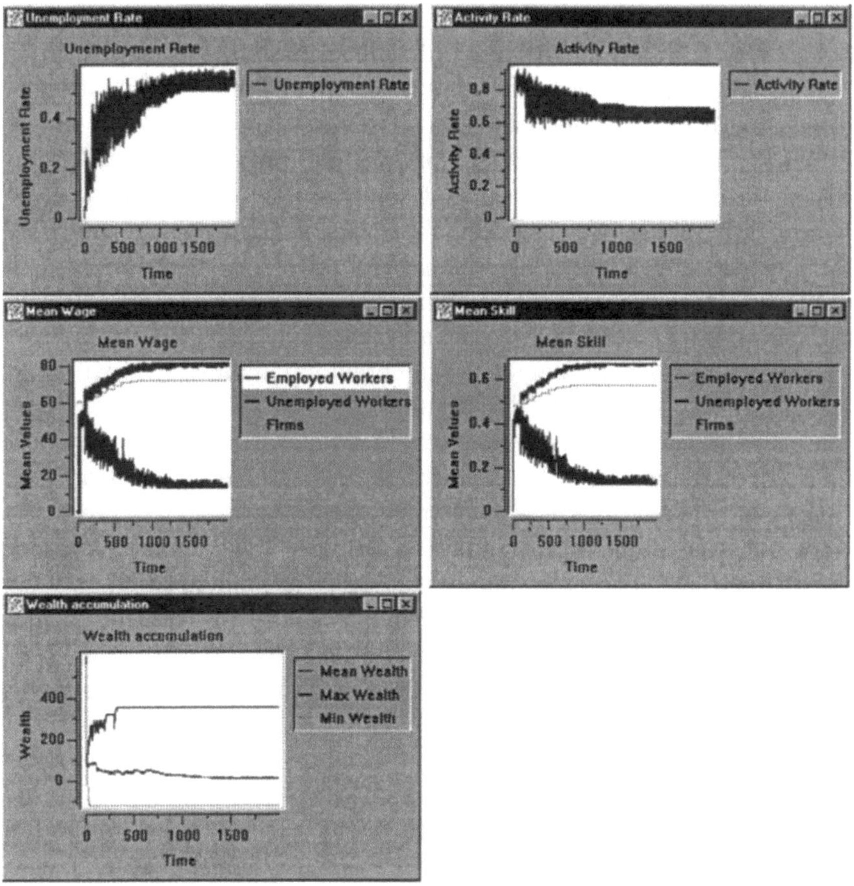


*Figure 11.4.* Information Bounds without selection (50 firm)

## 8. Learning and skill mismatch effects

As we started to illustrate in section 4, in order to assess the effect of different kinds of learning on the job on the dynamics of our artificial labour market, we have conducted experiments based on 3 different assumptions: 1- No learning on the job. Under this hypothesis, skill dynamics for employed worker follows [11]. 2- Non systematic learning on the job. This assumption concerns a non-maximising environment in which learning may be affected by managers decisions to train the staff that are mainly affected by some kinds of idiosyncratic random shocks. 3- Systematic learning on the job supposes that workers are able to learn by doing in any range of required skill. As table 11.2 summarises, results of these three experiments are consistently different with under many relevant aspects. In particular, we investigated the relationship between the degree of training on the job and skill mismatch, wage inequalities and long term unemployment. The basic model (no accumulation of human capital on the job) has been discussed as a benchmark in the previous section so we then focus more on the latest two. We will compare the three models at the end of some short considerations about experiment 2 and 3. We tested model 3 with firms investing massively in human capital. Essentially a worker obtains 5 of the skill used in the firm where she has been hired through training on the job. Human capital investments are sensibly smaller in model 2 where each hired worker could receive randomly a skill premium uniformly distributed over an interval [0, 1]. Models 2 and 3 exhibit very similar dynamic patterns. The effect of the investment in human capital is clearly positive on unemployment rate. If we compare the three different models, we may observe that there is a clear negative correlation between the rate of unemployment and training on the job. The same is true for wage inequalities. The more human capital is accumulated on the job, the more wage inequalities are reduced. It is interesting to note that, unless the system reaches a critical level of learning on the job policies, the fraction of highly marginalised workers still exists. It is also worth noting that positive effects of training on the job are clearly non-linear in capital accumulation effort. Even if in model 2 we simulate a much more massive investment policy (more than five times greater), we obtain just marginal improvements in the steady state welfare properties of the artificial system.

| **Scenario** | **Activity Rate** | **Unempl. Rate** | **Unempl. Employed Worker skill** | **Mean Employed Worker Wage** | **Inequality index [4]** |
|---|---|---|---|---|---|
| 1 | 85% | 25% | 0.7 | 81 | 4% |
| 2 | 97% | 2.5% | 0.95 | 90 | 0% |
| 3 | 100% | 0% | 1 | 92 | 0% |

Table 11.2 - A comparison among models

The inequality index is calculated among employed workers. Wage inequalities rise between employed and unemployed as learning on the job becomes more intensive. In this case the gap between the two states becomes greater and consequently marginalised workers condition is relatively worse. In the case of simulation 3, we reach the ideal situation of no unemployed worker, and no wage inequality among different workers. In other words heterogeneity is solved, and, due to the learning mechanism, the artificial system collapses to a simple representative agent model.

## 9. Concluding Remarks

Labour Sim attempts at providing a representation of the labour market in the spirit of agent-based modelling. This approach is not just a change in the technique of empirical verification, it also involves a thorough rethinking of the methodological issues within economics. Agent-based modelling studies economic facts as phenomena that can be tested in some kind of laboratory, namely the simulation performed according to the object oriented programming language and the ACE validation rules. This paper constitutes a first result of an ongoing research, which aims at encompassing further aspect of the labour market. A further step will consist in describing data from a quantitative/statistical point of view and in conducting standard sensitivity analysis. This first series of experiments aimed at testing the plausibility of the chosen assumptions and of the consequent results. It is our opinion, that, even if the adopted model is straightforward, results are interesting and encouraging. Firstly, we simulate the traditional competitive framework and stress the differences between the evolutionary and non-evolutionary versions. We then add frictions to the competitive setting to get closer to the traditional job search theory, and find that informational problems together with indirect search costs induce structural unemployment, lower participation rates, and over-skilled labour force. Different training on the job policies are then tested and the intensity in human capital investment is found to reduce unemployment.

## Notes

1. The number which equates marginal costs and marginal benefits of searching.

2. Contrarily to infinite horizon models, here the reservation wage varies as time passes even when agents have infinite life. The explanation echoes that of Mortensen (1986). Reservation wage responds to searcher's liquidity constraints (for instance, inability to borrow in the official credit market);

3. Askenazy (1996) provides a first example of the features enabled by the graph library in the original version of the BankNet simulator.

4. The inequality index is computed according to:

$$I = (Ewage_{max} - Ewage_{min})/Ewage_{mean}$$

where

$Ewage_{max}$ = Wage of the most well paid employed worker

$Ewage_{min}$ = Wage of the worst

$Ewage_{mean}$ = Wage of average employed worker

## References

Bean C. (1994), European Unemployment: A Survey, Journal of Economic Literature, 32, pp. 573-619.

Ashenfelter D. R. Layard (Eds) (1986), Handbook of Labor Economics, vol. 2, Elsevier, Amsterdam.

Burdett K. (1979), Unemployment insurance payments as a search subsidy: a theoretical analysis, Economic Enquiry, 42, 333-343.

Epstein J.M. (1999),Agent-Based Computational Models and Generative Social Science , Complexity, 4, pp.41-60.

Epstein J.M. Axtell R. ( 1996), Growing Artificial Societies, MIT Press, Cambridge (Mass.).

Manning A. (1998), A Simple Model of Labor Market with Frictions, CEIS, International Summer School on Unemployment Theory and Empirical Evidence, mimeo.

Marimon R. Zilibotti F. (1997), unemployment vs. mismatch of talents reconsidering unemployment benefits, Economic Journal, 109, 266-291.

Mortensen D. (1986), Job Search and Labor Market Analysis, in Ashenfelter Layard (Eds).

Pissarides C. (1992), Loss of Skill during Unemployment and the Persistence of Employment Shocks, Quarterly Journal of Economics; 107(4), pp. 1371-91.

Stigler G. (1962), Information in the Labour Market, Journal of Political Economy, 70, 5.

Sugden R. (1998), Spontaneous Order, The New Palgrave, forthcoming.

# Index

MIX
Papier aus verantwortungsvollen Quellen
Paper from responsible sources
FSC® C105338

If you have any concerns about our products,
you can contact us on
**ProductSafety@springernature.com**

In case Publisher is established outside the EU,
the EU authorized representative is:
**Springer Nature Customer Service Center GmbH**
**Europaplatz 3, 69115 Heidelberg, Germany**

Printed by Libri Plureos GmbH
in Hamburg, Germany